Sociology, Work and Organisation

The seventh edition of *Sociology, Work and Organisation* is outstandingly effective in explaining how we can use the sociological imagination to understand the nature of institutions of work, organisations, occupations, management and employment and how they are changing in the twenty-first century.

Intellectual and accessible, it is unrivalled in the breadth of its coverage and its authoritative overview of both traditional and emergent themes in the sociological study of work and organisation. The direction and implications of trends in technological change are fully considered and the book recognises the extent to which these trends are intimately related to changing patterns of inequality in modern societies and to the changing experiences of individuals and families. Key features of the text are:

- clear structure;
- 'key issue' guides and summaries with each chapter;
- identification of key concepts throughout the book;
- unrivalled glossary and concept guide;
- rich illustrative snapshots or 'mini cases' throughout the book.

This text engages with cutting-edge debates and makes conceptual innovations without any sacrifice to clarity or accessibility of style. It will appeal to a wide audience, including undergraduates, postgraduates and academics working or studying in the area of work and the organisation of work, as well as practitioners working in the area of human resources and management generally.

Tony Watson is Emeritus Professor of Sociology, Work and Organisation in the Nottingham University Business School, University of Nottingham.

Sociology, Work and Organisation

Seventh Edition

Tony Watson

Routledge
Taylor & Francis Group

LONDON AND NEW YORK

Seventh edition published 2017
by Routledge
2 Park Square, Milton Park, Abingdon, Oxon, OX14 4RN

and by Routledge
711 Third Avenue, New York, NY 10017

Routledge is an imprint of the Taylor & Francis Group, an informa business

First edition published by Routledge & Kegan Paul 1980,
entitled *Sociology, Work and Industry*
Sixth edition published by Routledge 2012

British Library Cataloguing in Publication Data
A catalogue record for this book is available from the British Library

Library of Congress Cataloging in Publication Data
Names: Watson, Tony J., author.
Title: Sociology, work and organisation / by Tony Watson.
Description: Seventh edition. | Abingdon, Oxon ; New York, NY :
Routledge, 2017.
Identifiers: LCCN 2016047466| ISBN 9781138941809 (hardback) |
ISBN 9781138941816 (pbk.) | ISBN 9781315673509 (ebook)
Subjects: LCSH: Industrial sociology.
Classification: LCC HD6955 .W38 2017 | DDC 306.3—dc23
LC record available at https://lccn.loc.gov/2016047466

ISBN: 978-1-138-94180-9 (hbk)
ISBN: 978-1-138-94181-6 (pbk)
ISBN: 978-1-315-67350-9 (ebk)

Typeset in Bembo and Gills Sans
by Keystroke, Neville Lodge, Tettenhall, Wolverhampton

To Diane, Emily, Lizzie, Clara, Lawrence and Albert

Contents

CONTENTS

Figures, tables and snapshots

Figures

Tables

Snapshots

FIGURES, TABLES AND SNAPSHOTS

Introduction

Never before, since the first industrial revolution, has sociology had so much potential as a resource that people can use in making sense of what is happening to the work aspects of their lives. Sociology is distinctive in showing us how issues at the global level of changing societies and economies interlink with matters relating to the lives and experiences of each one of us. This has been an argument that has inspired the various editions of the present book over the decades following the first edition in 1980. Over the life of the book, there have been enormous changes in the world that sociology studies, in the research that has been published and in the sociological 'apparatus' itself (concepts, research methods, the philosophical underpinnings of both of these). Change has been a constant theme over the various editions of the book, and we have come across new terminologies in each volume. In the seventh edition of *Sociology, Work and Organisation* for example, we come across terms such as 'fourth industrial revolution', 'gig economy', 'zero hours contracts', 'empty labour' and 'hybrid roles'.

As I was writing each of this series of books, I was also working as a research sociologist, university teacher, research supervisor and academic-journal and book reviewer. This means that the content of my textbooks is always informed by my daily learning as a sociological practitioner. My writing is also strongly informed by periods spent getting inside work organisations as a participant observer. Throughout all of this, I have been learning my trade. And I continue to do so. In teaching and training researchers, in particular, I have learned a lot about 'what works' in communicating sociological, organisation-theory and methodology ideas.

In the teaching and training aspect of my work, and also in examining and reviewing activities, I have inevitably come across some worrying trends. I can give two examples here of such issues, each of which I have tried to address in *Sociology, Work and Organisation*. The first is a tendency for students and research writers to fail to meet a key challenge that they are told they must face. This is the challenge of choosing and explaining the methodological assumptions which they are making when they are doing their sociology or their organisation-studies work. Time and again one sees essays, theses and draft articles in which the student/researcher has assumed that they must declare whether they *are*, say, a 'critical realist' or a 'social constructionist'. This sort of thing is simplistic and inadequate when it comes to the shaping of the substantive part of their essay writing or their choice of research procedures. The second problem is much more specific and concrete. It is a problem of the frequent and astonishing carelessness with which researchers focusing on identity matters use the term 'identity' in their academic writing. In everyday life, quite reasonably, we all shift around when speaking of identity or identities. We switch between applying the word to who a person thinks they are (*self-identities* here), identities available to us in the world around us (*social-identities* here) and how people present themselves to others (*personas* here). Conceptual clarity and consistency is of the essence in sociology – and this is a clear lesson from my own sociological practice that I wish to pass on in Chapter 10 of *Sociology, Work and Organisation*.

I was one of the earliest sociology students in the UK to study an option in what was then called 'industrial sociology'. The subject – which nowadays is most often referred to as either the 'sociology of work' or 'organisation studies' – thrilled me in those youthful years. It continues to do so. And I have been incapable, ever since, of stopping 'doing sociology' – whether it be in the university, in other people's workplaces or (being of an ethnographic bent) in the street and in the pub. I truly wish that *Sociology, Work and Organisation* will encourage my readers to join me in a process of continuous sociological learning. And I hope that they will find joy in applying the sociological imagination to the world around them.

1 Studying work, society and organisation

Key issues

- What is work?
- What is 'thinking sociologically'?
- How can we most helpfully think about 'social organisation', 'society' and 'societies'?
- What role has sociology played historically in understanding a changing world and what role might it play in understanding contemporary issues and transitions?
- In what ways can sociology be understood to be a science?
- In what ways do sociologists use theories, adopt various research methods and work within differing philosophical (or 'methodological') assumptions?

People, work and society

Sociology is a resource which people can use to understand better how the social world 'works', so that they can act more effectively in the various social spheres in which they lead their lives. One of those spheres is work. Yes, but already in the opening words of this book, we have used the word 'work' in two rather different ways. When we say, for example, 'I want to understand better how modern banking works', and when we state that 'my father used to work in a bank', we are not speaking of the same thing. 'Work' is one of those words that is used in many different ways. It is also used very frequently. It is the eighty-seventh most common word in English, occurring 3 million times in the *Oxford English Dictionary* (Hargraves 2014).

If we are going to study human work activities and how they are organised and experienced, we need to decide how we are going to use the term 'work'. This is not a matter of producing a final and absolute definition of work. Sociology, like all scientific and other forms of systematic study, proceeds by deciding what is likely to be the most useful way of characterising the topics being studied. Certain types of economic inquiry in a modern industrialised society might best be conducted by defining work in terms of task-based activities for which people are paid by an employer, client or customer. However, this would exclude all those tasks that we refer to as 'housework' for example. This would be a serious omission given that, in Brown's (1997) words, 'without the enormous volume and unremitting cycle of domestic labour the formal economy of jobs and pay packets would cease to function'. Pettinger *et al.* (2006) build on this insight in their suggestions for a 'new sociology of work', one which pays close attention to the 'blurry line between work and not-work'. Glucksmann (2006) suggests that such a sociology of work might look at such activities as the cooking and preparing of meals, recognising the fusion of work, non-work and skill acquisitions which such activities entail. But we have to careful here. If we include in the scope of the sociology of work all task-oriented activity in which effort is expended, then we risk extending our study to such activities as walking across a room to switch on a television set or packing a bag to take for a day on the beach. We need a compromise that gives sufficient focus to our studies without limiting them to activities with a formal economic outcome.

There are two main aspects of work that a sociological concept of work needs to recognise. The first is the task-related aspect of work and the second is the part played by work in the way people 'make a living'.

Work
The carrying out of tasks which enable people to *make a living* within the social and economic context in which they are located.

Thinking about work in this way associates it with the expenditure of effort to carry out tasks, but it limits it to something that has an economic element – in the very broad sense of dealing with problems of survival in a world of scarce resources. But the notion of 'making a living' implies much more than just producing enough material goods to ensure physical survival. People do not simply extract a living from the environment. Work transforms environments in many ways and, in the process, creates for many people a level of living far in excess of basic subsistence. But it does more than this. It also relates intimately to how people shape their very lives and identities. And people's lives are significantly shaped by the circumstances in which they have to work. The work people do becomes closely bound up with their conception of self. In looking at how people 'make a living', we are looking at how they deal with both the economic and the social or cultural aspects of their lives.

Work is a social, economic and cultural phenomenon. It is not simply a matter of behaviour. Work occurs in societies, and as with work, we have to conceptualise 'society' before we can systematically examine the role of work in human societies.

Society
The broad pattern of social, economic, cultural and political relationships within which people lead their lives, typically but not exclusively in the modern world as members of the same nation state.

Social organisation, work organisations and thinking about work sociologically

Sociology provides us with a range of insights, concepts, theories and research findings which help us understand the wide range of work and work-related activities that occur in the context of the broader social and cultural arrangements.

Sociology
The study of the relationships which develop between human beings as they organise themselves and are organised by others in societies and how these patterns influence and are influenced by the actions and interactions of people and how they make sense of their lives and identities.

This definition of sociology incorporates the basic insight which is shared by all the social science disciplines: that human life does not happen randomly or by individuals and small groups following their instincts in order to survive. Social life is organised. If there were no organised patterns in social life, there would be no predictability to our lives, no sense of order and nothing to stop people killing and robbing from each other as they pursued selfish interests. For this reason, we can identify various patterns of *social organisation* existing throughout human history. Hunter gatherer lives were socially organised as was life in the Roman Empire or in African nomadic tribes. However, a characteristic and dominant institution in contemporary industrial-capitalist societies is that of the bureaucratised work organisation. Thus, in the societies in which we currently live, there is general *social organisation* (a pattern of social structures, cultures, institutions and so on). Within this there is a set of *work organisations* that operate – sometimes in co-operation with each other, sometimes in competition with each other – to produce and provide goods and services and administer social, political and economic aspects of life.

Whether we are dealing with activities at the level of the individual, the group or the work organisation, the essential characteristic of the sociological perspective is that it *ultimately relates whatever it studies back to the way society as a whole is organised*. Sociology works on the assumption that no social action, at however mundane a level, takes place in a social vacuum. It is always linked back to the wider culture, social structure and processes of the society in which it takes place. These structures, processes, norms and values, with all their related inequalities, ideologies and power distributions, are the source of both constraints and opportunities which people meet in conducting their lives. The better and more widely these cultures, structures and processes are understood and the better the connections between specific actions or arrangements and these basic patterns are appreciated, then the greater is the opportunity for the human control over work, industry and every other kind of social institution.

Let us illustrate this argument by trying to make sense of a simple piece of 'everyday' work-related human behaviour. One might interpret this, first, as if one were simply a casual observer and, second, as if one were a sociologist.

If we were viewing this scene as strangers to this work organisation, whether or not we were formally trained as sociologists, we would be

Snapshot 1.1

A man and a woman arrive at work

A man and a woman get out of a car and walk into an office block. One of them goes into a large private office and closes the door. The other sits at a desk outside that office alongside several other people. The person in the private space telephones the one in the outer office, and a few minutes later, the latter individual takes a cup of coffee and a biscuit into the person in the inner office.

thinking about both the personal and the work relationship between these people: were they a married couple, lovers or simply people sharing a lift to work? We would wonder how this aspect of their relationship related to the authority relationship between them: presumably one of them was 'the boss', was the more highly paid, the more highly trained, and had the right to give instructions to the other. If we were more consciously sociological in our speculations, however, we would draw on our knowledge of 'sociological' matters such as social class, educational and career opportunity structures, bureaucratic authority structures, culturally normal patterns of workplace layout and the patterns of behaviour, rules, assumptions and expectations associated with work activities in this particular society and culture at this particular time in history.

If it were the man that entered the private office, we might note that standard 'norms' were being followed with regard to gender relationships. But if it were the woman who 'played the role' of the senior person – the presumably higher paid, more qualified individual with greater authority – we might begin to reflect on how this individual has come to challenge established patterns. How had she come to break established norms? What opportunity structures had she used, what barriers had she overcome? To what extent were her actions and her relatively unusual position in the workplace part of a broader pattern of social change?

In analysing this simple piece of mundane activity in this way, we are thinking sociologically. In asking these questions, we are asking sociological questions. And, in doing so, we are engaging with issues of power and life chances in a way that both enhances our 'academic' understanding of relationships at work and, at the same time, offers understandings of possibilities and practices which have the potential to inform human choices that might further – or, for that matter, resist – social change.

Choices, constraints and opportunities in work and society

Sociology's potential as a resource for informing human choice is something to which we will return shortly. First, however, we need to reinforce the point about working arrangements and social patterns being both the outcomes of human actions and factors helping shape those actions. Sociology has been defined here as something that looks at how human beings organise both themselves and each other. In looking at how people think and behave, it looks for cultural patterns and 'structures' in social life. These patterns are seen as both the outcome of the activities of individuals and as things that in turn, influence, encourage and constrain the individual. If, for example, it was the man in

Snapshot 1.1 who was the more senior of our two social actors, he might tell us in an interview that his current role as the organisation's head of information technology was the outcome of a series of *choices* that he personally made in his life. The woman, to whom he gives a daily lift in his company car, might talk to us about how she chose to train and work as an office secretary.

As sociological observers, we would not want to discount these claims to choice or 'agency' in these individuals' career patterns. Nor would we say that there were no individual choices behind the pattern whereby the great majority of the important 'decision-makers' in this organisation are currently men and most of the secretarial and 'personal assistant' workers are women. Choices have clearly been made. Nobody forced these people into these jobs. Each human individual is an agent, with wants, aspirations and a sense of identity which they bring to any decision to speak or act. But, at the same time, we are likely to be aware that the pattern we have observed is, in some sense, an outcome of the way the 'society' in which these people grew up channelled male and female children into different spheres of activity. There were clearly pressures on each child from the world around them: from role examples observed as they grew up to the opportunities made available to boys and girls in both education and initial employment.

It is easily possible to see two mutually exclusive alternative types of explanation emerging here: agency and choice on the one hand, and structural 'channelling' on the other. Sometimes sociologists talk of making a choice between *voluntarist* and *structural* frames of reference and modern sociological thought is characterised, as Swingewood (2000) observes, 'by a continual tension between ... a voluntarist model which emphasises the creative and active role of agents, and a structural model which focuses on institutions and processes which constrain and determine the course of action'.

To use terms which have been around as long as there has been social thought, we can speak of explanations which emphasise free will and explanations which stress determinism. This is something that sociologists try to go beyond. To develop an explanation of the patterns observed, we need an analysis which considers the way these individuals came to shape their career interests and 'choose' their aspirations in the light of their previous experiences in life and what they have learned from the cultural and parental influences upon them to be the appropriate and possible types of work for them to enter. There is an interweaving of individual and social factors, of free choice and of constraint. We might simplify this, as Figure 1.1 does, by saying that individuals make society and society makes individuals.

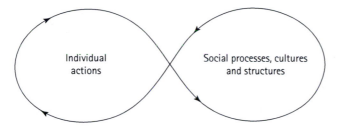

Figure 1.1 Individuals make society and society makes individuals

The analytical distinction between individual actions, on the one hand, and 'the social' on the other does not fully parallel the free will and determinism distinction, however, because it is possible to talk of an individual's actions being severely constrained, if not determined, by factors such as their individual genetic make-up. Equally, it is possible to see social structures as providing opportunities for individuals to realise their individual interests ('climbing the ladder' of the class structure, say), as well as seeing people constrained by such structures (being excluded from an activity because of one's gender or race, for example). Human beings are makers of social patterns and are also made by them. These patterns both constrain us and enable us to achieve our purposes. But these patterns or 'structures' are not objectively existing entities outside of human patterns of interaction, even though it may at times feel as if they have this kind of forceful presence.

Sociology is not simply the study of 'the social', of societies, of social structures. Neither, of course, is it a study of individuals' activities, aggregated in some way to give us a view of societies as little more than the sum of their parts. It is, rather, a study of the interrelationships between the individual and the social whose greatest potential lies in examining the processes whereby human initiatives and choices shape and are shaped by patterns of human interaction and power.

Work and the sociological imagination

In one of the most influential reflections on what sociology can contribute to human life, Mills (1970) identified the *sociological imagination* as a way of switching 'upwards' from an initial focus on the private problems of individuals. Such problems arise in the case of Mathieu and Valerie, who face losing their jobs, in Snapshot 1.2. It would be helpful if one were, first, to identify what some of the personal troubles of this couple might be in these circumstances. Second, one can go on to consider how their personal predicament might relate to broader 'public issues'.

The personal troubles of Mathieu and Valerie

Mathieu and Valerie are a couple in their thirties who have three young children: two at primary school and one at nursery school. For the past dozen or so years, they have both done assembly work at a car factory which, under a variety of owners, has been part of the industrial city in which they live for many years. The current owners have decided to move all the work to a newly built factory in Eastern Europe – arguing that the 'cost patterns' and the 'potential for innovation' in that setting make it imperative for them to cease operating in the city in which Valerie was born and into which Mathieu moved when he and Valerie first set up home together.

The first 'personal trouble' which is likely to confront the couple is that of a large drop in their family income. Neither of them is likely to know of alternative jobs in the city. They are likely to be distressed at the prospect of losing their heavily mortgaged home and to worry that, even if they choose to sell the house, they will have serious difficulties because many other redundant workers are likely to be putting their properties on the market at the same time. Also, if they are able to move, whether within the city or beyond it, they will worry about the children's education. They are likely to have struggled to get the children into the schools in which they are currently very happy. They are likely to hate to take their children away from these schools and from the various friends and relatives that are such an important part of the lives of the whole family.

Although, as human beings, we are likely to be very concerned for Valerie, Mathieu and for all the other families affected by this big business decision, our distinctively sociological interests move us to a further level of concern. The sociological perspective places human predicaments such as these in their broader context. Mills (1970) characterised this broader context as raising 'public issues' and this language immediately suggests to us a range of matters such as the levels of employment and unemployment in the city, the quality of educational provision for young children in this society and the nature of housing markets. These issues would require us to draw on other social sciences in addition to sociology – economics in particular. We would look at issues ranging from the state of the international market for manufactured goods and managerial, governmental and trade union policies, to patterns of technological change and patterns of business ownership. And within the analysis which we would undertake there is considerable potential for distinctly sociological matters such as patterns of urban change, gender

differences in careers and child-rearing, class and power in business decision-making, the relationship between work and personal identities, the
impact of globalising trends on different nation-states and so on.

Sociology, then, shifts the level of focus from that of the close-up
on individuals and their working life to that of the 'big picture' of the
society in which they live. Sociology is not simply 'painting a picture',
however broad that might be, however. It goes beyond this to look for
regularities, patterns, structures and processes. The events in Valerie and
Mathieu's city will be set in their historical context and the overall
structure of the several societies involved – the industrial bases, the
political-economic systems of both eastern and western Europe and
the ways in which these fit into patterns of global change. In analysing
these structures and processes, the sociologist would try to show how
they potentially both constrain people as well as enable people to further their personal wishes, whether these people be corporate managers,
politicians and trade union officers or 'ordinary' employees like Mathieu
and Valerie.

This distinctly sociological way of thinking means stepping outside
our normal 'everyday' common sense way of thinking about our working lives and adopting what is perhaps the most basic sociological insight
of all: that there is more than one way and one way only for men and
women to organise their lives. In other words, the way society *is* is not
necessarily the way society *has to be*. In the realm of work this means
that the way we currently organise production and distribution does
not possess some immutable inevitability. It is only one of a range of
possibilities. Baumann and May (2001) refer to sociology's ability to
help us appreciate its 'anti-fixating' power. We are reminded, they say,
that what we might think of as the 'natural, inevitable, eternal aspects
of our lives' have come into being as a result of the exercise of 'human
power and human resources'. This, in turn, suggests that social patterns
are not 'immune and impenetrable to human action – our own action
included'. A world that might have seemed 'oppressive in its apparent
fixity' is shown to be a world that could be 'different from what it is
now'. We are thus encouraged not to surrender to what might, at first,
seem to be irresistible pressures and circumstances.

The original sociologists were thinkers striving to make sense of the
dislocations of their age, as we shall shortly observe. The attempts by the
classical sociological thinkers to make sense of their time are invaluable
to us because, in an historical location more marginal than our own, they
were better able to look at the industrial capitalist world in the light of
conceptions of alternatives (Watson 2009b). This is the humanistic significance and the continuing relevance to us today of people like Marx,

Weber and Durkheim. They were perhaps more aware of alternatives on a societal level than we are because they were better placed historically to contrast the modern and the industrial with the traditional, the urban with the rural, and so on.

LOOKING FORWARD >>>>>

The elements of the contemporary sociology of work which have their roots in the thinking of Marx, Weber and Durkheim are examined in Chapter 2.

Sociology, industrialisation and contemporary transitions

Sociology and the historical coming to terms with industrialisation

The sociological imagination requires a strong historical awareness. The sociologist of contemporary work studying, for example, 'lean production' methods or 'high-performance work systems' is likely to consider these practices in the context of the continuing history of industrialisation. Work, as Warren (2016) puts it, 'was core to the birth of sociology and its founding theorists'. Sociology is, we might say, itself a creature of the modern industrialised societies, within which it developed as a form of critical reflection on the considerable social changes associated with industrialisation and the growth of capitalism. Sociology emerged in the nineteenth century as both a reaction to and a reflection of certain major social and cultural shifts which had been occurring for hundreds of years in Europe. For some centuries prior to the emergence of sociology, the glue which held together the fabric of European society, giving it stability and a widespread taken-for-grantedness, had been weakening:

- The Reformation in the sixteenth century saw a questioning of the authority of a centralised Catholic Church and, with the emergence of Protestantism and dissent, came a growing stress on the individual rather than the corporate, and the rational rather than the traditional.
- The Enlightenment in the late seventeenth and the eighteenth century brought under rational and critical scrutiny institutions of religion, inequality, kinship, property and monarchy.
- The Industrial and French Revolutions in the late eighteenth and the nineteenth century ensured that all of these institutions were further shaken and indeed often overturned.

A bourgeois revolution occurred in England in 1688 limiting the power of the monarchy and, in France in the following century, the monarchy was toppled. Notions of democracy were becoming increasingly popular in the early decades of the nineteenth century, but the problem of finding appropriate institutions for democratic politics was increased by the complications introduced by the Industrial Revolution. Capitalism had been growing in strength for centuries, but by the early nineteenth century, it had become combined with an industrial spirit and associated techniques which carried revolutionary structural implications. Arising partly within and partly from outside the established bourgeois class was the new industrial middle class and, even more threatening to stability, was the appearance of a new social phenomenon – an industrial working class.

Some sense had to be made of these massive processes of change. How could people come to terms with processes of urbanisation, industrialisation, a growing division of labour, secularisation, bureaucratisation, democratisation, national state centralisation and the rest? Sociology can be seen as an intellectual coming-to-terms with these processes and as an attempt to understand their impact.

The potential for a sociological way of coming to terms with these changes had developed during the eighteenth-century Enlightenment period, prior to the full emergence of sociology in the nineteenth century. The scientific aspects of such a venture were implicit in the Enlightenment and its characteristic belief that people would be better able both to understand and to control their destinies if they applied to them reason and systematic research. But also emerging in this period was the idea that human beings can only be understood in the context of the whole society in which they live. This was an insight that later sociologists were to take up from the eighteenth-century writing of Giambattista Vico. It was also a key idea of the Scottish Enlightenment, and two key figures in this – John Millar and Adam Ferguson – examined changing patterns of work specialisation and division of labour sociologically, stressing the social as well as the economic aspects of these changes and identifying their implications, both positive and negative, for human welfare and work experience (Swingewood 2000; Herman 2001).

A near total breakdown in old assumptions about authority and social order followed the Enlightenment and the Industrial and French Revolutions, a breakdown that called for a reconstruction of the social order. Piecemeal reconstruction was seen as inappropriate, according to Fletcher (1971), when the 'entire fabric of institutions was falling apart' and a need for a 'body of knowledge about society as a totality of institutions' became apparent. It was this need that the founders of sociology were to try to meet. The key concepts or 'unit ideas' of sociology, Nisbet

(1970) argued, were all developed as part of an attempt to achieve a 'theoretical reconsolidation' of the various elements on which social order had once rested – kinship, land, social class, religion, local community and monarchy – but which had now been 'dislocated by revolution' and 'scrambled by industrialisation and the forces of democracy'.

Sociologists, in this view, developed concepts like society and community to provide a consolidating or over-arching perspective which would counter the divisive, contradictory and individualistic tendencies of life in this period of emerging modernism. The founders of sociology were preoccupied with the analysis of industrialism and were engaged in creating a 'powerful vision or "image" of a society in the making' (Kumar 1978) and, says Giddens (1971), the overwhelming interest of Marx, Durkheim and Weber was in the 'delineation of the characteristic structure of modern capitalism as contrasted with prior forms of society'. Contemporary sociology has inherited this role and has 'as its main focus the institutions of "advanced" or "industrialised" societies, and of the conditions of transformation of those institutions' (Giddens 1971).

Contemporary sociology and the informing of democratic choices about work

The sociological imagination requires us to suspend our everyday common sense assumptions about the world and, indeed, about the future of the world. But it also means being wary of styles of intellectual analysis that are more concerned with solving the problems of particular sections of society than with developing an analysis that would be relevant to members of society more generally. Jacques (1996) points out, for example, that many of the attempts currently being made to theorise work relations are producing their own kind of 'common sense'. At the heart of this is a standard body of relatively unchanging US-created 'management knowledge' that takes for granted that the key 'work' issue is one of finding better ways to manage employees to enable organisations to achieve high productivity, international competitiveness and 'world class efficiency'. Questions are not asked about the nature and legitimacy of work organisations or, for example, the role of non-managers in 'managing' work, in shaping 'motivations' or acting as social citizens within work arrangements in which relationships are built and balanced. To ask these questions, we might add, does not preclude an interesting issue of efficiency and productivity but it does mean asking 'efficiency and productivity in whose interests?'

The notion of a public sociology incorporates such a concern. Burawoy and researchers from a variety of countries argue for a sociology which engages with issues in their various economic, social and political contexts in order to further social, political and economic changes (Burawoy 2014). A concern to counter the dehumanising tendencies of contemporary changes in polities, economies and work activities is at the heart of this enterprise. But we must be careful here. Burawoy's idea of a public sociology goes beyond an involvement in debate. He wishes public intellectuals to 'take the side' of particular interest groups in society. He welcomes the support being given by sociologists to organised labour in the US and links this with rejection of a 'professional industrial sociology'. A labour-focused public sociology of the type Burawoy writes about played a significant part in the anti-Apartheid period in South Africa, but this has not survived democratisation and the twenty-first century, Buhlungu (2009) argues, with little interest being shown by contemporary social scientists in the idea of a public sociology.

The question is one of whether this call for a public sociology is going too far in reaction to the long-recognised dangers of industrial sociologists taking a 'servant of power' role and working as specialist human manipulators by large organisations in the way Baritz (1960) saw beginning to happen in pre-war America, where such people were 'doing what they were told to do and doing it well – and therefore endangering those other personal, group, class and institutional interests which were opposed to the further domination by the modern corporation of the mood and direction of American life'. Sociological knowledge and insights inevitably have a relevance to practical problem-solving in large organisations and can be shown to help solve problems in certain relatively bounded situations (Klein 2005). One would be naive and wrong to deny the right of any group to make use of knowledge in this way. What can be objected to, however, is the exclusive development of industrial sociology as a manipulative instrument for the pursuit of sectional interests. Whether or not this justifies sociologists taking sides with groups opposed to the most powerful interests in society is another matter.

An alternative role for the sociology of work and organisation would be as a resource which helps those living in the industrial capitalist type of society to understand better the possibilities and choices which exist with regard to how work is organised and experienced in those societies. Its role is thus to inform choice. Here, the subject is not the sole preserve of the expert – be they 'servants of power' or marginalised utopian academics. Instead, it is something to be disseminated through both formal and informal educational institutions and communication media (*cf* Dallyn *et al.* 2015). It becomes something in whose development the individual is first involved as a student, and something which is subsequently drawn upon and further engaged with in their later life and career as employees, managers, voting citizens, trade unionists, self-employers or consumers. It is a resource vital to a democratic society. As Eldridge *et al.* (1991) said about the role that industrial sociology might play in coming to terms with economic and social issues emerging later in the twentieth century, 'To show what possibilities may exist for political choices in an active democracy is to exercise the sociological imagination'. Burns (1962), in discussing industrial sociology at a time when it scarcely had a foothold in Britain, argued that it is the sociologist's business 'to conduct a critical debate ... with the public about its equipment of social institutions'. If the sociology of work and organisation is going to play such a role, however, it must be careful not to preach to society from 'on high'. Beirne (2008, 2013) points out that the industrial sociologists operating at the time that Burns was writing these words were not working in the elitist and 'top-down' manner of contemporary 'critical' sociologists. He calls for a return to the kind of 'grounded realism' of earlier industrial sociologists and for a type of 'generative research' which 'connects with the grassroots and offers scope for collective engagement to address practical matters of innovating and changing work arrangements in the way exemplified by socio-technical systems thinking'.

LOOKING FORWARD >>>>>

Socio-technical systems thinking and some classic research carried out in that tradition will be examined in Chapter 6, p. 189.

The exercise of a critical but non-partisan sociological imagination is as relevant in the twenty-first century as it was in earlier periods of industrialisation. The twenty-first century presents us with challenges of coming to terms with social and economic changes that are no less significant than those faced by the creators of sociology almost two centuries ago. Industrialisation continues apace, if unevenly, across the globe, and links between different areas and cultures are becoming closer and more immediate with fast-developing information and communication technologies.

LOOKING FORWARD >>>>>

Past industrialisation processes which have, in so many ways, given us the world we live in are examined in Chapter 4 and the notion of a contemporary 'fourth industrial revolution' will be discussed in Chapter 6, p. 120.

It sometimes seems that there are few choices left to us about how we live, at the level of the nation state let alone at the level of the local community or family. As we see in Chapter 4, technology, international corporations and pressures for capital accumulation sometimes seem to be pushing everyone towards a globalised future within which some will be allocated rich, secure and fulfilling lives at the expense of a mass of materially and experientially impoverished insecure workers and an even more impoverished stratum of economically inactive groups. At other times, we are encouraged to believe that the best of all possible worlds is available to us all, if we take advantage of the great opportunities both for challenging work and exciting recreation made possible by the same technological, commercial and globalising forces. Sociology has to bring us down to earth with regard to all of this. It needs to analyse what is going on and help us make a balanced appraisal of trends. Such analysis and insight can be a valuable resource, informing us and encouraging us to think imaginatively about the alternatives and choices facing us in all aspects of our lives, in our families, our communities and the wider societies of which we are members. How we think about the part that work is to play in our lives is necessarily central to this.

Researching and theorising work patterns and experiences

Sociology as science

Sociology's history unfolded alongside the rise of democratic institutions in Western societies, as we have seen. It is also a result of the rise of scientific ways of looking at the world. Sociology is a science. But what makes it a science is not a sterile value-neutrality or a concern with amassing facts uncontaminated by subjectivity. Neither is it a pursuit of final laws. Sociology uses insight, imagination and even inspiration; it is motivated by moral concern and even by political commitment, and it is characterised by internal debate and rivalries of both method and interpretation, but, in the end, it falls into the category of the sciences rather than the arts.

Science and sociology

Science is a formal, systematic and precise approach to building up a body of knowledge and theory which is rigorous in examining propositions about the social world in the light of available evidence. Sociology is a science because it makes generalisations as systematically as possible in the light of available evidence.

Sociology is a scientific pursuit because it goes about detecting regularities and because it makes its generalisations on as systematic a basis as possible given its subject matter. This involves the 'testing' of propositions and the basing of statements on evidence – this being collected, explained and interpreted in such a way that others can scrutinise that evidence and make their own judgements on the generalisations that are offered.

Sociology as a science is not essentially different from shrewd practical reasoning about our social lives. It is not radically distinguishable from informed journalistic critiques of social institutions and trends in social change. It is different from these other endeavours in degree rather than in essence, in three ways. It is:

- more formal, systematic and precise in its observing, classifying, conceptualising and interpreting;
- more rigorous in the extent to which it submits its procedures to critical examination (seeking to falsify rather than prove its tentative explanations for example); and
- more committed to building up a body of knowledge and a series of generalisations which go beyond immediate and practical needs. This body of knowledge is, therefore, available to be drawn upon when there is a practical issue to which it may be relevant.

Theory, work and society

Science is concerned to make informed generalisations about the world. These are scientific *theories*. In part these are informed by rational and critical reflection about the world but, most characteristically, they are informed by careful and considered attention to systematically gathered evidence.

Sociological theories
Systematic generalisations about how the social world 'works'.

It is unfortunate that many people use the term 'theory' in a derogatory manner to refer to ideas that do not effectively connect with human practices in the world. Facts about work, some people say, are interesting and useful but once we start to 'get theoretical' we start to become self-indulgent and irrelevant. However, once we recognise that sociological theories are essentially attempts to make sense of how society 'works', the nonsense of this becomes apparent. Indeed, 'facts' about society and work activities cannot really exist separately from the theoretical frames of reference within which they are expressed. How could we in subsequent chapters, for example, talk about the 'facts' of work security and insecurity without a theory of what constitutes 'security' and 'insecurity' in this context? How can we consider the extent to which the world is in fact 'globalising' without some reference to theories of globalisation? How can we even talk about 'work' and 'society' in a theory-free way? The way we conceptualised work and society earlier in this chapter was the start of the broader process of theorising the role of work activities and experiences in modern societies (and, yes, we will have to theorise 'modern' at the appropriate stage). The point of all of this is to deepen our understanding of *what is going on* in the world of work. Surely such an appreciation is valuable to all of us in shaping our social practices.

Concepts, definitions and theories

The theoretical 'strands' that exist within the sociology of work and organisation and which will be examined in Chapters 2 and 3 are, in effect, broad conceptual schemes that we apply to particular work contexts to make sense of what is going on there. Whenever one sets about studying the world a 'bundle' of concepts are needed. These are what we might call the working definitions of the various phenomena and factors that are important in the aspect of the world that we are examining.

Concepts
Working definitions that are chosen or devised for use in scientific analysis. They are the way scientists define their terms for the purpose of a specific investigation. They therefore differ from dictionary definitions – these tending to have a more general and therefore much less precise applicability.

When beginning one's investigation of an area of social life it is vital to define one's terms. This is not a matter of seeking *correct* definitions from a dictionary, however. It is a matter of choosing or creating definitions which are likely to be most helpful to the particular project being developed. There are, for example, a variety of ways of defining or, more correctly, *conceptualising* organisations. Each of us has to select or create a concept of work organisations which we believe will be most helpful to our investigations of the organised aspects of working life. And we need, at the same time, to develop concepts that will work together with this central one in order to create a theoretical framework for our study. These might be organisational structure, organisational culture, strategy, negotiated order and so on. In *Sociology, Work and Organisation*, terms are defined, as the chapters proceed, through the device of the concept boxes. In every case, these are conceptualisations which are taken to be the most helpful for the investigation of the particular phenomena being examined. Readers may therefore choose to use these concepts themselves in their own work. Equally, they may develop their own versions of these conceptualisations in the light of their personally preferred theoretical priorities or methodological emphasis.

A range of research methods

Sociologists of work and industry use a variety of techniques of investigation when they undertake empirical research ('empirical' meaning dependent on observation and experience of phenomena rather than reflection on them 'at a distance'). At one end of a continuum are studies involving the manipulation of existing bodies of statistical information and research projects involving the analysis of quantitative information gathered through questionnaire-based surveys specially designed by the investigators. At the other end of the continuum is field research in which the researchers immerse themselves in the lives of the people, becoming participant observers in order to write ethnographies (Watson 2011, 2012).

Ethnography

A style of social science writing which draws upon the writer's close observation of and involvement with people in a particular social setting and relates the words spoken and the practices observed or experienced to the overall cultural framework within which they occurred.

Participant observation

A research practice in which the investigator gets 'close to the action' by joining the group or organisation being studied – as either a full or partial member – and both participating in and observing activities, as well as asking questions, taking part in conversations and reading relevant documents .

This kind of research is nowhere near as common as that closer to the other end of the continuum. It can be argued, however, that the activity should be considerably increased given the enormous potential which it has for helping us understand 'how things work' in organisational and work situations (Watson 2011).

The continuum of different research methods relates to the way in which research sometimes goes for *breadth* of coverage by looking at large numbers of instances of whatever is being studied, or by checking samples large enough to be statistically representative of larger patterns and, at other times, goes for *depth* of understanding by giving attention to close details of particular *cases*. Case studies might examine particular work organisations, particular events or even particular individuals. The logic of such work is to get a detailed understanding of the processes that occur when, say, two work organisations merge, a new occupation is established or an individual rises from being an ordinary worker to taking over the leadership of a trade union.

We will come across studies in subsequent chapters which use various of these different approaches to develop our understanding of what is generally 'going on' in the work and industrial aspects of societies and the work dimension of people's lives. As shown in Table 1.1, it is possible, however, for a variety of techniques to be used within one study, as we see in the following imagined research study, in which a group of sociologists has decided to combine their efforts in a major piece of research to investigate in depth the large and growing phenomenon of

Table 1.1 A range of research roles and associated techniques which might be used in a single research study

Researcher 1	concentrates on examining employment *statistics* across a range of developed and less developed economies in which call centres are located.
Researcher 2	*interviews* workers and managers in a carefully selected sample of call centre companies of different sizes.
Researcher 3	conducts a postal *survey* of members of the public who use or are contacted by such organisations.
Researcher 4	obtains a job in a single case-study call centre to work as a *participant observer* and learn first hand about working in such a setting.
Researcher 5	studies in depth at two *comparative case-study* call centres. One has been selected on the grounds that it has a generally good reputation as an employer. The other has a bad reputation. The researcher will use whatever methods she finds useful, from interviews and (non-participant) observation to documentary analysis and written questionnaires. The intention is to get as full a picture as possible of each of these work organisations so that the team can compare the two. The intention of the comparative case-studies is to give a focus to the group's broad interest in the variety of work designs and work experiences which they believe are the case in this employment sector.

work in telephone call centres (see pp. 195–197). After working together on reviewing the existing literature – academic and 'popular' – and agreeing on the concepts they want to use and the variables they want to examine, they divide up the investigative labour.

This design of this multi-technique research project is influenced by current theories of, for example, work design, organisational change and job 'choice'. The information it produces will be analysed to develop further the theoretical understanding of these matters as well as, of course, in order to present to the public and to policy-makers broad insights about what is occurring in an important aspect of contemporary employment. However, things are not as straightforward as our imagined case of a research project might imply. Sociologists who study work, industry, occupations, organisations and employment relations often differ from each other in quite significant ways in the assumptions which they bring to their studies.

Methodological assumptions

We have just noted the range of different methods that sociologists of work use. But they also vary in the *methodological* assumptions they bring to their research and theorising.

Methodology

A term often misused to refer to research techniques and which, properly, refers to the philosophical issues raised by the attempt to investigate the world scientifically and, in particular, issues relating to the assumptions that researchers make about the nature of societies, organisations and individuals.

It is unfortunate that the term 'methodology' is often used simply to mean 'method'. This usage tends to divert people from some very important issues that need to be considered before a 'method', in the sense of an investigative technique, is chosen. Methodological assumptions are ones about the very nature of the 'realities' (ontology) that we study, about how we can 'know' those realities, and how we can make valid or 'truthful' generalisations about the social world (epistemology) on the basis of the very limited materials that we gather (whether these be numbers from surveys or statements and observations collected in 'field work'). There are many complexities involved here, but it is vital to any student of the sociology of work and organisation to have a basic understanding of the main methodological choices that every researcher and theorist has to make.

LOOKING FORWARD >>>>>

The discussion here considers methodological issues in a broad and general way. More particular issues of the assumptions that we make about organisations and individuals are focused upon in Chapters 5 and 10 respectively.

The term 'positivism' is often used to refer to any research that uses quantitative methods and is sometimes condemned for a naive belief in the validity of the social facts that it collects, regardless of the theoretical assumptions to which those alleged 'facts' relate. But this is, as Turner (2001) stresses, a 'gross distortion' of what was intended by Auguste Comte, the original advocate in the 1830s of a positivist sociology (and, indeed, the inventor of the word 'sociology'). Comte conceived of sociology as a theory-driven activity. Data collection would be a means of formulating laws – laws that would enable positive social progress to be made and would replace superstition and guesswork as the basis for making decisions about the control of society. Positivists continue to seek 'covering law' types of generalisation about the social world, working on the assumption that the social world is not fundamentally different from the natural or physical world and that the social sciences can therefore adopt procedures similar to those of the natural sciences. Donaldson (2003), a leading proponent of 'sociological positivism' in the field of organisation studies, says that the aim is to 'reveal causal regularities that underlie surface reality', and he follows Durkheim (1982) in arguing that the subject matter of sociology is 'social facts' or 'causes that stand apart from people and constrain them, forcing them to behave in ways – even sometimes regardless of the ideas in the minds of the people involved'. And social facts 'should only be explained by other social facts, i.e. objective conditions, rather than in the consciousness of social actors'. His example here is the explanation that Blau (1963) develops of how organisations tend to become increasingly differentiated (broken down into more and more sub-units). The causal factor is not decisions or actions by organisational managers; it is *organisational size*. Differentiation is a social fact. And so is organisational size. Most non-positivist sociologists, however, would not exclude from their accounts of such processes the meanings brought into play and the initiatives taken by organisational actors.

In contrast to positivist principles, interpretive principles are based on a belief that the social world is not amenable to research procedures directly derived from the natural sciences. The social world is taken to be different in nature from the physical world. It must therefore be studied in a different way. Most significantly, this is because human beings are thinking, sensemaking, decision-making beings who could potentially choose to defy the predictions of social scientists. Humans, unlike physical entities, make interpretations for themselves of what is happening in the world. Close attention therefore needs to be paid to the *interpretive* or meaning-making interactions of people in societies.

So far, then, we have identified two alternative sets of methodological principles for social science: positivist and interpretive principles. In practice, sociologists do not straightforwardly fall into two camps based on these two sets of principles. If there is a single division to be seen in practice, it would be between

(1) *realists*, who work on the assumption that social reality exists independently of how people observe and make sense of it, and

Table 1.2 Four methodological positions in social science

Realist	**Positivism**
	Sometimes called 'naive realism' because it gives no recognition to the interpretive principle. Researchers seek causal regularities in the form of laws inferred from the analysis of observable and measurable data.
Non-realist	**Interpretivism/constructionism**
	Privileges the interpretive principle and denies the existence of social realities beyond the processes whereby people observe and interpret and 'socially construct' the world. Language has the role of 'constituting' the social world as opposed to simply describing it. Researchers seek to understand how this occurs in different spheres of social life.
Realist	**Critical realism**
	Incorporates the interpretive principle by recognising that interpretive, linguistic and 'discursive' processes of social construction ***play a part*** in bringing about a social world which then has a reality of its own. This reality has a 'thing-like' reality and properties which exist at a level deeper than the surface 'empirical' and 'actual' levels. Within this there exist 'causal powers' and 'generative mechanisms' which come into interplay with human agency to shape societies and social lives. Researchers attempt to reveal these powers and mechanisms.
Realist	**Pragmatic realism**
	Incorporates the interpretive principle, without privileging it. In this it is similar to critical realism. Unlike critical realism, it does not seek 'mechanisms' operating below the surface of social life. Instead, it follows the Pragmatist philosophers, Peirce, James and Dewey, in treating reality as the circumstances with which people have to come to terms in order to cope in the world. Researchers attempt to create knowledge about 'how the social world works' in different social spheres, the resulting knowledge only ever being relatively true. This 'truth' is judged by the extent to which it informs people's attempts to pursue their various projects in the sphere of life studied.

(2) *non-realists* (who variously call themselves 'interpretivists', 'social constructionists/constructivists', 'post-structuralists' or 'discourse theorists') who insist that the social world only exists insofar as it is 'constituted' by processes of interpretation and linguistic practice.

The complication in all of this is that, while non-realists tend to share the common position that there is no social reality beyond the processes whereby people make sense of the social world, realists vary in the extent to which they are willing to incorporate some interpretive principles within their shared view that social reality has an existence *sui generis* or 'in its own right'. This gives us four basic methodological positions as set out in Table 1.2.

As we noted earlier in this section, positivism has historical roots as deep as those of sociology itself in the early part of the nineteenth century. But recognition of what we have here called the 'interpretive principle' soon led to challenges to positivism, most famously by Max Weber and his attempt, later in the same and the subsequent century, to combine interpretive insights with realist considerations. The same can be said of Berger and Luckmann's classic twentieth century work, *The Social Construction of Reality* (Watson 2008c). Social constructionism, interpretivism and discourse theory – in spite of the use of terms with a longer history – can be seen as coming into sociology in the late twentieth century under the influence of French post-structuralist language-centred thought.

LOOKING FORWARD >>>>>

Post-structuralism and the heavy emphasis on the importance of language in social life are discussed in Chapter 3.

Snapshot 6.3 (pp. 210–211), *Angus, the posh wage slave*, is a demonstration of how a realist analysis can incorporate the interpretive principle.

Critical realism came into play during the same period, in part as antidote to the non-realism of so-called constructionists and interpretivist researchers (Bhaskar 1989; Sayer 2000). One of its attractions to sociologists of work is that it stresses the reality of the underlying mechanisms of the capitalist mode of production whilst recognising that, at a level above this, interpretive processes and social construction processes do play a significant role in shaping social patterns and processes (Ackroyd and Fleetwood 2000). It can be criticised, however, for its dependence on rather mechanistic or biological metaphors such as 'generative mechanisms' and 'causal powers'. Pragmatic realism shares with critical realism

Table 1.3 Four proposed studies, each with a distinctive methodological orientation, of the relationship between people's age and experience of work

Proposal 1 (working within positivist principles): A large survey will be designed in which a questionnaire will be posted to a sample of people, the sample being 'stratified' to ensure that there is a representative coverage of different age groups and occupations. Questions will be asked about respondents' age and about the extent of their agreement with a variety of printed statements about work satisfaction and dissatisfaction. Once collected, these responses will be treated as *data* – unproblematic 'givens' or 'findings' – which can then be statistically analysed to test the hypothesis that job satisfaction increases with age in high-status occupations and decreases with age in low-status occupations. If the 'data' or 'findings' support the original contention, then the researcher will be in a position where they can say they have developed a new 'theory' about age and job satisfaction. Strictly speaking, this will be a covering law. It will take the form of a statement about the relationship between work and age which has a degree of predictive power: suggesting to each of us, in our particular occupational context, how our happiness at work is likely to change as we get older.

Proposal 2 (working within interpretive/constructionist principles): A series of face-to-face interviews with people of different ages and in different occupations will be conducted. Additionally, time will be spent with some of these people in the workplace, or in a leisure context, in order to note how in group interactions they talk to each other about their work and their lives. The researcher will interpret what was said to them in the light of how they believe the subject was interpreting the context in which they spoke and how they were, at the time of their speaking, choosing to present a particular image of themselves to the researcher and perhaps to other people present. In the analysis of this research material, close attention will be given to the language used by the subjects, as well as other symbols like 'body language' and the clothing worn by subjects. This will be used to construct an understanding of how the people make sense, for themselves and for others, of the relationship between age and the experience of work. The 'reality' of the relationship between one's age and one's work experience is thus treated as something that emerges from human interactions, socially negotiated understandings and available discourses. It does not exist 'out there' separately from the people who bring that reality into existence.

Proposal 3 (working within critical realist principles): This project will be strongly influenced from the start by existing theories (in the sense of generalisations about how the social world 'works'). The study might use either, or both, quantitative and qualitative techniques to reveal how ideologies influenced by the interests of employers in capitalist societies influence younger, and hence fitter and more flexible, people to regard their work positively whilst older, and potentially less productive, workers are discouraged from wanting to stay at work. Drawing on both existing theoretical assumptions about the social world and on the information gathered in the research, attempts will be made to identify the causal or 'generative' mechanisms within capitalist class and employment relationships using concepts like capital accumulation, labour process and false consciousness. These mechanisms will be taken to have a 'real' existence of their own, a reality operating at a deeper level than the actions and interpretations of the employers and workers involved.

Proposal 4 (working within pragmatic realist principles): As with critical realism, the study might use either, or both, quantitative and qualitative techniques, but the researchers are likely to get as close as they can to the people involved in the study. They will analyse what they see and hear by relating it to wider historically pre-existing and real institutional patterns and discourses in order to understand how people have gone about 'learning the ropes' of the context in which they have been acting. The rules, 'definitions of the situation' and negotiated meanings which are observed and related to wider institutional patterns are presented as social realities; they constitute knowledge which has the potential to inform human practices and projects in areas of life similar to those studied.

an interest in realities existing beyond, but not separate from, processes of human interpretation (Johnson and Duberley 2000; Watson 2010, 2011; Van de Ven 2007). It avoids, however, making these too 'solid' in the way that critical realism does by utilising relatively 'hard' metaphors of 'mechanisms' or 'powers'. Pragmatic Realism still uses sociological notions of social structure, organisation, class and the like. It does not see them as 'things' with 'properties' but as pragmatically selected conceptual devices to help the sociologist to make sense of the patterns of human relationships, processes and understanding by which work and other human activities shape and are shaped. Sociological phenomena of organisational rules, occupational cultures and so on are experienced *as if* they were 'things out there'. In Pragmatist terms, however, they are patterns, processes, tendencies and tensions which human actors need to be aware of – if they are going to be at all successful in the practices and projects which they undertake (Watson 2013).

To avoid this discussion sounding too abstract or esoteric, as shown in Table 1.3, we can outline four different ways in which researchers, adopting different methodological positions, might go about studying the relationship between people's age and their experience of work. The four approaches take the form of research proposals that might, for example, be submitted to a research-funding body.

Our examples of four possible research studies make it clear that there are significant variations of *methodological orientation* within the sociology of work and organisation. These four philosophy-of-science stances do not necessarily each lead to the application of particular research methods or even to the adoption of particular theories or concepts. Nevertheless, as the examples suggest, the methodological position adopted may lead to a broad preference for one style of research rather than another (the positivist towards survey methods and the pragmatic realist towards participant observation, for example). The same might be said about theoretical positions with the positivists tending to look to Durkheim's sociology, for example, the interpretivists towards Foucault's ideas, the critical realists towards Marxian analysis and the pragmatic realists towards Weberian, interactionist and institutional theories. It is to the variety of *theoretical orientations* that we now turn in Chapters 2 and 3.

Summary

In this chapter, we have established that sociology developed historically as a discipline intended to help people understand and deal with processes of modernisation and industrialisation and that it has the potential to play an important role in informing the choices made about work in the twenty-first century. Sociology is a scientific discipline concerned with developing theories and insights which can inform human choices, and to this end, it uses a variety of different research methods and works within a variety of different methodological assumptions.

2 Analysing work and organisation: scientific management, human relations and negotiated orders

Key issues

- How can we map and appreciate the variety of different sociological approaches to work and its organisation?
- What are the key ideas and influences of the managerially and psychologically-oriented writers against whom, in part, the modern sociological researchers in the work and organisations field have reacted?
- In what ways does the work of Durkheim and those who have been influenced by him, alongside the contributions of interactionist thinkers and researchers, demonstrate essentially sociological ways of looking at and understanding the dilemmas of the modern world and the lives of people coping with the changing patterns of work and organisation?

Strands of thought and key theoretical perspectives in the sociology of work and organisation

We saw in the previous chapter that sociology originally developed to provide a critical understanding of industrial capitalist societies. Work and how it is organised and experienced has always been central to this project. In spite of this, a single and fully integrated industrial sociology or sociology of work and organisation did not emerge. Sociologists of work and organisation have varied in their methodological and theoretical orientations. They have also differed in their primary interests. Some researchers have focused on large societal patterns of work organisation whilst others have examined more 'micro' aspects of work behaviour and experience. Some sociologists have prioritised issues of conflict, exploitation and inequality whilst others have given greater emphasis to issues of workplace and team co-operation. Some have concentrated on structural factors influencing work activities and others have concentrated on the role of human agency and 'subjectivity'. It is nevertheless possible to see some pattern in all of this. To avoid the artificiality of allocating different researchers and writers to 'schools' whilst still recognising the need somehow to bring together contributions which appear to have something in common, we can use the notion of *strands* of thought. This metaphor is not ideal, but it recognises that some sociologists might work with just one of these strands in doing their research whilst others may pull together two or perhaps more strands to create a conceptual rope to take the weight of their analytical endeavour.

Six strands of thought that we need to be aware of if we are to appreciate both the variations and the continuities in the sociological study of work are identified in Table 2.1. The arrows crossing some of the 'boxes' in the table indicate developments which have been influenced by more than one of the theoretical strands. In the case of three of the

Table. 2.1 Six strands of thought in the sociology of work and industry

Strand of thought	Application and development
Managerial-psychologistic	Scientific management (Taylorism)
	Psychological humanism
Durkheim-human-relations-systems	Human relations
	Systems thinking in organisational analysis
Interactionist-negotiated-order	Occupations and professions in society
	Organisations as negotiated orders
	Ethnomethodology
Weber-social-action-institutional	Bureaucratic principles of work organisation
	Orientations to work
	Institutionalist organisation theories and social construction
Marxian-labour-process	Individual experiences and capitalist labour processes
	Structural contradictions in society and economy
Poststructuralist and postmodern	Discourse and human subjectivity
	Postmodern organisations

strands, we see approaches which have been especially influenced by a particular founding figure of sociology, Durkheim, Weber or Marx. The first of these will be considered in the present chapter and the other two in Chapter 3. The managerial-psychologistic strand, which we consider first, contains what are usually seen as quite separate and indeed contrasting elements. What they share, however, is the fact that they are ways of thinking about people and work to which the five more sociological strands can be seen as reacting and going substantially beyond.

The managerial-psychologistic strand

Strictly speaking, neither of the two approaches brought together here are part of a sociology of work and organisation. Yet they are vitally important to an understanding of the development of industrial sociology, as it became a significant area of study in the twentieth century. They have provided an ever-present broad style of thinking with which sociologists have to come to terms and to which they provide a critical alternative. Scientific management and psychological humanism are the ghosts at the banquet, in effect. It is much easier to appreciate the sociological guests at the feast if we have a good view of these strictly non-sociological approaches which tend to haunt such events.

Scientific management and psychological humanism are, at first sight, diametrically opposed in underlying sentiment and assumptions about human nature. But they are both relatively individualistic styles of thinking about work and are both concerned to prescribe to managers how they should relate to their employees and should organise workers' jobs. They both concentrate on questions of 'human nature' and fail to recognise the range of possibilities for work organisation and orientation that people may choose to adopt, depending on their priorities in life. To this extent, they can be regarded as *psychologistic*.

Psychologism
A tendency to explain social behaviour solely in terms of the psychological characteristics of individuals.

The concern of each of the approaches is to harness scientific method to discover and make legitimate what are, in effect, techniques of manipulation rather than disinterested concerns with understanding.

Scientific management

The leading advocate and systematiser of what he named scientific management (and others frequently call 'Taylorism') was F.W. Taylor (1856–1915), an American engineer and consultant. Taylor's importance to the modern organisation of work has to be set in its historical context. The increasingly rationalised division of tasks and the mechanisation of work reached a point at the beginning of the twentieth century where the need to co-ordinate human work efforts not surprisingly invited the attentions of individuals interested in applying scientific and engineering criteria to the human sphere as they had to the mechanical. Taylorism encouraged a view of the industrial worker as an economic animal who could be encouraged to act as a self-seeking hired hand and who would allow managers to do their job-related thinking for them. If this could be achieved, especially through the use of output-based and potentially high-level rewards, the management would work out the most efficient way of organising work, tying the monetary rewards of the work to the level of output achieved by the individual. This would produce results which would benefit employer and employee alike, removing the likelihood of conflict and the need for trade unions.

Scientific management involves:
- the scientific analysis by management of all the tasks which need to be done in order to make the workshop as efficient as possible;
- the design of the jobs by managers to achieve the maximum technical division of labour through advanced job fragmentation;
- the separation of the planning of work from its execution;
- the reduction of skill requirements and job-learning times to a minimum;
- the minimising of materials-handling by operators and the separation of indirect or preparatory tasks from direct or productive ones;
- the use of such devices as time-study and monitoring systems to co-ordinate these fragmented elements and the work of the deskilled workers;
- the use of incentive payment systems both to stabilise and intensify worker effort; and
- the conduct of manager–worker relationships at 'arms-length' – following a 'minimum interaction model' (Littler 1982).

Taylor's successors within scientific management modified his refusal to accept a place for organised labour in the workplace, but the approach has always retained its individualistic emphasis. Books on management thought and much management teaching imply that scientific manage-ment, on being shown to fall short psychologically, was consigned to the history of management as a thing of its 'classical' past. This is far from the case, however, when it comes to the practicalities of job design in the modern world. Systematic research carried out in the 1950s and followed up in the 1970s (Davis and Taylor 1979) on a representative sample of American companies showed that job design practices in manufacturing continued to be dominated by a concern to minimise the unit production time in order to minimise the cost of production. Job design criteria included skill specialisation, minimal skill requirements, minimum training times, maximum repetition and the general limiting of both the number of tasks in a job and the variation within those tasks and jobs. Braverman (1974) claimed that scientific management and its associated deskilling, because of its association with the logic of capital accumulation, will continue to dominate the capitalist working world. Research carried out in a wide variety of contexts to test Braverman's analysis has shown that alongside attempts to give workers greater choice and relative autonomy in certain work contexts, the deskilling logic of scientific management is still applied to many easily routinised work activities.

The psychologistic assumptions of scientific management are illustrated by reference to Taylor's concept of 'soldiering' as described in *The Principles of Scientific Management* (1911a). Soldiering in Taylor's sense is 'the natural instinct and tendency of men to take it easy'. When this is combined with people's economic interests and the failure of managers to design, allocate and reward work on a scientific basis, it leads employees to get together and rationally conspire to hold production down. They do this to maximise their reward without tempting the incompetent management to come back and tighten the rate (which only needs tightening because it was originally guessed at and not fixed scientifically). This is 'systematic soldiering' and is an inefficient evil. It is not, however, an inevitable phenomenon. If the management relate directly to each individual and satisfy their personal self-interest, then they will get full co-operation. A proper understanding of human nature, it is implied, would demonstrate that this is the case. And the application of technical solutions to human problems in this way makes it unnecessary to tackle them politically. Taylor, and other engineers of his time, aspired to taking politics and contest out of work relationships, effectively 'redefining industrial conflict as a mechanical problem' (Shenav 1999). These aspirations were cultural as well as political. Scientific management fostered a social movement which, as Taksa (1992) puts it, 'would facilitate the creation of a unified industrial culture unmarked by class divisions or conflict, a culture characterised by imposed notions of consensus'. Although scientific management is not spoken of in these terms in contemporary times, it is important to recognise the extent to which its working principles continue to underlie the design of 'knowledge work' activities across the world.

Psychological humanism

The prescriptions offered to managers by this group of writers and researchers are based on rather different assumptions about human psychology than those seen in scientific management. Psychological humanists argue for achieving organisational efficiency not through the exclusion of workers from task-related decision-making but by encouraging their *participation* in it with, for example:

- non-managerial workers becoming involved in setting their own objectives;
- jobs being 'enriched' by reducing the extent to which they are supervised and monitored; and
- more open and authentic colleague relationships being developed, particularly in 'teams'.

These ideas have become popular with more 'enlightened' managers since the writings, manuals and training films of a group of American psychologists and management consultants encouraging such an approach began to have an influence in the 1960s. It can be seen as the opposite of scientific management, but in some ways, it is a mirror image of it. It bases its approach to human work behaviour on a theory of human nature, and one of the popular early writers of this school made quite clear the equivalence of the two opposing propositions by labelling them, alternatively, Theory X and Theory Y.

McGregor (1960) characterised the scientific management type of approach, which is adopted by unenlightened managers, as based on Theory X. This sees human beings as naturally disliking work and therefore as avoiding it if they can. People prefer to avoid responsibility and like to be given direction. They have limited ambitions and see security as a priority. The manager therefore controls and coerces people towards the meeting of organisational objectives. The effect of this is to encourage the very kind of behaviour which managers wish to avoid: the employees' passive acceptance of the situation may be encouraged, leading to a lack of initiative and creativity on their part, or their resentment may be fuelled and hence their aggression and lack of co-operation. But Theory Y, which McGregor advocated and which social science research was said to support, states that people are not at all like this but would generally prefer to exercise self-control and self-discipline at work. He believed this would occur if employees were allowed to contribute creatively to organisational problems in a way which enabled them to meet their need for self-actualisation.

The notion of a *self-actualisation need* within all human beings is central to the writing of Maslow (1954) whose starting point was the belief that scientific investigation of human behaviour should be oriented towards releasing in people the various potentials they possess. The basic scheme, which has been taken from Maslow and used by numerous 'enlightened' management writers and teachers, is the 'hierarchy of needs' model. This suggests that there are five sets of genetic or instinctive needs which people possess and that as one satisfies most of the needs at one level one moves up to seek satisfaction of the needs at the next level:

- At the first level, there are *physiological needs*, such as for food, drink, sex and sensory satisfaction.
- At the second level, there are *safety needs* which motivate people to avoid danger.
- At the third level, there are what Maslow calls *love needs*; these include needs to belong and to affiliate with others in both a giving and a receiving sense.
- At the fourth level, there are *esteem needs* which cover prestige, status and appreciation coming from external sources as well as internal feelings of confidence, achievement, strength, adequacy and independence.
- At the fifth level, there is the need for *self-actualisation*, which is the desire to realise one's ultimate potential.

Self-actualisation

To become self-actualised is 'to become more and more what one is, to become everything that one is capable of becoming' (Maslow 1943).

The needs–hierarchy model was influenced by Maslow's earlier studies of monkeys and of the way certain individuals, human or primate, come to dominate others. He believed that some individuals have a greater inherited propensity to self-actualise than others. Natural biological elites would thus come to rise to the top in society and, Cullen (1997) argues, Maslow's theory effectively 'justifies managerial power, and enables managers to adopt motivation practices that appear to be responsive to employee needs while at the same time absolving them of accountability for the ineffectiveness of their practices'. In spite of these ideological undertones, or perhaps because of them, Maslow's model is frequently used as a stick with which to beat traditional managerial approaches, these being seen as failing to obtain employee co-operation because they do not provide the intrinsically and naturally sought rewards which employees 'need' once they have satisfied their basic low-level requirements. The immense popularity of the Maslow theory has to be explained in terms other than ones of scientific credibility (Watson 1996a). The weakness of the theory, in both sociological and 'critical commonsense' (Watson 2006) terms, is brought out by the words of a practising manager who had thought carefully about 'motivational' aspects of his job. It might be an interesting exercise to check how applicable Maslow's hierarchy idea might be to your own 'real life situation'.

Snapshot 2.1

'The hierarchy of needs theory doesn't stack up, does it?'

'When you think hard about the so-called hierarchy of needs, it doesn't stack up, does it? I am Jewish and I get a good deal of my self-esteem and an awful lot of the social rewards in my life from belonging to my culture. The meeting of these social and esteem needs, I have to say, comes before I meet my need to eat or my need to make love to whoever I fancy. The rules of my religion and my community define what and when I eat and who I can have sex with. If I was in the Israeli army, like my cousin recently was, I would put the need to belong to my community and my personal prestige needs, as a fighter for freedom, way before even my need for safety. Yet Maslow's simplistic scheme has us all working up through the satisfaction of the more basic physiological and safety needs towards the higher social or esteem ones. It is nonsense – there is simply no straightforward sequence to how people pursue their needs. And Maslow's whole notion of human beings seems to be one in which people live outside of culture'.

An influential example of a practical application of this 'needs-based' type of motivational thinking is Herzberg's 'Motivation-Hygiene' or two-factor theory of work motivation (1966), which was originally based on a study of engineers and accountants who were asked to describe events in their working lives which made them feel good or made them feel bad. Herzberg suggested that the factors which made them feel good when they were present were different from those which made them feel bad when they were absent.

Herzberg went on to differentiate between:
- contextual or 'hygiene' factors like salary, status, security, working conditions, supervision and company policy which can lead to dissatisfaction if 'wrong', but which do not lead to satisfaction if 'right'; and
- content or 'motivation' factors such as achievement, advancement, recognition, growth, responsibility and 'the work itself'. These have to be present, in addition to the contextual or 'hygiene' factors, before satisfactions can be produced and people motivated to perform well.

These 'motivators' clearly relate to Maslow's 'higher level needs' whilst the hygiene factors only satisfy the 'lower level' ones. Managers are therefore encouraged to see that getting 'right' such matters as wages, supervision and working conditions would produce little by way of positive motivation. Instead, the 'motivators' have to be built into the very way jobs are designed. Jobs should be enlarged and managerial controls over how they are performed reduced. Workers themselves would set targets, plan the work and, as far as possible, choose the working methods to be used. This represents a complete reversal of the job design principles advocated by scientific management.

Discussion

At first sight it might appear that those interested in scientifically investigating work behaviour have a fairly simple task here: that of testing these two propositions about work and human needs to find the validity of either scientific management's 'Theory X' or the psychological humanists' 'Theory Y'. Alas, says the sociologist, this cannot be done. Such an attempt would involve reductionism and psychologism in its belief that understanding work behaviour is a matter of reaching a correct understanding of human nature – a set of principles about people which would apply to all human beings in all circumstances. In so far as there is such a thing as human nature, it is much more complex than this and leads people to act very differently in different circumstances. To a much greater extent than other animals, humans are what they make of themselves. They are not without instinctive drives or innate physiological needs. But these are overridden by cultural norms, social rules and identity related preferences. Within these, individuals may sometimes seek the assurance of safety and sometimes seek the stimulation of danger, sometimes pursue self-aggrandisement and sometimes indulge in self-abasement. This was the logic of the argument put forward by the reflective manager in Snapshot 2.1. Our socially or culturally defined nature is far more important than any universal 'human' or species nature. We have socially mediated wants rather than built-in needs.

In evaluating scientific management and psychological humanism, we confront a paradox. In effect, both are right and both are wrong. To make sense of this statement, we must add the words *depending on the circumstances*. By circumstances, we mean the structural and cultural factors that are central concerns of a sociological approach to analysis. Many of these factors are concentrated at the organisational level (as following the previously indicated links show). However, they also apply at the societal level, for example:

- If a society or a part of a society has a culture which puts major value on money and it has an industry structured on the basis of mechanisation and minute task-specialisation, it is possible that people in that social/cultural situation would deliberately choose to do such work and will happily accept close supervision and a degree of boredom in return for cash.
- If, on the other hand, there is a wider culture which places central value on personal autonomy and sees work as a key to identity, then we might expect the scientific managers to lose out to the self-actualisers as guides to appropriate managerial policy.

These two social possibilities are vastly over-simplified, in order to make a point about the importance of factors of a sociological nature which exist alongside psychological ones. In practice, we find a mixture of these circumstances in modern societies. Consequently we need a more sophisticated sociological approach to studying work behaviour and attitudes. The work orientations perspective that we will meet in Chapter 3 was in part intended to meet this need but, for the moment, we must stress that the choice which is made to adopt either cash-reward-oriented or self-actualising work organisations is not a scientific one. It is to a large extent a value or a political choice. The role of sociological analysis is to inform that choice with a consideration of what is possible in what circumstances.

The Durkheim-human-relations strand

In contrast to the psychologism of the first strand of thinking, there is a rejection in the second strand of attempts to understand social patterns through a focus on human individuals and the 'needs' which they are all said to share. Instead we see an emphasis on the social system of which individuals are a part. The social system may be that of the society as a whole or, alternatively, it may be that of the work organisation or even a sub-unit of the organisation. The key idea is the essentially sociological one of concentrating on the patterns of relationships which exist between people rather than on the people as such. This insight is apparent in the proto-sociologists of the Scottish Enlightenment with Adam Ferguson, for example, noting the system-like character of the emerging industrial workshops whose logic was one in which the workers' minds were less significant than their acting as components of a social 'engine' (Swingewood 2000). But the broad emphasis on patterns of human relationship reaches its peak in the history of sociology with Emile Durkheim, and it provides the theoretical underpinning of what is often identified as the first recognisable 'school' of industrial sociology, that of 'human relations'.

Emile Durkheim

Emile Durkheim (1858–1917) can be seen as the sociologist *par excellence*. In this, we see both his importance and the major problem with his work. His position as the first sociologist to hold a university professorship meant that there was considerable pressure on him to establish the distinctiveness of the new discipline. This fact probably explains in part his over-heavy stress on science (which, he believed, can give moral guidance) and his over-emphasis on the 'reality' of an autonomous and externally existing 'society'. Ideas which stress the primacy of community over the individual have a strong ideological and conservative potential, but to picture Durkheim as an intentionally conservative thinker in this way is quite wrong. He was concerned neither to return to the past nor to justify the status quo. Yet he was strongly reacting to certain aspects of the prevailing individualism of his age. On a methodological level, he was opposed to psychological reductionism, showing that even a highly individual act like suicide has to be understood in terms of the extent of the individual's bonding with others in a community or group rather than by simple reference to the individual's mental state. Further, as Dobbin (2009) points out, Durkheim's ideas have influenced contemporary organisational sociologists in two ways in their stress on, first, the 'social underpinnings of cognition' and, second, 'our inclination to act collectively to make sense of the world by classifying things and attaching meaning to them, [which] informs much of the cultural work in organizational sociology'.

Durkheim argued that to study social life one had to isolate and examine 'social currents' and 'social facts'. These are *things* that exist externally to individuals and exert constraint over them. Values, customs, norms, obligations and suchlike are to be considered in this way. If there is a degree of over-emphasis on the structural side of the agency–structure relationship here, we can perhaps explain it by putting it in the context of Durkheim's morally inspired reaction to the disintegrating effects of the egoism and self-interest which he saw developing in the European societies of his time.

> ### LOOKING BACK AND FORWARD <<<<< >>>>>
>
> Durkheim was just one of the early sociologists reacting to what they saw as fundamental changes in the nature of modern societies, as we saw in Chapter 1, pp. 12–14. A key work was his study of the changing division of labour coming about with industrialisation (Chapter 4, pp. 91–94).

Durkheim saw the organic solidarity so necessary for a healthy society being threatened by laissez–faire economics and a utilitarian philosophy which encouraged an egoism strongly contrasting with the healthy kind of individualism which could exist in an industrialised society. For Durkheim, as Hookway (2015) puts it, 'The purpose of society is to maintain stability and cohesion through successful regulation and integration of the pre-social self into the prevailing norms and values of a society'. A 'healthy' individualism could exist as long as that society provided regulation, directing principles or norms. Without this, we have the pathology of anomie.

Anomie
A form of social breakdown in which the norms which would otherwise prevail in a given situation cease to operate.

The particular form of anomie which worried Durkheim was one in which the 'organic' integration of society would be threatened by unrestricted individual aspirations and hence a lack of any kind of social discipline, principle or guiding norms.

Durkheim's emphasis was on social life at the societal level and, as P. Hirsch *et al.* (2009) observe, contemporary globalisation trends echo Durkheim's thoughts on 'social transformation at the turn of the twentieth century'. His ideas, and his concepts of anomie and 'social solidarity' in particular, can also be applied at the organisational level, as we see in the case of a project in a local government organisation.

Snapshot 2.2

Her mind turned to 'Suicide': social solidarity and anomie in two organisational departments

A researcher studying employment relations in a local government organisation noticed that there were distinctive differences between two of the organisation's clerical departments. In Department A, there was a low level of staff turnover, a low level of sickness absence and very few disputes requiring the union representatives to present grievances to the management. In Department B, however, there were regular disputes, some of these leading to short strikes. Staff turnover had reached a level which seriously impaired the effectiveness of the department and the levels of absence from work were similarly very high. When the researcher investigated this, she was surprised that find that there was little apparent difference in the sort of work that the staff were doing in the two departments. The age, qualification and gender distribution patterns were also similar. No specific factors could be identified that might explain either the differences in absence or leaving the authority's employment. It was only when the researcher spent several days getting to know people in the two departments that she saw any kind of pattern. In Department A, she observed strong patterns of friendship between colleagues, with a number of them being related both by blood and by marriage. Most of the workers were local people, and there was a lot of sharing of lifts to work as well as groups going out in the evenings together. The office manager and the two section leaders frequently took part in these informal leisure activities. In Department B, however, it seemed to the researcher that staff were rather like 'strangers to each other'. She found it much more difficult to get into more than superficial conversations with these people – in clear contrast to her experiences in Department A. A much higher proportion of the Department B staff, compared to the other department, had moved into the city in recent years, and there seemed to be no tradition of their spending time with each other outside work. The manager and the section leaders operated what the researcher felt was a 'remote' form of control of the department: tending to send emails to staff when, in similar circumstances, their opposite numbers in the other department would speak directly and informally to staff.

The researcher in this 'snapshot' initially had difficulties with analysing the difference between the two departments. She was sure that what would commonly be called 'management style' was a factor in what was occurring. But she also, as a result of her sociology training, felt that there was something more 'structural' or 'cultural' about the situation. This took her back to her days as a sociology student and her reading of Durkheim's classic work *Suicide*. Durkheim explained the different rates of suicide prevailing among different social groups in terms of the degree to which the members of those groups were bonded with each other in a family, group or community way. Divorced people killed themselves more often than non-divorced people, single people more than married people, members of individualistic (Protestant) religions more than members of more communal religions and so on. Taking time off work or leaving one's job was hardly the same as committing suicide, our researcher thought, but it nevertheless seemed to her that these actions were equivalent to some degree: Department A displayed a much higher level of social solidarity than Department B which, in comparison, was somewhat anomic. Durkheim showed that suicide occurred less in contexts of social solidarity than in more anomic circumstances. By the same token, people were more disposed towards coming into work, regardless of how well or unwell they felt, were more disposed to stay with the employer and were less disposed towards developing grievances about their work experiences in Department A, where there were strong shared norms than were in Department B where there was less normative and social support.

Human relations and the Hawthorne studies

Durkheim's analysis of anomie and his concern about social solidarity was a major influence on the work of Elton Mayo (1880–1949), who has come to be seen as the leading spokesman of the so-called human relations 'school' of industrial sociology. Whereas Durkheim's sympathies were not with the ruling or managerial interests of capitalist society, Mayo's were. In place of Durkheim's seeking of social integration through moral communities based on occupations, Mayo put the industrial work-group and the employing enterprise, with the industrial managers having responsibility for ensuring that group affiliations and social sentiments were fostered in a creative way. Like Taylor, Mayo was anxious to develop an effective and scientifically informed managerial elite. If managements could ensure that employees' social needs were met at work by giving them the satisfaction of working together, by making them feel important in the organisation and by showing an interest in their personal problems, then both social breakdown and industrial conflict could be headed off. Managerial skills and good communications were the antidotes to the potential pathologies of an urban industrial civilisation.

The context of the contribution of the human relations group was the problem of controlling the increasingly large-scale enterprises of the post-war period and the problem of legitimating this control in a time of growing trade union challenge. The faith of the scientific management experts in a solution which involved the achieving of optimum working conditions, the 'right' method and an appropriate incentive scheme proved to be too blind. Practical experience and psychological research alike were indicating the need to pay attention to other variables in work behaviour. Here we see the importance of the Hawthorne experiments.

The Hawthorne investigations had been started in Chicago by engineers of the Western Electric Company's Hawthorne plant. They had investigated the effects of workshop illumination on output and had found that, as their investigations proceeded, output improved in the groups investigated, regardless of what was done to the lighting. In 1927, the Department of Industrial Research of Harvard University, a group to which Mayo had been recruited, were called in. Their enquiry started in the Relay Assembly Test Room where over a five-year period a wide range of changes were made in the working conditions of a specially segregated group of six women whose job was to assemble telephone relays. Changes involving incentive schemes, rest pauses, hours of work and refreshments were made, but it was found that whatever changes were made – including a return to original conditions – output rose. The explanation which was later to emerge has been labelled 'the Hawthorne effect'. It was inferred that the close interest shown in the workers by the investigators, the effective pattern of communication which developed and the emerging high social cohesion within the group brought together the needs of the group for rewarding interaction and co-operation with the output needs of the management. This type of explanation was also encouraged by the other stages of the investigation. The employee interviewing programme was seen as showing that many of the problems of management– worker relationships could be put down to the failure to recognise the emotions and the 'sentiments' of the employees, and the study in the Bank Wiring Observation Room was taken to show the part played by informal social group pressures in worker restriction of output. The workgroup informally set their own 'output norm' and subsequently found ways of punishing any member who performed at either a higher rate ('ratebuster') or a lower rate ('chiseller') than the norm.

The Hawthorne studies were most fully reported by Roethlisberger and Dickson (1939), and their reports and interpretations can be compared with those of Mayo (1933) and Whitehead (1938). We have already noted the relationship between Durkheim's ideas and those of Mayo but perhaps a more important influence on all of these interpreters was the classical sociologist Pareto (1848–1923). A key figure in the Harvard sociological circles of this time was the biologist and translator of Pareto, L.J. Henderson. He introduced the thinking of this former Italian engineer to those Harvard thinkers who, at the time, were highly receptive to ideas that might counter those of the liberals or Marxists (Gouldner 1971). The effects of Pareto (via Henderson) on this early form of industrial sociology were two-fold:

1. The suggestion that workers' behaviour can be attributed to their 'sentiments' rather than to their reason. Apparently rational behaviour, like Taylor's 'systematic soldiering', referred to earlier, could be better understood as deriving from irrational fears, status anxieties and the instinctive need of the individual to be loyal to his or her immediate social group. The problems did not arise from economic and rationally perceived conflicts of interest and were therefore not open to solution through scientific management.

2. An emphasis on the notion of *system*, this conveniently according with the holistic tendencies of Durkheim. Here we have the organic

analogy with its stress on integration and the necessary interdependence of the parts and the whole. Only by the integration of the individual into the (management-led) plant community could systemic integration be maintained and the potential pathologies of the industrial society avoided.

Human relations industrial sociology has been widely criticised for such things as its managerial bias, its failure to recognise the rationality of employee behaviour and its denial of underlying economic conflicts of interest (see Landsberger 1958). The investigations which were carried out have also been examined and found wanting (Carey 1967). Some of the writers in the tradition are more vulnerable to criticism than others, but what cannot be denied is the enormous influence these researchers, and especially Mayo, had on subsequent social scientific investigation of industrial behaviour (Smith 1987). The 'Mayo legacy' remains in management thinking, especially in human resource management (HRM) and the concern of that approach with getting workers to 'adjust' so that they are 'integrated' into organisations whose 'goals' they identify with (O'Connor 1999).

LOOKING FORWARD >>>>>

HRM will be examined in Chapter 6, pp. 178–183.

Although the Hawthorne works in Chicago have now been replaced by shopping malls, researchers on work organisations are turning back to the classic studies carried out there as they debate a range of theoretical and methodological issues which were initially raised by this work (Schwartzman 1993). Gillespie (1991) argues that we can most usefully regard the accounts and discussions of the Hawthorne experiments as 'manufactured knowledge' in which Mayo and his fellow human relations writers drew on their social scientific investigations to construct a 'message' – one which played down the possibility of an active role for workers, especially a collective role and which stressed the role of managers as experts in control.

Corporate cultures

In recent decades, corporate managers have time and again been encouraged to develop 'strong' cultures in their organisations (Peters and Waterman 1982; Deal and Kennedy 1982). This, in part, took up the recognition by Barnard (1938), a management writer associated with the Human Relations group at Harvard in the 1930s, of the importance of developing a sense of belonging and common purpose within organisations. Barnard contrasted the type of social integration he felt necessary for the successful performance of industrial organisations with Durkheim's notion of *anomie*. This was manifesting itself within industrial enterprises where there was a lack of clear corporate norms of conduct pulling people into managerially desirable co-operative social action. The later advocates of strong corporate 'cultures' similarly wanted to create conditions in which people's individualism would flourish through their finding meaning as members of a corporate community. In this, there would be a reconciling of the social and the individualistic aspects of human beings along the lines that Durkheim envisaged as a component of social solidarity at a societal level (Ray 1986).

The association by critics of the management culture writers of their tendency to 'subjugate the individual to the collective' (Ray 1986; Dahler-Larsen 1994) with Durkheim's understanding of social solidarity is not warranted, according to Starkey (1998), if we recognise how Durkheim's later work gave fuller attention than his earlier work to how an interplay between different interests, as opposed to an overcoming of differences, contributes to the achievement of social integration. Lincoln and Guillot (2006) encourage us to engage in a fine-grained reading of Durkheim's work. This would show that he accepted that 'all consciousness of necessity resides in individual minds' but 'it converges and coalesces through a dynamic process of interaction and so becomes exterior and constraining in the incontrovertible sense that individuals find themselves enmeshed in thick and unyielding webs of social pressure that leave them little recourse but to join the crowd'. And, as sociological research shows, 'work organizations . . . often contrive to spin these ideological webs, which enable them to put aside the hard structural controls whose source is easily pinpointed and against which resistance can readily form'.

LOOKING FORWARD >>>>>

The sociological concept of *organisational culture* was discussed in Chapter 2 (p. 44), and the interest of corporate managers in developing strong corporate cultures is examined in Chapter 6 (pp. 197–200).

Discussion

Although they can be accused of using over-simplified versions of Durkheim's ideas for critical purposes rather than fully appreciating the sophistication of his thinking (Stedman Jones 2001), later sociologists have seen the key weakness of the Durkheimian strand of thinking as a tendency to over-emphasise integration and consensus, both within societies and within work organisations, at the expense of attention to underlying conflicts and fundamental differences of interest. Differences of interest are recognised, but interest groups tend to be conceived within a 'pluralist' political model which sees the parties in conflict as being more or less evenly matched in power terms. As we shall see in later chapters, contemporary approaches to understanding industrial capitalist societies, work organisations and industrial conflict, attempt to give a more balanced view through attending to basic power structures and patterns of inequality as well as to matters of co-operation and shared norms.

In making human individuals secondary to or derivative of the social system in which they are located, Durkheimian approaches tend to pay insufficient attention to the degree of interplay which goes on between individual initiative and social constraint in human societies. Systems-oriented models tend to fall especially short when it comes to taking into account the extent to which the social world is the creation of interacting individuals and groups assigning meanings and making interpretations of their situations. To consider an approach which gives prime emphasis to meanings and to interaction rather than to systems and structures existing outside the individual, we now turn to a quite different strand of the sociology of work and organisation.

The interactionist-negotiated-order strand

The interactionist strand has its roots firmly in the sociology department of Chicago University in America. Theoretically, the interactionist perspective, with its focus on the individual, the small group and on meanings, is almost a polar opposite of the Durkheim systems strand described in the previous section. Yet in the contributions of interactionist sociologists to the study of work, we find important continuities with the work of Durkheim. This continuity can be seen in a common interest taken in occupations as central social institutions and also in recognition of the importance of the division of labour in society. But to appreciate fully the interactionist approaches to work, it is necessary to give an account of the theoretical approach of the wider tradition in sociology of which these sociologists of work are a part – that of symbolic interactionism.

The Chicago school and symbolic interactionism

The particular brand of sociological theory that came to be known as symbolic interactionism has developed alongside the more empirical study of work which has taken place within the same Chicago circles. The origins of the approach lie in the work of Cooley (1864–1929) and Mead (1863–1931) and its basic position is that the individual and society are inseparable units; their relationship is a mutually interdependent one, not a one-sided deterministic one. Human beings construct their realities in a process of interaction with other human beings. Individuals derive their very identity from their interaction with others. Carter and Fuller (2016) characterise this 'micro-level theoretical framework and perspective' as addressing the way in which society is created and maintained through face-to-face repeated, meaningful interactions among individuals (before going on to look at varieties of the perspective and how these have influenced several recent branches of theorising).

Symbolic interactionism
The study of social interaction which focuses on how people develop their concept of *self* through processes of communication in which symbols such as words, gestures and dress allow people to understand the expectations of others.

According to the symbolic interactionists, all interaction and communication is dependent on the use of symbols such as words, gestures, clothes, skin colour and so on. The infant acquires an identity – a consciousness of *self* – through the socialisation or social learning process. This process involves the internalisation of symbols, which are organised around the concept of self to make social life meaningful. Awareness of self is acquired through 'taking on the role of the other'. It is through taking on the role of the other, particularly what are called 'significant others', that we learn about the expectations which others have of us. This helps us in deciding what role we will play in any given situation. Similarly, by taking the role of the other, we learn what to expect of that other. To orient us as we make our way through life we look to a variety of what are termed reference groups and as we move through a series of situations which bestow identity on us we are said to follow a subjective *career*. If we look at an individual's work life objectively, we see them moving through various structural 'statuses' which may be viewed as making up occupational careers (Chapter 8, pp. 254–256) or organisational careers (each organisation has a series of positions through which individuals may move in typical sequences). However, individuals also have their own view of the process which their life is following. Hughes (1937) refers to the 'moving perspective in which the person sees his life as a whole and interprets the meaning of his various attributes, actions, and the things which happen to him'. This is the individual's subjective career.

Subjective career
The way an individual understands or makes sense of the way they have moved through various social positions or stages in the course of their life, or part of their life.

Robert Park (1864–1944), who established the investigative programme of the interactionists, was a former journalist who encouraged researchers to make detailed ethnographic observations of both normal and deviant Chicago life in the participant observation tradition previously confined to anthropological studies of tribal life. In this and in his Durkheimian interest in what he called the 'moral order' (an ordering of expectations and moral imperatives which tend to routinise interaction) he influenced Everett Hughes (1863–1931) (Hughes 1958). Where Durkheim tended to look to occupations as offering possible solutions to the problem of social order, Hughes tends to take the study of occupations as his starting point; his way into learning about society. He has been an inspiration to contemporary researchers whose 'workplace studies' in settings such as news rooms, hospitals, air traffic and rapid urban transport control centres are closely examining how 'the social and interactional organisation of workplace activities, ranging from paper documents to complex multimedia systems, feature in day-to-day work and collaboration' (Heath *et al.* 2000).

Hughes' approach is to focus on the social drama of work – the interaction which takes place at work – taking note of the problems or tensions which are created by the work itself and by its social situation. The concern then turns to how the individual copes with or adapts to those problems, and especially, relates them to the problem of maintaining their identity.

LOOKING FORWARD >>>>>

Identity is a key concern of Chapter 10 and Hughes' interest in 'dirty' and 'deviant' work informs part of Chapter 8.

Hughes paid great attention to how members of different occupations cope with the particular problems of their work. He especially encouraged his students to focus on the offbeat, the 'dirty' or the deviant types of occupation (in the notorious Chicago 'nuts and sluts' tradition). This was not only because these occupations are interesting in their own right but because their study can highlight factors of general relevance to work experience which we might not notice in more conventional kinds of work where we too easily take them for granted.

Organisations as negotiated orders

Interactionism has also contributed to how we understand work organisations. Its most significant contribution here is its conception of the organisation as a *negotiated order* (Watson 2015). The concept was developed by Strauss *et al.* (1963) as part of a study of a psychiatric hospital showing how 'order' in the hospital was an outcome of a continual process of negotiation and adjustments between doctors, nurses, patients, social workers, patients' families and administrators. Organisational rules and hierarchies play a part in the patterning of life in organisations, but the overall organisational order is one that emerges out of the processes whereby different groups make use of rules, procedures and information in the day-to-day negotiations that occur between them about what is to happen in any given situation at any particular time.

Negotiated order

The pattern of activities which emerges over time as an outcome of the interplay of the various interests, understandings, reactions and initiatives of the individuals and groups involved in an organisation.

The hospital study was criticised for a failure to ground organisational analysis in its wider political, social structural and historical context (Day and Day 1977). Strauss (1978), however, took up the criticism of the earlier study and developed a style of organisational analysis which would cover not just mundane and local differences between parties involved in an organisation but would identify more basic or 'endemic' conflicts affecting them. The original hospital study was influenced by an earlier interactionist study of asylums in which Goffman (1961) showed that within 'total institutions' like prisons, monasteries and mental hospitals, in which inmates' lives and identities are almost totally dominated by organisational rules, even those in the least powerful positions in organisations nevertheless 'make out' and defend their identities in spite of the determination of the 'system' to reduce them to a cipher. Strauss' later work made use of Dalton's (1959) classic participative observation study of managers and how they make covert deals and secret bargains and generally engage in 'sub-processes of negotiation'. Such matters are clearly shown by Bishop and Waring (2016) to be central to the managing of tensions in a public–private hybrid health organisation. In this study the 'negotiated order' perspective is expanded and developed by combining it with the powerful notion of institutional logics (Chapter 3, pp. 63–65).

Ethnomethodology

Ethnomethodology might be seen as taking interactionist insights to their logical conclusion. It combines the thinking of the Chicago school with ideas from the European tradition of phenomenological philosophy and with insights from Weber's methodological thinking.

> ### Ethnomethodology
>
> The study of how ordinary members of society in their everyday lives make the world meaningful by achieving a sense of 'taken-for-grantedness'.

Ethnomethodology denies any objective reality to social phenomena. It suggests that there are no such things as societies, social structures or organisations. Instead, there are conceptions of this type within the heads of ordinary members of society which are made use of by these 'members' in carrying out their everyday purposes. Thus, as Bittner (1965) suggested, for example, we should see the idea of 'the organisation' as a commonsense construct of ordinary people rather than as a scientific concept, and we should concentrate on how people exploit the concept to make sense of what it is they are about. We do not follow organisational rules and procedures but carry out a whole range of personal projects which we then 'make sensible' by claiming to be acting in accordance with the organisation's requirements. Rules are seen by ethnomethodologists as resources that people draw upon to legitimise their actions and further whatever projects they are pursuing in the work context. We see that happening in Snapshot 2.3.

Snapshot 2.3

Putting ethnomethodology and 'negotiated order' to work on a factory yard

A delivery van belonging to the business in question was being driven up a narrow alley way in the middle of the company's large factory site. The driver was waved to a halt by one of the company's security officers. The security man pointed out to the van driver that he had been spotted on several occasions taking an illegal 'shortcut' across a large industrial plant. He asked what the van driver had to say for himself.

The van driver said, 'The company says that all employees should use their initiative. They say we should put the customer first in everything that we do. By driving up this road, I can get the goods out to the customer more quickly than if I follow the site's one-way system. The other security men know this, and don't stop us'.

Ethnomethodological analysis of the factory episode would draw attention to how the van driver uses for his own purposes a notion of 'the organisation' ('the company') as a resource to legitimise his behaviour to the security man. He also utilises the 'rule' about using initiative and putting customers first. And the concept of 'negotiated order' can also be made to analyse what is going on here. Informal negotiations between van drivers and security officers which allowed people to drive along an illegal route through the plant had become part of the normal 'order' of life in the organisation. It suited both parties in that it helped give the security staff a 'quiet life'. And it saved both time and effort for the drivers. For all concerned, it 'got the job done'. Negotiated order thinking, however, recognises that such deals are continually liable to change. This, if we can return briefly to the story, is what was happening on the day in question. The security man was new to the organisation. Consequently, he believed that the one-way rule (which made the shortcut 'illegal') was a necessary one for protecting the safety of employees working in the plant. Just like the van driver, he made use of a notion of 'the organisation'. He also 'drew on a rule' of what he saw as fitting his definition of the situation when he said, 'You should realize that the company puts employee safety before even customers. Don't drive down here again'. But this, we can speculate, was unlikely to have been the end of the story.

Ethnomethodological thinking has been applied by a number of researchers to work and organisational settings. It was applied by Silverman and Jones (1976) to show how interviewers in a job selection process 'made sensible' the decisions they reached by utilising 'typifications' like 'acceptable behaviour' or 'abrasive behaviour'. It plays a key part in the new workplace studies which examine the minutiae of workplace activities (Llewellyn and Hindmarsh 2010), and give particular attention to the ways in which technologies are developed and used (Luff *et al.* 2000). A collection of studies brought together by Rouncefield and Tolmie (2011) includes the 'managing' of customers by bank workers, the management of workflow and divisions of labour in printing and engineering and profit–loss decision-making in a catering context.

Ethnomethodology has also had an impact in the occupational sphere in the study of the work of scientists and the ways in which knowledge emerges from the processes whereby scientists work together to produce 'accounts' of the physical world (Woolgar 1988). Neither the science produced by scientists nor the decisions arrived at by the job selectors are to be seen as outcomes of a rational analysis of an objective 'reality'; instead they reflect the mundane sensemaking work which all human beings do all the time. The same applied to both the van driver and the security officer in our small case study. At the heart of ethnomethodology, as McAuley *et al.* (2007) put it, 'is the study of the "common sense" methods that members use to solve problems, make decisions, make sense of their situations and undertake fact finding in their everyday lives'. These insights can perhaps most usefully be combined with other ideas to give them analytical power at the levels above the 'microscopic' as we have done here in our case study by connecting ethnomethodology to the idea of negotiated order.

Perhaps ethnomethodology's importance is far greater than is implied by the very limited number of people in the sociology of work and organisation who wholeheartedly adopted it. The impact of the ethnomethodologists' powerful critique of conventional sociology which was mounted in the early to mid-1970s was to make sociologists much more sensitive than they had been to the dangers of turning conceptual abstractions like 'society', 'class' or 'organisation' into concretely existing 'things' which have a life of their own outside people's minds.

Discussion

The interactionist strand of the sociology of work and organisation clearly pays great attention to individuals and their role in social life, and it pays very necessary heed to the human interpretative process which more structural or systems-oriented approaches are sometimes seen to neglect. Yet, interactionism itself has been neglected in British sociology, according to Atkinson and Housley (2003). It is certainly made less use of in the sociology of work and organisation than it might be, in spite of its continuing value, as Hallet *et al.* (2009) point out, as a way of stressing that organisations are populated by people, individuals and groups who bring meanings, interests and agency to bear on organisational activities. Thus we avoid the danger which Gouldner (1955) warned of long ago, whereby organisational sociology operates pessimistically within a 'metaphysical pathos' which treats organisations as structural entities subject to impersonal forces. Nevertheless, although the interactionist approach is clearly not psychologistic, it may be necessary, to do sufficient justice to the influence on human interaction of ongoing historical processes and 'structures' of power and material interest, to combine interactions insights with ideas from the more power-conscious and historically aware perspective of Max Weber. The strand of thinking inspired by Weber opens Chapter 3.

Summary

It is difficult to appreciate the distinctiveness of sociological thinking about work without first appreciating the more psychological-oriented ideas of various management writers and thinkers. Examining the assumptions of this style of thinking sharpens one's appreciation of the more sociological way of looking at the world generally and at the sphere of work and organisation particularly. The next chapter will move on to look at three further strands of thought, each of which is currently making key contributions to the sociology of work and organisation.

3 Analysing work and organisation: institutionalism, labour process and discourse analysis

Key issues

- How has the classic sociological thinking of Max Weber been developed by sociologists studying work and organisations to produce notions like work orientation and institutional logics – concepts which play a central role in contemporary studies?
- How has the contemporary study of work and organisation developed certain basic ideas of Marx and Engels to establish a strong and flourishing strand of research which investigates labour processes in the modern world?
- How has the study of work and organisations been influenced in recent decades by post-structuralist and postmodern thinking?
- Taking the example of the widely used concept of *discourse*, to what extent can one draw on ideas from across the different strands of sociological thought to tackle issues and answer questions about work, organisations and human experience?

The Weber-social action-institutional strand

This strand of sociological thinking takes into account both the meaningful activity of the individual and the larger-scale questions of historical change and economic and political conflicts. As we saw in Chapter 2, interactionist thinking showed an early interest in the societal 'moral order' and the overall division of labour. Their interests subsequently proved to be largely confined to the group, organisational or occupational levels. They tend not to relate meanings at the micro level to historical and cultural patterns at the macro level. A concern with such a relationship is basic to the work of Weber.

Max Weber

The work and ideas of Max Weber (1864–1920) have been much misunderstood and misrepresented. This is partly because of the incompleteness of his written works, his awkward style of writing, his ambiguity on various issues, his tendency to separate his political writing from his sociological work and, especially, because of the fact that his work was brought back into contemporary sociology largely via American sociologists who wished to use the name of this impressive European figure to legitimate their own positions or interests. Thus we find Weber misinterpreted at times as one who totally opposed Marx's position on the nature and rise of capitalism, who denied the importance of class divisions in society by arguing that a plurality of interest groups counter-balanced each other, who 'advocated' bureaucracy as 'efficient', who was an armchair thinker without interest in carrying out empirical investigations and who encouraged the sociologist to be a neutral and uncommitted individual. There is some element of truth in each of these interpretations, but each of them tends to suggest quite the opposite of what was his essential position.

Weber's advocacy of value-freedom and his attempts to fill out (rather than totally contradict) the one-sidedness of Marxian thinking have to be understood in the light of his social and historical context. In trying to separate scientific analysis from political interpretation and advocacy, he was reacting to contemporary academics whom he believed were abusing their academic status, and he was interested in relegating sociological study to a role which was secondary to moral thinking and political activity. His reaction to the Marxist thinking of his time was not to try to demolish it but to take from it what was most useful in understanding modern capitalism whilst balancing its emphasis on material factors with fuller consideration of the role in history of ideas, individual agents and culture. It is true that, in his more political writings, he showed a clear preference for capitalism over its socialist alternative, but his enthusiasm for capitalist social organisation was not much greater than that for socialism. Both of them involved the threat to individual freedom which he saw in bureaucracy. Such was the fatalism and pessimism that runs through Weber's world view (Turner 1996).

Weber defined sociology as the study of *social action*. The discipline should examine the ways in which people, through the attribution and inference of subjective meanings, would be influenced by each other and thereby oriented in their actions. Weber avoided talking of 'structures' or 'systems', and he related these social meanings to the wider society through the concept of a 'legitimate order'. This is a patterning in social life which individual actors *believe* to exist and to which they may conform. To understand how the order becomes valid to actors, it has to be seen within the human meaning-creating processes which, in turn, have to be related to the conflicts and power struggles which take place in a world where there are a variety of material interests. The interplay between ideas and interests is basic to Weber's sociology. The sociologist,

- as a first stage of investigation, attempts to gain an interpretative understanding (verstehen) of actors' behaviour, and
- as a second stage of investigation, moves to a causal explanation. Since the actors who are being studied think in causal terms about what they are doing and because they base their actions on certain rationally based assumptions of regularities in the world, some causal explanation of their behaviour is possible.

LOOKING BACK <<<<<

In the discussion of methodological choices in Chapter 1, it was argued that Weber rejected positivist thinking and strove to combine recognition of the 'interpretive principle' with recognition of a social reality which exists beyond people's interpretation of it.

Although Weber labelled part of his work 'interpretive sociology', he cannot be seen as 'interpretivist' in the non-realist constructionist or post-structuralist sense that has now become common. His intention, as Freund (1972) puts it, 'was certainly not to assign a higher place to interpretation than to explanation'. Weber gave primacy neither to the objectively existing 'real' world nor to human subjectivity. Nevertheless, as Radkau (2009) shows, reality was 'a central concept for Weber': he frequently used the term *Wirklichkeitswissenschaft* – a 'science of reality'.

Weber's sociology is informed by a set of philosophical assumptions about the world which include a view of reality as infinitely diverse and as involving the existence of fundamental differences of value, interest and perspective. Social life is thus characterised by perpetual conflict, struggle and the exercise of power. Humans are seen as rational beings pursuing ends, but there is no direct relationship between their efforts and the resulting social order. There is a paradox of consequences in social life which, say Symonds and Pudsey (2008), is an idea at the centre of Weber's work (in spite of its having been somewhat neglected in the secondary literature).

Paradox of consequences

The tendency for the means chosen to achieve ends in social life to undermine or defeat those ends.

LOOKING FORWARD >>>>>

The tendency for means to defeat ends is profoundly important for our understanding of the role of bureaucracy in modern societies, as we shall see in Chapter 5.

The phenomenon of unintended consequences of human actions is fundamental to Weber's most famous substantive work. In his study, *The Protestant Ethic and the Spirit of Capitalism* (1965), to which we will return in Chapter 4, pp. 89–91, we see how the ideas developed by individuals such as Luther and Calvin, who were primarily concerned with religious and spiritual ends, had the unintended consequence of helping to foster a 'spirit of capitalism' and an increasingly rationalistic world view, one of the consequences of which was the eventual undermining of religious belief. The ideas which encouraged asceticism contributed to a later materialism in Western culture which would have horrified those who first set out these ideas. But Weber, in this kind of analysis, is not suggesting that ideas autonomously wing their way through history, changing their form as they go. It is their coming together with the material interests of historical actors which gives ideas force. Weber talks of an 'elective affinity' between ideas and interests: people tend to choose, develop or adopt ideas which fit with their material interests – these interests in turn being influenced by available ideas. Weber is by no means replacing Marx's stress on material interests as a force in history with an equally one-sided stress on ideas. Instead, he is showing that the cultural or subjective aspects of social life have to be seen as equal partners in any analytical scheme.

> ## Rationalisation
>
> A trend in social change whereby traditional or magical criteria of action are replaced by technical, calculative or scientific criteria.

Weber sees a process of *rationalisation* underlying Western history. With rationalisation, social life is 'demystified' or disenchanted, rational pursuit of profit motivates work behaviour and efforts are increasingly co-ordinated through bureaucratic means. All this means that people more and more use calculative devices and techniques as means towards the achieving of ends (these are formally rational means) – the division of labour, sets of rules, accounting methods, money, technology, and so on. However, because of the ever-present tendency for unintended consequences to occur, these often turn out not to lead to the goals for which they were intended (thus making them materially irrational). In fact, the means may subvert the very ends for which they were designed. This may be difficult to understand and it is perhaps not surprising therefore that many writers on organisations have taken Weber to mean that bureaucracy is 'efficient, thus implying that he was unaware of its tendencies to develop 'dysfunctions' – tendencies towards inefficiency (Albrow 1970). Weber was in fact pointing merely to the potential superiority of bureaucracy as an administrative instrument (its formal rationality) whilst being fully aware that it could manifest features which rendered it materially irrational, even going so far as to threaten individual freedom in a society with an attachment to such a goal or value. But this misunderstanding of Weber (perhaps partly deriving from a failure to realise that his ideal-type construct of bureaucracy was an intentionally one-sided representation) has been such that it has led to the development of one whole area of industrial or organisational sociology, and therefore part of the present strand. This is the work in the tradition of Merton's analysis of the so-called dysfunctions of bureaucracy.

LOOKING FORWARD >>>>>

The concept of bureaucratic dysfunction, and related ideas, is discussed on pp. 147–149.

Weber's perspective allows us to take into account the individual social actor whilst locating ideas and actions in the context of the vast political and dynamic patterns of history. The great sweep of Weber's interests (note that he applied his historical and comparative approach to both Western and non–Western societies) does not mean, however, that he was uninterested in detailed empirical investigation. He was, in fact, closely involved in what might have become one of the classical studies of industrial sociology – factory studies which predated the Hawthorne studies by twenty years or more. Weber was interested in investigating a range of issues which are very close to those which have become central to industrial sociology in practice only some fifty or sixty years later (Eldridge 1971). Weber's 'Methodological Introduction' to the proposed study shows an intention to study the effects of large-scale industry on the 'individual personality, the career and the extra-occupational style of living of the workers', thus taking into account the 'ethical, social and cultural background, the tradition and the circumstances of the worker'. All this is set in the context of economic, technical and capital-investment patterns in a way which is still very relevant to the sociology of work and organisation today.

Orientations to work

A Weberian strand of specialised industrial sociology could well have started early in the century had Weber's intended research investigations not foundered (Radkau 2009). But more recent sociologists have applied a generally Weberian perspective to industrial questions and carried out studies very much in the spirit of Weber's own projected work. Especially important here were the *Affluent Worker* studies of Goldthorpe *et al.* (1968) which gave sociology the important concept of 'orientation to work', a notion which links actions in the workplace and the external community and cultural life of employees.

> ### Orientation to work
>
> The meaning attached by individuals to their work which predisposes them both to think and act in particular ways with regard to that work.

The orientations perspective takes the employee's own definition of the situation as an 'initial basis for the explanation of their social behaviour and relationships' (Goldthorpe *et al.* 1968). Much earlier thinking about industrial behaviour tended to focus on the assumed 'needs' of workers, whether these be the economic needs focused on by Scientific Management (pp. 32–33), the social needs focused on by Human Relations writers (pp. 42–44) or the self-actualisation needs focused on by the psychological humanists (pp. 34–37). And there was a trend in the 1960s for the technological context in which people worked to be a determinant of people's attitudes to work (Chapter 9, pp. 284–285). Goldthorpe and colleagues reacted against all of this, stressing the importance of the meanings that workers take into the work situation in the first place.

LOOKING FORWARD >>>>>

Orientations to work are returned to in Chapter 9.

Thus an individual in a life situation where earning money might be a priority over personal work satisfaction might choose to undertake unpleasant but highly paid work but, at another stage of their lives, where economic imperatives are less significant to them, they might opt for work that allowed them more scope to express their own identities, develop their capacities or simply enjoy the company of other people at work.

Snapshot 3.1

John's changing orientation to work

John tells us how his approach to work (which we would conceptualise as his 'orientation to work') changed over time: 'When I was in my first year at university, I worked hard because I had come to love economics when I was at school. But in the second year I got a part-time job in a bar in the financial district and I became cynical about economics. I just did the minimum of studying and put a lot of hours in at the bar. I didn't like the job, mind. I just wanted to get as much money as possible to finance my skiing trips. I did the job well. As long as they paid me I was willing to do whatever was necessary. I confess that this approach to work stayed with me through my final year and into my first job, the one I got after I scraped a reasonable degree. In that first job, I just treated work as a way of financing my leisure activities. The job, in an accounting firm, just wasn't me. But after a couple of years, my girlfriend persuaded me to take a pay cut and go to work with her in this charitable trust. We work well together and I really believe that we are making a difference to the African villages that we deal with'.

What this piece of autobiography illustrates is the way that so-called 'motivations to work' need to be understood as involving a lot more than the meeting of 'needs'. Work meant different things to John at different times, as his values changed, his life priorities changed and his personal relationships changed. To understand how people approach their work, we need to look at their whole life situation, their notion of who they take themselves to be ('the job . . . wasn't me') and at the social, economic and value contexts through which they move in their lives.

Institutional theories of organisation and the social construction of reality

The rationalisation process identified by Weber, in which deliberately calculated means are adopted in the pursuit of consciously selected ends, has led to the pervasiveness of bureaucratised organisations across the world. Organisations are thus, in a sense, expressions of some of the basic cultural characteristics of modern societies. This is emphasised in *institutional theories* of organisations (Selznick 1949; Tolbert and Zucker 1996; Scott 2008) where a central argument has been that organisations take the shape they do, not because of their efficiency or proven effectiveness, but because people draw from the culture around them value-based notions of how things should be organised. 'New institutionalism', as its more recent (1980s onwards) manifestations are often called, emphasises the extent to which common understandings in the culture outside the organisation come to be 'culturally embedded' within the organisation (Zucker 1988). Organisations are part of the socially constructed reality through which people relate to the world.

Social construction of reality
The process in which people, through cultural interaction, give meaning to the world – a world that exists beyond language but which can only be known and communicated by people through language-based processes of cultural interpretation and sensemaking.

The notion of the 'social construction of reality' (Berger and Luckmann 1971; Watson 2008c) recognises in a broadly Weberian way that, through processes of institutionalisation, people 'make the social world' at the same time as their own notions of who they are and what they are doing are 'made by' the social world.

Social institutions
Regularly occurring meanings, rules, activities and relationships which have become 'normal' or taken-for-granted in any given society.

Organisations are not institutions themselves. But they operate within this 'institutionalised' social world (the key institution for them being bureaucratic administration). We shape the organisations we are involved with, but these organisations, in part, shape us. The organisations in which we work, shop, are born and die are 'real'. But they are not real in the sense that they are entities that we can touch, feel, hear or smell. They become real to us as we confront the institutionalised patterns of rules, norms, procedures and expectations that we *take for granted* as 'reality'. And that 'taken-for-grantedness' is the outcome of historically grounded processes of human *interpretation* of the world. We might say that it is only by putting 'constructions' on our world that we can relate to it and achieve both personal sanity and social 'order'.

The societal pattern of expectations at the heart of the socially constructed realities which confront us is not to be seen as a politically neutral matter. Meyer and Rowan (1977) point to the significance in the modern world of the *rational myth*. This element of the social construction of reality would suggest that, for example, rules in organisations are institutionalised in a form where they appear to be neutral technical matters. Their connection to values or interests is thus obscured. In spite of the importance of this insight in the Meyer and Rowan article (which was an early and influential part of the 'new' institutionalist attempt to reinvigorate an older and essentially sociological institutionalist perspective), critics have suggested that the neo-institutional theory 'quickly lost its focus on power' (Clegg *et al.* 2006). This has been encouraged by the stress that DiMaggio and Powell (1983) put, in a particularly influential article, on change 'as being driven towards established and legitimized practices in a given organisational field' (Delbridge and Edwards 2008) through processes of coercion, normative conformity and *mimetic isomorphism* (where, organisations become more and more alike as a result of the tendency of organisers to imitate each other). The problem is that the actual practices of human agents are put into a 'black box'. Scott (2008) observes, however, that the tendency for institutionalism to emphasise 'convergence, conformity and isomorphism' at the expense of attention to power and conflicting interests has been countered by a new emphasis on human agency in institutional shaping. Important here is the growing attention being paid to the activities and influence of *institutional entrepreneurs* (DiMaggio 1988; Dorado 2005; Leca and Naccache 2006; Greener 2009).

Whilst this move recognises that there are always outstanding individuals who make exceptional interventions in how society is organised, it should not divert attention from the fact that ordinary managers in the everyday life of organisations regularly make interventions in

> ## Institutional entrepreneurs
>
> Individuals with sufficient resources and interests to be able to stand back from existing institutional arrangements in order to create new institutional patterns or change existing ones.

institutional patterns, however modest these may be. In effect, they make interventions in the wider processes of the social construction of reality by attempting to create definitions of situations among the employees which *legitimise* institutionalised patterns of power and advantage. The notion of legitimacy is the key concept linking Weber and institutional theorists.

An alternative to focusing on institutional entrepreneurs is to consider the ways in which social change arises from the tensions which inevitably arise between different social institutions – or, rather, between different institutional logics. The concept of institutional logics had been available for some time (Friedland and Alford 1991) before it was represented and extended (Thornton and Ocasio 2008), to the extent that Thornton *et al.* (2012) wrote of their intention not to 'revive neo-institutional theory but to transform it' – thus producing what they call an 'institutional logics perspective' which should be treated as a 'new approach to culture, structure and process'. Another way of looking at this important theoretical development is to see it as simply a major advance in sociology – an advance in which the deep Weberian roots of the discipline are being strengthened and its aspirations are better fulfilled.

> ## Institutional logics
>
> The sets of values, rules, assumptions and practices associated with key institutions of a society (such as the family, the market, politics, religion, bureaucratic administration) which have been socially constructed over time and through which patterns of social organisation and human activity are shaped and given meaning.

Each major social institution has its own central logic, a logic that both enables and constrains human actions and the shaping of organisations. But, in many situations in social life, more than one institutional logic may exert its distinctive pressure at the same time. If, in any given situation, there are tensions or contradictions between these logics, change will necessarily occur as social actors interpret, accommodate to, or succumb to, those tensions. Currie and Spyridonidis (2016) observe two major institutional logics in tension with each other in the hospitals they studied: a professional logic and a managerial policy-driven logic. Each of these was characterised by ambiguity and variation, and members of the key occupational groups (nurses, doctors, managers, nurse consultants etc.) worked, sometimes in co-operation, sometimes in contention, to 'blur' and 'blend' these logics to enable the hospitals to function successfully as well as to defend or further the interests of the different groups, each having its distinctive 'social position in the hospital hierarchies'.

In Snapshot 3.2, we see a large agricultural work organisation and the district in which it is located undergoing changes that arise because of a tension between the institutional logic of an emerging global market and the logic of more traditional kin-based institutions.

Snapshot 3.2

Clashing institutional logics and the reorganisation of an African farming district

'Our farm covered a really large area of land and almost everybody in the district worked on the farm, including most of the members of our family. I worked alongside my parents and my three brothers and two sisters in running the farm. About ten years ago, my eldest brother and younger sister started to argue that our attachment to family and tribal values was compromising the future success of the farm, and especially its ability to expand production to meet growing global markets. These meant, they insisted, that we were not appointing the most able people to fill certain roles. We were giving jobs to friends and to the children of favoured tribal families and were ignoring the talents that were available on the wider labour market which was developing in colleges and universities across the continent. The whole thing came to a head when my parents insisted on giving a new job as head of marketing to a cousin of ours, a character that I admit was unlikely to put a lot of effort, let alone expertise, into this new role. I argued that we had to find a way of balancing our ancient values and belief in family, kinship and tribal history with the pressures of the markets that were opening up to us.

After just one family row too many, my parents came to the conclusion that the farm – and that meant the whole district, in effect – would have to be split into two units. So that area over there, from the foot of the hills that you can see down to the side of the lake is now run by my eldest brother and my youngest sister in what they call their 'scientific agricultural' style. Legally, their business has become a separate one from ours, and we carry on here in a similar but not identical way to before. Life is different in the valley now, many people feel. There are definitely problems within some of the families where only certain family members have been 'selected' to work in the new farming and food distribution business. But we have not stood still in the 'old' business. We are upgrading our own operation. We are working with the local schools and a new small agriculture college to improve the overall levels of education and skill in the valley. On balance, then, the changes are for the better. But that's my view. Others are distressed that life in the valley is becoming more stressed and competitive and that the improvements in material benefits that are slowly occurring do not compensate for the decline in traditions and the idea of one big valley family. As my mother said, we could not resist certain inevitable changes coming about in society but we could try to handle those changes in as creative a way as possible. I think that is what we have done'.

The main clash of institutional logics which came about on the farm in Snapshot 3.2 is one between the logic of family and kinship, on the one hand, and the logic of the competitive market on the other hand. Other institutional factors no doubt played a part too: religion and science being perhaps two of these. But these 'structural' tensions have not come about independent of human 'agency'. Human activities elsewhere have influenced the institutional pressures that are being exerted upon this African district. But most clearly we can see that human agency is equally important in how these tensions are handled at the district level. People are both constrained and enabled by the pressures. The brother–sister pair were feeling especially constrained and, in the new situation, some of the more traditional citizens of the valley are feeling pushed about. But it is likely that a variety of people in the valley will have taken initiatives in the light of the changing circumstances – in addition to the agency exerted in Snapshot 3.2 by the brother–sister pair and their parents. We would fail to do justice to this fact if we were to pick out any one individual as an 'institutional entrepreneur' (p. 63). A more useful concept to apply specifically to Snapshot 3.2 and more generally all processes of institutional change would be that of *institutional work*.

Institutional work

The efforts made by social actors to maintain, disrupt or create institutional patterns, sometimes individually and sometimes in concert with others, sometimes through large interventions and sometimes through small initiatives, sometimes successfully and sometimes unsuccessfully and, often, with unintended consequences.

The concept of institutional work, say its key proponents, encourages us to study 'the efforts of individuals and collective actors to cope with, keep up with, shore up, tear down, tinker with, transform, or create anew the institutional structures within which they live, work, and play, and which give them their roles, relationships, resources, and routines' (Lawrence *et al.* 2011). The concept has close affinities with that of institutional logics. Both concepts emerged out of dissatisfactions with certain aspects of neo-institutional theory. And they can be valuable deployed together (Zilber 2013) in a manner which has relevance far beyond so-called institutionalism ('neo' or otherwise). These two notions, brought together can sharpen up conceptually, in a much more general way, the subject matter and procedures of Wright Mills' sociological imagination (Chapter 1, pp. 9–12).

Actor-network theory

Actor-network theory does not fit neatly into any particular strand of theory, being influenced by both the Weberian tradition in sociology and by post-structuralism. Nevertheless, it can be considered in the present setting as a distinctive way of bringing together the human-agency and the 'mechanical' aspects of our lives. Although technologies do not have inherent properties or essences of their own (Grint and Woolgar 1997), we often experience them as if they did have an independent kind of 'existence' equivalent to that which we see in other human beings. *Actor-network theory* (ANT) recognises this and challenges the taken-for-granted distinction that we tend to make between human and inanimate actors. ANT encourages us to analyse people, machines, techniques and operational principles as equivalent *actors* in a network of activities (Latour 2005). Latour (1993) says that the distinction between the natural and the social world can be regarded as a myth of modernism. The distinction is apparently not one that would have meant a great deal to Theresa Smurfit after a particularly frustrating day.

Snapshot 3.3

'The computer won't let me do my job'

'When I got up this morning', Theresa tells us, 'I was looking forward to a productive and enjoyable working day. But it all started badly when I simply could not get my son going. He wouldn't get dressed, and he wouldn't eat his breakfast. And then the car wouldn't start. I felt as if everything was conspiring against me. Because I wanted to get the computer training lab sorted out before any clients arrived, I got to work really early. In the past, I would have had to wait until the reception opened to get into the building. But I presented my new swipe card to the reader on the door, and the security system let me in. That was great. But I got into the computer lab only to find that whoever had used it before me had done something with the passwords, and the ones I had simply didn't work. I was locked out of the system for half of the morning. I was supposed to be training people to use the computer system. But the computers wouldn't let me do my job. Aaaaargh!'

In actor network terms, Theresa, her son, the car and the computer system are all *actants*, living out their day within a network of numerous other actants – human and nonhuman – in the home and in the work organisation. Notice how similarly Theresa talks of her son and the car, neither of which would easily 'start'. She goes on to talk of the security system precisely as if it were a person who 'let me in'. She speculates about human actions in relation to the passwords. But, then, her being 'locked out' of the computer system is spoken about in terms of the computers not 'letting her' do her job. There is a constant interplay between 'hard' technological artefacts and their human partners, we might say. And this insight is central to an analysis of an industrial dispute in a university where 'artefacts such as cars, minutes of meetings, emails, mobile phones, posters or leaflets and their complex ties with humans were integral' to the staff resistance to management initiatives (Knights and McCabe 2016).

In spite of useful insights such as these which actor network theory offers, it is necessary, as Chugh and Hancock (2009) suggest, to 'distance ourselves from the idea that material objects possess agency in and of themselves'. The alternative, following Dant (1999), is to treat material culture and artefacts as actants only in the sense that they are mediators between the people who design the machines or the buildings and the people whose actions are extended or limited by their occupying the material spaces or their use of devices.

Discussion

Recent developments in theorising with the notions of institution and human agency at their centre represent a significant step forward in the effectiveness of sociological analysis generally and to the sociology of work and organisation particularly. The roots of this work are clearly in the thinking of Max Weber and his concern with the interplay that occurs between the agency or voluntaristic aspects of social activity and the wider cultural or structural patterns within society (Chapter 1, p. 9). Such concerns also make Marxian thinking of continuing relevance. Especially in the light of the emphasis on the concept of institutional logics, it is important to note that there is a close relationship between Weber's concern with the 'paradox of consequences' and the Marxian notion of the contradictions of capitalism.

The Marxian-labour-process strand

Since its first appearance on the intellectual and political scene, Marxist and Marxian thought has influenced the development of sociology (Marxist to mean after Marxism, a politically oriented programme, and Marxian to mean after Marx's more analytical work). Marx and Engels created one of the most influential theories of social life ever made available to those trying to make some kind of systematic sense of the modern industrialising world. Its influence in contemporary sociology can be understood as part of a reaction, alongside that of Weber's, to an earlier tendency of much academic sociology to be consensus-oriented, to be non-critical at best and justifying the status quo at worst, and also to its tendency to restrict its attention to the 'social' at the expense of the economic and political. Much of the older sociology was also seen to be too static and tending to ignore history.

Marens (2009), having argued that to take a Marxian 'intellectual approach' entails no commitment to Marxist revolutionary politics, points out that Marxian political economy is especially relevant to contemporary global circumstances. We live, he argues, in a period in which 'market relations are . . . extending their geographic reach' at the same time as they are 'intensifying within virtually every region of the globe'. These are two tendencies which, in an earlier period, Marx studied in a relentless and 'famously single-minded' way.

Marx and Engels

Underlying the ideas of Karl Marx (1818–1883) and Friedrich Engels (1820–1895) is an assumption about the nature of human beings. This is the assumption that human beings achieve the fullness of their humanity through their labour. It is through labour – an essentially social process – that the human world is created. This is the basis of Marx's 'materialism'. However, the conditions under which labour is performed make a crucial difference to the extent to which the human being is fulfilled. Under capitalism workers are forced into an unequal relationship with the owner of capital, to whom they sell their labour power. The relationship is unequal, since the owner of capital always has sufficient means of subsistence whether production goes ahead or not, whilst wage workers are dependent on work being available to them. Furthermore, the employer requires workers to do more work than the workers themselves would need to do to meet their own needs; that is, the capitalist *extracts the surplus value* and in this way exploits the workers. Work within a capitalist context does not allow the workers the creative fulfilment which labour could potentially give them. Since the workers do not use tools and materials which are their own and since they neither own nor control the products of their labour any more than they have control over the methods which they apply in their work, they cannot achieve their potential self-realisation. They are thus *alienated* (Chapter 9, pp. 285–287). Although this condition clearly has subjective implications, fundamentally it is an objective condition. A contented worker is no less alienated in this sense than a frustrated one.

Marx sets these ideas in a historical model of the way in which one form of society develops to a point where it is superseded by another (for example, feudalism is transcended by capitalism which, in turn, is transcended by socialism). These ideas are also set in a structural model of capitalist society – or, more accurately, a capitalist mode of production. This is represented in Figure 3.1.

According to Marx, it is the nature of the economic base which characterises a society. The way in which production is organised and the social relations accompanying that organisation are the more decisive factors – ideas, culture, law and politics being secondary. This again illustrates the materialist basis of Marx's work and perhaps indicates how the rather crude accusations of 'economic determinism' have come to be made against him. His approach is often described as 'dialectical materialism', and the dialectical element of the analysis can be illustrated here by pointing to the tendency of the base to contain within it conflicts

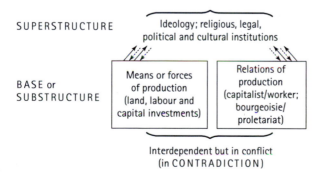

Figure 3.1 The capitalist mode of production

and contradictions which represent the seeds of its own destruction (or, rather, supersession). The dialectic operates in history by the growth of one thing out of another in such a way that the new comes into conflict with the old, leading to its overthrow. Thus the bourgeoisie, we might say, created the proletariat but, in so doing, created the condition for its own overthrow.

Marx sees the capitalist mode of production as inherently unstable and ultimately doomed. A close reading of Marx's later economic writing makes it clear that this demise of capitalism could well be a very long way off and that the dominance of capitalism in the early twenty-first century is quite consistent with Marx's long-term thinking (Desai 2002). Capitalism may be a long way from coming into full bloom. The roots of the eventual superseding of capitalism have been in the ground from the start, however. They lie in the fact that the social relations of bourgeoisie and proletariat are relations of fundamental conflict since their relationship is a one-sided and exploitative one. All of those who sell their labour power are, objectively, members of the proletariat. They are all 'exploited'. The proletariat is thus a 'class in itself', but they will not act as a class – so releasing themselves from exploitation – until they overcome their 'false consciousness' and become aware of their common interest. Class action is therefore dependent on the growth of class consciousness. The proletariat will become a 'class for itself' and act out its historical destiny through creating socialism. To recognise the full force of the notion of contradiction in Marx, we have to note that the efforts of the bourgeoisie themselves, to a considerable extent, hasten their own demise. For example, the bringing together of larger and larger numbers of employees into ever larger work units will create the very conditions in which workers, through being thrown together, can become aware of shared economic and political interests. Thus class-consciousness increases and the challenge to the prevailing order is invited.

Marxian industrial sociology and labour process analysis

Marx's key concepts of class, exploitation, labour process and alienation played a growing part in the sociology of work and organisation after the mid-1960s, sometimes being used as analytical instruments and sometimes in a more directly Marxist way when their discussion is tied to an interest in actually affecting consciousness. There has been an especially strong Marxist attention to various aspects of conflict at work (Beynon 1984; Nichols and Beynon 1977), and Hyman (1989) has exerted considerable influence through his persuasive attempts to establish a Marxist political economy of industrial relations. The greatest impact of the ideas of Marx on modern work and organisational sociology has undoubtedly been through the use of his concept of 'the labour process' to develop a perspective which combines interests in employee behaviour, employment relations and questions of work design and organisation. In essence, labour process theory focuses on the point of production to analyse patterns of control, consent and the ways in which workers resist control.

The capitalist labour process

The design, control and monitoring of work tasks and activities by managers acting as agents of the capital owning class to extract surplus value from the labour activity of employees.

It is assumed that capitalist employment is essentially exploitative in attempting to take from working people the 'value' which they create through their labour and which is properly their own. In managing the labour process to fulfil this function, managers follow the logic of the capitalist mode of production whereby the need for capital accumulation demands employers' constant attention to subjugating labour, in order to extract enough profit from it to enable the employer to survive within the capitalist market economy.

A central role in stimulating this kind of analysis was played by Braverman's (1974) application of it to various trends in work design. Braverman's thesis was that the pursuit of capitalist interests has led to a general trend towards deskilling, routinising and mechanising of jobs across the employment spectrum, from manufacturing to retailing and from design to clerical work. Industrial engineers are seen as going from strength to strength as they apply the deskilling logic of Taylorism to work tasks. They are helped along in this by the personnel and human relations experts who act as fellow manipulators and as a 'maintenance crew for the human machinery' rather than as any kind of check upon or reaction to work degradation. Braverman links these work design processes to class analysis by reference to Marx's argument that the working class will become increasingly homogeneous. He suggests that, through the process of deskilling and work degradation, all employees will find themselves in increasingly similar positions and distinctions between blue-collar and white-collar, technical and manual, production and service workers will become increasingly blurred. Taylorism continues to be rampant and is aided and abetted by modern electronic techniques which are continually reducing the need for capitalist employers to depend on human skills and hence reducing their need to reward employees in any but a minimal and straightforwardly economic way.

Research following up Braverman's resurrecting of an interest in the capitalist labour process has shown trends of deskilling and up-skilling occurring simultaneously, the existence of these opposing trends not necessarily being seen as undermining the basic assumptions of labour process analysis but, instead, as refining it by showing that in some circumstances capitalist interests are better served by upgrading work and in others by downgrading it (Friedman 1977; Edwards 1990). At the theoretical, as opposed to the empirical level, effort has been made to overcome the weaknesses of the basic Braverman version of labour process thinking. Not only did that perspective fail to recognise that owning interests may, in certain circumstances, see it as advantageous to upgrade rather than downgrade jobs, it also portrayed managers as much more omniscient and united than they really are, tended to romanticise the skilled craft worker of the past and underplayed the ability of workers to defend themselves against managerial strategies. The trend within labour process thinking has therefore to recognise that a range of contingencies or circumstances intervene between the deeper tendency of labour to be managed in the interests of capital and the actual practices that are followed. Burawoy (1985), for example, recognises that the extraction of surplus value with its implications for employer–worker conflicts at a deeper level necessarily requires a degree of aligning of employer–worker interests at the level of the workplace. Thompson (1989) acknowledges that whilst there are basic structural pressures to accumulate capital this does not directly determine patterns of control and resistance in the workplace. And Edwards (1990) stresses that the way events unfold at the level of day-to-day behaviour is pressured by 'structured antagonism' rather than fully shaped by it.

Thompson and Smith (2009, 2010) argue forcefully for the 'critical materialist' labour process theory (LPT) which has emerged from post-Braverman LPT studies should be at the heart of a non-fragmented sociology of work. It is rooted, they say, in classical sociological thought, especially that of Marx and Weber, its research methods have continuity with a long tradition of workplace research, and it is at the forefront of contemporary research into the new sources of labour power, especially those of emotional and aesthetic labour.

LOOKING FORWARD >>>>>

Emotional and aesthetic labour are examined in Chapter 10, pp. 322–326.

A post-structuralist variant or development of labour process analysis is examined in a later section (pp. 79–81).

Discussion

Marxian thought constitutes more than a sociological theory. It can be seen as providing a method of analysis which does not divide polity, economy and society. Despite the fact that Marx wanted to bring together theory and practice and encourage revolution, sociologists who do not share these political goals can derive a great deal of *analytical* value from Marxian thinking.

Nevertheless, a major source of difficulty with this strand of thought for sociologists of work and organisation who do not share Marxist political ambitions, arises from its primary concern with problems of class, exploitation and large-scale historical change and the implicit (sometimes explicit) interest in seeing existing political-economic patterns overthrown. The concepts, which are deployed to analyse specific situations, therefore tend to be selected to highlight issues relevant to these problems and associated political interests and, consequently, risk playing down issues which are not felt to be of strategic political relevance. However, many of the issues which are under-emphasised within the Marxist frame of reference or a 'problematic' are areas of considerable importance when it comes to examining actual work or employment problems at a particular point in history – even if in the 'final instance' they may not be regarded as crucial to those hoping for the overthrow of capitalism. There are people who will look to the sociology of work and organisation for insights relevant to their concerns with such matters as organisational redesign, the improvement of workplace relations and the attempt to reduce ethnic or gender discrimination within the existing basic social and economic system. Marxian thought has useful insights to offer on questions such as these. Such insights are perhaps more likely to be taken up if they are offered alongside insights and concepts from other theoretical and value traditions within the sociology of work and organisation. This is demonstrated by the increasing influence of Pierre Bourdieu whose writing synthesises Marx's emphasis on power and domination, Durkheim's concern with the relationship between cultural categories and social structures and Weber's attention to legitimacy as an institutional process (Sallaz 2010; see also Emirbayer and Johnson 2009).

LOOKING FORWARD >>>>>

Ideas from Bourdieu will be considered later when use is made of his concept of *habitus* in later chapters, pp. 210, 258, 326 and 396.

The value of drawing on Marxian ideas alongside ideas from other 'strands' of thought, more generally, will be particularly apparent in Chapters 5 and 12. It became apparent to Jean Parker as she learned some lesson about the relevance of Marxian thinking – learning these, as her Marxist friend told her, 'the hard way' (Snapshot 3.4).

Snapshot 3.4

Jean learns a sociological lesson – the hard way

Jean Parker used to work in a large textile company where she was a union representative. In the evenings and at weekends, she was studying for a degree by open learning and especially liked the sociology modules she studied. She tells us, 'I used to come to work in the morning full of my studies from the night before and I used to have some great discussions with Frank, an old-style trade union man who had more-or-less grown up with Marxism. He liked to listen to me going on about the cultural analysis that we were doing and things like people's identity dilemmas and the changing pattern of consumption in postmodernity. He then used to argue that it was a pity that we were not reading Marx. And I used to argue that Marx was no longer relevant in the 21st century and that, anyway, the labour theory of value was flawed. He used to say to me, 'Aha, young woman, but you will see'. And, indeed, I did eventually begin to see what he meant without, let me stress, my getting converted to Marxism and believing that Marx was the key thinker in sociology (which he kept trying to persuade me was the case). In the union, I argued strongly for partnership agreements with the employer, and I spent a lot of time in the consultation process which preceded the move to teamworking arrangements.

I still believe that the managers I was negotiating and consulting with were as sincere as I was about making the factory a better place to work in and the business a more competitive one. Frank just used to say that I was "falsely conscious" and that I was being taken in by the 'servants of capital'. I laughed at this. But I stopped laughing when, one day, the very managers who I'd got to know so well, and to trust, called me and the other reps into the boardroom. They announced to us that "the board" had decided that it had no choice but to close down our whole factory. They said that the shareholders would no longer tolerate the "inevitably high cost base" of its UK factories and that this meant that all production had to move to the far east. After the meeting, I started to rage about how these managers, the men and women that I knew and liked, had betrayed us. Frank told me that I should stop this. "You cannot put this down to the choices of managers", he said, "it's all to do with the logic of capitalist accumulation. The company can extract a much higher rate of surplus value from Chinese workers than from us. As it is a capitalist business at the mercy of capital markets, it has got to go that way."

Frank then said that my sociological studies should make me aware of the power of this kind of "determining force". "You don't have to take on my Marxist politics", he said, in a very kindly tone. And, even more kindly, he said, "And you can go on liking our manager friends over in the office block." He pointed out that most of them were going to lose their jobs. "They are just as much victims of capital as us", he said. Now, let me say that I don't go all the way with Frank here. My university module on globalisation made me aware that things are much more complicated than this. However, I think I learned an important sociological lesson from my experiences in that company – a lesson about the significance of big structures and the logic of the political economy of the modern world. And as Frank said to me, "It's a pity you had to learn this lesson the hard way". Indeed it was'.

LOOKING FORWARD >>>>>

The 'partnership agreements' to which Jean refers are explained in Chapter 12 (pp. 360–361), and the 'globalisation' issues she mentions are discussed in Chapter 4.

A note on feminism and sociology

In the present text, we are using the notion of 'strands' of thinking in the sociology of work and organisation. These could alternatively be labelled 'dimensions' (Watson 2015). Such terms are felt to be less misleading than the notion of 'schools' of thought, with the latter's hint of greater coherence within groupings of thinkers and researchers than is realistic. However, Vallas (2012), in his overview of the sociology of work, is happy to use the term 'schools of thought' (synonymous, it would appear, with 'approaches') and to identify four of these: Marxist, interactionist, feminist and institutionalist. But two of these 'schools' – the Marxist and the feminist – are, in the terms used earlier in this chapter, closely tied to political rather than theoretical-analytical positions. And while it can reasonably be argued that every social-scientific theoretical scheme has a value-political underpinning, the scientific aspirations of sociology imply a requirement of every researcher or theorist to be constantly vigilant about allowing their political preferences – how they would like the social world to be – to undermine the integrity of their analysis of how the social world is. This Weberian position means that one may be a socialist, a feminist or a political conservative in one's non-scholarly life and, indeed, may be inspired by these concerns but that one cannot be a socialist, feminist or conservative *sociologist*. Hence, a feminist strand or dimension of the sociology of work and organisation is not being identified here. And this is emphatically not to deny that there is a great deal of theoretical research work being carried out, especially on gender-related issues, by sociologists of work and organisation who do identify themselves as feminist researchers and writers. And this major contribution is fully recognised in later chapters with this work being treated, first and foremost, as a contribution to sociology.

LOOKING FORWARD >>>>>

The section of Chapter 7, 'Women, men and work', considers the issue of how we might explain patterns of gender inequality, and Chapter 9 looks at women's preferences, choice and work orientations.

The post-structuralist strand and postmodernism

The ways in which the terms post-structuralism and postmodernism are used are inconsistent and highly confusing. Sometimes they are treated as the same thing and sometimes attempts are made to differentiate between the two expressions. The authors of one organisation theory book accept that, while they find it 'hard to clearly delineate' between the two, they are nevertheless certain that central to both approaches is 'a focus on language, subjectivity and knowledge' (McAuley, Duberley and Johnson 2007). And Hatch and Cunliffe (2006), in their text, suggest that 'postmodernism embraces poststructuralist suppositions such as that there are no structures underlying human existence'.

Postmodernism

The idea of postmodernism embracing post-structuralist presuppositions helpfully positions post-structuralism as the theoretical basis for what Hatch and Cunliffe (2006) identify as the postmodernist belief that 'the world is formless, fragmented and intertextual: there is no hidden order, what you see on the surface is all that there is'. And the post-modernist perspective, with its roots in the French intellectual tradition of *post-structuralism*, puts human language at the centre of the study of all aspects of human existence. This gives us a postmodernist way of looking at the world.

Postmodernism

A way of looking at the world which rejects attempts to build systematic explanations of history and human activity and which, instead, concentrates on the ways in which human beings go about 'inventing' their worlds, especially through language and cultural innovation.

Although, as its name suggests, post-structuralism rejects the notion of structure, a concept which was central to the predecessor *structuralist* tradition in French social theory, it does take as its starting point the key insight of the structuralist linguistics about the 'arbitrariness of the sign'. This is the recognition that there is no necessary connection between a word (or other sign) and what it stands for. The word 'book', for example, does not connect with the item which you at this moment have in front of you apart from the social convention that such a sound, to an English speaker, is conventionally taken to stand for such objects. The same would apply to 'work' or to 'organisation'. In post-structural or postmodern thinking, reality itself comes to be treated as if it were a text, as a set of arbitrary signs which are not tied into a pre-existing reality. This implies that there is no basic truth outside language and that there is no reality separate from the way we write and talk about the world. There are no universal human values, and we cannot rely on overarching systems of thought, like science or religion, to give us a basic understanding of the world and to provide guidance on how to act within it.

LOOKING BACK <<<<<

The idea that there is no reality separate from the way we write and talk about the world underpins the interpretivist/constructionist methodological principles examined in Chapter 1 (pp. 22–27).

LOOKING FORWARD >>>>>

Postmodernism is a way of looking at the world. 'Postmodernity' is something different – it is more about the state of the world than about how we think about the world. Postmodernity is considered in Chapter 4 (pp. 101–102).

Postmodernism rejects the main ideas of the Enlightenment, the change in Western thinking that led among other things to the emergence of sociology itself, as we saw in Chapter 1. There is a turning away from the Enlightenment principles that constitute modernism.

Modernism
A way of looking at the world which believes that the application of rational and scientific analysis to social, political, economic and industrial institutions can lead to greater human control over the world and thus bring about general progress in the condition of humankind.

In modernism, expertise becomes important in achieving human progress with key roles going to scientists, technocrats and administrators. And grand narratives like those of Marxism or Freudianism emerge to offer blueprints for making the world a better and more easily controlled place. Postmodernism reacts against all of this. It encourages what Lyotard (1984) calls a stance of 'incredulity towards metanarratives' and, in effect, encourages us to look at the world in terms of the way we 'make it up' through talk, speech and other communicative behaviour.

After twenty years of influence and controversy, postmodernism may be disappearing from the broader intellectual agenda. Matthewman and Hoey (2006) argue that the word *postmodern* is dropping 'out of academic book and conference titles at an ever accelerating rate'. Nevertheless, it continues to play a role in the sociology of work and organisations. Chia (2003), for example, in arguing for a postmodern organisational science, sees an important critical role for the 'postmodern critique' of contemporary organisational practices. This, Chia says, 'attempts to reveal modern rationality as the . . . effect of a reductionistic operation whereby the phenomenal flux of lived experience is forcibly carved up, conceptually fixed, and systematically subjugated by the . . . organizing impulses of division, naming, classification, and representation'. These impulses are, of course, central to work organisations. This means that organisations can be understood as sites where human beings are subjugated by the language of modernism, management and bureaucratic organisation. There is a need to liberate people from this subjugation and, in Chia's words, give 'voice and legitimacy' to other tacit or buried forms of knowledge upon which modernist practices 'inevitably depend . . . yet conveniently overlook or gloss over in the process of knowledge creation'. And, to help with this, we can now turn to the thinking of Foucault and the concepts of *discourse* and *subjectivity*.

Post-structuralist labour process thinking, Foucault, discourse and human subjectivity

Postmodern and post-structuralist perspectives are said to 'decentre the subject'. They question the notion of an autonomous thinking and feeling human subject who acts upon the world from a position of confident belief in an essential and unique personality or 'self'. Post-structuralists stress the way the human being's notion of who and what they are is shaped by the *discourses* which surround them.

There is a variety of ways in which 'discourse' has come to be used by different theorists, since it first appeared in the work of Foucault (Alvesson and Karreman 2000; Grant *et al.* 2004a). Discourses are elements of human culture which arise over time and *frame* the way various aspects of the world are understood so influencing the way people act with regard to that aspect of their reality.

Discourses

Discourses are sets of concepts, statements, terms and expressions which constitute ways of talking or writing about a particular aspect of life, thus framing the way people understand and act with respect to those areas of existence.

Foucault (1980) observes historically how various discourses have exerted power over people by creating the categories into which they are fitted: 'the homosexual', 'the criminal', the 'mentally ill'. Such notions help people define what they are and create notions of how such people should be treated by others. This is clearly relevant to people as workers and employees. To designate a worker as 'a loyal employee' for example, is clearly to frame for that person a reality that supports particular workplace power relations and encourages certain behaviours as well as beliefs that are consonant with that order.

From a Foucauldian perspective, say McKinlay and Starkey (1998), 'truth and knowledge are weapons by which a society manages itself', and they argue that perhaps the greatest impact of this perspective on the study of work organisation and management has been on the critical study of accounting where accounting is seen as 'a set of practices and a discourse which aims to disaggregate the organisation and lay the actions of all its members open to critical scrutiny, comparison and modification' (Miller and O'Leary 1987; Hoskin 1998).

LOOKING FORWARD >>>>>

Research on the role of discourses in shaping human subjectivities at work will be examined in later chapters, pp. 197–199, 262, 306, 301–309, 317 and 370.

In the 1990s, two key members of the labour process analysis camp, Knights and Willmott, led a move away from examining the implications of the indeterminacy (uncertainty, unpredictability, 'fickleness', contingency) of labour to attend to the indeterminacy of the much broader notion of human *subjectivity*.

Subjectivity

The sense which people have of who they are and how they fit into the social world – a sense which is continually developing and redeveloping in the light of the shifting discourses which surround them.

The employee's subjectivity is, say Knights and Willmott (1989), 'directed narrowly, and in a self-disciplined fashion' towards actions that give people a 'sense of security and belonging'. This subjectivity is 'a product of disciplinary mechanisms, techniques of surveillance and power-knowledge strategies' and the tendency is for individuals to become isolated from each other or 'individualised' (Ezzy 1997; O'Doherty and Wilmott 2001). This emphasis on subjectivity has been sharply attacked by authors who share the labour process background of these writers but who see the change of focus 'beyond the political economy of capitalism to some existential self' as a serious *diversion* from the important issue of understanding the potential role for human agency within the constraints of capitalist employment relationships (Thompson and Smith 2001; also, Tinker 2002; Friedman 2004). A particularly significant result of the diversion away from issues of capitalist political economy, the critics argue, is that the potential for workers to challenge, resist or generally 'misbehave' is seriously underestimated (Thompson and Ackroyd 1995; Ackroyd and Thompson 1999). This line, in turn, is contested by Knights and McCabe (2000), as we see in Chapter 12 (p. 370).

Discussion

Postmodernism as a way of looking at the world has been received with varying degrees of acquiescence and disdain by industrial and organisational sociologists. Early on, Thompson (1993), for example, characterised it as a 'fatal distraction' and a retreat by sections of the intelligentsia from engagement with important issues in the world. He described postmodernism as a reactionary trend. Although there are progressive dimensions to postmodernist thinking – the decentring of the sovereign subject, the exploration of multiple identities and the challenge to traditional hierarchies of knowledge – the interest in 'multiple realities' and the making of multiple interpretations of the world leaves a situation where, in effect, the world becomes 'all things to all people'. If we let this become the case, Thompson argues, it would allow us no opportunity to take action to change that world.

An alternative approach is to applaud post-structuralism and post-modernism for bringing into sociology in general, and the sociologies of work and organisation in particular, a more central role for language than it had previously taken. The most significant idea in the postmodernist style of analysis is the notion that, as Hassard and Parker (1993) put it, 'the world is constituted by our shared language and . . . we can only "know the world" through the particular forms of discourse our language creates'. This has appeal to many social scientists who have, as Gergen (1992) suggested, a yearning for an alternative to modernist and romanticist beliefs that there are 'essentials of the universe' which can be discovered through observation and reason and which are then *reflected in* or represented by language. Within modernism, language is in some way secondary to that which it 'describes'. Postmodernism reverses 'the modernist view of language as picturing the essentials of reality'. Language loses its 'servant' or 'picturing' role and is seen, instead, as part of a process whereby people, through joint action, make sense of the world. In effect, we cease to speak of language as something which *describes action* and see language as *action in itself*. Such a shift in thinking is often referred to as a 'linguistic turn' or a 'cultural turn' in the social sciences. However, the bringing of language into the centre of sociological analysis can surely be decoupled from the 'baggage' of postmodernism.

A 'core proposition' of full-blooded postmodernism, as Hancock and Tyler (2001) point out, is the idea that all knowledge claims are relative to their linguistic and cultural context, which means that 'all claims to knowledge . . . become contingent and temporary'. But this tendency to make all truths relative inevitably threatens the very idea of a social science. What Parker (1993) has called the 'extreme ethical–political relativism' of 'hard' postmodernism, together with its tendency to refuse to see a social world beyond the 'texts' that people write and speak, makes it unacceptable to many sociologists. Indeed sociology is an enterprise to which we might expect fully committed postmodernists to deny legitimacy. Sociology can dissociate itself from postmodernism by retaining a concern with reason and analysis, at the same time as recognising, along with Weber (p. 58), the limits of formal rationality. Sociology can recognise the centrality and power of language, without suggesting that there is nothing in the world beyond the words we use to talk about it. The best sociology has always come fully to terms with the plurality of interests and perspectives in the social world without descending into a moral relativism where any one idea or activity is said to be as good or as right as any other.

Sociology, discourses and working lives

The concept of *discourse* and the analysis of discourses have become central in studies of work and organisations. Organisational discourse analysis involves the study of 'the structured collections of texts embodied in the practices of talking and writing . . . that bring organizationally related objects into being as these text are produced, disseminated and consumed' (Grant *et al.* 2004b), and such work has produced valuable insights, from researchers working within critical realist principles (Fairclough 2005) as well as the interpretive/constructionist tradition. However, a concept of *discourse* can also take its place in sociological analyses where language, as such, is not the main focus. The notion of discourse can fill a serious conceptual gap in sociology. It is a device which helps us deal with the level of social reality that mediates between that of *culture* at the relatively 'macro' level and the social interactions and interpretive actions of individuals and groups at the more 'micro' level. In our lives, we are influenced by a wide range of different discourses that surround us, rather than by a single overarching 'culture'.

Discourses, are the building blocks or *elements* of culture in the inevitably plural, complex and conflict-ridden societies in which human beings exist. They are multiple, dynamic and often in contradiction with each other. For example, we might identify a discourse in a particular society which 'speaks of' a human right to find personal fulfilment in one's work. Certain people might be encouraged by this way of 'framing' work realities to strive in their working careers to train themselves and gain employment in jobs in which they feel they might achieve 'self-actualisation'. Yet there may exist in the same society, at the same time, a contradictory discourse that speaks of work as an unpleasant necessity, the only purpose of which is to produce a level of income which enables people to support their families and to find personal satisfaction in the non-work part of their lives. People accepting the latter way of framing the realities of work will be more inclined to look for a job that pays well but from which they can psychologically disengage. Members of societies do not simply and passively 'read' these discursive framings, of course; they also contribute to the shaping of these ideas and ways of talking about the world and the ways in which they change – with their language-use affecting their actions and their actions affecting their language-use. Discourses also provide rhetorical resources which people may use to persuade others to act in particular ways (Watson 1995). All of this occurs within a political economic context, within patterns of material advantage and disadvantage and within processes of conflict, contest and change.

Discourses sometimes constrain us in our projects and purposes and sometimes they enable us or inspire us to act in particular ways. All of these possibilities are apparent in the story which Janet tells us in Snapshot 3.5.

Snapshot 3.5

The life of Janet: discourses as constraining and enabling

At first sight, I may look and sound like the other women lawyers in these chambers. But I come from somewhere quite different from all of them. My colleagues all come from what you might call professional homes; indeed they are mostly from families of lawyers. They were brought up with the assumption that girls could stay on at school, go to university and enter legal practice in the same way as boys. They were brought up with the language of 'career success' and 'making it to the Bar' for men and women alike. There were five children in our family, and the way that our families, our neighbours and our teachers spoke left me quite unaware that education beyond sixteen could be on my life agenda. If it were not for what I have achieved, it still would not occur to my brothers and sisters that any such thing was possible for 'people like us'.

I, together with one of my brothers and two of my sisters, was certainly spoken of as 'clever' at home and at school. What this meant was that we could expect to enter an office job rather than go to work in a factory when, like everyone else on our estate, we left school at sixteen.

I often think that if I had actually enjoyed the office job that I started three days after my six-teenth birthday, I would have settled for this. But, as my luck had it, it was a horrible job with horrible people. I hated it and, in my restlessness, I found myself reading a lot of magazines and novels that had women in them who had broken free from the sort of background I came from. Here was another way of looking at the world, one in which your origins and your gender need not hold you back if you were clever and determined enough. Well, I changed my approach to the world. I did A levels in the evenings and got to university whilst I was still in my teens. And here I am now. And, let me add, the stories I tell my son and my little girl about education, work, careers and gender are very different from the ones I heard as a child.

Janet, her siblings and her work colleagues all grew up in the same society and engaged with the same culture. Or did they? Janet and her family, on the one hand, were in a quite different social class, neighbourhood and educational setting from her women lawyer colleagues. In principle, the two different *discourses* or 'work career languages' that Janet alludes to were accessible to them all. But the structural circumstances of each group 'pushed' them towards two rather different discourses of work, education and career. And this 'pushing' or channelling took them towards quite different career destinations. Yet these structural and discursive pressures were not totally determining. Janet talks of other siblings being 'clever' like her. It was a chance thing, she tells us, that her dislike of her first job pushed her to reading materials which drew her attention to a 'new' discourse. This framed the world rather differently from the discourse which had framed her earlier 'reality'. A sociological analysis of Janet's life has to use concepts such as those of class, culture, educational opportunity, gender and the rest. But the use of the concept of discourse strengthens this essentially sociological analysis, with its attention to both 'structure' and 'agency' in the shaping of society and human lives. The concept has been imported from post-structuralism, we might say, and sharpened our analytical sensitivity through drawing attention to the centrality of language to the social world.

LOOKING FORWARD >>>>>

Significant use will be made of the notions of *discourse* and *discursive resources* when we look at *identities* and *identity work* in Chapter 10. A concept of identity which has both an internal (self) and an external (social) analytical dimension is offered in the spirit of producing a theoretical account which balances the roles of both agency and structure in the dynamics of social life.

Sociology emerged as a characteristically modernist activity with the project of applying reasoned analysis to the changes which were coming about with industrialisation and helping people make a better world within the new possibilities which were emerging. This aspect of the 'enlightenment project', so powerfully defended by Habermas (1987), need not be totally abandoned, as a postmodernist position would suggest. But social science is inevitably going to play a much more modest role in helping social change and achieving human control over circumstances than its creators might have hoped. The sociology of work and organisation can itself be characterised as a bundle of *discursive resources* that people can use in various ways to create their own interpretations and understandings of the world. This is a world full of ambiguities, paradoxes and contradictions which will never finally be 'sorted out', classified or pinned down in terms of sociological laws. The various perspectives or strands of thought in the sociology of work and organisation covered in this chapter all have something to offer and provide us with powerful analytical resources which we can apply in subsequent chapters.

Summary

Following the examination in Chapter 2 of the more 'managerial' and psychological strand of thinking to which sociology has reacted and the presentation of these 'reacting' sociological strands, attention has now been paid to three further strands, each of which has been central to more recent work in the sociology of work and organisation. In looking at these strands of thinking, an introduction has been given to a range of theories, concepts and orientations which will be made use of in subsequent chapters.

4 Industrial capitalism, change and the possibility of a fourth automation-based industrial revolution

Key issues

- What are the distinctive characteristics of the industrial-capitalist type of society and economy that is dominant in the modern world?
- How did this modern industrialised type of world come about?
- What transitions have sociologists identified as having occurred in the latter part of the twentieth century and the early part of the twenty-first century?
- What continuities and changes are occurring in twenty-first-century post-financial-crash societies?
- What part in change processes does technology play?
- What can be said about the future of work? And might we be entering a fourth industrial revolution?

The nature of modern societies

Sociology emerged and developed as a way of coming to terms with fundamental changes associated with industrialisation and the rise of capitalism, as we saw in Chapter 1. Changes in the way work is organised and experienced have been at the heart of the social and historical shifts with which sociology has always engaged. The most significant historical shift identified by sociologists was the rise of technology-based industrialism and capitalist forms of political economy. But, within this, sociologists and other social commentators have identified a variety of subsequent shifts in how the working aspects of societies are organised, using terminology like post-industrialism, post-Fordism, postmodernism and globalisation. Most recently, there has been speculation about a forthcoming fourth industrial revolution.

These shifts, or alleged shifts, cannot be understood without their first being located in the historical process through which the basic form of modern societies emerged. And the most useful way to characterise the basic modern form of social organisation is as 'industrial capitalism'.

> ### Industrial capitalism
>
> A form of society in which privately-owned large-scale and/or complex technologies are widely applied (within supportive states) to the pursuit of economic efficiency on a basis whereby the capacity for work of the members of some social groups is sold to or otherwise acquired by profit-seeking social groups who control and organise it in such a way that the latter groups maintain relative advantage with regard to those resources which are scarce and generally socially valued.

> ## LOOKING FORWARD >>>>>
>
> At this stage, we are looking at industrial capitalist societies as a broad type of social order. We consider later in this chapter, however, the argument that there currently exist a variety of 'capitalisms' or business systems (pp. 108–109).

The emergence of industrial capitalism

From feudalism to capitalism

Sociologists have conventionally accentuated the characteristic features of industrial capitalist societies by comparing them with some notion of a feudal society. The most famous attempt to do this is that of Ferdinand Tönnies (1855–1936) who contrasted the modern form of

Table 4.1 Tönnies' notion of a transition from community to association

Community (Gemeinschaft)	Association/society (Gesellschaft)
• Small-scale, intimate, stable	• Large-scale, individualised, rapidly changing
• Rural	• Urban
• Religious and traditional	• Scientific and rational

association or society (*Gesellschaft*) with the older, traditional, small-scale community (*Gemeinschaft*), as shown in Table 4.1.

To build upon this simple image of transition we can look back to the pre-industrial and pre-capitalist world, remembering that in doing this we are considering a world that has left us images of life that still underlie many of our contemporary ideas about how human lives could be lived in the future.

People undoubtedly worked very hard to survive in the medieval period. But this work was performed within principles that are fundamentally different from those which we take to be normal today. Work was seen more as an inevitable burden than as a way of 'developing' oneself. It was not a duty to work hard nor was hard work a way of improving oneself. Hard work was done because survival demanded it. Further, there was little separation of home and workplace, and a quite alien notion would have been that of 'working for' an employer. This does not mean that the rich did not exploit the poor but that even the poorest and most exploited serfs tended to have their own land to work – even if they were forced to supplement the income derived from this with some wage labour. However exploitative relationships might have been between social groups, the hierarchical relationship existing between people was nevertheless based on a certain recognised mutual dependence and some sense of reciprocity. There was a commitment from both sides of the master–servant relationship of a diffuseness quite lacking in the modern employment relationship (Fox 1985). The essential feature of work was that it was performed to meet clearly and generally recognised needs and its rhythms were given by natural and immediate human needs, like the need for food, shelter and clothing, or by the rhythms of nature in the shape of the changing seasons, the needs of animals to be milked or crops to be harvested.

The most advantaged groups of this period not only had the greatest share of wealth, which was predominantly in the form of land and the comforts which accrued from that land, but they were also served by a church which provided ideologies helping to stabilise social order. Christianity itself contained much which might have encouraged challenge to the feudal order and such challenges indeed did arise in combination with Christian 'heresies' and millenarian hopes on a number of occasions. However, the Roman Catholic Church and its doctrines, which put its priests as intermediaries between individuals and their destinies, was able to counteract challenges with organic models of society like that developed by Aquinas in which each person plays his natural part in the wider scheme of things. In an organic view of society, each person serves or contributes to this scheme for the sake of the whole community. Those who rule are merely doing so for the benefit of the community. Given a largely illiterate society and the insecurities resulting from dependence on agricultural production and dangers of war and disease, it is easy to see how the Church, with its near monopoly on literacy, could maintain a stabilising affinity between ruling interests and the realm of ideas. The rise of Protestantism challenged this stability.

Protestantism and the spirit of capitalism

Weber's emphasis on cultural factors in his immensely important study, *The Protestant Ethic and the Spirit of Capitalism* (1965) must be seen in its wider political, economic and historical context. If one looks at his *General Economic History* (1927) and at *Economy and Society* (1978), especially his chapter on 'the city', it is clear that he regards the influence of Protestantism as just one factor to be put alongside the type of change in city life alluded to in the previous section, the growing separation of home and workplace and many other technical and commercial factors. Weber's main significance results from his bringing into historical analysis the variable of human agency, countering any tendency towards determinism with an emphasis on human initiative. Weber recognised that interests, not ideas, govern human conduct (Bendix 1965). Nevertheless, he sees world views created by ideas frequently acting 'like switchmen indicating the lines along which action has been propelled by the dynamics of interest'. In his version of Goethe's concept of *elective affinity*, Weber suggests that people adopt ideas to fit in with their interests.

The spirit of capitalism, aided by the Protestant ethic, brought a new force and a new legitimacy to the proto-capitalists of the European cities. It encouraged hard work, not just in order to meet basic needs or to produce short-term capital gain, but as a virtue or duty in its own right. A religious doctrine which suggests that one is serving God by following one's mundane tasks in a self-disciplined and efficient way and which combines this with a demand for an ascetic or frugal form of existence has obvious potential for fostering such a spirit and indeed encouraging the accumulation of capital. One makes money by hard work and application but confidence of membership of the elect is risked if one slacks in one's efforts or if one over-indulges in the fruits of one's labours. The fruits of labour are not now hedonistic ones but confidence of salvation. Under Catholicism, a 'calling' from God involved transcendence of the mundane, but the novel Calvinist notion of seeing one's mundane work itself as a 'vocation' overturned this. The almost revolutionary change in religious thought brought about by the Reformation was its removal of the Church and its priests as intermediaries between the individual and God. In a sense, every one was to be their own priest, and the demand was now less that one should be guided in one's actions by the Church hierarchy than that one should look to one's own conscience in deciding how one should act.

There had been earlier tendencies in Christianity which looked to 'motives of the heart' in this way, but such ideas were only able to take root once there were social groups well placed to sustain opposition to prevailing values, and 'in a society where custom and tradition counted for so much, this insistence that a well-considered strong conviction overrode everything else had a great liberating force' (Hill 1974). Protestantism does not cause capitalism but gives force and legitimacy to the pursuit of economic interests by already emerging social groups. As Hill puts it, 'the protestant revolt melted down the iron ideological framework which held society in its ancient mould. Where capitalism already existed, it had henceforth freer scope'. Weber's whole point is to show how the ethical posture of inner-worldly asceticism engenders within certain groups 'already involved in the practice of business . . . a certain occupational ethic' (Poggi 1983). This is 'the spirit of capitalism'. And this 'spirit' saw the unleashing of the process of rationalisation.

Rationality and change

The criterion of rationality involves submitting decisions and actions to constant calculative scrutiny and produces a continuous drive towards change.

This process involves a replacement of the criterion of *tradition* (we do this because it is the way it has always been done) with a criterion of instrumental rationality (we must work out the most efficient means of achieving this end).

The essence of rationality is calculation, and historically, this process led to the undermining of the primacy of religious or magical thought (including, ironically, those forms which gave impetus to this process) and is a force pushing forward the growth of science and technology together with an accompanying expansion of the technical division of labour and the bureaucratic organisation of work.

> **LOOKING FORWARD >>>>>**
>
> Socio-technical systems thinking and some classic research carried out in that tradition will be examined in Chapter 6, p. 189.

Industrialisation and the changing division of labour

Central to the development of the Industrial Revolution was the bringing together of the now available *wage labour* in special premises to work under the supervision of the employers (or their agents), using the employers' tools and machinery and their raw materials. The impression is frequently given, following the lead of Adam Smith's Wealth of Nations (1776), that the splitting down of work tasks among the employees in these factories simply follows some 'logic of efficiency'. In contrast to this, it can be argued that this division of labour was not the result of a search for a 'technologically superior organisation of work but for an organisation which guaranteed to the entrepreneur an essential role in the production process' (Marglin 1980). There is thus no determining force making the appearance of the factory inevitable. There is, rather, a choice on the part of certain people to provide themselves with a niche in society – one which involved the control and co-ordination of the labour of others in the pursuit of capital accumulation and their own material advantage. It was no technological imperative that brought people into factories and set under way new methods of work organisation. Human interests and ideas, including ideas about how technologies could be developed, worked together to change societies and the division of labour within societies.

A key concept used in the analysis of social organisation and social change since the early stage of industrialisation has been that of a division of labour. The concept focuses attention on how particular tasks are carried out by particular people – this pattern being seen as undergoing significant change with industrialisation.

The division of labour

The allocation of work tasks to various groups or category of individual.

Durkheim (2014, originally 1893) saw the division of labour as central to the nature of a society's solidarity – the way in which a society achieves integration. In a simple society, there would be little occupational differentiation with, say, most of the women carrying out one basic task, most of the young men occupied in another general task and so on. A similarity of outlook would develop between people, most of whom are engaged in more or less similar activities. Social order and stability would thus be maintained through *mechanical solidarity*. However, in the vastly more complex industrialising world where a large range of specialised occupations have developed, each with distinctive ideas, norms and values, a similarity of outlook cannot be depended upon to hold society together. The source for stability is to be found, instead, in the inevitable interdependence of members of occupations one with the other. Bakers depend on butchers for their meat, butchers on the bakers for their bread, and so on. We thus have integration through *organic solidarity*.

Although Durkheim saw the occupational principle as offering a basis for integration in modern society in this way, he nevertheless began to note how the increasing emphasis on material advancement and sectional interests of his own time tended to undermine social solidarity, leading, in particular, to the moral confusion and purposelessness which he conceptualised as *anomie*. But Durkheim treated such tendencies as pathological rather than as essential features of industrial capitalism. The more closely we look at Durkheim's assumed source of social order in modern societies – the organic solidarity achieved by interdependent occupations – the more we come to realise that the structure and dynamics of industrial capitalism can be better understood in terms of interests, power and control. The attachment of people to the prevailing social order is more realistically seen as deriving from their dependence on the material rewards to be gained from their relationship, not to occupations, but to bureaucratic work organisations, whether this relationship be more one of submitting to control within an organisation, exercising such control or servicing the organisation in some direct or indirect way.

Consideration of the division of labour in the Marxian tradition has seen the increasing specialisation of tasks that accompanies the capitalist labour process as essentially disintegrative. As shown in Table 4.2, an

Table 4.2 The social and technical division of labour

Social division of labour	Technical division of labour
The allocation of work tasks at the level of society, typically into trades and occupations	Task specialisation within an occupation or broad work task

important distinction is made between the general or *social* division of labour and the detailed or *technical* division of labour.

The technical division of labour has generally been seen as involving a splitting down of tasks within a former craft at the initiative of employers or their agents in order to increase the efficiency of the enterprise – efficiency as conceived by those extracting a surplus (Braverman 1974). The dividing of tasks within occupations, with its alienating effects, is often seen as fundamentally different from the dividing of tasks between occupations – the latter constituting a healthy and necessary part of any human society.

Marx would no doubt have seen the modern violin-factory workers as less fulfilled ('more alienated') than the 18th century craft-based violin makers, as described in Snapshot 4.1.

Snapshot 4.1

Violin-making in Poterton

When violins were first made in the small town of Poterton, we could say that the social division of labour was in operation. There were wheelsmiths, a baker, a butcher and several weavers living and working alongside two or three violin makers in the main street. The violin makers worked on each instrument all the way from the initial woodcarving stage to the varnishing and the adding of the bridge, pegs and strings. Violins are still made in the town, but they are produced in the violin factory. Here a technical division of labour prevails. Where, in the past, the violin makers were able to deal with every stage of the production of the instruments, we now find that any particular worker in the violin factory is only able to work the wood cutting machine, glue the front, sides and backs of the instrument together or varnish the violin when it reaches the varnish shop. Many more violins can now be produced by a given number of people. And a much higher rate of profit is achieved than in the past. The one man with real craft expertise spends most of his time instructing and monitoring the workers.

The occupational principle of work structuring that underpinned the social division of labour saw individual workers playing their part in society as a violin maker or a butcher, and each of these possessed the cluster of skills that went with their particular occupation or craft. They would undertake 'whole tasks' – the design, production and selling of a violin or the killing, preparing and selling of meat, for example. With the rise of industrial capitalism, the rationalising force of bureaucratisation and the growth of the institution of formal employment came the splitting down into deskilled jobs of the old occupational roles of the declining social division of labour. Industrialisation brought about the technical division of labour which saw the creation of jobs in which individuals did only one specialised part of what had previously been an occupational 'whole task'.

These new principles of work design were first written about by Adam Smith in his *Wealth of Nations* in 1776. Smith recognised that enormous gains in efficiency were to be obtained if the 'whole' task such as the making of tacks (or 'pins' as he called them) could be split up into a number of smaller scale and less skilled tasks or jobs. Each job would be easy to learn, and each operation readily repeatable. The employer would benefit enormously from the increased dexterity of the worker, the reduction of time spent in preparation and changeover from one operation to another and from the possibilities which were opened up for further mechanisation. But it was Charles Babbage, in 1832, who pointed out that this kind of deskilling also reduced the cost of labour. If 'whole' tasks were carried out then you had to pay each worker a rate which was appropriate to the most skilful or physically demanding element of the task. You could, however, 'by dividing the work . . . into different degrees of skill and force . . . purchase the precise quantity of both that is necessary for each purpose'.

Modern industrial capitalist social organisation: dimensions of change

In the same way that early sociologists observed a transformation occurring in societies as they industrialised, thinkers have suggested further transformations in industrial societies which are significant enough to warrant recognition of the approach or the arrival of a new type of social order, in one sense or another.

Post-industrialism and the information society

Post-industrial society
A type of economically advanced social order in which the centrally important resource is knowledge, service work has largely replaced manufacturing employment and knowledge-based occupations play a privileged role.

One of the most influential claims about a new kind of social organisation was made by Bell (1974). He suggested that advanced industrial societies were entering a new phase in their development in the latter part of the twentieth century. Out of this has come the still influential notion of a post-industrial society. The characteristic features of the post-industrial society are to be found in the spheres of technology, the economy and the social structure. The economy undergoes a shift from being a predominantly manufacturing one to a service one in which 'knowledge workers' (Drucker 1968) play a central role. In technology, the new science-based industries become central. And in the social structure, we see 'the rise of new technical elites and the advent of a new principle of stratification' (Bell 1974). The suggestion is that a new type of occupational structure develops in which white-collar workers outnumber blue-collar ones and in which the professional, scientific and technical occupations become predominant.

In this new type of society, 'theoretical knowledge' becomes the basis for innovation and policy-making. Post-industrial society is thus a 'knowledge society', and those occupations that possess theoretical knowledge are expected – on the principle that knowledge is power – to come to exert a controlling influence on society. With the diminution of the manual working class, a relatively stable order is expected to follow as social and economic policy is rationally formulated and as individuals are tied into the social order, through the operation of the meritocratic system of rewards which must accompany an occupational structure dependent on recruiting individuals with high ability. The potential for satisfaction at work is increased, it is claimed, by the increased opportunity created by the expanding service sector for people to relate to other people in their jobs rather than to machines.

Bell's assumptions about the changing nature of the work people *actually* do can be strongly questioned. Qualitative inferences about the nature of occupational life are made on the basis of statistical trends whereby tasks are allocated to official categories which tell us little about what people actually do in their work (Gershuny 1978). The greatest weakness in Bell's thesis, however, lies in his assumption that there is anything novel about the centrality of knowledge to economic and working life. The growth of industrialism and the rise of capitalism were both dependent on the increasing application of rational–calculative thinking to social life. Thus the growth of scientific and technical qualifications among the population is all part of the rationalisation process which Max Weber saw as characterising Western history over several centuries. This is recognised in Castells' (1996, 1997, 1998) major overview of the sociological implications of information and communication technologies (ICTs) and his notions of 'the information age' and 'the network society' (Castells 2000).

LOOKING FORWARD >>>>>

Knowledge workers, along with workers in the creative and cultural industries are discussed, in the context of the occupational principle of social organisation, in Chapter 8, pp. 247–249.

Castells (1996) distinguishes between the 'information society', which is not new, and the *informational society* which differs from what has come before because the generating, processing and transmitting of knowledge-based information has become 'the fundamental sources of productivity and power'. Acknowledging the 'globalisation' dimension of changes here, Castells sees this new picture merging in the 1980s with the emergence of 'informational capitalism' – something which has since taken on a global form (albeit with considerable regional differences). It is the 'networking logic' of ICTs that gives them a 'planetary' significance – with the gains made from global flows of capital becoming more significant than those that were made from the production of goods. And whereas, in the older forms of capitalism, the challenge to capitalism came from members of working classes resisting their exploitation, the challenges to informational capitalism come from a variety of social movements concerned to protect or advance their *identities*, rather than their material interests. However, opposition from, say, environmentalist, feminist or gay groups does not come from outside the networked social order; such groups will only be able to pursue their identity projects through the use of information technologies and networks.

Castells' work has been challenged on the grounds that it is not supported by empirical evidence and is poorly theorised (Abell and

Reyniers 2000). McLennan (2003) questions whether the identification of the series of factors that have brought the informational society into being 'amounts to a causal explanation, or whether it is rather more in the way of an evolutionary description of how things happen to have happened'. And in pointing to significant continuities between the role played by ICTs and modern technologies generally and noting the continuing salience of long-standing patterns of social inequality, Golding (2000) argued that the sociology of the future, in these areas, is very much the sociology of the present. This is not to say, however, that new information and communication technologies are not having a significant impact at the level of work experience and work organisation, as we shall see shortly.

Post-Fordism

Like the concepts of post-industrialism, information or network society, post-Fordism has been used to characterise changes in work and society since the late 1970s. Although Fordism is clearly connected to developments made in the earlier part of the twentieth century in Henry Ford's car factories, 'Fordism' has come to be used as a term describing a whole way of organising industrial societies that came to prominence in the second part of that century (Beynon and Nichols 2006). At the level of the workplace, Fordism follows such scientific management or 'Taylorist' principles as the use of a detailed division of labour, intensive management work-planning and close supervision (Chapter 2, pp. 32–34), and extends these considerably in the close attachment of the individual to their work station and in the mechanising of work handling. But it goes beyond Taylorism, which tends to treat labour strictly as a commodity, by making a connection between labour management policy and attention to markets. Fordism was essentially a mass production process which recognised that the people it employs are part of the market for its products. It therefore recognises the necessity of taking an interest in the lives of workers as consumers as well as producers. And this involves nation states in adopting policies and creating institutions, such as those of the 'welfare state', that develop citizens as both fit and healthy producers and acquisitive consumers.

> ## Fordism
>
> A pattern of industrial organisation and employment policy in which
> (a) mass production techniques and an associated deskilling of jobs is combined with
> (b) treatment of employees which recognises that workers are also consumers whose earning power and consumption attitudes – as well as their workplace efficiency – affect the success of the enterprise.

Fordism involved a recognition of the need to develop working-class 'social consumption norms' which would stabilise the markets for the products of mass production industries (Aglietta 1979). The mass consumption market has to be created and stabilised to fit the mass production organisation of the factory. But such regimes are seen as being replaced by post-Fordism.

> ## Post-Fordism
>
> A pattern of industrial organisation and employment policy in which skilled and trusted labour is used continuously to develop and customise products for small markets.

In 'regulation theory' (Lipietz 1987; Boyer 1988), post-Fordism is related to the ways in which particular 'regimes of accumulation' in capitalist societies are supported by specific 'modes of regulation'. Different relationships are said to emerge between these two structural elements as Fordism begins to fail and is replaced by post-Fordism:

- *The Fordist regime of accumulation* in which standardised products for price-competitive mass markets are mass produced with largely semi-skilled labour is supported by a Fordist mode of regulation in which there is state macro-economic regulation, public welfare provision and the institutionalising of collective bargaining.
- The *post-Fordist regime of accumulation* replaces the Fordist one with an emphasis on quality-competitive production for shifting and differentiated markets, using qualified and highly skilled flexible labour, and is supported by a post-Fordist mode of regulation in which there is reduction in state intervention in labour markets, a shift of responsibility for welfare provision from the state to employers or private individuals and a more flexible and varied approach to employment relations.

Fordism is widely seen as hitting difficulties in the later part of the twentieth century. The economic recession of the 1970s and 1980s could be seen, for example, as part of a general economic downswing associated with a crisis in the Fordist approach to production and consumption. Jessop (2002), in his analysis of north-west Europe, the USA and Australia, argued that Fordism as a form of capitalist accumulation became incompatible with the Keynesian welfare state with which it was linked as a result of various crises and contradictions. It has been replaced with a 'Schumpeterian Workfare Postnational Regime' at the centre of which is state prioritisation of the pursuit of competitive advantage through enterprise, innovation and technological change.

Although this analysis still has overtones of economic determinism, it usefully draws attention to possible links between the economic and the political spheres – as long as these are not seen as too mechanistic and as operating in only one direction. Such theorising is, however, also vulnerable to criticisms of over-simplification because of its dualistic style of analysis. When we look at more detailed and local studies of restructuring such as that of Bagguley *et al.* (1990), who examined restructuring in two particular towns, there is less evidence of changes being 'driven by capital' than the neo-Marxist theories would suggest. These researchers argue that, although economic factors are central to what they saw occurring, they are far from the whole story. Local, ethnic, political, gender and class factors play a significant role.

In spite of the need for careful empirical study of what is actually occurring 'on the ground', the idea of a new kind of post-Fordist social organisation has led to some influential speculative analyses and prescription. With the collapse of Fordism and the growth of a de-standardised, fragmented, deregulated and plural 'underemployment system' in which neither the state nor trade unions can protect people from risk and insecurity, Beck (2000) pointed to an opportunity for a 'multi-activity society' to be developed. In this 'brave new world of work', housework, family work and voluntary work would be 'prized alongside paid work', and new communities of interest developed outside the formal world of organised work and industry. Gorz (1999) also argued for movement towards a multi-activity society and culture along such lines, seeing this as an alternative to the pressure which post-Fordist employment puts on the worker to sell their 'whole self' to the corporation. Whereas under Fordism the worker simply sold their labour-power to the employer, the post-Fordist employer would seek a level of commitment and initiative that would threaten workers' identity and personal autonomy. No significant evidence for anything along these lines actually happening has been forthcoming. Yet this does not mean than such arrangements might not be a possibility in the future.

Flexible specialisation

Flexible specialisation (Piore and Sabel 1984; Piore 1986; Hirst and Zeitlin 1991) is similar to post-Fordism but extends the idea in several ways.

> ## Flexible specialisation
>
> An approach to employment and work organisation which offers custom-ised products to diversified markets, building trusting and co-operative relationships both with employees, who use advanced technologies in a craft way, and other organisations within a business district and its associated community.

Those identifying a trend towards flexible specialisation see the breakdown of the mass markets associated with Fordism leading to a use of computer-controlled production equipment for the small batch pro-duction of high-quality, customised products for discrete or specialised market niches. The speed and economies possible with microelectronic technology allows firms to respond rapidly to changes in demand and to combine low unit costs with non-repetitive manufacturing. For this to succeed, workers have to be competent across a range of tasks and be prepared to switch between these as demand requires. Recomposition of tasks leads to reskilling of labour and the revival of craft traditions. Co-operative relationships are developed not only with the employees, however, but with other organisations and institutions within the firm's business district. Collective services relating to training of labour, low-cost finance, marketing and research and development are shaped in the district in such a way that firms both co-operate and compete with one another.

Patterns of flexible specialisation in this sense have arisen in districts of Germany and Italy, and its advocates see a potential for its principles spreading into larger organisations as these perceive a need to react to changes in consumer demand. Little evidence is available, however, of these principles having been taken any further. But, again, there are ideas here which might become relevant again in the future.

Postmodernity

Postmodernity is a term used to characterise a recent stage in human history.

LOOKING BACK <<<<<

Whereas 'postmodernity' is an historical epoch, 'postmodernism' is a style of social and cultural analysis – a way of looking at the world, as we saw in Chapter 2.

Postmodernity

An alleged state into which the world is moving which departs from the key organising principles of modernity.

Postmodernity sees a reshaping of activities across the globe with trends towards both globalisation and more localised activity. A greater plurality of interest groups appears, 'image' and consumption play a key role in people's consciousness with pleasure replacing the old emphasis on work as a virtue in its own right. Work organisations become much more decentralised and people's experience within them changes.

Discussions of postmodernity pay attention to various ways in which fragmentation of existing patterns can be seen to be occurring in the world – although there is also attention to some countervailing trends within this. As the association of a concept of postmodernity with post-modernism as a way of thinking about the world (explained in Chapter 3) would imply, a concern with changes in human knowledge plays a key role here, as it did with claims about post-industrialism. Lyotard's (1984) claim that the basis of legitimacy of 'modern' knowledge is withering away is crucial here. Postmodernity is associated with 'heterogeneity, plurality, constant innovation and pragmatic construction of local rules and prescriptives agreed upon by participants, and is thus for micropolitics' (Best and Kellner 1991).

Like the idea of globalisation and Castells' notion of the network society, 'postmodernity' tends to be associated with increasing movements of capital across the world and the way this puts considerable limits on what nation states can do. Such trends, say Lash and Urry (1987), lead to a 'disorganisation of capitalism' as economic activities within a nation state become decreasingly amenable either to state management or to working-class-based political initiatives. The claim of these authors that there is a general move from an era of 'organised capitalism' to one of *disorganised capitalism* has a cultural element as well as an economic one. Lash and Urry observe the 'disorganising' effects of a postmodern culture, with its fetishising of cultural images which they see as tending to fragment people's cultural or class identity. In spite of the fact that analyses such as these touch on significant changes occurring in contemporary life, especially in the cultural field, they are vulnerable to the same criticism made earlier of information-related attempts to identify a new epoch in human history. And, inevitably, there arises a question of the quality of the evidence that is put forward in support of some of the large generalisations that are made about a new kind of society. This applies to the often cited generalisations made about contemporary life by Baumann (2005, 2007). Nevertheless, his reflections on social life and its organisation in the twenty-first century world are provocative and stimulating. This has been especially the case since he replaced his previously favoured term 'post modern society' with the concept of the *liquid modern society*. In 'liquid modernity', there are two dominant processes of social change: globalisation and individualisation. Every aspect of social life is dominated by the logic of free market economics and this leaves individuals in a state of fear and uncertainty. The habits and routines which previously gave people comfort and security failed to survive the speed of cultural change. Consumption thus comes to take a central role in human lives as people seek solutions to their existential problems from the market place. In this, goods and services alike play their parts.

McDonaldisation and the blurring of the manufacturing-service distinction

Those societies in which industrialisation first came about have seen a moving away to other parts of the world of a significant proportion of their manufacturing capacity. Britain, for example, has in a single generation changed from being a manufacturing nation to one where most employment is in services (White *et al.* 2004). However, it is important when looking at statistics indicating shifts from manufacturing to service work to note that much of the apparent increase in service employment (increases in numbers of managers, technologists and other professionals) is associated with an increase in activities aimed at improving the efficiency of systems of material production. In pointing this out, Gershuny (1978) also noted that service requirements are often being met by increased production by manufacturing industry. For example, people tend to buy a washing machine, putting demand on the manufacturing sector, instead of taking the washing to a laundry and creating laundry service employment. And when it comes to the experience of work in the two sectors, there are both continuities and differences.

The fast-food restaurant is a prime example of principles of industrial manufacturing being applied to service work, thus giving us continuity between experiences in the two sectors. Taylorist principles underpin the operation of the fast-food restaurant.

Labour in such restaurants is 'highly rationalised, and the goal is the discovery of the best, the most efficient, way of grilling a hamburger, frying chicken, or serving a meal' (Ritzer 1993). As Ritzer (1993, 1998) observes, McDonald's, the best-known fast-food business, did not invent these ideas but combined them with the principles of bureaucracy and the assembly line 'to contribute to the creation of McDonaldisation'. And industrial manufacturing principles of mechanisation, rationalisation and routinisation are not only applied to fast-food service work but also to banking, retailing and other services work in a way which means that service work is tending to extend 'manual industrial labour' rather than erode it (Beynon 1992). Yet, as Ritzer points out, in response to Smart's (1999) criticisms of his McDonaldisation thesis, these tendencies towards 'McDonaldised standardisation' are occurring in the world at the same time as post-Fordist moves towards greater flexibility may be occurring in other 'sectors of society' (Ritzer 1999). This would suggest that there is no trend of convergence here towards a single pattern.

In contrast to this, Bryman (2004) is willing to make bold claims about convergence, arguing that the contemporary world is converging towards the features of Disney theme parks. This Disneyization of culture and society involves the growing use of branding and the 'theming' of shops, hotels and restaurants. On the work side, it involves increasing proportions of employees being required to give theatre-like 'performances' in the course of doing their jobs. This analysis fits with other writing which stresses the differences between the newer types of service work and older standard manufacturing type employment. Allen and du Gay (1994), for example, talk about a 'hybrid' type of activity in that it combines with its economic function a cultural one (culture being involved with the 'production of distinct meanings'). Thus, a profitable service relation 'is one in which distinct meanings are produced for the customer' and service work can be seen as developing its own technologies – 'soft' ones of 'interpersonal and emotion management'. This means that service work has its own characteristic types of skill, involving predispositions and capacities which are aimed at making it possible for them 'to win over the "hearts and minds" of customers'.

The view that service work has its own distinctive characteristics is open to challenge. A great deal of work in manufacturing organisations, for example, especially in the managerial and marketing spheres, involves the types of 'people skills' that are traditionally associated with service work. Frenkel *et al.* (1999), in recognising a general rise in the proportion of people engaged in service rather than manufacturing work, observe the increasing importance of *front-line service workers*, both as a proportion of the workforce and as a reflection of the 'strategic' role they play 'at the interface of the organisation and its customers'. Work, these researchers argue, is generally becoming more complex. In part, this is because of increasing demand for more customised products and services and is partly the result of the growing use of ICTs combined with the increasing costs of labour. An important consequence of this shift, Frenkel *et al.* suggest, is that higher-level skills will be required of an increasing proportion of workers, with a consequential shift in bargaining power on the part of those workers. Nevertheless, a basic tension will continue to be present in a great deal of service work between, on the one hand, the need for workers to use discretion, individuality and flexibility in order to please customers and, on the other hand, a need for their work to be closely directed and routinised in order to maintain tight managerial control. Korczynski (2002) sees this in terms of a new form of what Bell (1976) called the cultural contradictions of capitalism and he points to a contradiction between the 'dual logics of rationalisation and customer-orientation'. One of the ways in which this is managed is through the promotion of 'the enchanting myth of customer sovereignty' in which service interactions are structured so that 'it appears to the customer that he/she is in charge whilst the customer may be substantively directed and influenced' (Korczynski and Ott 2004).

If, as we saw earlier in this section, it can be argued that there is high-skill, service-like work being done in so-called manufacturing contexts, there may, at the same time, be low-skill, manufacturing-like work going on within so-called service settings. Retail work, for instance, is typically regarded as service work. Yet Pettinger (2006) argues that it is wrong to label retail work in this way. She demonstrates that customer service interactions are not central to sales but are 'an adjunct of a more general confluence of production and consumption'. At the 'core of retail work' in fact are 'domestic-style tasks of cleaning and tidying'. And when it comes to the 'back office' type of service work, of which call centre work is the best known example, all the evidence points to the continuation of close, bureaucratic or 'mass production' modes of control (Poynter 2000; Batt 2000; Korczynski 2004).

Yet another way of questioning the whole notion of 'service work', and perhaps the most radical approach so far, is to look at how the distinction between service and other work is used in practice in the work context. Sallaz (2010) applied the concept of *nomination struggle* (from Bourdieu's theory of *political representation*) in his ethnographic study of a South African entertainment complex, a business which incorporates a hotel, a shopping centre, a casino and several food courts. The management fully 'bought into' the idea that customers' emotions 'would be managed by the firm' and that the service provided would lead to a 'world class' leisure experience. The workers, for their part, were keen to be identified with these principles and made a claim to be classified as service workers. The management, however, resolutely resisted this. They insisted, on essentialist race-based grounds, that the black workforce were incapable of providing customer service. They were to be treated, in effect, as 'objects', alongside the lights, the music and the wine which the business would use to manipulate the consumers' emotions and satisfaction. Here we see a 'nomination struggle' which had both material and symbolic significance for the managers and for the workers. In the light of this study, it is difficult to treat the notion of 'service work' as a neutral analytical concept.

LOOKING FORWARD >>>>>

Further aspects of service work are discussed when we look at issues of identity and emotional labour in Chapter 10, pp. 322–326, and worker resistance to customer pressures in Chapter 12, pp. 386–388.

Globalisation

It is probably most helpful to start here with a relatively open conceptualisation of 'globalisation', one which commits its user to little more than recognising that different parts of the world are increasingly linked with each other.

This fits with the characterisation of 'an empirical condition of the modern world' offered by Tomlinson (1999). This is a condition of *complex connectivity* in which there is 'the rapidly developing and ever-densening network of interconnections and interdependencies that characterise modern social life'. Similarly Clegg and Carter (2009) refer to an 'intensification of political, financial and informational connectivity'. Walby (2006) too keeps things initially simple with a definition

> ### Globalisation
>
> That trend in which the economic, political and cultural activities of the people in different countries increasingly influence each other and become interdependent.

of globalisation as 'a process of increased density and frequency of international or global social interactions relative to local or national ones'.

Going beyond these basic simplicities, we have to come to terms with the fact that there is a great deal of variation in how the 'globalisation' term is used. It seems often to be used as a flexible debating device rather than as a useful social scientific concept. To bring clarity to the issues which arise, Child (2005) focuses on the economic sphere, saying that globalisation 'actually refers' to various developments occurring since the mid-1980s, including 'an accelerated growth of world trade and direct investment, the global integration of currency and capital markets, and the spread across the world of value-added chains made possible through decreasing transport costs, the widespread application of new information technologies, and the dissemination of "best practice" management concepts'. He nevertheless notes that the term globalisation is used in such a variety of ways that it is 'in danger of losing any useful purpose'. This sentiment is echoed by Van der Bly (2005) who says that the concept is 'quintessentially ambiguous, thus creating an accumulation of confusion rather than an accumulation of knowledge'. To deal with this, Van der Bly attempts to go beyond what she sees as the dominant economic approach to a more sociological one, saying that sociologists might switch away from economists' defining of globalisation as 'an open economy', towards a more sociological idea of 'an open society', with the degree of openness being something they might empirically examine. Drori et al. (2006) adopt an institutionalist style of analysis (see Chapter 3, pp. 61–64), to paint a picture of a world of more and more organisations, and of increasingly elaborate organisations. The 'recipe' of rationalised organisation creates a 'pervasive system' which 'penetrates and transforms all sorts of social domains everywhere, over and above variations in issues, locations, and resources'. Echoing Weber's rationalisation thesis (Chapter 3, p. 58), they see the 'myth of organisation' being increasingly imposed on domains previously structured in traditional ways. This 'hyper-rationalisation' is, however, accompanied by 'hyper-individualism', and in what these authors suggest might be called 'postmodernity', they see a dialectic between the tendency for individuals to be subjected to tighter social controls and the tendency for the 'grounds of empowerment' to increase 'for the same social actors'.

It is clearly important for sociologists to go beyond examining economic trends when considering alleged trends towards globalisation. Political and cultural changes must be considered alongside the economic. We need to note, for example, the importance of *political* changes following the end of the Cold War and changing patterns of international tension (Bobbit 2002) which brought about new patterns of military alliance which influence contacts between peoples in different parts of the world. And the *cultural* dimension of international changes is stressed by Robertson (1992) who defined globalisation as 'the compression of the world and the intensification of consciousness of the world'. He analyses the ways in which the trend towards global consciousness develops at local levels as people look outwards towards the world. He questions the thesis that globalisation represents a growing domination of the world by Western rationality. The considerable role of religious movements across the globe, examined by Robertson, is strong evidence of the survival of a powerful 'local' level of consciousness. This exists, however, alongside the international popularity of various forms of entertainment and the ubiquity of certain fast food 'outlets' (Waters 1995). And there is empirical evidence for convergence of time-use patterns, at least in the developed world, with Gershuny (2000) showing that, across the twenty societies he studied, there has been a *national convergence* and shared general increase in leisure (as opposed to work), a *gender convergence* in which women do a greater proportion of domestic work than men, and a *status convergence* in how time-use varies between social groups.

In spite of the multi-dimensionality of the globalisation phenomenon, economic factors remain central to globalising trends, not least because they have enormous significance for politics and indeed for culture, insofar as economic interests press upon the world homogenised cultural products in spheres such as those of food and entertainment. And very important to debates about globalisation has been the recognition that, if full economic globalisation were to come about, national governments would become powerless in the face of the international market, and national and local elites would lose their power and influence to international 'capital'. Multi-national corporations – ones with a base in a particular country – are undoubtedly increasingly influential in the world, moving people, money and jobs around the world to suit their own interests (Gray 1998). Globalisation would entail these being replaced by transnational corporations whose management is internationally recruited and who move business activities about the world regardless of interests in any one country. However, it is clear that the major business corporations in the world are still located in particular countries. Although large corporations move investments about the world and build international markets, they are still recognised as being 'Japanese companies' or 'American corporations'.

It is perhaps most helpful to say that an international economy certainly exists but not a 'globalised' one (Hirst and Thompson 1996). Indeed, these authors observed that markets were more open and flows of immigration were greater between 1870 and 1914. Thus we are not looking at a new trend. And Evans (2007) refers to the 19th century 'making of the global economy' in which 'the marketplace, and even more the social relations of the market economy of Europe, put in place a new map of the world'. And moving into modern times, Hirst and Thompson (1996) demonstrate that national and international markets have not been replaced by a global free market. Similarly, Whitley and Morgan (2012) argue that, in spite of the expectations of some thinkers that neoliberalism would 'signal the withdrawal of the nation-state from key areas of economic life in the industrialized world' states remain the 'key source of political legitimacy' in that world.

Business systems theory attempts to identify the 'varieties of capitalism' to be seen across the world with Whitley (2000) identifying five types of business system – fragmented (Hong Kong), co-ordinated industrial districts (parts of Italy), compartmentalised (Anglo-Saxon countries), state-organised (Korea) and highly co-ordinated (Japan). He then produces evidence to suggest that little convergence is occurring between these, in spite of financial and economic internationalisation. Lane (2007) applies similar thinking to post-socialist societies and shows considerable variation in the extent to which the state retains a significant role *vis-à-vis* the market across Central and Eastern Europe (CEE). Martin (2008) supports the picture of diversity in the CEE states whilst stressing, to a greater extent than the business system theorists, the role of history, process and contingent circumstances in the way different trajectories have been followed in different societies.

These variations with capitalist social organisation support the general failure to identify a pattern of convergence. This clearly questions the work of those contributors to globalisation debates whom Held *et al.* (1999) characterise as 'hyperglobalists'. The evidence is, however, consistent with Held *et al.'s* own 'transformational' perspective. This recognises 'transformation in the spatial organisation of social relations and transactions . . . generating transcontinental or interregional flows and networks of activity, interaction and the exercise of power' but does not define a clear end point for 'globalisation'. It is left as an open question as to where ongoing transformations will take the world. So again, the notion of convergence is rejected, as it is by Smith (2005). In order to explain variations in organisational practices and forms Smith presents a system, society and dominance (SSD) model. At the *system level*, we can see the effects on organisations of the political economy or mode of production of capitalism (which in its generic form is based on 'distinctive property rights, accumulation through competition, and incessant innovation of the means and forces of production'). But mediating this generic pressure is the effect of unique national institutions, cultures, and histories (societal effects) and the diffusion of best practices or modernisation strategies by the society-in-dominance at any particular period of global competition (dominance effects). These dominance effects, in recent decades, have been exercised by Japan and the USA. Such effects are observed by Jacoby (2004) in his detailed study of matched companies and associated HR practices in American and Japanese companies. Whilst both business communities have responded to certain globalising pressures, they have nevertheless retained different national characteristics. And this is in spite of the dominance effect's pushing every other country, Japan included, towards American practices.

These emerging analyses suggest, then, that there are increasing connections and similarities across the globe but that these continue to exist alongside national and local differences. Having said this, however, we are left with a crucially important question for sociology: where does the concept of 'society' fit into all this?

LOOKING BACK <<<<<

In Chapter 1, society was defined as the 'broad pattern of social, economic, cultural and political relationships within which people lead their lives' and it was observed that this was 'typically in the modern world as members of the same nation state'.

The process of globalisation raises the question of whether people's attachment to a 'society' is going to remain as 'members of the same nation state'. This is recognised by Walby (2006) who, whilst not calling for our abandoning the concept of society, suggests that we treat *societalisation* as a matter of degree. And by this, she means 'the extent to which the economic, political and cultural domains map onto each other in a given territory and mutually affect each other'. The idea is to treat the mapping of the economic, political and cultural domains of social life onto one another not as a matter of presumption but as 'a matter of degree'. This is valuable sociologically because it encourages us, as we look at increasing linkages across the globe, to study linkages that involve notions of nation, religion and ethnicity as well as class. These are all important factors in how individuals relate to the social world, and we need to understand the roles they play as people across the globe increasingly come into contact with each other, at the level of ideas as well as economic arrangements. Studies which look closely at specific work organisations and the people working in them are going to be very important if we are going to understand these matters.

One such study is an ethnographic investigation carried out by Ailon-Souday and Kunda (2003) in an Israeli high-tech corporation which was undergoing a merger with an American former competitor. The researchers show how the members of this organisation made creative use of ideas of national identity which they 'tailored' and 'mobilized' in 'social struggles of resistance that were triggered by globalization'. The notion of national identity that they developed in this context was used to signal 'a strong sense of similarity' among organisational members and it served as 'a marker of distinction that was used to differentiate them from their merger partners'.

LOOKING FORWARD >>>>>

The concept of identity is a major concern of Chapter 10 where it will be recognised, as in this Israeli study, that identities are not simple 'givens' in people's lives. A concept of *identity work* will feature in Chapter 10, and we could, in the present context, characterise what these researchers observed as a case of collective identity work.

As researchers have begun to examine more closely the impact of globalisation processes on workers and organisations in different countries, it becomes clear that there is little commonality of employee response. Emerging evidence suggests that the impact of globalisation on workplaces and workers is highly diverse (Debrah and Smith 2002). Whilst recognising such diversity, however, Amoore (2002) identifies a clear logic underlying globalising processes as they affect workplaces and workers. Globalisation, she says, is best understood as a 'contested, contingent and politicised process that is expressed, first and foremost, through everyday social practice'. And at the centre of these practices are attempts to increase labour flexibility. Labour regimes vary from country to country, and globalisation is an 'interested discourse that is used in different ways by actors contesting and negotiating the reform of labour relations'. It is used in Britain, for example, to advance the particular version of hyper-flexible Anglo-Saxon capitalism. And it is used in Germany to support the restructuring of various state and non-state institutions, as well as to accelerate workplace reform.

The restructuring of work, neoliberalism and financialisation

Especially since the abandoning of socialism in Central and Eastern European states following the removal of the Berlin Wall there has emerged an 'ultra-competitive world' (White *et al.* 2004). International competitiveness and trade threats have forced employing organisations and states to seek ways of not only increasing the cost-effectiveness of labour *per se*, but of increasing the overall capacity of the organisations within which that labour is used to innovate at a rate which will enable them to produce goods and services that are competitive in the international context. Work and work experience are widely seen as caught up in processes of restructuring.

The restructuring of work
The changing patterns of work experience, organisational and occupational activity both resulting from and contributing to economic, political and cultural changes unfolding across the world.

Restructuring within the older economies has involved a move away from traditional heavy industry activities such as steel-making, textiles, mining and heavy industry towards, on the one hand, service industries and, on the other, the production of both consumer goods and capital products using advanced electronic technologies. Employment has shifted with this and white-collar employment has grown as manual work has decreased. Central to the growth of service work has been the expansion of financial services work and major changes in patterns of retailing, these two trends being made visible by the dominance of banks and building societies in British high streets and the way the superstores, away from city centres, have 'done much to rearrange the shopping and leisure habits of large proportions of the population' (Beynon *et al.* 2002). Increasing numbers of jobs are part-time or short-term, and governments, whether nominally of the political left or right, tend towards tight control of public spending and the freeing of labour markets from tight controls. Industries previously controlled by the state have been privatised, deregulated or 'put into the market', especially in Central and Eastern Europe and in Britain.

At the heart of the move towards an ultra-competitive world has been a shift towards a *neoliberal* political and economic ideology.

Neoliberalism

A set of principles for shaping economic institutions, business practices and states across the world based upon a belief in the centrality to human life of individual human choices in a context of competitive markets.

An examination of the intellectual development of neoliberal thinking, with its emphasis on the relatively autonomous human individual and on the alleged effectiveness of free markets, shows how, as Gane (2014) puts it, neoliberalism, 'emerged out of a critical engagement with classical sociology', and, in particular, Max Weber's methodological writing ('methodological' here in the sense explained in Chapter 1). More broadly, the *individualistic* intellectual assumptions of liberalism clash with those at the heart of the whole sociological project; the notion that human beings are essentially *social* animals whose abilities to make choices and decisions arise from the set of social institutions, structures and cultures which are humanly created. This sociological stance, which is in clear contradistinction to a neoliberal one, has not been adopted simply because sociologists (and writers outside the discipline but working with a sociological orientation) emotionally prefer it. It has emerged because their scientific and critical engagement with 'how societies work' – through both theorising and empirical investigation – leads them to such a position. This point can be illustrated by considering the issue of the role of the state in political-economic matters.

Neoliberal policies 'liberalise' or loosen the regulation of market activities. Although neoliberalism ideologically presses the case for private enterprise over state 'intervention', it is observed by Mirowski (2013) that neoliberalism, as it operates in practice, incorporates a strong role for the state in shaping a political economy in which markets are also powerful. To argue in this way is an outcome of careful scholarly examination of how the social, political and economic world 'works', as opposed to ideas espoused by neoliberal ideologists. In a similar and systematically research-based manner, Mazzucato (2013) has produced a study which 'debunks' what she calls 'public versus private sector myths', a central plank in the neoliberal platform. Extensive case study research shows that states play a major role in technological and economic innovations (from biotechnology and the internet to touch screen devices and GPS) often setting the stage for private sector investors who would have baulked at the risks involved in the early stages of these innovations.

It might be too simplistic to paint a picture of sociologists and the like acting in a purely objective neutral manner whilst neoliberals proselytise and act in ways especially favourable to the holders of significant wealth. Yet it is clear that neoliberal thinking and practice focus strongly on the interests of shareholders. Enormous pressures are put upon businesses to concentrate on building *shareholder value*. Business institutions are regarded primarily as the creatures of their share-holding owners rather than as social institutions with multiple purposes and social as well as financial obligations.

A process which can be understood as the motor within the neoliberal machine (Gamble 2009; Willmott 2011) is that of financialisation in which profit-making increasingly comes from the trading of financial assets rather than the producing of goods and services in the traditional or 'real' economy' (Dore 2008).

Financialisation

A process whereby financial institutions come to dominate economic activity with increasing emphasis on the trading of financial assets (shares, bonds, options, mortgages and other debts) as opposed to the exchange of goods and services produced in the traditional economy.

Whereas previously financial institutions, financial instruments (and the 'derivatives' of those instruments) could have been regarded as *means* towards the effective performance of goods-and-services-producing economies, they have instead tended to become *ends* in themselves. A simple transaction such as one person lending some money to another to help the latter, say, pay for a holiday can, with financialisation, become 'securitised'; the debt is turned into a 'security' which the lender may sell to someone else. That debt is now a *tradable* financial asset from which the new owner may later profit when they eventually collect the debt and its interest from the original borrower. But as Taleb (2007) explains, financialisation can misrepresent reality. House mortgages which do not 'accurately represent the risk to the lendor or the promise of future income from the borrower' can be issued, for example.

The financialisation phenomenon was most notoriously seen in the case with the 'sub-prime' mortgage crisis in the USA, a crisis that was at the centre of the world financial crash. This had massive repercussions in the form of a 'credit crunch' across the world which, from 2007 on, has been followed by massive global instability, as individuals, families, business and whole economies find themselves with enormous burdens of debt (Streek 2015). A falling proportion of credit had gone to productive business investment which would have enabled sustainable economic growth with the remainder going to financial activities, property and consumer credit, creating asset price 'bubbles' (CRESC 2009). The social consequences of all this include 'exacerbating inequalities, greater insecurity, misdirection of talent, and the erosion of trust' (Dore 2008). And when it comes to matters of work organisation and experience, financialisation has, Thompson (2013) argues, exacerbated trends towards achieving 'shareholder value goals' through such means as 'taking labour out and squeezing extra performance from those who remain'.

LOOKING FORWARD >>>>>

Neoliberal and financialisation practices have profound implications for social inequalities across the world and these will be examined in Chapter 4, pp. 111–114.

Technology and change

Sociological analysis recognises the importance of human interests in introducing changes in the division of labour and instigating technological change. It also recognises that new technologies are not just new machines. In spite of this, technology is frequently spoken of in terms of the physical devices or 'hardware' that people use when carrying out tasks. Sociologically, it is seen as involving much more than this.

Technology
The tools, machines and control devices used to carry out tasks and the principles, techniques and reasoning which accompanies them.

The view of technology as having causal power is often encouraged in the educational process. Many of us in our early history lessons at school are encouraged, for instance, to see the scientific inventions which were made in the period of the Industrial Revolution as key causal factors in the occurrence of that revolution. Technical changes in both of these cases might indeed constitute *necessary conditions* for the social changes with which they are associated, but it is mistaken to regard them as *sufficient conditions* for change. It was pointed out by Hobsbawm (1969) that the early Industrial Revolution was technically rather primitive. He suggested that what was novel was not technical innovation but 'the readiness of practical men to put their minds to using the science and technology which had long been available and within reach'. The motor of change was not the machinery itself or new scientific knowledge but, at the global level the forces of trade expansion and colonial expansion and, at the more 'micro' level, the motivation of these practical individuals. The novelty was 'not in the flowering of individual inventive genius', says Hobsbawm, 'but in the practical situation which turned men's thoughts to soluble problems'. Hill (1988) goes as far as to claim that science did not play a role as a leading edge in industrial progress until after the Second World War when existing markets for capitalist expansion were saturated. The early inventors were, in fact, 'more motivated by curiosity than "practical intent"'. Sociologically, however, we tend to avoid issues of individual 'motivation', seeing it more helpful to look at the 'social shaping of technology' (McKenzie and Wacjman 1985) and to recognise that in the emergence of any given technology a whole range of social factors, individual and group interests come into play and interact with each other. Boreham *et al.* (2008) take the view that dangers still exist of technological determinism, especially where non-evidence-based claims are made about a further industrial revolution or a 'new economy' (a matter to which we shall return shortly).

Technology may be a means towards certain ends, then, but the meeting of ends implies the fulfilling of human material interests. And all human material interests do not coincide. One man's airfield takes another man's land and one woman's capital requires another woman's labour. Thus the importance of technology in human life can only be appreciated once it is set in the context of social, economic and political relationships.

The future of work, digital technologies and the notion of a fourth industrial revolution

Work institutions, organisations and processes, as well as technologies, are created by human beings, both in co-operative and in competitive relationships with each other. They are not the outcomes of immutable historical forces. Recognition of this should make us cautious about associating the sociology of work with the popular activity of making *predictions* about the 'future of work'. Prediction is often seen as a key aim of scientific research and theorising. But, until recently, many of the predictions about the future of work have been speculative, sometimes highly pessimistic and sometimes highly optimistic. Handy, beginning with his influential *The Future of Work* (1994), put forward the notion of a revolutionary level of change in the so–called emerging 'knowledge economy'. This envisaged bureaucratically hierarchical work organisations being replaced by networks and partnerships in which people would undertake a variety or 'portfolio' of jobs instead of having a traditional career in a single employing organisation.

LOOKING FORWARD >>>>>

The alleged 'end of bureaucracy' is critically examined in Chapter 5, pp. 149–151, and the idea of portfolio jobs discussed in Chapter 9.

This flavour runs through a great deal of the writing on work's future. In optimistic versions of this kind of futurology we see visions of a world of rewardingly co-operative, creative and socially useful work. On the pessimistic front, Beck (2000), on the European side of the Atlantic, wrote about a world of growing insecurity and risk, this being matched by the pessimism, on the American side of the ocean, of Bridges (1995) and Rifkin (1995), with the latter entitling his book *The End of Work*. However, all of these 'grand narratives', as Nolan and Wood (2003) call them, are produced with an 'almost complete absence of any grounded theory or systematic data' (*cf* Wilson 2004) – not that this necessarily rules out the possibilities of changes coming about along the lines identified by the speculative writers.

In any attempt to use sociology to reflect on the future of work, it is important to remember that we can only ever research what 'is', as opposed to what 'might or will be'. Inferences about the future from whatever 'evidence' we gather about the present must be made with great care. Whilst it is necessary, however, to avoid the exaggerations of much of the futurology and guru writing, this should not rule out the application of a degree of imagination in our writing on the sociology of work and industry. Williams (2007) points out that recognising that the future is not 'cast in stone' frees us to 'imagine all manner of alternative futures of work' and that this, in turn, can help to stimulate 'greater discussion of how to open up the future more for those who currently have little choice'. And Parker *et al.* (2014) make it clear that such imaginative thinking must necessarily involve raising complex questions about current industrial capitalist assumptions and practices. Kostera (2014) not only echoes the view that imaginative thinking about the future is inevitably political; she also invites her readers to work with others to change the world using 'insight, imagination and practical action'.

Bearing in mind both the warnings about the over-speculative nature of writing about the future of work as well as the value of thinking imaginatively about what might happen, we turn to look at significant developments in computer/digital technologies and the increasingly popular notion that a fourth industrial revolution is upon us.

Current and imminent changes in the application of computer-based technologies or ICTs ('information and communication technologies') are discussed under a variety of headings ranging from 'AI' (artificial intelligence) to 'advanced automation' to 'robotics'. Thoughts about robots may be the most susceptible to the type of imaginative thinking referred to earlier but, as important as devices with humanoid features and capabilities might be in the home and some workplaces, we must recognise that many of the outcomes of the most significant shifts from human-based work activities to computer-based task performance will not even be visible, let alone involving swirling arms, legs and heads.

> ## Automation
>
> The application of machinery which is controlled and co-ordinated by computerised programmes to tasks previously done by direct human effort.

Whereas in earlier stage of computerisation, it was predominantly routine tasks that were automated, the power and sophisticated nature of both hardware and software increasingly means that non-routine tasks, problem-solving and decision-making are coming within the scope of digital technology (Autor 2015). In an unusually scholarly and rigorous research study, Frey and Osborne (2013) emphasise the significance of emerging large and complex data sets ('big data') and advanced algorithms that can manipulate this material. Thus, diagnostic tasks are already being computerised in the health care sector and the same is coming about in legal and financial services. Already, law firms are using computers that can scan thousands of legal briefs and precedents to assist in pre-trial research. And when we turn to the robots proper, improvements in their sensors enables them to produce goods more reliably and at higher levels of quality than human beings can achieve. Machines that handle goods in docks, depots and warehouses and machines that work farmers' fields are 'imminently automatable' with hospitals already employing autonomous robots to transport food, prescriptions and samples. Frey and Osborne (2013) argue that it is 'largely already technologically possible to automate almost any task, provided that sufficient amounts of data are gathered for pattern recognition', and they apply their own methodology to estimate the probability of computerisation of 702 US occupations, concluding that 47 per cent of total US employment is potentially automatable over twenty years or so.

This research has been drawn on and built upon by reports and speeches from various leading consulting firms and banks – including Bank of America Merrill Lynch, the Bank of England, Price Waterhouse Cooper and Deloitte, with the latter, in collaboration with Frey and Osborne, estimating that '35% of jobs in the UK are at high risk of automation in the next ten to twenty years' (Deloitte LLP *et al.* 2014; Deloitte 2015). The Bank of England's chief economist reported in a speech (Haldane 2015) that the Bank had applied Frey and Osborne's research methods to the UK, concluding that 15 million British jobs (compared to 80 million in the USA) are at risk of automation. The jobs most at risk were judged to be in administrative, clerical and production domains.

Three past transitions in economic growth (or 'industrial revolutions') are often identified by economists and economic historians: the first industrial revolution seeing the arrival of steam engines, water and mechanical production equipment; the second revolution bringing electricity, mass production and a more complex division of labour in the second half of the 19th century and the third revolution in the second half of the twentieth century being the era of electronics, information technology and automated production. In each of these, jobs were lost and new ones created. But the future may be different, as smart machines, unlike in the past, 'have the potential to substitute for human brains as well as hands' (Haldane 2015). And the effect of this could be as radical as bringing about the demise of those occupations claiming the status of 'professions'.

LOOKING FORWARD >>>>>

'Professions' are a key topic in Chapter 8, pp. 262–269.

This status derives from what Susskind and Susskind (2015) call a 'grand bargain' whereby 'society' awards a mandate in light of the profession's expertise and specialist knowledge. But, these authors claim, future technologies may destroy this monopoly of knowledge, thus undermining the standing – and associated benefits – of occupations including lawyers, doctors, teachers, accountants, architects, tax advisers and clergy.

Turning to manufacturing, in Germany the term 'industrie 4.0' is increasingly used, by industrial experts and politicians alike, to cover what are seen as highly significant fourth industrial revolution changes. The various elements of the manufacturing and value chain process are connected to each other. Machines, systems and factories are interlinked so that they can automatically control each other, thus helping to achieve the highest possible levels of efficiency, quality and cost-saving. Efficiencies and cost-savings – and the production of new products such as 3-D printing machines, driverless cars and domestic/service robots – extend these allegedly revolutionary changes beyond manufacturing itself.

Sociologically, one has to be wary of using the term 'revolution' too glibly. The risk of hyperbole is considerable. Exaggerating either the promise or the threats of a new digital world can draw attention away from careful analytical research like that of Frey and Osborne, discussed earlier. This does not mean, however, that we should not pay attention to the arguments being put forward about the implications of changing technologies. And especially interesting here are well-publicised statements being made about these potential changes from bankers, business leaders and business consultants. Whereas we might expect warnings about the dangers of growing inequalities to come from politically 'left' commentators, it is significant to see warnings coming from those who we might reasonably see as associated with the wealthier and more powerful elements of society.

A good example of this phenomenon is a paper presented to the World Economic Forum in 2016 at Davos by the Swiss bank UBS (UBS 2015). This envisages polarisation of the workforce, with inequalities between developed and undeveloped countries, between the rich and the poor and between the young and the old being exacerbated by 'extreme automation and connectivity'. The Bank of America Merrill Lynch (2015) considers a range of possible effects of what it calls the 'creative disruption' threatened by emerging technologies, and among these is disruption of the labour market with the possibility of large scale 'technological unemployment' and general 'winner takes all' outcomes. None of this is inevitable and one positive possibility is that there might emerge a large enough sector of the economy where humans have a comparative advantage – perhaps in arts and entertainment, personal care or areas that involve 'deeper analytical thinking' of a type that artificial intelligence cannot replace. But just what efforts can be made to bring about benign rather than disastrous outcomes of what he calls the 'fourth industrial revolution' are difficult to see, argues Schwab, the founder and head of the World Economic Forum. Like a number of economists and social analysts looking at trends in the broader political economy (Atkinson 2015; Hutton 2015; Piketty 2014; Stigliz 2010; Wilkinson and Pickett 2009), Schwab points to the dangers of inequalities growing and societies fragmenting and expresses worries that shaping the fourth industrial revolution so that it is empowering and human-centred rather than divisive and dehumanising is 'not a task for any single stakeholder, or sector or for any one region, industry or culture' (2016). In spite of this, Schwab argues that the profound uncertainty being faced across the world gives a responsibility to governments, business, academia and civil society 'to work together to better understand the emerging trends' (2015). This, however, is not a level of co-operation and effort about which we currently have any evidence.

LOOKING BACK <<<<<

Chapter 1 considered the view that sociology itself originated, in part, as a reaction to the disruptions and instabilities being caused by the first industrial revolution. One might reflect on why it is that the identification of the instabilities and disruptions threatened by a potential 'fourth industrial revolution' has largely been done by organisations and individuals associated with the wealthier sections of contemporary societies.

Summary

Events and characteristics of modern work institutions can only be understood if they are connected to an appreciation of the distinctive characteristics of the industrial capitalist way of organising social life and how this itself is an outcome of historical processes going back several centuries. Such processes include the rationalisation of social life and the use of science and complex technologies to produce a new type of social order and division of labour. A variety of further recent transitions have been written about, these being various and characterised in such terms as post-industrialism, informationalism, post-Fordism, postmodernism and McDonaldisation. 'Globalisation' is a much discussed process, but the extent to which it is a useful way of characterising current world trends is open to debate and one possibility that must be contemplated is that its role has been more an ideological or legitimising one than an analytical one. However helpful it is to consider these various trends and processes, it is nevertheless vital to recognise the way in which the restructuring of work in the modern world is occurring in the context of two phenomena. The first is the political economic phenomena of neoliberalism and financialisation. The second is that of major potential changes in the application of computer-based or digital technologies. Discussion of advanced automation, robotisation and networking is increasingly being set in the context of an alleged trend towards a fourth industrial revolution. Although there is a valuable but limited amount of scholarly investigation of advanced technological trends, a great deal of the reflection of possibilities has been put forward by bankers, business consultants and leading figures in the World Economic Forum rather than by sociologists. The possibility of considerably greater social and employment inequalities emerging across the world with advanced automation of work plays a key part in worries expressed by these members of the currently most privileged sections of modern societies.

5 Work organisations

Key issues

- How can we most usefully conceptualise work organisations?
- What are the main 'design' principles underlying the organisational way of structuring work activities?
- How central is 'bureaucracy' to the idea of the work organisation, and to what extent is it possible to envisage work organisations or 'alternative organisations' that, to any significant extent, go 'beyond bureaucracy'?
- To what extent do work organisations' structures and cultures vary according to the circumstances within which they operate, and what is the relationship between the pressures created by the particular circumstances of different organisations and the choices that are exercised by the managers who are placed 'in charge' of those organisations?
- How significant are the politicking and career advancement activities of organisational actors to what occurs, officially and unofficially, in organisations, especially in the light of the ambiguities, uncertainties and unintended outcomes that affect all decision-making processes?

The organisational principle of work structuring

Work organisations are crucial to the way modern industrialised societies are structured. Central to the history of modern societies was a trend whereby work tasks were increasingly carried out within bureaucratised corporations and formally structured enterprises that employed people to work under the instructions of organisational managers. And the work tasks performed by organisations are not just those of industrial production but ones involved in the administration of government and the birth, education, leisure and welfare of people throughout their lives. A high proportion of people in modern societies earn their living through their employment by a formal work organisation, and after work, they go to shops owned and run by similar organisations, they enjoy entertainment provided by organisations and they seek help from them when they find themselves in difficulty. Thus, much of the 'structuring' or patterning of modern lives, both within work and outside it, involves what we might call the organisational principle of work structuring, at the centre of which is the performance of work tasks with some people conceiving of and designing work and then recruiting, paying, co-ordinating and controlling the efforts of other people to complete work tasks. 'Recruitment' may involve, at one end of a continuum, establishing long-term, close, secure and reciprocal relationships between the organisation and 'employees' and, at the other end of the continuum, engaging in short-term, arms-length and insecure labour relationships.

> ### The organisational principle of work structuring
>
> Work is patterned as the outcome of institutional arrangements in which some people conceive of and design work tasks and then recruit, pay, co-ordinate and control the efforts of other people to complete those work tasks.

As was observed in Chapter 4, the dominance of this aspect of modern societies is closely associated with the historical shift from a *social division of labour* in societies (where tasks are shared out *across* a range of occupations) to a *technical division of labour*. The technical division of labour involves task specialisation *within* what we still tend to call occupations but where, in practice, 'who does what and how' is decided by organisational managers, engineers, supervisors and other technical experts rather than by the guardians of occupational, guild or trade traditions.

The trend over recent centuries has been for the organisational principle of work structuring to push aside the *occupational principle* of work structuring, one which emphasises the way in which people with similar skills, traditions and values co-operatively conceive, execute and regulate work tasks. The occupational principle has not disappeared from the way work is structured in modern societies, as we will see in Chapter 6. At present, it most visibly survives in trade-based trade unions, in 'professional' groups and in public perceptions of distinctive types of job.

However, as we shall note in that chapter, this may change in the light of changes brought about by the widespread use of the computer-based technologies discussed in Chapter 4.

To study work organisations sociologically, we have to meet the very basic requirement of sociological thinking identified in Chapter 1 of fully recognising the interplay which occurs between the patterns, regularities or structuring of social life and the varied interests, initiatives and values of the individuals who create and operate within this structuring. To understand work organisations sociologically, therefore, we need to see them as patterns of regular behaviour which include a whole range of informal, unofficial and even illegitimate actions and arrangements. This is why the characterisation of the organisational principles of work structuring discussed at the start of this chapter recognised that the work structures we see in modern societies are the result of both intended and unintended efforts by organisational managers. It is highly inappropriate and partial (in both senses of the word – inadequate and biased) to see organisation structures as just the formal arrangements which are portrayed in the management's organisation chart, rule book and official operating procedures. This all too often happens in standard organisation and management writing and teaching, and it is as unhelpful as a way of conceptualising organisations to those who are interested in managing organisations as it is to those who simply wish to study how they work. Some careful attention to how we conceptualise organisations is therefore vital.

The nature of work organisations

The notion of 'organisation', used in a general sense, is fundamental to sociological analysis, as was stressed in Chapter 1. A basic insight of sociology is that the whole of life is socially organised in various ways: it displays certain patterns and exhibits regularities. Hence, the study of work organisations (or 'formal organisations') is to examine just one aspect of the wider *social organisation* of society. We are focusing on patterns of activity which have been deliberately set up at some historically distinguishable point in time to carry out certain tasks and which, to do this, make use of various administrative or bureaucratic techniques. Organisations thus include such things as manufacturing and service-providing enterprises, banks, hospitals, and prisons but exclude families, tribes, social classes and spontaneous friendship groups.

Organisations have become increasingly diverse, and the interests and concerns of their members are often less than clear; what ultimately distinguishes them from other aspects of social organisation is some initially inspiring purposiveness. Important here is the existence, at least in the organisation's early history, of some kind of relatively explicit charter or programme of action. Organisations are elements of human social structure that are much more deliberately or consciously designed than other forms of human association. And the pervasiveness of organisations in modern history is to be understood as part of the wider trend of increasing rationalisation discussed in Chapter 4, which underlies the development of industrial capitalism – the process identified by Max Weber whereby deliberately calculated means are adopted in the pursuit of consciously selected ends. Organisations are thus, in a sense, expressions of some of the basic cultural characteristics of modern societies.

Organisations can be understood as purposive and characteristically rational constructs. But purposiveness and 'rationality' is massively compromised by two things:

- the tendency within social life towards conflict between different interests, and
- the tendency towards insitutional tensions and unintended consequences.

The fact that organisations are more purposively conceived than other social forms has led to a degree of emphasis on their 'rationality' which has seriously exaggerated the extent to which, in practice, they operate as machines or systems efficiently pursuing specific purposes. Such an exaggeration has permeated business and management thinking but has also been present in much organisational sociology. This is revealed by the tendency of many writers on organisations to define organisations in terms of 'organisational goals'.

The danger with focusing on goals in this way when defining organisations is that attention is drawn away from the sociological fact that organisations, in practice and despite any clarity of purpose of those in charge of them, involve a wide range of people who have different goals or purposes. As well as the co-operation which must occur for an organisation to survive there will be considerable differences and conflicts of interest. What common purpose there is in the typical modern work organisation is as likely to be the outcome of the power behaviour of those in charge and of compromises reached between differing interest groups as it is of any consensual recognition of 'neutral' or collective organisational goals.

A conceptualisation of organisations is required which recognises the existence of a multiplicity of interests and of a power structure in the typical organisation whilst nevertheless accepting that organisations are purposive or task-based arrangements.

Work organisations

Social and technical arrangements in which a number of people come together in a formalised and contractual relationship where the actions of some are directed by others towards the achievement of work tasks carried out in the organisation's name.

Productive co-operation, processes and practices

The conceptualisation of organisations presented earlier in this chapter encourages a view of the organisation less as a pre-given structure into which people are 'slotted' and more as an ongoing and ever-changing coalition of people with quite different and often conflicting interests and purposes who are willing, within rather closely defined limits, to carry out tasks which help to meet the requirements of those in charge. And those people in charge are paid to achieve a level of *productive co-operation* in the carrying out of tasks which will enable the organisation to continue in existence under its formal identity and legal corporate status or 'name' as a furniture maker, a software company, a hospital or a university.

LOOKING FORWARD >>>>>

The matter of the organisations' 'name' will be returned to when we consider the idea of organisational identities later in this chapter (pp. 200–202).

Since the late 1960s, the sociology of organisations has increasingly moved away from a previously dominant conception of organisations as goal-based systems (Silverman 1970, 1994). Sociologically, organisations are more realistically seen as patterns of activity in which the effective production of goods and services is something that the 'organisers' have to strive for in the face of the multiplicity of interests and purposes that organisational actors bring to the enterprise. This is recognised by one of the managers at Barkermills in Snapshot 5.1.

Productive co-operation

The achievement, in the light of the tendency of people involved in organisations to have their own projects, interests and priorities, of a degree of working together that ensures that tasks carried out in the organisation's name are fulfilled to sufficient a level to enable the organisation to continue in existence.

Snapshot 5.1

Herding cats at Barkermills?

I remember when I was first in a management grade and the company sent me on this training course which was called something like 'managing people'. I came back from this full of enthusiasm and bounced into my boss's office to tell him all about how I thought we could get all our staff much more committed and much more willing to follow our leadership. I went on about motivation, commitment, leadership, strong culture and all this stuff. Frank then leaned back in his big chair, put his hands behind his head and sighed. 'Facts of life time', he said. 'You must have heard people say how trying to manage their pharmacists is like trying to herd cats or how managing their technicians is like herding cats or managing their junior managers is like herding cats'. I said that I had heard this all over the place. 'You've heard it time and again', he said, 'because there is a basic truth there. It's nothing to do with pharmacists or techies or whatever, though. It's to do with people. You cannot manage people'.

'So I've been wasting my time on the course, have I?', I asked. 'Well', responded Frank, 'Not entirely. Some of those ideas are helpful. But if you think that you are going to be seen as a "leader" here and that people will follow you wherever you try to take them, then you'd better start to think again. Nobody will "follow your leadership" or let you herd them. But they know they have signed up to work for Barkermills and that we will only stay in business if we get done the jobs allocated to our department. We've got to get these pills and potions packed and out on time. So they will co-operate with each other and with us as long as they feel that we are honouring the basic deal whereby they do a limited range of tasks, within certain clearly limited times, on clearly stated terms. And you need to remember, all the time, that these people have lives and purposes of their own – purposes that they don't all readily share. So you can use some of the skills that you've covered on your course to steer things along – basically getting them to be co-operative enough to get out on time and in good order the products that people expect from Barkermills. We know, and they know, that if we fall short on this, our days are numbered in the marketplace'.

Organisations, then, are not best understood as pre-given structures into which people are slotted but as the outcome of the interactive patterns of human activity. Organisations are often experienced *as if* they are 'things' which exist outside and prior to human activity, but what is really being experienced are institutional processes. And human actors as makers of meanings are always implicated in those processes rather than existing merely as a passive object upon which the process works. Such a view was inherent in the notion of the organisation as a negotiated order: a pattern of activities which emerges over time from the interplay of the variety of interests, understandings, initiatives and reactions of individuals and groups within organisations. And it accords with some of the insights that the ethnomethodological tradition brings to the study of organisations.

LOOKING BACK <<<<<

The concept of 'negotiated order' and the nature of the ethnomethodological approach of organisations are explained in Chapter 2. The story told in Snapshot 2.4 of the delivery van in the factory yard illustrates the insights common to both of these ideas.

In all this, there is an emphasis on human and social *processes* rather than on systems or 'things'. It is important to recognise, however, that when organisation theorists talk of processes they are not referring to such things as recruitment processes, manufacturing processes or sales processes – sets of procedures with which the everyday organisational practitioner is concerned.

LOOKING BACK <<<<<

The following discussion builds upon the introduction in Chapter 1 to 'methodology' (pp. 22–27).

Process-oriented theorists and researchers, instead, adopt a particular ontological position (see Chapter 1, p. 22) or 'take' on reality. In Chia's (2003) terms, they adopt an ontology of *becoming* as opposed to an ontology of *being*. Organisations are not 'things' and flux, change, instability and impermanence is normal, and in Weick's (1979) terms, it is more helpful to talk about *organising* rather than *organisations*. It would be reasonable to expect that this way of thinking would be relevant to any study in the sociology of organisations. It is, however, a quirk of organisation theorists to take a potentially universally relevant notion like 'process' and turn it into some kind of specialist activity or a special 'perspective' ('lens' or 'turn'). Thus we see collections of work on 'process organisation studies' (Hernes and Maitlis 2010). Alongside these we see collections of 'practice-based studies' – all depending on one or other kind of 'practice theory' (Nicolini 2013) – the key emphasis here being not just upon the things that people 'do' in organisations but on the roles of knowledge and knowledge reproduction within organisational practices.

Yet another 'perspective' or theoretical orientation which, alongside 'process' and 'practice' perspectives, is increasingly recommended as a way forward for the study of organisations is that of relational sociology (Donati 2011; Mische 2011; Prandini 2015). This can be regarded as containing nothing essentially new to sociologists in the Weberian and symbolic interaction traditions and to those influenced by Pragmatist philosophical and 'pragmatic realist' thinking (Chapter 1, pp. 24–26), whereby one treats reality, not in terms of properties and underlying mechanisms, but as the circumstances with which people have to come to terms in order to cope in the world. The essential principles of relational thinking underpin the characterisation of sociology offered in Chapter 1. It is a simple matter to modify that conception to define the sociology *of organisations* as the study of the relationships which develop between human beings as they organise themselves and are organised by others in work organisations, and how these patterns influence and are influenced by the actions and interactions of people and how they make sense of their lives and identities. The renewed emphasis on relationality in organisation theory is valuable because it recognises that a lot of thinking about organisations (from rational-actor theories to statistical variable analysis) depend on analysing substances (organisations as entities) rather than processes, and in static things (like 'organisations') rather than dynamic, unfolding sets of relations (Emirbayer 1997, in his 'manifesto' for a relational sociology). Table 5.1 pulls together the various elements of both process, practice and relational thinking as it can be applied to organisations, contrasting this to what might be characterised as 'orthodox', 'rational-system' or 'managerialist' views of organisations.

LOOKING FORWARD >>>>>

These matters of methodological and theoretical perspectives, and the notion of 'managerialism' in particular, will be taken up again in the discussion of the management occupation in Chapter 8, pp. 241–245.

Table 5.1 An emergent-relational view of organisations contrasted with a rational-system view

A rational-system view of organisations	An emergent-relational view of organisations
Organisations are *entities*, systems of managerially designed rules and roles existing in their own terms.	Organisations are *relational* phenomena, sets of relationships and associated understandings.
Organisations are outcomes of a managerial *organisation design* and possess a set of structural and cultural characteristics.	Organisations are *emergent patterns* resulting from processes of exchange, negotiation, conflict and compromise as well as an element of managerial design.
Organisations operate to ensure the completion of the *organisational goals* they were designed to fulfil.	Organisations are *strategically oriented* in the sense that those in charge of them strive to ensure that they survive into the long term.
Organisations are rational *systems of rules and procedures* which ensure the completion of tasks that ensure corporate goal fulfilment.	Organisations operate with *both reason and emotion*, the feelings of managers, workers and customers are as relevant to their behaviours as is their rational pursuit of material interests within formal corporate procedures.
Organisations are expressions of universally applicable organisational and managerial principles.	Organisations all follow modernist bureaucratic principles, but their functioning also reflects the economic, cultural and political circumstances of their societal location.

An emergent-relational view of organisations avoids a fallacy that philosophers have warned against for a long time: that of *reification* (where a non-concrete entity is treated as a thing) or *personification* (where a non-human entity is treated as a person). At first sight, this might seem like an unlikely error for scholars to make. But, if one reads certain economists or listens to certain business analysts, it soon begins to look normal to hear of 'firms' or businesses or organisations 'choosing to develop new products' or 'moving into new markets'. There is little problem here if these statements are merely 'short-hand' allusions to something much more complex and if the speaker or writer is well aware that closer analysis of these events needs deeper probing to ascertain just which individuals or groups – in conflict or competition with other individuals and groups inside and outside the organisation – are 'behind' these events.

> ### Reification/personification
>
> An error in which an abstraction is treated as a 'thing' or a living person. The error is committed, for example, when one talks of 'society' or an 'organisation' *doing* something – or *making* people act in certain ways.

Official and unofficial aspects of organisations

A pair of concepts that has been used throughout the history of industrial and organisational sociology has been that of *formal* and *informal* organisation. It emerged in the 1930s as a way in which both social scientists and some management writers engaged with what we might call the 'two-sidedness of organisational life'. One side of every work organisation is the set of bureaucratic roles, rules and procedures that we see represented in rule books, organisation charts and formalised sets of operating procedures. This is the aspect of organisations that encourages us to conceive of them as entities that remain in existence even when the individuals who take particular organisational roles are completely replaced by another set of individuals. However, this first side of the work organisation can only come into being when human individuals enter the set of roles indicated on the organisation chart. When they enter the organisational scene, they bring with them their own interests, purposes and understandings. And they are likely soon to want to shape certain aspects of their working lives for themselves, regardless of what the managerial blueprint dictates. Thus a second side of organisational life comes into being as people form relationships and coalitions of interests with others, play games, develop 'shortcuts', create 'pecking orders' and generally seek ways of expressing and defending their humanity and pursuing personal priorities. This second side of organisational life was given the label of *informal organisation* by writers and researchers associated with Human Relations thinking (discussed in Chapter 2).

The bank wiring observation room experiment at the Hawthorne plant is one of the best-known illustrations of how informal organisation develops (the setting of informal output norms by the work-group's members) in opposition to the formal organisation (the incentive system designed to encourage workers each to produce the level of output fitting their personally desired level of financial reward). Roethlisberger and Dickson (1939), in reporting this research, emphasised that informal organisation does not necessarily undermine the formal in this way – it sometimes operates to support the formal system. This point is emphasised in Barnard's (1938) analysis of executive activities and the extent to which the 'informal society' that develops among managers is vital to the effectiveness of the executive process. Similar arguments emerged from later research on managerial processes with Mangham and Pye (1991) reporting that senior managers often stressed to them that 'informal organising' was as important, or more important, to their work than the 'articulation of a formal organisation'.

Aspects of this second or 'informal' side of organisation will be considered later in this chapter when we look at organisational micropolitics and will be important again when we look at a range of 'oppositional' activities in the final chapter of the book. At this point, however, it is necessary to recognise that industrial and organisational sociologists have tended in recent times to turn away from the use of the formal/informal distinction to deal with the phenomenon (Watson 2015). In large part, this has been because of the association of the pair of concepts with human relations thinking and with the systems thinking that, to a certain extent, developed out of it. The distinction became associated with analyses that were seen as too 'unitary' – as insufficiently locating workplace activities within wider patterns of conflict and inequality beyond the formal and informal arrangements of the workplace. A further, and perhaps more significant, reason for moving away from the formal/informal distinction is in recognition of a trend for organisational managers (in line with the recommendations of Barnard [1938]) to integrate what was once separable into the 'formal' and the 'informal' into a single 'strong culture' organisation in which, for example, 'empowered' workgroups or 'teams' are encouraged to develop their own 'informal' norms and practice – as long as, of course, these support and further formally stated corporate values and objectives.

LOOKING BACK AND FORWARD <<<<< >>>>>

Organisational cultures were discussed in Chapter 2 (p. 44) and will be examined again in Chapter 6 (p. 97).

The rejection of the formal/informal dichotomy does not mean that we have to abandon any distinction between the 'two sides' of organisational life identified earlier. But to overcome the ideological associations of the formal/informal dichotomy, we can adopt, instead, a slightly different distinction: that between *official* and *unofficial* aspects of organisations. This concept pair encourages us to distinguish between – and examine the interplay between – the managerial aspirations expressed in official management statements, policies and claims and the observable patterns of belief and behaviour that prevail across the organisation in practice.

The official and unofficial aspects of organisation structures are best seen as only conceptually or analytically distinct aspects of what is really one overall organisational structure. The two are dialectically related. They are influenced by each other with activities in one often encouraging activities in the other.

> ## Official and unofficial aspects of organisations
>
> *Official* aspects of organisations are the rules, values and activities that are part of the formally managerial-sanctioned policies and procedures. *Unofficial* aspects are the rules, values and activities that people at all levels in the organisation develop but which do not have formal managerial sanction.

Snapshot 5.2

Mutual influences of official and unofficial practices at Barkermills

The managers of the Barkermills packing department, part of the organisation which we visited in Snapshot 5.1, some years ago devised a bonus-based payment system in the hope of increasing work output. The officially stated purpose of this was 'to share with employees the rewards of the high-performance production system that we all want to see'. The introduction of the scheme, however, was met with unofficial strategies among workgroups, along the lines of the so-called 'informal' ones observed in the Hawthorne experiments (Chapter 2, pp. 42–44). Workers resisted managerial pressures to work harder, as a group, than they felt was reasonable. In reaction to this, the managers introduced a new, and official, workshop layout which segregated workers from each other, thus breaking up the unofficial relationship and communication patterns existing under the old arrangement. Very soon, the workers devised an unofficial signalling arrangement whereby they let each other know just what each one was producing. The unofficial output norm stayed in operation.

This illustration of how official and unofficial aspects of organisations interrelate also illustrates the very important point that all of these facets of life within the organisation relate to patterns prevailing in the society outside organisational boundaries. There is a clear difference of priorities between those managing the workshop and those working the machines, these differences relating to the broader economic, social status and social class positions of these people.

Organisational structures and cultures

Organisational structures, seen sociologically, are part of the wider social structure of the society in which they are located. But if we wish to look at organisational structures in their own terms, we need to conceptualise them in a way that ensures both official and unofficial aspects of organisational activities are covered.

> ## Organisational structure
>
> The regular or persisting patterns of action that give shape and a degree of predictability to an organisation.

The structure of any organisation, seen in this way, will partly be the outcome of the efforts of managers and other organisational designers to structure tasks, activities and establish a controlling hierarchy of command. And it will partly be an outcome of the efforts of members of the organisation to find their own way of doing things, to establish their own coalitions of interest and, to some extent, to develop their own power hierarchies. Those involved in particularly strategic roles are especially likely to shape the organisation to fit with their own life projects (Watson 2003a).

Snapshot 5.3

Official and unofficial structure at Begley's

There is an official supervising role of office manager in the sales department of Begley's – a food wholesaling organisation. But alongside this is the unofficial role of office 'wise old lady' which is played by a popular and generally well-regarded clerical worker (who liked her unofficial designation, in spite of only being in her mid-thirties). There is also an unofficial role of 'office clown'. This was played by the same man for many years before the role was taken over, on this man's retirement, by another individual who, it seemed, had understudied his friend for many years. There was an official rule in the office that a tie must be worn by any male employee when meeting a customer. But this was accompanied by a rigidly enforced unofficial rule that men would always undo their tie when a manager was not watching them. And alongside official procedures, such as that whereby all letters sent out from the office should be signed by the manager, is the unofficial procedure that office workers use a rubber stamp of the manager's signature on letters they write, both to get the mail despatched more quickly than they would if they waited for the manager to sign each letter and to make life easier for everyone concerned.

When we look at organisational structures, as in the Snapshot 5.3, we are focusing on regular activities and behaviours. And when we turn our attention to the meanings that people attach to these activities we tend to use a concept of organisational culture.

In so far as we can identify a distinctive culture in any organisation (remembering that, as with structures, cultural patterns within an organisation are to a large extent facets of the culture of the society of

> ## Organisational culture
>
> The set of meanings and values shared by members of an organisation that defines the appropriate ways for people to think and behave with regard to the organisation.

which the organisation is a part), it will in part be shaped by managerial attempts to devise official 'corporate cultures' with sets of managerially propagated 'values', mission statements and the like. Managerial talk about corporate cultures tends to treat cultures as things that organisations 'have'. But it is probably more helpful to talk about the cultural dimension of organisations rather than of 'organisational cultures' as such. And this dimension of organisational life has significant unofficial aspects.

Snapshot 5.4

Official and unofficial culture at Begley's

Officially, the culture of Begley's is one in which every employee is guided by the moral rule or 'value' that 'the customer is always right'. Unofficially, however, the cultural pattern is one in which complaining customers tend to be treated with contempt and only treated politely when it is deemed likely that they will take their complaint to a supervisor or manager.

To understand the cultural dimension of an organisation, it is helpful to analyse a variety of expressions of culture, remembering that each of these can support either the official or the unofficial aspect of culture:

- *artefacts*, such as the tools, documents, building layouts, logos, badges and furnishing;
- *jargon*, the linguistic terms that are peculiar to that organisational setting;
- *stories* about how people have acted within the organisation, and with what effect;
- *jokes* and *humour* generally;
- *legends* about events that might or might not actually have happened but that have a sense of wonder about them and which point to activities that organisational members are encouraged to admire or deplore;
- *myths* about events that are unlikely ever to have happened but which illustrate some important 'truth' about the organisation;

- *sagas* about the organisation's history and how it has become 'what it is';
- *heroes* and *villains* that people speak of – inspirational figures that organisational members are encouraged to emulate and 'bad people' illustrating types of behaviour to be avoided;
- *norms of behaviour*, regularly occurring pieces of behaviour that become accepted as 'the way things are done' in the organisation;
- *rituals*, patterns of behaviour that regularly occur in particular circumstances and at particular times in an organisation;
- *rites*, more formalised rituals that tend to be pre-planned and organised; and
- actions leading to *rewards* or *punishments*, behaviours that lead to positive or negative sanctions because they accord with or clash with cultural values.

LOOKING FORWARD >>>>>

Several of these aspects of culture – stories, jokes, legends, myths and sagas – take a narrative or a 'story' form. The significance of narratives and stories in social life and human identities is considered in Chapter 10, pp. 306–309.

We can apply some of these culture-related concepts to life in Begley's Foods. As we look at each facet of the culture, we can each build up for ourselves an impression of the overall culture of the organisation: the meanings and values shared by people at Begley's that define how people should think and behave when working in the company.

Snapshot 5.5

Some cultural features of Begley's Foods

Artefacts: The front office of Begley's sales department is clean and well furnished, unlike the 'back office' which has not been decorated or re-furnished for almost twenty years. The directors' offices are on an upper floor and are spacious with large windows, unlike any of the other offices on the site. All staff wear badges, and it is common practice for warehouse workers to pin their badges to their clothes upside down.

Jargon: Products are classified in terms like 'wet' and 'dry', which most people can guess at the meaning of. Others, however, are 'P&P' or 'P&N' – the meaning of which is privy to 'insiders'.

Stories: The most popular stories are currently ones about the long lunch breaks taken by company directors and the luxurious life-styles of the members of the Begley family.

Legends, heroes and villains: The original James Begley is often spoken of as a very generous individual, and there are several legendary accounts of individual acts of generosity to workers. The meanness of James Begley, Jr, who only recently retired, could be described as legendary. And there is a legend of his going round the site one weekend removing any chairs or other seats that he thought were unnecessary and which might encourage workers to takes rests during working hours.

Behavioural norms and rituals: The wearing of upside-down badges by staff was normal in the warehouse as was the daily ritual of workers removing their badges and throwing them into a large plastic bucket at the end of each working day. The supervisor would then remove them from this receptacle and set them out on a table just inside the employee entrance ready for the next morning.

The distinction between organisation structure and organisation culture which we have been using so far, with the former focusing on activities and the latter on meanings and values, is a useful one. But it can only be taken so far. Many aspects of organisational life can as readily be regarded as structural, and they can be treated as cultural. A good example of this would be *rules*. An organisational rule can be seen as an element of an organisation's structure. But it can equally be seen as an expression of an organisation's culture. We need to recognise, in fact, that organisational structures and cultures are not really separate phenomena at all. The two concepts derive from two different metaphors that we use to try to give some solidity to the abstract phenomenon of 'organisation'. When we talk of an organisational structure we are utilising a metaphor of the organisation as 'something built' and when we talk of an organisational culture we are using an agricultural metaphor rather than a construction one and applying a metaphor of organisation as 'something cultivated'. The way in which we tend to switch about between these metaphors can be illustrated by the fact that we sometimes talk of 'the bureaucratic structure' of an organisation whilst, at other times, we talk about that organisation's 'bureaucratic *culture*'. This suggests that it might be wise to move away from the traditional sociological practice of treating such matters as bureaucracy as structural phenomena and recognise that they are both structural and cultural.

It is thus helpful when examining how modern work organisations have developed in the way that they have to consider the efforts of 'organisers' simultaneously to design official structures *and* cultures. There are certain key principles which have been applied in the shaping of modern organisations, 'bureaucracy' being a central one.

Official structure and culture: basic organisational design principles

Although, to understand organisations sociologically, we need to see them as involving both official and unofficial practices, at the core of any work organisation will be the *official control apparatus* which is designed and continuously redesigned by those 'managing' the enterprise.

The official control apparatus of an organisation
The set of roles, rules, structures, value statements, cultural symbols, rituals and procedures managerially designed to co-ordinate and control work activities.

In designing the organisation, the managers seek to establish such things as:

- how the tasks to be done within the chosen technologies are to be split into various jobs;
- how these jobs are to be grouped into sections, divisions and departments;
- how many levels of authority there are to be;
- the nature of communication channels and reward structures;
- the balance of centralisation to decentralisation and authority to delegation;
- the degree of formalisation and standardisation of procedures and instructions;
- the values or principles that organisational members should be guided by in their behaviour; and
- the beliefs about the organisation and the legitimacy of managerial authority that organisational members should hold.

The most basic set of principles underlying modern structural and cultural organisation design efforts are those of *bureaucracy*. We can consider what this entails first and then go on to look at two prescriptive 'schools' of organisational thinking: classical administrative principles and Taylorism/Fordism, which have provided managements with design guidance, respectively, for the organisation as a whole and for the part of the organisation most directly involved with productive tasks.

Bureaucracy

Organisations are *authoritatively co-ordinated human enterprises* (Watson 2007a). This characterisation recognises that the task-based activities of

social arrangements such as businesses, schools, churches, public admin-
istrations and armies are all bureaucratically co-ordinated. And Weber's
(1978) conceptualisation of bureaucracy put authority, in the sense of
legitimised power, at the centre of these organising processes.

> ### Bureaucracy
>
> The control and co-ordination of work tasks through a hierarchy of
> appropriately qualified office holders, whose authority derives from
> their expertise and who rationally devise a system of rules and pro-
> cedures that are calculated to provide the most appropriate means of
> achieving specified ends.

The bureaucratisation of work has to be seen as part of a wider set
of historical processes in Western industrial capitalist societies whereby
more and more aspects of life were being subjected to more instrumental or calculative styles of thinking.

> ### LOOKING BACK <<<<<
>
> Rationalisation processes were introduced in Chapter 4. See also the discussion of Max Weber
> in Chapter 3.

The rationalisation process involved the rapid development of scientific
and technological thinking and, with regard to work organisation, it was
increasingly felt that by carefully calculating the most appropriate way of
achieving tasks and then basing on this formalised roles, procedures and
arrangements within which people would be rewarded only in terms
of their contribution to officially set tasks, the efforts of large numbers of
people could be co-ordinated and controlled and large and complex jobs
done. Thus we see the increasing influence of the institutional logic of
bureaucratic administration. The appeal of this logic to those pushing the
modernisation of the world was two-fold. Bureaucracy could bring about:

- *fairness* in the distribution of posts and rewards, particularly in the
  sphere of public administration, this increasingly being expected in
  the democratising societies of Europe and America. By the following
  of procedural neutrality and impartiality, the old evils of favouritism,
  nepotism and capriciousness would be removed;
- *efficiency* both in state administration and in industrial enterprises.
  Great promise was seen in terms of output and quality if large

organisations could be administered on the basis of clear procedures, expertise and co-ordinated human efforts.

To help analyse the process of bureaucratisation, which he saw as central to modern societies, Weber in *Wirtschaft und Gesellschaft*, published after his death in 1921, presents a model of what a bureaucracy would look like if it existed in a pure form. In doing this, he used the device of the *ideal type*. Weber's ideal type of bureaucracy is often taken to be the conceptual starting point in organisation theory and much of the effort expended by sociologists and other social scientists to understand organisations has been an attempt to refine or take issue with what Weber was taken to be implying in its use.

In an ideal-type bureaucracy (that is, in an imagined pure case of the phenomenon):

- all operating rules and procedures are formally recorded;
- tasks are divided up and allocated to people with formally certified expertise to carry them out;
- activities are controlled and co-ordinated by officials organised in a hierarchy of authority;
- communications and commands pass up or down the hierarchy without missing out steps;
- posts are filled and promotions achieved by the best qualified people;
- office-holder posts constitute their only employment and the level of their salary reflects their level in the hierarchy;
- posts cannot become the property or private territory of the office-holder (the officer's authority derives from their appointed office and not from their person);
- all decisions and judgements are made impersonally and neutrally, without emotion, personal preference or prejudice.

Although bureaucratisation is a general societal and historical process, it is sometimes possible to see its key principles clearly illustrated when an organisation that has been run on relatively traditional grounds is 'rationalised' or 'modernised'. This was the case with the *Merryton Echo*, described in Snapshot 5.6.

Snapshot 5.6

The rationalisation and bureaucratisation of an Australian newspaper

It was never clear in the old days of the *Merryton Echo* newspaper just how any particular person got appointed to any given job. But after the old lady who owned the paper died, the person who inherited the business declared that he would 'rationalise the rag from top to bottom'. The main outcome of this pledge was the employing of an editor who was a trained journalist and who was selected after competitive interviews with other aspiring editors. Previously, the editorial role had seemed to go to whoever was in personal favour with the old lady and belonged to the local Masonic lodge. One of the first tasks that the new editor was required to do was to prepare a document called the 'Office and Operating Procedures Manual'. Job specifications were drawn up for all the tasks that needed to be done to produce the paper and, once persona specifications had been prepared for each of these, all staff were interviewed and selected for jobs against these formal criteria. All but the most routine communications were made by being referred 'up the line' to the editor who passed them back 'down the line' as he felt appropriate. Pay scales were no longer based on how long an individual had been employed or how well the editor liked the person. Scales now related to qualifications and the possession of proven skills. Unlike in the past, it was made clear that the editor could be removed if the paper was not successful (previously it was regarded as a job for life). And decisions about what would and would not be printed were now made on the basis of how they would influence sales. Previously, stories seemed to be selected on near-random grounds or on the basis of how they would be helpful to relatively influential people in the local community. Stories that might have harmed local worthies, but sold extra copies, in the past were suppressed. This was no longer the case.

Weber's ideal type of bureaucracy is in no sense a model of what he thought *ought* to be the case administratively. It is a device to help us analytically by providing us with a sketch of an impossibly pure and unachievable structure against which reality can be compared. Weber was concerned to contrast characteristically modern forms of administration (which he saw based on a legal-rational form of authority in which orders are obeyed because they are seen to be in accord with generally acceptable rules or laws) with earlier forms (based on traditional or charismatic authority). As du Gay (2005) points out, Weber saw little sense in either abstractly celebrating or denouncing 'bureaucracy'. There is no point in applying 'global moral judgements to bureaucratic conduct *tout court*: to praise it for its impartiality or condemn it for its conservatism; to approve its efficiency or damn its amorality'. The point is to examine specific cases of bureaucratic organisation and to see in which direction bureaucratisation has taken in that case. This means that Weber was in no way advocating bureaucracy. Neither was he addressing himself to the managers of organisations, as some managerial and organisational behaviour textbooks seem to imply. The bureaucratic principle which he was analysing in his historically based political sociology was, however, put into prescriptive form by a number of writers who were probably quite unaware of Weber's existence and who can be grouped together as the advocates of classical administrative principles.

Classical administrative principles

> ### Classical administrative principles
>
> Universally applicable rules of organisational design – structural and cultural – widely taught and applied, especially in the first half of the twentieth century.

Largely drawing on their own experiences and reflections, writers such as Fayol (1916), Mooney and Riley (1931) and Gulick and Urwick (1937) attempted to establish universally applicable principles upon which organisational and management arrangements should be based. Fayol can be seen as the main inspirer of this approach and the following suggestions for practice can be found among the mixture of exhortations, moral precepts and design principles that make up his writings. He said, for example, that:

- there should always be a 'unity of command' whereby no employee should have to take orders from more than one superior;
- there should be a 'unity of direction' whereby there should be one head and one plan for a group of activities having the same objective; and
- there should be regular efforts to maintain the harmony and unity of the enterprise through the encouragement of an 'esprit de corps'.

The advocates of principles like these for the designers and managers of work enterprises vary in their sophistication and in the extent to which they see their principles as relevant to all conditions. However, there is a pervasive underlying principle of there being a 'one best way'. This can be seen in the suggestion that there should always be a differentiating of 'line' and 'staff' departments (those directly concerned with producing the main output of the organisation and those who support this process) and in the various attempts to fix a correct 'span of control' (the number of subordinates any superior can effectively supervise). This kind of universalist prescribing is of importance because it influenced a great deal of twentieth-century organisational design.

LOOKING FORWARD >>>>>

The 'contingency' concept in organisation theory can be seen as having been introduced to counter this 'universalist' tendency. Different circumstances or 'contingencies' are seen as requiring different structural arrangements. This is explained later in this chapter (pp. 153–158).

Taylorism and Fordism

Whilst the classical administrative writers were advocating what amounts to a set of basic bureaucratic design principles for work organisations as a whole, F. W. Taylor and his associates were putting forward principles for job and workshop design which would apply to the 'lower parts' of these organisations (Taylor 1911a, 1911b).

LOOKING BACK <<<<<

Scientific management or 'Taylorism' was introduced and explained in Chapter 2.

It is easy to understand how Weber came to see in these principles the most extreme manifestation of the process of work rationalisation and the 'greatest triumphs in the rational conditioning and training of work performances' – 'triumphs' he anything but admired but which he saw as fulfilling its 'dehumanising' potential.

Although Taylorist principles of work organisation can be understood as part of the general rationalising process hastening the bureaucratisation of work organisations after the turn of the twentieth century, it is very important to note that these principles are only partly to be understood as bureaucratic. This was pointed out by Littler (1982) who noted that the 'minimum interaction model' of the employment relationship implied in Taylorism contrasts with the career aspect of the principle of bureaucracy. An official in a bureaucracy has the potential to advance up the career hierarchy, but a shop floor worker, under scientific management, has no such potential. Different conditions therefore apply to people employed in the lower half of the industrial organisation's hierarchy than apply to those located in the upper part – which is therefore more fully bureaucratic.

LOOKING BACK AND FORWARD <<<<< >>>>>

Taylorism or 'scientific management' is a phenomenon that we encounter time and again when studying work and work organisation both historically and sociologically. It can be looked at as a contribution to intellectual and theoretical thinking about work organisation and was, accordingly, treated as part of the managerial-psychologistic strand in the sociology of work and industry in Chapter 2. But, as was noted in Chapter 2 and is stressed later in Chapter 6, understanding Taylorism and its legacy is vital to an appreciation of how job design practices have changed over time and, especially, to understanding what the various attempts to rethink the way work tasks were shaped and allocated over the past half century were reacting against. If we look back to the account provided in Chapter 2, Taylor can be seen as a thinker and managerial innovator who combined a 'psychologistic' style of analysis (one which focuses on the psychological characteristics of human individuals) with a socio-political concern to influence the organisation of the work-related aspects of early twentieth-century industrial society.

When it comes to our understanding of patterns at the level of the work organisation, we can see the principles of the scientific management that Taylor initiated as significantly shaping the particular bureaucratic forms that work organisations came to take on as the twentieth century unfolded. Especially important here, and continuing to be significant in the twenty-first century, is the notion that scientifically orientated managerial experts should take control over task performance in work organisations, thus reinforcing the strength of hierarchical power in those organisations.

To some observers, the growing twentieth-century significance of the assembly line alongside the spreading influence of Taylorism is sufficient to warrant the recognition of a set of work design and management principles which came to exist in their own right. This is Fordism.

LOOKING BACK <<<<<

As the discussion in Chapter 4 shows, Fordism has a significance way beyond the workplace. It has nevertheless had considerable impact on the way workplaces have been shaped, across the world.

At the workplace level, an important aspect of the innovations that Henry Ford made in his car factories was an extension of scientific management principles of a detailed division of labour, intensive management work-planning and close supervision. Fordism, with its assembly line, creates an even closer attachment of the individual to their work station and increases the mechanising of work handling. On the cultural side, however, it departs from Taylorism – which tends to treat labour strictly as a commodity – by making a connection between labour management policy and attention to markets. Fordism is essentially a mass production process which recognises that the people it employs are part of the market for its products. It therefore recognises the necessity of taking an interest in the lives of workers as consumers as well as producers. A mass consumption market has to be created and stabilised to fit the mass production organisation of the factory. It is in this context that we can understand Ford's particular innovation of the Five Dollar Day – a relatively high wage level which could be obtained once the worker had a minimum of six months continuous service and as long as they complied with certain standards of personal behaviour. Fordism accepts that the workforce should be treated as more than a commodity to be dealt with at arm's length whilst, nevertheless, keeping them under the close control and instructions of the management in a machine-paced environment.

The limits of bureaucracy and the paradox of consequences

Modern employing organisations, all of which are more or less based on the bureaucratic principle, use rational calculative techniques of various kinds as means towards the ends pursued by their controllers. They also use the work efforts of human beings as resources, as devices, as means-to-ends. However, human beings are assertive, creative and initiating animals with a tendency to resist being the means to other people's ends. This potential means that they are always problematic when used as instruments – as the means to other people's ends. Every organisation is thus confronted by a basic paradox.

> ## A basic paradox of organising
>
> The tendency for the means adopted by organisational officials to achieve particular goals to fail to achieve these goals since these 'means' involve human beings who have goals of their own which may not be congruent with those of the officials or 'managers'.

This paradoxical reality not only accounts for many of the 'motivational' and 'industrial relations' problems which organisational managements continually experience in their work; it also provides the starting point for explaining many structural features of organisations themselves. It provides the key to explaining the growth of quality control and auditing functions and aspects of the human resourcing and employee relations structures within organisations. It also accounts in part for the existence of government and quasi-government agencies involved in regulating the activities of employing organisations. All of these are involved in coping with potentially destructive contradictions.

This view of organisations caught up in a paradox is very much in the spirit of Weber's view of modern society and is developed from his key distinction between formal and material rationality.

Ironically, many writers on organisations – who frequently look back to Weber as some kind of founder of organisation theory – completely miss the point of Weber's view of bureaucracy. They assume that when he wrote of the high degree of formal rationality achievable by bureaucratic organisation he was claiming that it is necessarily 'efficient' in its meeting of goals. As Albrow's (1970) important reappraisal of Weber's position showed, Weber did indeed recognise, in pointing to the high formal rationality of bureaucracies, their 'technical superiority' and their virtues of calculability, predictability and stability. But he was nevertheless well aware that, although these were necessary conditions for 'efficient' achievement of goals, they in no way constituted a sufficient guarantee of such success. Formal rationality (choice of technically appropriate means), does not guarantee material rationality (achievement of the original value-based goal). In the light of this argument, it is indeed ironic that attempts to refute Weber's imputed belief in the efficiency of bureaucratic organisations have provided a key motivation behind much organisational sociology.

At this point, we can introduce some of the key studies which have been done in this tradition, noting that their mistaken intention of 'correcting Weber' does not in itself invalidate their findings. In a sense, they are extensions of the Weberian view rather than refutations of it. The basic mistake made by many writers on organisations is to take Weber's ideal type of bureaucracy as if it were some kind of prescription of what an efficient organisation should be.

One of the first sociologists to point to negative aspects of bureaucratic administration was Merton, who concentrated on what he termed *dysfunctions of bureaucracy* – a dysfunctional aspect of any system being some aspect of it which undermines the overall functioning of that system. Merton (1957) argued that the pressure put upon the individual official by bureaucracy, which encourages accountability and predictability through the use of rules, could encourage a counter-productive inflexibility on the part of the officials themselves. Rules and operating procedures thus become ends in themselves rather than means towards organisational goal achievement. We thus get, for example, what Merton called the 'bureaucratic personality'. There was at least one of these at Melkins.

Selznick (1949) observed an equivalent form of goal displacement arising from a different source. The sub-units or departments resulting from delegation of authority within organisations may set up goals of

Snapshot 5.7

Melkins' own 'bureaucratic personality' – and the broken cricket bat

'Look, mate, it's more than my job's worth to let you into the building before half past eight'. This was the first time I had come across this type of person since I started at Melkins. When I mentioned this individual to my friends that evening, they all gave examples of what they called 'jobsworths'. I then remembered this expression from back at school when a teacher called the groundsman at our playing fields a 'jobsworth' because he was always invoking one petty bureaucratic rule or another. I remember him refusing to replace a broken cricket bat in the middle of a game one Saturday afternoon because we didn't have the properly filled in form signed by a teacher. 'We'll get you one on Monday', we said, 'Oh no you won't; it's more than my job is worth to let out a new bat without proper authorisation'. This really messed up the cricket match. But he didn't care. He had that little bit of power and he relished it. It was the same with the security man at work. I urgently needed some papers from that building to take to a meeting which was beginning in my own building at 8.30 am. But, because of him, and his 'sticking to the letter of the law' I was prevented from making as effective a contribution to the business meeting as I might have made, had he worked in a more flexible and helpful manner.

Snapshot 5.8

Marketing at Melkins: a means to business success or an end in itself?

When I left the meeting I sat and reflected on this 'jobsworth' experience. This bloke was more concerned with his own personal importance than with helping us all get our work done. And, as I was thinking about the man, I started to realise that he was not alone in this kind of thing. It isn't just the relatively powerless who indulge in organisationally unhelpful practices, for their own purposes. My meeting was about developments in the marketing of our products. And the clear impression that I got was that the marketing people were something of a 'law unto themselves'. They flash around all these so-called creative ideas and seem to me to be more concerned with impressing other people in the marketing profession than in helping Melkins succeed in the marketplace. There has been a lot of fighting about a recent advertising campaign. This apparently won the marketers a couple of prizes, but according to some of the Head of Marketing's rival directors, the campaign has actually harmed our sales. But instead of reining in the marketing people, it looks as if they are going to set up a separate advertising department – one that will devise more 'realistic' advertising materials. I cannot believe that anything so stupid can really happen. It will simply make the problem worse.

their own which may come to conflict with those organisational purposes behind the setting up of that sub–unit. Responses to such problems involving the setting up of further departments to cope with these difficulties only exacerbate the situation as further sectional interests or goals are created. This appeared to be happening in Melkins, the organisation in which we have just met the 'jobsworth'.

Gouldner's classic factory study *Patterns of Industrial Bureaucracy* (1964) illustrates in a corresponding way how attempts to cope with contradictory tendencies within the organisation may merely set up a kind of vicious circle of increasing organisational dysfunctions. Impersonal rules in the workplace contribute to control and predictability in task-performance, and they also function to reduce the visibility of the power relations between supervisors and workers. But the tendency of rules to be interpreted as minimum standards of performance may in certain circumstances reduce all activity to an apathetic conformity to this 'official' minimum. Should this happen, there is likely to be a managerial response whereby rules are tightened or direct supervision increased – with the effect that power relations become more visible and overt conflict between managers and managed is increased. Through this the achievement of management's overall goals is increasingly threatened as their control is challenged. We see this, too, happening in Melkins.

Snapshot 5.9

Hitting the targets and endangering Melkins' future

Another issue which arose within the arguments over marketing and advertising was about sales. Apparently, the Sales Director (yes, all these senior people at Melkins seem to be called 'directors') has been managing his function through a ruthless sales target system. He keeps his distance from his sales staff and judges them almost solely on the sales figures they produce at the end of each month. But this, it turns out, has created some serious problems. Orders have been taken which simply cannot be met. The sales people say that they are pressed to 'get the numbers, get the numbers'. They feel they would lose 'good selling time' if they checked with the factory just what could be delivered and when. And if they were told that certain things could not be produced on time, their figures would immediately suffer. So, what is the result of this? The company is getting a bad reputation for non-delivery. The outcome of a system in which sales figures are everything is that a high level of 'sales' are made in the short-term – but with the consequence that actual sales are going to be severely damaged in the long-term.

The virtues of bureaucracy, virtual organisations and the fantasy of the post-bureaucratic organisation

The rules, procedures and administrative devices shown in the academic studies and our own snapshot examples to create problems for those in charge of organisations, are all means by which power is exercised. The so-called 'bureaucratic dysfunctions' are, in effect, limitations on the successful exercise of power within the organisation. However, the problems which arise with bureaucracy have not just been a concern of sociologists wishing to deepen our analytical understanding of bureaucratic organisations. An attack upon bureaucracy has been central to newer managerial discourses which place an emphasis on innovation and enterprise. Du Gay (2000) observes that bureaucratic modes of organisational governance are frequently criticised as inefficient and ineffective because they fail to draw upon people's personal involvement and ideas. He questions the assumptions behind this with particular regard to the administrative aspects of democratic societies. He draws on Weber's observation that the 'impersonality' of the bureaucratic role is an alternative to the pre-bureaucratic situation in which office-holders could readily do their work in a way which prioritised their private advantage. Bureaucracy is thus defended by du Gay as an important ethical and political resource in liberal democratic regimes because it separates the administration of public life from 'private moral absolutisms'. Bureaucracy's 'indifference to certain moral ends' is its strength and not its weakness. This is not to deny the advantages of reducing the size and costs of certain bureaucratic bodies but to remember that in part bureaucracy is a 'positive political and ethical achievement'.

In spite of attempts made to recognise the positive aspects of bureaucracy, an outpouring of anti-bureaucratic thinking and an advocacy of post-bureaucratic forms continues to flow both among managerial writers, social scientists and socio-political theorisers (Reed 2005; Thompson and Alvesson 2005; Alvesson and Thompson 2005). Post bureaucratic organisations are variously characterised

- as 'networked', as in the Castells type of analysis covered earlier (p. 96);
- as 'entrepreneurial' or 'market led', rather than bureaucratic and 'production led';
- as manipulated by strong corporate cultures, as opposed to command structures; and
- as featuring organic or 'indirect controls', rather than mechanistic or 'direct' controls.

This style of thinking began to acquire force in the 1980s with Peters and Waterman (1982) who suggested that 'simultaneous loose–tight controls' will increasingly be developed whereby a basic simple structure (probably divisional) and a strong organisational culture will be combined with a tendency to 'chunk' the organisation into 'small-is-beautiful' units, 'cabals' and other problem-solving and implementation groups. As part of the same wave of thinking, Deal and Kennedy (1982) envisaged a future in which small task-focused work units are bonded like molecules into a 'strong corporate whole'. The need to achieve this bonding through integrated business and manufacturing *systems design* was also central to Drucker's (1992) analysis of management in the future and of the *postmodern factory*. Where the traditional factory was seen as a battleship, says Drucker, the new enterprise will be more like a *flotilla* – 'a set of modules centred around stages in the production process or a set of closely related operations'. Castells (1996) writes in a similar vein about the *network enterprise* which not only uses flexible rather than mass production and emphasises horizontal rather than vertical relationships, but also becomes intertwined with other corporations within a pattern of strategic alliances.

The term *virtual organisation* has become popular as a way of referring to post-bureaucratic organisations made up of networked relationships in which people tend not to be physically located in the same place or relate to each other as co-employees. In the virtual workplace, 'employees operate remotely from each other and from managers' (Cascio 2002).

> ### Virtual or networked organisations
>
> Sets of work arrangement in which those undertaking tasks carried under a corporate name largely relate to each other through electronic communications rather than through face-to-face interaction.

When Alvesson and Thompson (2005), Reed (2005) and Thompson and Alvesson (2005) examine the evidence for an alleged move away from basic bureaucratic principles, they conclude that the announcement of the death of bureaucracy is highly premature. There never was a single and monolithic phenomenon of 'bureaucracy', and what we are currently seeing in certain cases of contemporary organisational change are reconfigured or hybridised versions of the more traditional bureaucratic forms. Hales (2002) helpfully talks of newer manifestations of bureaucratic controls as 'bureaucracy-lite', and his case-study research shows managerial work continuing to be preoccupied with 'monitoring and maintaining work processes, routine direction and control of staff and processing information'. Vie's (2010) study of middle managers concludes similarly. Hybridisation, say Courpasson and Clegg (2006), is actually rejuvenating, rather than superseding, bureaucracy. It continues, albeit it in a modified way, to intermingle political principles of oligarchy and democracy within the context of the 'perpetuation of elite power'. Whilst these authors emphasise the political significance of bureaucracy, Kallinikos (2004) stresses its modernistic significance, claiming that many of the essentially modern features of bureaucracy, especially its concern with standardisation, are not 'suspended by the trends subsumed under such catchwords as network, virtual or entrepreneurial forms of organisation'. This argument, we can add, would apply to public management as much as to industrial organisations, in spite of an increased 'marketisation' of public services. What is happening here, say Farrell and Morris (2003), is the emergence of a 'simultaneously centralised and decentralised form of bureaucracy'. These authors suggest that apt terms for the new state model would be 'neo-bureaucratic' or a 'bureaucratised market form'.

Bureaucratic and market logics: an inevitable tension

LOOKING BACK <<<<<

Institutional logics and how tensions between them influence social and organisational change was explained in Chapter 3, pp. 63–64.

One way in which we can understand the trend towards bureaucracy/market 'hybridisation' is to draw on the idea that tensions between institutional logics in societies are important factors in processes of both social and organisational change. Institutional logics are the sets of values, rules, assumptions and practices associated with key institutions of a society which have been socially constructed over time and through which patterns of social organisation and human activity are shaped and given meaning. And work organisations are shaped by the logics inherent in two of the key institutions of industrial capitalist societies: the institution of the competitive market and the institution of bureaucratic administration. The logic of the institution of market competition puts pressures on organisational managers to be creative and devise new exchange or 'trading' relationships to cope with the essentially dynamic nature of the industrial capitalist context in which they exist. This presses them to engage in *entrepreneurial action* and the greater the market pressures and pressures to innovate are upon any given organisation at any given time, the greater will be the emphasis on entrepreneurial action (Watson 2013).

> ### Entrepreneurial action
>
> The making of adventurous, creative or innovative exchanges (or 'deals') between the entrepreneurial actor's home 'enterprise' and other parties with which the enterprise trades.

However great the pressures might be on an organisation to operate in an innovative and entrepreneurial manner, it cannot abandon the institutional logic of bureaucratic administration: the logic whereby a hierarchy of appropriately qualified managers use their technical expertise and a rationally devised system of rules and procedures to maintain control, co-ordination and efficiency, (see the definition of bureaucracy, earlier, p. 139). Without a bureaucratic apparatus, entrepreneurial action could not occur and, without a degree of entrepreneurial action, an organisation would fail to cope with its inevitably changing context and would eventually collapse. The two logics will nevertheless always be in tension, as Table 5.2 illustrates.

Organisational managers will handle the tensions between these two logics in different ways in different circumstances. In particular, they have the option of adopting either relatively *tight* or relatively *loose* forms of bureaucratic structure and cultures. This takes us to the relationship between managerial choices and the circumstances ('contingencies') which enable and constrain those choices.

Table 5.2 Two institutional logics and two types of social action

Societal and global level institutional logics	Market competition	*Tension/contradiction* ⟷	Bureaucratic administration
Corporate level social action	Creatively devising new exchange relationships	*Tension/contradiction* ⟷	Maintaining stability and predictability in exchange relationships

Contingency and choice in the shaping of organisational structures and cultures

As we saw earlier, sociologists like Merton, Selznick and Gouldner raised problems about the practical functioning of bureaucracies in general. Other researchers have raised doubts about the universally relevant prescriptions of the kind suggested by Fayol and others. The classical administrative writers offered universally applicable guiding principles on the best vertical and horizontal span of hierarchies; the best degree of specialisation, formalisation, centralisation, delegation and the like. However, the *contingency approach* to the design of the official control aspects of organisational structures, which has grown in popularity in organisation theory since the late 1950s, suggests, instead, that managements tend to seek the most *appropriate* shape of organisation to achieve their purposes given prevailing situational *contingencies*.

Contingencies

Circumstances which influence the ways in which organisations are structured.

Two studies which were particularly important in establishing this new flexibility in thinking were those of Woodward (1994, originally 1965) and Burns and Stalker (1994, originally 1961). Woodward's study of a hundred manufacturing firms in Essex started with an interest in seeking relationships between successful business performance and organisational structure. However, it was only when the variable of technology was introduced into the researchers' thinking that sense could be made of the variations which were found in such features as the spans of control within firms, the number of levels in the hierarchy and the extent to which communications were verbal or written. When firms were examined in terms of their place on a scale of complexity of production technology (a scale ranging from unit and small-batch production, through large-batch and mass production to process production), it became clear that different structural configurations were appropriate to different technologies. Thus it would be appropriate for, say, a petrochemical company to have a relatively tall and narrow hierarchical shape whilst a firm turning out custom-built perambulators might be better suited to a short and wide configuration.

Burns and Stalker's study can also be taken to show the importance of technology as a contingent factor, although technology itself is emphasised here less than is the environment to which the technology relates. The authors observed that a different organisational pattern is likely to be appropriate in an industry like textiles where the environment is relatively stable compared to the pattern appropriate to an industry like electronics where the environment produces a constant pressure for innovation. To cope with pressures for innovation, an organic type of structure will be appropriate. The structure here will be loose and flexible with a relatively low degree of formalisation and task prescription. Where conditions are more stable, however, mechanistic structures may be more appropriate, these approximating far more to the ideal type of bureaucracy and the prescriptions of the classical administrative writers.

Contingent factors of *technology* and *environment* are stressed in these now classic studies, but other contingencies are emphasised by later contributors. Researchers at Aston University (Pugh and Hickson 1976; Pugh and Hinings 1976; Pugh and Payne 1977), for instance, argued that Woodward's analysis did not sufficiently take into account the *size of the organisation*. The Aston studies were interpreted by their authors as indicating that Woodward's generalisations about organisational shape and technological complexity may only apply in smaller organisations and in those areas of larger organisations close to the production process itself. Generally valid organisational principles may well be applicable, it was argued, at the higher levels of management. Thus, once you move away from the 'shop floor' or operating level of any organisation the structural pattern will be more influenced by the organisation's size and its degree of independence from other organisations (within and without a parent group).

Lawrence and Lorsch's (1967) work concentrated on environmental contingencies, stressing the influence of the degree of certainty and diversity in the environment on ways in which organisations are structured in terms of *differentiation* and the *integrating* mechanisms used to cope with problems arising from the operation of differentiated units. Perrow (1970b), on the other hand, argued for the centrality of technology, something which he conceptualised in a much wider way than have other writers. Perrow concentrated on the nature of the 'raw material' processed by the organisation, whether this be a living material as in an educational organisation, a symbolic material as in a financial institution or an inanimate material as in manufacturing. These raw materials clearly differ in their variability, and hence their processing will create different problems to be faced by the organisational structure. The more routine such materials processing is, the more a formal centralised structure is appropriate, and vice versa.

There are important insights to be derived from these various studies. However, there are a number of difficulties that arise, not the least of which is the tendency for the studies to rival each other in the particular contingency which they emphasise. An overview of the contingency literature strongly suggests that a variety of contingencies are likely to be relevant to any given organisation. But if we accept this, we are still left with the problem of incorporating the insights of this literature into a general sociological theory of organisations which sees organisational structure as arising out of the interplay between official and unofficial activities within what is an essentially humanly initiated and political competitive process. In his influential critique and refinement of the contingency approach, Child (1972) stressed the dangers of seeing organisational structures as automatically reacting to or being determined by contingent factors like environment, size or technology. He pointed out that those effectively managing the organisation, whom (following Cyert and March 1963) he calls the *dominant coalition*, do have a certain leeway in the structures which they choose to adopt in their strategic directing of the organisation. A range of contingent factors will always limit the decision-making of senior managements, but their strategic choices are not limited to establishing structural forms. They also include the manipulation of environmental and the choice of relevant performance standards. In pointing to the strategic choices made by a concrete group of motivated actors as part of an essentially political process, Child provided a 'corrective to the view that the way in which organisations are designed and structured has to be determined largely by their operational contingencies' (Child 1997) and, in applying the perspective in research on a major organisational change process, developed it to demonstrate the significance of corporate ideologies and organisational learning processes in the shaping and reshaping of organisations (Child and Smith 1987).

Donaldson (1996) says that the core assumption of 'contingency theory' is that whilst 'low uncertainty tasks are most effectively performed by centralised hierarchy since this is simple, quick and allows close co-ordination cheaply', higher 'task uncertainty' makes it necessary for the hierarchy to loosen control and 'be overlain by participatory, communicative structures'. This insight can be incorporated into a more fully sociological model of how organisations come to be shaped as they are by treating contingent factors as ones which managers, to a greater or a lesser extent, *take into account* when choosing organisational structures and cultures.

The model represented in Figure 5.1 takes the contingency insight out of the systems-thinking tradition of organisation theory and

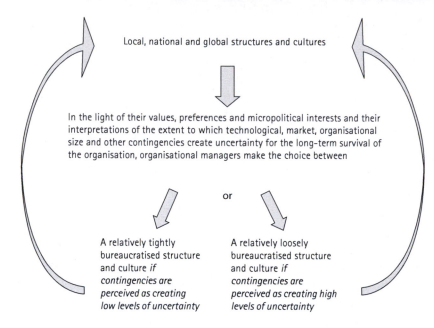

Figure 5.1 Contingencies and managerial choices in shaping organisational structures and cultures

incorporates it into a more political–economic and sociological type of theorising which recognises that:

- organisational structures and cultures are the outcomes of human initiatives and choices (as opposed to relatively automatic reactions to system needs);
- these choices are influenced by (and themselves influence) the broad institutional context of the organisation, that is by societal patterns of social structure and culture; and
- organisational design choices are influenced by the preferences, values and interests of the managers who make them as well as by the interpretations which those managers make of the organisation's circumstances ('contingencies' like the volatility of its markets, the complexity of its technologies, the size of the enterprise, etc.) and the degree of uncertainty about the future that those circumstances create.

LOOKING FORWARD >>>>>

A version of Figure 5.1 appears in Chapter 6 (Figure 6.1, p. 182) applying this thinking to human resourcing strategies.

Contingencies, underwear and the fight for survival

For many years, Lastica had produced large volumes of standard men's and women's vests and pants for a large retailing chain. The designs changed very little from one year to another and the size of the order book varied very little from season to season. The company was successfully managed in a traditional 'top-down' and bureaucratic manner, with the standard rules and procedures being well fitted to a standard product range and a steady pattern of demand. Almost overnight, however, the company found that its major customer had turned to overseas producers for standardised products. Lastica simply could not match the prices offered by these new competitors. The board of directors made the decision to reduce the size of their operation and to produce smaller volumes of higher-value garments. Designers and marketing experts were recruited, and the redundancy programme was used to increase the average skill level of the remaining manual workforce. But what the directors did not do was to change the tightly bureaucratic structure and culture of the organisation. As a result, tensions between managers and designers, between supervisors and skilled workers and between sales staff and factory managers increased to a level that threatened the very survival of Lastica. A new managing director was brought in to save the business, and for the first year of his appointment, his major effort went into persuading the fellow directors and the managers to loosen the formality and rigidity of the structures of command and communication. He argued that the various grades and types of employee in the firm needed to work much more closely and informally with each other if they were going to be responsive to rapid changes in customer taste and the need to produce

In the way of looking at organisational shaping put forward in the model represented in Figure 5.1 and illustrated by the Lastica snapshot, managers are not seen as technical experts making politically neutral decisions about their organisations. They are seen as people with a variety of personal and group interests who, inevitably, act in a 'micropolitical' way as they simultaneously carry out the tasks they are paid to perform and manage their organisational and 'life' careers.

Micropolitics, careers and unofficial management practices

In turning to organisational *micropolitics*, we are focusing on the 'upper' part of organisations. And we are looking at everyday aspects of how *power* is exerted and experienced within the bureaucratic hierarchy. 'Politics', Buchanan and Badham (1999) suggest, can be seen as 'power in action' with power itself being viewed as a 'latent capacity, as a resource, or a possession'. But power is a multi-dimensional phenomenon:

new products at great speed. Although he talked about 'getting rid of bureaucracy', what he was doing, in effect, was moving to a much looser type of bureaucracy in which people were given the discretion to work out, with each other, the best and quickest way to solve the problems that arose from being in this completely different type of business situation. Theoretically, we would say, the contingencies affecting the organisation had changed and, with a change in the politics and power distribution of the board room, managerial choices had been made which produced a better 'fit' between contingencies and structures.

- At an interpersonal level, some individuals have power over others to the extent that they can get those others to do things they would not otherwise do.
- At a societal level, power is more a matter of a pattern of relationships and understandings – a 'structure' which enables certain social groups to exert pressures on others (through the wealth or the armaments they possess or through the authority that the culture vests in them).
- At an organisational level, power structures involve rules, hierarchies and cultural norms that people agree to comply with by joining the organisation, and which make it 'reasonable' and normal for some people to get others to do what they would not otherwise do.

What runs through all these three dimensions of power is the capacity of groups or individuals to affect *outcomes* of situations to their advantage. Those in charge of large modern corporations have, from the time of the British East India Company through to the lobbying undertaken by contemporary corporations, made considerable efforts in an interlinked or 'institutional field' manner, to exert considerable power in their relationships with governments (Barley 2010). And, *within* organisations, power is exerted and resisted through 'micro political' processes. Micropolitics are the processes whereby competition occurs for the 'good things' of life in any particular organisation at a particular time: salaries, promotions, company cars, smart offices, status or simply opportunities to influence other people. Studies of micropolitics tend to see organisations as political arenas in which people both co-operate

Power
The capacity of an individual or group to affect the outcome of any situation so that access is achieved to whatever resources are scarce and desired within a society or part of a society.

and compete with each other to further and defend their interests. Micropolitics are part of the unofficial 'side' of the organisation and involve individuals, groups and members of organisational 'sub-units' (departments, functions, divisions and so on) forming coalitions and alliances, helping friends and defeating rivals and bringing about the organisation's *negotiated order* (pp. 49–50). This power, as McCabe (2009) stresses and illustrates with research in a financial institution, is 'exercised in ambiguous and contradictory ways' – ways that both support and thwart efforts to direct the organisation in a particular direction.

> ## Micropolitics
>
> The political processes which occur within organisations as individuals, groups and organisational 'sub-units' compete for access to scarce and valued material and symbolic resources.

Vertical aspects of micropolitics

Noting that 'interests, influence and the resulting politics . . . are the very stuff of decision-making in organisations', Hickson (1999) asks, 'How else could it be when organisations are made up of so many people with diverse viewpoints and are surrounded by so many people who have a stake in what they do?' But organisational politics do not come about simply as a result of the diversity of human interests in an organisation, and organisational power is more than a matter of what von Zugbach (1995) calls 'deciding what you want and making sure that you get it'. A sociological analysis of politicking looks at how it is related to the broader structures and processes of which it is a part. It can be seen as an inevitable outcome of the way organisations are designed.

The bureaucratic structure of organisations, as a reading of Weber's ideal-type of bureaucracy would reveal, provides not only a control mechanism but a potential career ladder and thus a reward mechanism for individuals. Burns (1961) in early and influential work on micropolitics pointed out that organisational members are 'at one and the same time co-operators in a common enterprise and rivals for the material and intangible rewards of successful competition with each other'. The bureaucratic structure thus has both an integrative and a disintegrative aspect. The fact that the career rewards available to individuals are necessarily scarce ones means that those who are officially intended to work co-operatively are likely to find themselves in conflict with each other.

The narrowing ladder in the Ministry of Technology

I thought that life in the civil service would be much more civilised than the dog-eat-dog world of business that I had read about and seen in films when I was a student. And it did feel like that when I joined the technology ministry. There were seven of us new graduates in the department I joined and we all became very good friends. We went out a lot together and we helped each other out at work. But after a year or so, I noticed that one of my friends was choosing not to pass onto me certain pieces of information which would have prevented my getting into difficulty with my seniors. I then realised another friend was listening a lot to my ideas about work but was not sharing with me any of her own ideas. I spoke to my father about this. He is very experienced in government service, and he said to me that I should have recognised that the bureaucratic structure we work within is not just a 'management device' but is also a career ladder. And he drew this ladder on the paper napkin of the restaurant where we were eating. The ladder he drew had wide rungs at the bottom and narrower and narrower ones as you moved up. 'Didn't you realise', he asked me, 'that your friends are both your work colleagues and your career competitors?'. You are not all going to move up in the next round of promotions and these two friends are simply manoeuvring to get up onto the next career rung ahead of you.

Although a certain amount of competition between individuals may be 'functional' for the organisation, it equally may create organisational problems. And individuals' political behaviour readily takes a group form as coalitions, cliques and cabals arise. Sectional interests may be served at the expense of those of senior management. Burns (1955) notes the tendency for two types of group to arise:

- *cliques*, which develop norms and values contrary to the dominant organisational ones, especially among older managers who lack promotion prospects and feel a need to act defensively, and
- *cabals*, which develop among younger managers whose individual interests may be better served by compliance with dominant norms and values.

The managers working in modern organisations are seen by Jackall (1988) as the 'paradigm of the white-collared salaried employee' and his study of managers in several American corporations portrays them as experiencing the corporation as 'an intricate matrix of rival and often intersecting managerial circles'. He says that 'the principal role of each group is its own survival, of each person his own advancement'. Individuals are forced to surrender their personal moralities when they enter the world of the bureaucratic career and the meaning of their work – especially if they are ambitious – 'becomes keeping one's eye on the main chance, maintaining and furthering one's own position and career'. In this pessimistic view of organisational politics, all higher moral principles retreat in the face of a logic of bureaucratic priorities and the self-interests of those who seek careers in modern organisations. Such a view can be contrasted with the points made earlier about the ethical basis of bureaucracy as a form of governance. It is also challenged by evidence that managers may be able to bring personal ethical values to bear on managerial decisions as long as they can successfully argue that the decision they are arguing for will benefit the organisation (be 'good for business'), in the longer run (Watson 2003b, 2007b).

Snapshot 5.12

The very model of a modern moral manager

Glenn Ferness worked in a senior post in a large chain store organisation. The idea of being a 'moral person' was at the core of her self-identity. 'I am', she sang to a tune from a famous operetta, 'the very model of a modern moral manager'. She said this with a tone of self-mockery, stressing that her 'understanding of the modern world' included recognition of the fact that, as a manager, she was being paid to advance the interests of the business that employed her. 'But that does not mean that I don't bring my personal values into my work – as long as I can establish with the bosses that the things that I believe are "right", are "good for the business"'. She went on to speak about her belief in gender equality and explained that she was slowly increasing the proportion of women managers in her own store. 'But', she explained, 'my stated justification for this is that it is best for the business to use all the talents available to us'. She spoke about a 'profound personal moral belief that we should treat everybody with equal regard and that it is desperately wrong to judge people on the basis of their sex, ethnicity or age'. However, she understands that if she were to 'argue the moral case in those terms' she would 'get nowhere'. Instead, 'I argue the case for using all the talents we have got or I argue that it would be "bad for business" to be known as an employer who unfairly discriminates against various groups'.

The provision by organisations of career advancement as a motivational inducement is frequently systematised in administrative procedures such as 'career development' programmes, annual assessments, promotion boards and the like. Yet again Weber's 'paradox of consequences' manifests itself since such systems may well create unrealistic expectations of advancement with consequential demotivating results when these expectations are not met. The potentially disruptive effects of internal promotion procedures were well illustrated in Burns' (1977) study of the BBC, where promotion procedures were so highly stressed that the corporation appeared to put a 'positive value on careerism, on the energetic pursuit of promotion' with the effect that performing well at appointment boards became more important than actually being successful in one's job. Burns also showed how individuals attempted to appear as 'BBC types' through carefully managed impressions of self, thus contributing to 'a latent system of approved conduct and demeanour'. Although this was by no means uniform, it was nevertheless 'always consonant with the prevailing code by which individuals . . . were selected and gained approval and promotion'. At the point of recruitment, vague criteria of approval are often adopted, such as recruits' 'likeability' or, as Finlay and Coverdill (2002) show, in their study of 'headhunters', the presence of the right 'chemistry'. And Brown and Hesketh (2004), in their study of the recruitment of graduates, confirms just how important the rather general opinions that managers have of recruits' abilities are, not just at the point of recruitment but also in the later assessment of the quality of their work performance.

Horizontal aspects of micropolitics

We have to take care here not to stress the interpersonal career competitions and the striving for individual power outside the context of the departmental structures in which people are located. Research on the horizontal dimension of organisational power activity has attempted to explain how it comes about that departments or organisational 'sub-units' are rarely equally powerful – in the sense of the access they allow to scarce and valued resources. In the 1960s, Crozier (1964) identified power with the ability to resist the removal by others of uncertainty in one's sphere of activities. He showed how maintenance workers in a tobacco factory had more power than those who operate the machines they maintain. At the managerial level, Perrow (1970a) showed that in eleven of the twelve industrial firms he studied, managers felt the sales department to be the most powerful. Perrow explained this in terms of the 'strategic position with respect to the environment' and subsequent research and theorising has developed the insight that organisational uncertainties may be the key to power within organisations.

Uncertainty
A state in which the understanding of a future situation or event is unclear or confused and is therefore open to a variety of interpretations.

The insight about the connection between power and uncertainty was developed and applied by Hickson and his colleagues (1971) to produce a *strategic contingency theory of power*. This theory suggests that as long as a sub-unit is central enough to an organisation's activities and non-substitutable enough for others to be dependent upon it, its influence over decision-making is significantly enhanced if it can show that it can deal with *strategically important uncertainties*. In other words, the 'ability to manage uncertainty on behalf of others provides a vital power base' (Miller *et al.* 1996). Thus, if any individual or departmental grouping within an organisation wishes to increase their access to the material and qualitative rewards available within the organisation, a successful claim must be made to being independent of other parties, irreplaceable by other parties, and capable of dealing with uncertainties that potentially threaten the survival of the enterprise.

The location of individuals within the administrative structure clearly influences their relative autonomy and their access to rewards, but it is important to note that these structures are not pre-given patterns into which people are simply slotted. Organisational structures are the outcomes of interplay between official and unofficial influences. The organisational structures within which individuals both contribute to organisational performance and pursue sectional interests are in part the outcome of their own initiatives. Pettigrew (1973) showed in his study of organisational decision-making, 'by their ability to exert power over others, individuals can change or maintain structures as well as the norms and expectations upon which these structures rest'. Pettigrew's study shows how the head of a management services department is particularly able to influence key organisational decisions on computerisation through being in a 'gatekeeper' role – one which enabled him to bias the information which reached the formal decision-makers. The effective converting of 'potential power into actual influence' involves a great deal more than being in the right place at the right time, however. It requires considerable skills of 'matching power sources' to the various different situations that arise and the 'drawing on the right mixture of analysis, persuasion, persistence, tact, timing, and charm' (Pettigrew and McNulty 1995).

One of the power sources some organisational actors are able to deploy is specialist functional or professional expertise, making it possible for such specialists simultaneously to enhance the influence of their sub-unit and improve their personal careers. Research in the British personnel management field also observed how it is possible to watch personnel departments 'expand ("empire build") as career advantages and structural uncertainties are brought together by individual personnel specialists who see the need for a job evaluation manager today and a remunerations manager the next' (Watson 1977). Similar issues have been tackled by Armstrong (1986, 1993) in a series of studies of 'professional' functional groups such as engineers, accountants and personnel managers. Armstrong makes the 'structural uncertainties' which provide these groups with opportunities to increase their influence more specific than other theorists and ties them into the interests of 'capital'. He interprets his own and others' research in this area as suggesting that 'there is a link between certain aspects of organisational politics, the process of professionalisation of managerial occupations and changes in the nature and intensity of the crises confronting capitalist enterprises'.

Within these structural circumstances, a considerable range of behaviours which fall under the 'political' heading can be seen to occur. In a biographical case study of a single manager, for example, the following activities were identified (Watson 2006):

- doing mutually advantageous personal deals with particular individuals;
- seeking patrons to help advance one's careers;
- making alliances;
- conspiring;
- mobilising groups and assuming informal leadership roles;
- lying and cheating;
- making strategic retreats;
- using charm and skills of persuasion to get one's own way;
- networking and 'schmoozing';
- talent spotting, selective recruiting and adopting protégés; and
- gathering information that might potentially be used against a rival or otherwise advance one's interests.

The individual in this study was something of an extreme case (chosen for study precisely because of his reputation as a ruthless 'political' animal). This focused research study is balanced and complemented by Buchanan's (2008) much broader survey study of 250 UK managers. This not only suggested that these kinds of behaviour are common but that they are regarded as both necessary and ethical. The survey responses indicate, says Buchanan, 'willingness to engage in politics, the need to act ruthlessly and the appropriateness of reciprocity when faced with political behaviour' – this implying an attitude of 'You stab my back, I'll stab yours'.

Unofficial practices and bureaucratic dysfunctions

Not all unofficial or informal managerial behaviour is primarily concerned with sectional interests. Because of the contradictions and dysfunctions of bureaucratic structures (see p. 147) managers often depart from formal or official procedures to help fulfil rather than compromise the overall goals of the dominant interests in the organisation. To illustrate this we can again refer to Gouldner's (1964) classic study which was used earlier to illustrate the dysfunctional aspects of rule-conformity. The same study illustrates how, conversely, unofficial rule-breaking may in fact help meet the ends which those rules were originally intended to serve. Gouldner noted the existence of an *indulgency pattern*.

Indulgency pattern

The ignoring of selected rule infringements by supervisors in return for those being supervised allowing supervisors to call for co-operation in matters which, strictly speaking, they could refuse.

Here supervisors avoided the potentially negative effects of workers taking certain rules as minimal performance standards by their own demonstrating of flexibility in conniving at the breaking of certain other rules by subordinates. Such a pattern is very common, and team leaders and supervisors frequently find that one of the few devices left to them to obtain flexible and more than grudging co-operation from those they supervisor or 'lead' is to be willing to connive at minor rule infringements. Albie Cooper illustrates this for us in Snapshot 5.13.

Snapshot 5.13

Indulging the team

I am nowadays called a team leader, but I don't think that the job is very different from when I was called the supervisor. When I was first promoted, I realised early on that whatever formal authority I had to tell people what to do and what not to do was very tightly limited. If you simply went 'by the book', giving people formal instructions and punishing them for breaking rules or cutting corners on technical procedures you would soon find them failing to 'play the game' with you. Let's take overtime for instance. It happens every now and again that we get a rush order in the factory, and I have to ask people at very short notice to stay on and do an hour or two's overtime. But the rules say that I should ask people at least two days in advance if I want them to do extra hours. Now, if I was not willing, as I am, to turn a blind eye to some of the overlong tea breaks that they take or to the occasional late arrival at work when the weather is bad, they would simply refuse to stay late – in spite of the very good overtime rates that we pay – without the two days' notice. I could not do the job if I slavishly followed every little rule.

A study of two government agencies by Blau (1963) revealed what he called the *dynamics of bureaucracy* through observing the various ways in which employees avoid what could become 'dysfunctional' aspects of official procedures. 'Procedural adjustments' constitute one form of adaptation in which the officials, when faced with alternative courses of action choose the one more congenial to themselves, typically justifying this choice as the one more in the interests of successful organisational performance. Law enforcement agents, for instance, justified their preference not to obey the rule of officially reporting bribes which were offered to them on the grounds that keeping the offer to themselves gave them a psychological advantage over the offender which would help them complete their investigations. Another tactic is to redefine a rule or procedure in a way which 'deliberately sacrifices the original objective of a procedure in order to achieve another organisational objective more effectively' as in the case of the employment agents who more or less abandoned counselling clients in order to concentrate on getting them speedily placed in jobs. In reaction to this type of unofficial activity, Blau observes, managerial attempts are made to elaborate or 'amplify' procedures. These, in turn, lead to further unofficial adjustments. Here we see an ongoing dialectical relationship between the official and the unofficial aspects of the organisation. In the end, all this helps the functioning of the organisation through accommodating the interests and preferences of employees to the wider purposes of those in charge of the organisation.

Ambiguity and decision processes

It is increasingly being recognised by organisation theorists that social scientists are prone to seeing far more rationality in organisational activities and arrangements, in the sense of fully calculated goal-oriented and purposive thinking, than is justified. As Perrow (1977) put it, 'a great deal of organisational life is influenced by sheer chance, accident and luck';

that most decisions are ambiguous and 'preference orderings incoherent'; that sub-systems are very loosely connected and that 'most attempts at social control are clumsy and unpredictable'.

Bounded rationality

Human reasoning and decision-making is restricted in its scope by the fact that human beings have both perceptual and information-processing limits.

A theoretical starting point for this kind of thinking is often found in the suggestion of Simon (1957) that human rationality is bounded. Human beings can only 'take in' so many data and can only mentally manipulate them to a limited extent. As Weick (1979) expresses it, there is little viewing of all possible circumstances and a criterion of 'sufficiency' is applied with people dealing with the 'here and now in a way which involves least possible effort'. This kind of insight was incorporated into the 'behavioural economics' of Cyert and March (1963) where 'search procedures' are shown to be essentially 'simple-minded' (in that the search for a new solution to a problem stays close to the old solution) and as taking place within the overall process of coalition manoeuvring which constitutes the norm in organisations.

Ambiguity

A state in which the meaning of a situation or an event is unclear or confused and is therefore open to a variety of interpretations.

Ambiguity is significant here. March and Olsen (1976) put their main stress on the ambiguity of organisational situations, arguing that there is typically ambiguity about what objectives are meant to be set; the nature of the technologies which are used; the state of the environment; people's knowledge about the past; the involvement of the individuals working in the organisation – given that people's attention to what is going on varies and the pattern of participation is uncertain and ever-changing. And, because individuals have a range of interests of their own, they come to use decision-making situations or 'choice opportunities' as occasions for doing a lot more than simply making decisions, say March and Olsen. Decision processes are occasions in which people:

- fulfil duties;
- meet commitments;
- justify themselves;
- distribute glory and blame;
- exercise, challenge and re-affirm friendships;
- seek power and status;
- further personal or group interests; and
- simply have a good time and take pleasure in the decision-making process.

On the basis of their study of American universities, which they describe as 'organised anarchies', Cohen *et al.* (1972) developed their 'garbage can model of organisational choice' – a model which continues to be influential decades later (Lomi and Harrison 2012). The decision opportunity operates like a bin because the eventual outcome is a result of what happens to have been thrown into the container. The things that are 'thrown in' include problems which are around at the time, solutions which are available and might be attached to those problems, the people who happen to be around and the amount of time those people have available. On decision-making occasions we therefore get choices looking for problems, issues and feelings looking for decision situations, solutions looking for issues and decision-makers looking for work. All of these factors can be seen in the meeting of the trade union branch committee in Snapshot 5.14.

Snapshot 5.14

The union committee decision bin

There were only five of us at the meeting and the task, at first sight, was a simple one. We had to decide whether or not to recommend to the members of our union branch that we should go on strike in support of the national claim for a general salary rise. Gerry, always our most powerful advocate of strike action tended to see a strike as the solution to any problem of consequence. Strikes, for him, were the solution to most problems, it seemed. We knew that he would pressure all of us to agree to the strike recommendation. Normally, he would be opposed by Sue, who saw withdrawal of labour as the absolute final resort in any dispute. She was also a former girlfriend of Gerry and, for whatever reason, greatly disliked him. However, she was ill that week and was not at the meeting. Her absence was going to make a big difference, making it much more likely that there would be a 'yes' decision than a 'no' one.

Norman was much older than the rest of us, and he loved meetings like these. He would stretch out any meeting for as long as he could and, as Sue always says, he loves the sound of his own voice too much. He started to make one of his interminable speeches soon after the meeting started but was cut short after ten minutes or so by Joe, the regional organiser. Joe had to be at a meeting at another branch that same afternoon, and this meant that he was pressing us for a quick decision. As for me, well, I am really a very indecisive type, and I wanted to hear all the arguments. But, you can guess what happened. After only three-quarters of an hour, we had resolved to recommend strike action to the branch. Gerry and Norman wanted this outcome, and Joe was very keen to make the meeting as quick as possible. This is what happened. Norman got upset at being shut up and said he would go along with whatever the rest felt. I was embarrassed by this, and without Sue there to put the case against action, I decided to 'go with the flow' and say yes.

I am not sure how happy I was with the decision that was made. I was not surprised how it turned out, given who was there that afternoon – and who was not there as well. And, of course, there was the pressure of time and, well that's just how it panned out.

Because there are so many types of garbage being thrown into decision-making situations, conventional rational and analytical processes will have difficulty in coping. Hence, March and Olsen (1976) advocate supplementing the 'technology of reason' with a 'technology of foolishness'. In this, organisational participants relax the normal rules and 'playfully' experiment. Conceptual work of this kind fits with the findings of those who have empirically examined the nature of the work done by managers in organisations.

LOOKING FORWARD >>>>>

This empirical research is examined in Chapter 8, pp. 243–245.

Summary

The most useful way of understanding organisations is to see them as patterns of work activity which are the outcomes – intended and unintended – of social and technical arrangements in which some people conceive of and design work and then recruit, pay, co-ordinate and control the efforts of other people to complete work tasks. In both their structural and their cultural aspects, organisations are much more complex than the 'official' design (represented in the organisation chart and the administrative rule book) would imply. Theoretically, it is more helpful to study organisations within a practice-relational frame of reference. This helps us see that organisations have both official (formal) and unofficial (informal) aspects which are always in interplay with each other. The principles of bureaucracy provide the key design principles of all organisations but the 'paradox of consequences' means that bureaucratic devices never operate in the way originally intended. In spite of this, and in spite of frequent claims that post–bureaucratic or 'network' organisations are emerging, bureaucracy remains at the heart of all organisations. Where variations can be seen is with regard to how tight (mechanistic) or loose (organic) the bureaucracy form is in any given instance – such variations being influenced by the way managers interpret and take into account the various 'contingencies' which affect their particular organisation. The managements of organisations are neither homogenous nor united, however. An inevitable outcome of the way organisations are structured, together with the high degree of ambiguity and uncertainty which pervades organisations is that managers will compete with each other for resources and career advancement. This means that 'micropolitics' are a significant part of the unofficial life of every work organisation.

6 Control and variation in organisational shaping and human resourcing

Key issues

- What basic logic do the managers of corporations follow in the shaping and reshaping of their enterprises?
- What part do 'human resourcing' strategies and practices play in managerial attempts to control organisations and their employees?
- What are the key options facing the managements of organisations in the ways they go about seeking control and flexibility?
- To what extent are there varieties in the design and experiences of call centres?
- What part is played by 'culture change' programmes and 'spirituality' initiatives in contemporary attempts to shape work activities and worker subjectivities?
- What are benefits of looking at organisations' identities and the attempts made to shape these?

Variations in working patterns and the logic of corporate management

The focus of this chapter is on the ways in which the officers of bureaucratic corporations – the managers of organisations – vary the ways in which work is carried out as they strive to exert control over task performance in order to assist the survival of the enterprise that employs them. This striving to achieve a level of *productive co-operation* – the achievement, in the light of the tendency of people involved in organisations to have their own projects, interests and priorities, of a degree of working together that ensures that tasks carried out in the organisation's name are fulfilled to sufficient a level to enable the organisation to continue in existence in a context of competition and power struggle, at every level, across the world.

The underlying logic of managerial work

The managerial control of work is always partial and temporary: the term 'struggle to control' is vitally important here. In their case studies of seven employing organisations, Beynon and his colleagues (2002) showed that the managers implementing changes neither had a clear sense of direction about changes they were bringing about nor a ready capacity to 'meet their desired ends'. They were, rather, 'buffeted this way and that, dealing with uncertainty and risk by displacing it down the organisation – most normally through adjustment of employment policies'. Managers work day-to-day in a context where the survival of the organisation can never be taken for granted, whether it is a profit-oriented business corporation or a public service organisation.

A stress on organisational survival has been increasingly recognised by organisation theorists. One approach has been to see the relationships between organisations and their 'environment' as a matter of natural selection: a fight for survival within the ecological system of which they are a part. In *population ecology* thinking (Hannan and Freeman 1989; Morgan 1990; Baum and Shipilov 2006, Aldrich 2011), organisations are seen as adapting and evolving in order to survive within the organisational population of which they are a part. They go through both planned and unplanned 'variations' in their form, and, largely through processes of competition, the environment 'selects' the form which best suits the organisation. Organisations then 'retain' the form which best suits their particular 'niche' or domain, this retention process including all those normal organisational practices – from the use of operating manuals to socialisation activities – which organisations follow to maintain stability.

The population ecology way of looking at organisations offers useful insights, but it tends to give limited attention to the role of human agency in the way organisations come into being and go out of operation. The important insight that organisations tend to be managed within a strategic logic of fighting for corporate survival in a turbulent and competitive world can nevertheless be retained without treating organisations as if they were biological entities like plants or animals. But why is this survival insight so important? On what grounds can we argue that the logic of corporate management is one of seeking long-term organisational survival? One answer is to point out that it avoids all the difficulties of debating whether the primary goal of businesses is one of maximising profit, growth, return on capital or the creation of human welfare. All of these criteria of corporate effectiveness are relevant to organisational managers operating businesses, but instead of seeing these as alternative criteria that managers apply, they are better understood as means towards the single criterion of survival. Thus, instead of arguing over whether, say, profitability or share of the market is the focus of managerial efforts, we can see both or either of them as important, to varying extents at different times, as means to survival (i.e. not as means in themselves). A similar argument can be applied to a non-business organisation like a hospital: we do not debate whether hospitals are run to cure patients, provide healthy workers for the economy or please the politicians who fund them. Instead, we look at the range of pressures on those in charge of hospitals – of which we have mentioned just a few – and which they have to handle to keep that hospital operating into the future.

The *resource dependence* style of organisational analysis (Pfeffer and Salancik 1978; Watson 1986; Morgan 1990; Hillman *et al.* 2009) examines the role played in the survival of organisations by the *exchanges* or 'trades' which organisations make with all of those parties upon whom it is dependent for survival. We can draw from this a recognition that organisations do not simply compete with other organisations. They also depend on a whole series of other organisations (state, client bodies, pressure groups, trade unions and so on) as well as on various managerial and employee internal constituencies for the supply of resources upon which their continued life depends. Internal micropolitical and industrial relations processes are thus intertwined with market and other macro-political ones. We can identify the logic of corporate management as one of dealing with resource dependence relationships.

The logic of corporate management

The logic of corporate management is one of shaping exchange relationships to satisfy the demands of the various constituencies, inside and outside the organisation, so that continued support in terms of resources such as labour, custom, investment, supplies and legal approval is obtained and the organisation enabled to survive into the long term.

LOOKING BACK <<<<<

The logic of corporate management is an institutional logic in the sense introduced in Chapter 3 and taken up in Chapter 4 where work organisations were characterised as manifestations of the institutional logic of bureaucratic administration. The logics of bureaucratic administration and corporate management operate together, in effect, as 'twin logics', the former having a relatively internal emphasis and the latter a relatively external one. Corporate managers are, technically speaking, bureaucratic officials.

The need to exchange and to follow a survival-based criterion of corporate 'effectiveness' guides the practices of organisational managers: the logic of strategic managerial work is one of setting up and maintaining exchange relationships in such a way that the organisation continues into the future. And a further answer to the earlier question about why it is helpful to conceptualise corporate managerial priorities in terms of long-term survival lies in the vital recognition that it is not a feasible option to run an organisation of any reasonable size as a short-term operation. Little support for an organisation, in its day-to-day or short-term task performance, will be given by either investors or workers if they perceive that the enterprise with which they are involved lacks a secure future. This means that it is better to see the logic of corporate action, not as the making of profits, the curing of patients, the educating of pupils *per se*, but as the satisfying of the demands of resource-supplying constituencies to the level below which the constituencies would withdraw resources from the organisation and thus threaten its survival. Such a logic is recognised by Andrew Swan, the Chief Executive of a commercial organisation in Snapshot 6.1.

Snapshot 6.1

Keeping the Liffatec show on the road?

When I reflect on what I do as the Chief Executive of Liffatec, I recognise that I and my company are part of a much bigger scheme of things. We operate within a particular economic system with its markets, its patterns of wealth, its broadly capitalist culture and so on. That system both constrains what we do and gives us opportunities to do new things. Yeah? If we don't play to those rules, we get pushed off the scene. All that's very clear to me. OK? But when it comes to running a company – and this is the third one I've been in charge of – it's much more a matter of constantly paying attention to all the different people that we deal with to make sure we – how can I put it? – 'keep them sweet' so that they continue to 'do business' with us. Pretty obviously it's the customers that are always at the fronts of our minds. If we don't give them what they want, they won't give us what we want: their money. But it actually doesn't feel very different when it comes to dealing with the shareholders. If we don't give them the rate of return that they want, well, you know what happens: they withdraw their investment and – kaput! So obviously profitability is vital – but from my position sitting in the driving seat, it is just one of the balls that I have to keep in the air if I am going to keep the business going – keep the show on the road, you might say. The people who work for us also want things from the firm – so we trade with them, in effect, in the same way that we trade with the customers and our suppliers. And there's no way I can give any of these different people (some people call them 'stakeholders' but it's not a term I like) everything they want – shareholders included. I give them what I have to give them to be sure that they continue to 'do business' with us. And I suppose it's just the same with how we deal with the tax people, the press and all the rest.

Corporate effectiveness is best understood as a contingent matter (a matter of the circumstances in which it finds itself). It is not an essential quality that an organisation either possesses or lacks. At particular times, certain groups would have more 'pull' than others so that managements have to deal first with the most *strategic constituency* – with the one that is currently perceived as creating the highest level of strategic uncertainty. And, as we shall now see, the extent to which the various employee constituencies within an organisation are managerially perceived to be sources of greater or lesser uncertainty, is a major factor influencing the type of employment or 'human resourcing' strategy that is followed.

Managerial choices in these matters, we must remind ourselves at this point, can all be understood in terms of the pursuit of *control*. Poole *et al.* (2005) show that their surveys of managers' attitudes over the years have shown continuity in the concern of managers to resist to control being taken from them, whether it be by the state, at one level, or domestic trade union activity at the workplace level. In spite of this, Child (2005) has observed that although 'control is an essential and central process of management', it is 'strangely neglected by many writers on organizations'. Indeed, 'without (some form of) control organising is not possible; notions of "structuring", "job design" and "co-ordination" are redolent of control' (Delbridge and Ezzamel 2005). It is important to note the phrase 'some form of control' here. This, we can infer, is a recognition of the point made earlier in this chapter that managerial control is something that can never be fully achieved.

Choice and circumstance in the shaping of employment or 'human resourcing' practices

The struggle to control the activities which occur within employing organisations has at its heart a struggle to control the labour 'input'. As Marchington *et al,* (2004) emphasise, not only is it necessary to bring together concepts and evidence from organisation studies and employment studies to understand what is occurring, it also is vital to avoid seeing changes in work arrangements arising simply as a result of global competition and technological changes. It is vital to pay attention to the balance of *power* between employer and employer interests, across organisations as well as within them. It is also necessary to recognise that the twenty-first century has seen, in White *et al.*'s (2004) terms, a 'cultural revolution' in management. These writers found from their case study research that management, at least in the more successful organisations, 'no longer waits around for changes to hit them'. Change is continuously promoted in organisations, be they large or small organisations, business enterprises or government departments and agencies. Relations with labour are central to this.

Labour or human resource 'inputs' into organisations are clearly not equivalent to inputs of gas, electricity or raw materials. To achieve sufficient productive co-operation between people involved in completing work tasks, appropriate *relationships* have to be established between employers and employees and constructive bargains over efforts and rewards struck.

LOOKING FORWARD >>>>>

The nature of employment relations, the role of institutional tensions and conflicts and processes of negotiation are examined in detail in Chapter 8.

At this stage, as we concentrate on managerial initiatives, as opposed to bargained outcomes, we see that there are important variations of managerial strategy with regard to employees. This is recognised in labour process analysis. It has come to the fore, however, with academic interest in human resource management (HRM). We will look at each of these approaches to understanding variations and try to reach some conclusions on the relationship between managerial choices and structural circumstances in how variations in patterns of employer–worker relationship come about.

Labour processes and employment practice options

Having recognised that managements may follow different control strategies with regard to their employees, we are left with the question of which circumstances lead to the adoption of which type of strategy. One approach to answering this question has been that developed by theorists in the labour process tradition who wanted to develop a more subtle and 'dialectical' approach to analysing capitalist labour processes which affords much greater recognition of the challenge offered to employers by organised labour than was the case in Braverman's (1974) seminal work.

LOOKING BACK <<<<<

Labour process analysis is discussed in Chapter 3, pp. 70–73.

It is argued that managerial activity should be understood not as straightforwardly imposing upon employees the work tasks 'required by capital' but as engaging in a competition for control with employees, albeit in the same long-term interests of the owners of capital. Friedman (1977) showed how some employees are better able than others to resist managerial controls, and hence deskilling. Here the emphasis is on the longer-term aspect of the capitalist profit motive and it is stressed that the managerial treatment of labour and the way jobs are designed may vary according to the circumstances. Working on the assumption that managements operate in the ultimate interests of long-term profitability, he introduces what, in Chapter 5, we called the 'contingency insight' and suggests that management may choose either:

- a *direct-control strategy* which is consistent with Taylorist deskilling policies, or
- a *responsible autonomy strategy* in which employees are allowed a degree of discretion and responsibility in their work.

This latter approach is followed where management fear that the introduction of Taylorist controls would risk a loss of what they see as necessary goodwill. Workers who are central to long-term profitability, in that they have skills, knowledge or union power which renders their opposition dangerous, have to be treated carefully and are therefore candidates for responsible-autonomy treatment. Peripheral workers, on the other hand, who are less critical to longer-term profitability, can be more directly controlled. Their work is much more vulnerable to deskilling and 'degradation'.

HRM and 'high-commitment' and 'low-commitment' options

The term 'human resource management' has gained increasing currency over the past two decades. However, the term is used rather confusingly. Sometimes it is used to refer to all kinds of employment management or labour management and sometimes it is used to refer to a 'new' kind of employment management. The former is the most useful way of proceeding, it is suggested. This means treating HRM as 'a broad generic term equivalent to "labor management"' (Boxall 2007) recognising, as Kaufmann (2007) puts it, that 'viewed as a generic activity involving the management of other people's labor in production, human resource management (HRM) goes back to the dawn of human history'. We therefore provide a generic definition of HRM.

> ### Human resource management (HRM)
>
> The managerial utilisation of the efforts, knowledge, capabilities and committed behaviours which people contribute to work organisations as part of an employment exchange (or more temporary contractual arrangement) to bring about the completion of work tasks in a way which enables the organisation to continue into the future.

If we conceptualise HRM in this way, it becomes possible to locate what is sometimes called the 'new HRM paradigm' as a particular variety of the generic HRM phenomenon – a distinctive way of approaching the employment aspects of work organisation which emerged in the later twentieth century. In the later part of the twentieth century. The idea of a 'new' HRM, which was often contrasted with the 'old' personnel management, originated with various American academic commentators (Tichy *et al.* 1982; Beer and Spector 1985; Walton 1985), and was later taken up by British academic researchers (Storey 1989, 1992; Hendry and Pettigrew 1990; Guest 1991; Legge 1995). Jacques (1999) identifies three themes in this new approach: 'comprehensive as opposed to patchwork direction of the human function in organisations; linking operational HR issues to the firm's strategy and structure; learning to regard expenditures on labor and worker-embodied knowledge as an investment rather than an expense'.

The 'new' HRM phenomenon is, as Storey (2001) put it, 'an amalgam of description, prescription, and logical deduction' and it is based on the assumption that 'it is human capability and commitment which in the final analysis distinguishes successful organisations from the rest' and that,

LOOKING BACK <<<<<

The claim that the 'new paradigm' HRM represents, in effect, a 'post-personnel management' era in employment relations is directly parallel to and closely connected to the argument that 'new' forms of organisation represent a 'post-bureaucratic' shift. This was criticised in Chapter 5. The 'new' HRM can more usefully be seen as a variant of the old styles of employment or labour management in the same way that 'hybrid forms' were identified in Chapter 5 as variants of standard bureaucracy.

therefore 'the human resource ought to be nurtured as a valued asset'. But the single feature that distinguishes these 'new HRM' approaches from earlier ones is their concern with nurturing a high level of psychological and social commitment towards the employing organisation on the behalf of the workforce (Walton 1985). To avoid all the difficulties that arise with the notion of HRM as some kind of new managerial paradigm (Watson 2004, 2010), it is useful to bring a focus to the issue of choice of managerial strategy in the employment area by utilising this distinction between high- and low-commitment approaches and identifying two *ideal types* of human resourcing strategy, as we see in Table 6.1.

LOOKING BACK <<<<<

The *ideal type* was an analytical device used by Max Weber, and it is a model of an aspect of the social world which extracts the essential or 'pure' elements of that phenomenon. It shows us what, say, capitalism or bureaucracy would look like if it were to exist in a pure form – as we saw in the case of bureaucracy in Chapter 5. A useful technique which will be used several times in the present book – with Table 6.1 being the first occasion of its use – is to create pairs of ideal types which can be envisaged as two ends of a continuum. 'Real' HR strategies (Table 6.1) or patterns of work design (Tables 6.2 and 6.3) fall at various points along these continuums. These paired ideal types, it must stressed, are not the type of dualistic categories into which some writers force social phenomena (Williams 2007).

No 'actual' organisation follows either of these impossibly 'pure' types. But a significant way in which organisations differ from each other is in the extent to which they lean towards one of these pure types or the other. And the matter of which end of the continuum between the two types any particular organisation will lean towards is likely to be influenced by the values and preferences of strategic managers but, as we saw in Chapter 4 with regard to organisational design choices, these

Table 6.1 Two ideal type human resourcing strategies

High-commitment human resourcing strategies	Low-commitment human resourcing strategies
Employers seek a close relationship with workers who become psychologically or emotionally involved with the enterprise. Opportunities for personal and career development are built into people's employment, which is expected to continue over a longer-term period and potentially to cover a variety of different tasks.	Employers acquire labour inputs at the point when it is immediately needed. Workers are allocated to tasks for which they need very little training, with the employment being terminated as soon as those tasks have been completed. The organisation-worker relationship is an 'arms-length' and calculatingly instrumental one.
Work tasks are *indirectly* controlled: workers are given discretion about how tasks are carried out.	Work tasks are *directly* controlled: workers are closely supervised and monitored.

choices are very much constrained by circumstances and organisational 'contingencies'.

LOOKING BACK <<<<<

It was pointed out in Chapter 5 when we examined the dual role of contingencies and strategic choice in the shaping of work organisations that the level of uncertainty that managers see arising in their organisation's circumstances is an important factor in pushing them towards the adoption of either a tightly bureaucratised structure and culture (when uncertainties are perceived as low) or a loosely bureaucratised structure and culture (when uncertainties are perceived as high). A corresponding analysis can be applied to the approach that is taken to managerial relationships with employee groups.

In the final analysis, what encourages managers to move in one strategic HRM direction rather than the other is the fact that a low-commitment type of human resourcing strategy (combined with the 'direct controls' which we will shortly look at more closely) is probably more appropriate to a situation where employees are not a major source of strategic uncertainty for the employing organisation, and a high–commitment strategy (combined with indirect controls) is likely to be more helpful in dealing with employees if those employees do create uncertainties for corporate management. If, for example, an organisation has a simple technology and a relatively straightforward business environment that makes workers easily obtainable and replaceable, that organisation will not require a highly participative set of working practices. However, if the future of an organisation appears to managers to be at risk if they do not meet the much higher demands that might follow from employing a highly skilled or educated workforce to operate a complex technology or deal with an especially tricky business environment, they are more likely to lean towards a high-commitment employment strategy. In this type of situation, workers are not easy to obtain or replace and thus relatively sophisticated employment practices are needed to attract them to the organisation and encourage them to stay and work creatively and flexibly towards corporate purposes. Figure 6.1 adapts the model introduced in Chapter 4 for analysing broad organisational shapes and practices to focus on the employment strategy dimension.

Figure 6.1 recognises that managerial discretion and micropolitical debate about choice of human resourcing strategy occurs, first, in the context of technological, market and other contingencies and, second, in the context of local, national and global structures and cultures (Watson 2010; Bratton and Gold 2015). To understand what goes on in any specific work organisation, it is vital to get inside the 'black box of HRM' in that particular setting and examine the complexities of the relationship between formal HR policies, mediating factors and actual outcomes (Boxall *et al.* 2011). Nevertheless, HRM is, as Janssens and Steyaert (2009) put it, a 'set of practices, embedded in a global economical, political and socio-cultural context'. And it has been argued that these global factors are increasingly dominating the national-level and more immediate contingency ones. Thompson's (2003) 'disconnected capitalism' thesis, for example, argues that the increasing emphasis on increasing shareholder value, on top of financial deregulation and market globalisation trends, significantly limits managers' ability to choose high-commitment or indirect control strategies. Short-term pressures to produce returns to investors on capital markets undermines the more considered relationships which previously existed with UK and US national business systems. And these tendencies are exacerbated according to Clark (2009), as what he calls the 'private equity business model' creates circumstances in which 'the interests of owners are now paramount . . . to the relative exclusion of other stakeholders'. Research by Bacon *et al.* (2008), focusing on managerial buyouts in the UK and Holland, suggests a considerably smaller impact of private equity on HRM. An international comparative study by Morris *et al.* (2008), however, confirms the intensification of 'shareholder capitalism' in the USA and notes a shift in Japan in this direction (away from the normal Japanese 'managerial capitalism'). When it comes to the matter of Japanese 'progressive' HRM practices, however, Morris *et al.* find that these have been largely retained. This suggests that managerial options are not totally overridden by the pressures of global capital. In fact, the pressures of global restructuring may *increase* rather than decrease managerial interest in high-commitment HRM practices. Roe *et al.* (2009) suggest precisely this: that organisational commitment has become a more important issue for organisations since 'shareholder interest took dominance over employee interests' because of the 'increasing degree of estrangement of employees from their employing organizations'. These authors also point to the pressures coming from the 'contingency' factor of employees' education and qualification levels. This increases managerial dependency on employees and hence encourages them to take high-commitment measures.

We can see some of the factors identified in Figure 6.1 in an account that Andrew Swan (whom we met earlier) gives us in Snapshot 6.2 of strategic choices at Liffatec.

We see in Snapshot 6.2 a clash of values between Andrew and his HR director, Angela Hurn. More significant, however, is the difference between the 'contingencies' that apply in the case of Liffatec and the contingencies that applied in the case of Angela's former company (and appear to apply to the company to which she has now moved). Also coming into play are political–economic and cultural issues, in the form of the availability of relatively compliant migrant labour in the area.

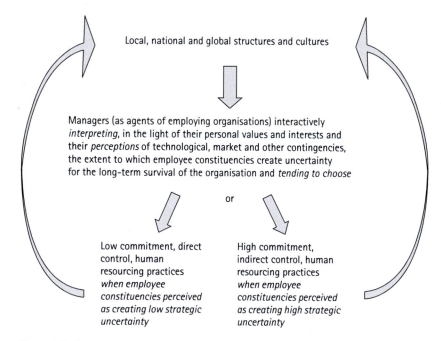

Figure 6.1 Choices and constraints in the shaping of organisational human resourcing practices

HR strategy-making at Liffatec

One of the most difficult things I had to decide about when I took over running Liffatec was the basic approach we were going to take towards our labour force. A new HR director had been appointed not long before I came on board. Angela Hurn was a very capable person who had previously worked in a high-tech business and built an excellent reputation. But we clashed rather badly over the extent we should introduce into Liffatec all the consultative, teamworking and what she called 'high-commitment' things that had worked so well in her previous company. Her main argument was that this was both the morally 'good' way to treat human beings and the most effective way, in terms of getting them to do a really good job. Now, I tried not to get into too many arguments with Angela about morality. But we seriously differed on the extent to which, as I used to put it to her, we have to be hard-headed in the business world. As I told you earlier, I see employees as just one of the groups that the business 'trades' with. You reward them only up to the level that you need to in order to keeping them providing you with the quantity and quality of labour that you need. In Angela's former company, they had to use very skilled labour, and they had to work hard to get everyone to contribute to the constant innovations that had to be introduced to stay ahead of the market. If I had been running that business, I would have supported all these progressive HR things that Angela favoured. But, as I kept saying to Angela, we simply did not need to 'invest' in people to the same extent in Liffatec. Our products are much simpler, and the main job that the workers do is one of putting together the little modules that we buy-in into our own casings. It only takes a few days to train people to do this work, and in our area, there are plenty of East European workers willing and able to come and do exactly what we instruct them to do. So, as far as I am concerned, we don't have a big problem with labour, and we don't have to spend all the time and effort that Angela wanted to put into 'developing' people and setting up teams and things. In the end, she left the company, and I now have a much lower-key HR manager doing things that work perfectly for us. I'm pleased to say, though, that Angela is back in the high-tech world where the sort of HR policies she favours are very necessary.

In Figure 6.1, the choice between low- and high-commitment human resourcing strategies is closely linked to a choice between what are identified as 'direct' and 'indirect' controls. This latter choice is central to issues of flexibility and managerial control generally, as we shall now see.

The pursuit of flexibility and direct and indirect managerial control options

Given the international dynamics of modern industrial capitalism, the shifting patterns of demand for goods and services and the innovative potential of information technologies, it can be argued that those economies and those work organisations which are going to perform relatively well in terms of generally accepted industrial capitalist criteria will be those whose work and employment institutions are the more responsive or flexible and are thus better able than their rivals to innovate. However, the concept of flexibility has tended to conflate a variety of different organisational innovations, and as Putnam *et al.* (2014) point out, research findings reveal 'tensions and contradictions in the ways that employees, managers and organizations develop, enact and respond to these flexibility initiatives'. To avoid any tendency to identify a single phenomenon of 'flexibility', it is helpful to recognise that there are, in practice, two quite different types of flexibility: flexibility for short-term predictability and flexibility for long-term adaptability.

Flexibility for short-term predictability

The ability to make rapid changes through the use of job designs and employment policies that allow staff to be easily recruited and trained or easily laid off – as circumstances require.

This fits with *direct control* managerial practices (and low-commitment styles of HRM).

Flexibility for long-term adaptability

The ability to make rapid and effective innovations through the use of job designs and employment policies that encourage people to use their discretion, innovate and work in new ways for the sake of the organisation – as circumstances require.

This fits with *indirect control* managerial practices (and high-commitment styles of HRM).

The emphasis put by any given organisation on either flexibility for predictability or flexibility for adaptability (or a mix of the two) will vary with the circumstances and policies of each employing organisation. And this variation can be understood in terms of a leaning towards either direct control or indirect control managerial practices – two alternative emphases in the ways managers attempt to maintain control over work activities, represented as two ideal types in Table 6.2.

Associated with these two approaches to control at the level of the whole organisation are two sets of principles for work design at the level of task performance. These are set out in Table 6.3.

Table 6.2 Direct and indirect approaches in the pursuit of managerial control

Direct control attempts	Indirect control attempts
• Close supervision and monitoring of activities	• 'Empowerment' and discretion applied to activities
• Tight rules	• Loose rules
• Highly prescribed procedures	• Flexible procedures
• Centralised structures	• Decentralised structures
• Low-commitment culture	• High-commitment culture
• Low-trust culture	• High-trust culture
• Adversarial culture	• Culture of mutual interests
• A tightly bureaucratic structure and culture	• A loosely bureaucratic structure and culture

Table 6.3 Direct and indirect work design principles

Direct control work design principles	Indirect control work design principles
• Jobs are deskilled and fragmented.	• Jobs are whole, skilled and 'rich'.
• 'Doing' is split off from 'thinking', the latter being done elsewhere.	• 'Doing and thinking' is combined in the job.
• The worker has a single skill.	• The worker has a range of skills.
• The worker does the same task most of the time.	• The worker does different tasks at different times.
• The worker has little choice over pace or order of task completion.	• The worker has choice over the pace and order of task completion.
• The worker is closely supervised.	• Workers supervise themselves.
• The quality of work is checked by an 'inspector'.	• Workers are responsible for their own quality.
• If there is a group dimension to the work, the supervisor allocates roles and monitors the workgroup's performance.	• If there is a group dimension to the work, the workers operate as a team with members allocating roles and monitoring team performance.

The factors which influence managerial choice of one approach to gaining control or the other are the same ones identified in Chapter 5 (Figure 5.1), as 'fitting' with relatively tightly bureaucratised structures and cultures or relatively loosely bureaucratised structures and cultures, respectively. They are also the same factors identified earlier in this chapter as 'fitting' either a low-commitment or a high-commitment human resourcing strategy. Thus, for example, an organisation with a simple technology, a stable market and a steady supply of labour, would be more likely to seek flexibility for predictability. If, however, the nature of the product, technology, market situation and the rest were such that long-term survival depended much more on the active commitment and initiative-taking of employees, then the emphasis would be on flexibility for adaptability.

In practice, most organisations are likely to experience pressures for both types of flexibility and their managers would have to handle the tension between them. This tension can be very significant as Snapshot 6.3 shows.

Snapshot 6.3

Two types of flexibility in a telecommunications company

In an ethnographic study of a telecommunications company (Watson 2001a), the high-tech nature of the business and its need for significant innovation to achieve long-term survival led to the pursuit of 'flexibility for adaptability' through a major culture-change programme together with a range of indirect control innovations in order to gain the long-term commitment and creative enthusiasm of employees. However, the corporation owning the company closely monitored costs and regularly insisted on reducing the numbers of employees to achieve certain accounting ratios. The effect of this imposition of a pursuit of flexibility for predictability was to undermine the pursuit of flexibility for adaptability because it created a sense of insecurity across the workforce and undermined the type of high-trust relations upon which flexibility for adaptability depends.

Flexibility and changing work control practices

Much of the pressure on managements to increase the flexibility of their organisations in the 1980s came from perceived competitive threats from Japan, primarily to enterprises involved in manufacturing. Competition from Japan came to provide a symbolic focus for many of the changes coming about both within the private manufacturing sector and beyond it, in spite of the fact many of the claims made for Japanese innovations are somewhat 'mythic' (Coffey 2006). Although these developments can be seen as an extension of Fordist principles, rather than an overturning of them (Beynon and Nichols 2006), Kenney and Florida (1993) heralded them as a new form of labour process at the heart of which was the use of team commitment and effort to achieve innovation mediated production. Team pressure not only encourages people to work harder but to improve continuously both products and processes, as well as develop new ones. The term high-performance work systems is often used in the USA to refer to the bundling together of workplace practices which differ from mass production regimes (Applebaum *et al.* 2000).

> ### High-performance work systems
>
> High discretion, skill and collaborative problem-solving is applied in a team-oriented way and is rewarded with relatively high pay, security and the provision of high-quality training.

The indirect control attempts at the heart of these practices are, as we saw earlier, closely associated with the 'high-commitment' style of human resource management. They involve 'high–dependency relationships' between managers and workers, something also central to just-in-time (JIT) and Total Quality Management (TQM).

> ### Just-in-time (JIT) production processes
>
> A way of organising production processes so that no buffer stocks are held in the factory, with materials and components only being delivered immediately before they are required.

JIT arrangements mean that production is vulnerable to disruption and this makes necessary the maintenance of stable employment relations and flexible and co-operative behaviour on the part of workers. TQM requires the building of a commitment to continuous improvement of processes and the quality of the product. This makes the manufacturing system further dependent on employees' positive attachment to the employer.

> ### Total Quality Management (TQM)
>
> An approach to the production of goods and services in which employees at all levels focus on 'satisfying customers', use statistical and other techniques to monitor their work and seek continuous improvement in the processes used and the quality of what is produced.

Many of the innovations in the area of quality improvement have been primarily associated with detailed changes of practice at the level of production processes and their full implications only emerge when they are linked to broader changes in organisational cultures and human resourcing practices. This relates to the point made earlier in this chapter that TQM, like JIT, creates a higher level of dependence on employee constituencies than more traditional approaches to manufacturing. Successful implementation of these practices is thus dependent on a shift towards the more 'high–commitment' style of human resource strategy discussed previously. In practice, the fulfilment of the espoused TQM values of 'autonomy, participation, responsibility and trust' are precluded by being introduced within an employment context 'characterised by job insecurity, hierarchical power relations, attempts by management to secure control, reduce costs and enhance short-term profitability' (Knights and McCabe 1998). Nevertheless, what is often called 'world class manufacturing' is distinctive in the way principles are brought together into 'a new, mutually reinforcing, whole'. Hence, JIT 'places a premium on right-first-time' and the continuous improvement theme of TQM 'requires involvement from everyone and some form of team-working'. Teamworking, in turn, 'implies a need for flexibility, while flexibility means a better trained and more competent workforce'.

Teamworking and control

Teamworking has existed as long as there have been situations in which people have worked together in a co-operative manner to complete work tasks. But 'management-initiated' teams 'have become the hallmark of contemporary organizational practice' (Hodson 2010). The concept nevertheless covers a range of possibilities; it has what Buchanan (2000) calls 'plasticity' so that, as Procter and Mueller (2000) put it, 'teamwork is intrinsically indefinable, adopting different expressions over time and in different contexts'. In spite of this, one can attempt a conceptualisation which recognises that whilst work 'teams' do indeed range from ones in which the choices left to team members are very circumscribed to ones in which there is a considerable degree of freedom about how to act, there is always implicit in the notion a degree of freedom of co-operative choice-making.

> **Teamworking**
>
> A form of group-based work activity in which a degree of discretion is left to group members, acting in a co-operative manner, about how they perform the tasks allocated to them.

A 'team' could thus be a group of senior managers in charge of a large enterprise (a 'top team' as some management writers would have it) or it could be half a dozen retail workers who are left by a shop manager to take a joint responsibility for ensuring that customers are served according to who is available at the time, without the manager having to direct particular workers towards particular customers. A study in the German engineering industry carried out by Saurwein (Minssen 2006) found nearly half of the companies surveyed claiming to be using teams in their production processes. Yet when this was examined more closely, it transpired that only 3 per cent of the companies were following the full teamworking principles associated with the notion of the semi-autonomous workgroup.

The idea of the semi-autonomous workgroup was derived from Tavistock Institute's notion of the organisation as a *socio-technical system*.

Socio-technical systems

An approach to work design in which the technical and the social/psychological aspects of the overall workplace are given equal weight and are designed at the same time to *take each other into account.*

Socio-technical systems thinking discourages managers from designing a technology and then fitting a social organisation to it and, instead, encourages them to devise each of these alongside the other in order jointly to optimise the two. It is assumed that the precise technical form required to achieve tasks is variable, as is the social structure to accompany it. Both can therefore be chosen to get the best fit, one with the other.

Snapshot 6.4

Coal and organisational choice: a classic study

Trist *et al.* (1963) showed how technical innovations introduced in post-war British coal mines failed to give either the social and psychological satisfactions traditionally expected by miners or the levels of productivity and uninterrupted working sought by management. This was because the technical pattern of such things as new occupational roles and the shift arrangements associated with new machinery took away the relative autonomy of work-groups and removed the opportunity for the coal miner to use a variety of skills. The researchers devised a different approach to the use of new machinery which allowed retention of some of the traditional features of the social and cultural arrangements preferred by miners. A better fit having been obtained between the social and technical arrangements, there was said to be a marked improvement in productivity, worker–management co-operation and absenteeism levels. And at the heart of this approach, in practice, was the semi-autonomous work-group.

In the semi-autonomous work-group tasks are grouped together to form a logical 'whole task' which can be performed with minimal interference.

Semi-autonomous workgroups

A work-group or 'team' in which individual jobs are grouped to focus work activities on an overall 'whole task', with group members being fully trained and equipped so that they can be given discretion over how the task is completed.

The work designer attempts to devise 'a group consisting of the smallest number that can perform a whole task and can satisfy the social and psychological needs of its members', this being 'alike from the point of view of task performance and of those performing it, the most satisfactory and efficient group' (Rice 1958). A parallel movement towards devising work-groups organised around 'whole tasks' which can be carried out relatively autonomously was a 'group technology' approach increasingly initiated by work engineers. Typically, workplaces were rearranged so that machines (or desks) are grouped together not on the basis of their doing similar work (drilling, grinding, invoicing or whatever) but on the basis of a contribution to a certain product or service. Thus a group of people all involved in making, say, small turbine blades or dealing with house insurance are brought together in such a way that greater integration is obtained and a greater degree of job satisfaction is facilitated by members' greater relative autonomy and through their productive co-operation with colleagues.

Some of these principles can be seen within modular or *cellular* work organisation arrangements, in which people and machines are grouped around information or product flows and in which these 'cells' are, to a greater or less extent, integrated with statistical quality controls and strategic manufacturing management accounting. In this approach, sometimes labelled MSE (manufacturing systems engineering), cells have a degree of independence from each other and from the organisation as a whole which not only reinforces identification of the team with their own product or service but also increases the flexibility of the whole organisation.

For some time, there has been a polarisation in the literature on modern teamworking innovations, as Geary and Dobbins (2001) noted at the height of the notion's popularity, with managerially oriented 'optimistic' writers pointing to the ways in which workers would benefit from becoming empowered teamworkers and more pessimistic critical observers arguing that managerial motivations were essentially directed towards the 'intensification' of workers' efforts. Geary and Dobbins then identify a trend towards a 'more nuanced and context-sensitive understanding' of these matters which recognises both the costs and the benefits of teamworking and other innovations to all the parties involved, the balance which these benefits take varying from circumstance to circumstance (Edwards et al. 2001; Knights and McCabe 2003, for example). This is labelled a 're-regulation' point of view and Geary and Dobbins' own case study is interpreted within this perspective. They observed in their case study company that whilst there was clear evidence of 'considerable intensification of effort and pressure levels', many workers actually welcomed the new pressures placed upon them. This supported the findings of an earlier study of TQM innovations by Collinson *et al.* (1997), in which workers were observed to appreciate the experience of working harder, given that it was occurring in a context of a welcome sense of order and direction in the workplace that had come about with the re-organisation of work.

How changes in work management regimes are experienced by workers is something that has to be analysed in the light of the complex set of factors that influence the meanings that people attach to their work. The importance of these orientations to work is something that we will return to at the end of this chapter. Nevertheless, as Harley (2001) stressed, after noting the limited survey evidence of any clear link between the adoption of teamworking and 'positive' employee experiences, 'unless teams entail a fundamental reconfiguration of dominant patterns of work organisation' (challenging, that is, hierarchical structures of power and influence in organisations and society) then 'they are unlikely to make a difference to employee discretion and via this to orientations to work'. Such a view is supported by Hodson's (2010) examination of 254 ethnographic workplace studies in which teamworking was introduced. The balance of power in these work settings was 'pivotal'. Positive outcomes for employees were observed, for instance, when there was trade union involvement ensuring that both job satisfaction and effort could 'be maximized by bargaining for job security and for the provision of the resources needed by employees to do their jobs effectively'. By the same token, teamwork innovations tended to 'backfire' on managers who acted in an 'abusive' or exploitative manner.

Problems are likely to arrive when teams contain individuals coming from rival status groups within an organisation. Finn's (2008) ethnographic study of the adoption of teamworking principles in an operating theatre showed 'rather than unifying the professions, teamwork produces unintended divisive effects'. The professional groups working in the theatre discursively constructed 'different versions of team work' and made 'competing legitimacy claims' with the result that 'the privileged position' of surgeons and anaesthetists over nurses and other staff' was 'legitimated and maintained'.

When we turn to the relationship between teamworking and organisational performance, a review by Delarue *et al.* (2008) of the survey-based research literature suggests there is a positive link between teamwork and 'operational or financial outcomes. Further, most of the studies which examined the link between employee behavioural and attitudinal outcomes found teamworking leading to 'improvement' – something which was also related to the incorporating of teamwork into wider structural changes.

Lean production, downsizing and delayering

What is clear from the range of research available to us is that, although many of the newer approaches to the organising of work incorporate elements of indirect controls and high-commitment employment practices to bring about 'flexibility for adaptability', they nevertheless also have built in elements of tight and direct control to ensure the degree of 'flexibility for predictability' – these being most obvious in the task schedules arising from the pressures of just in time logistics. This mixture of direct and indirect controls is most obviously a characteristic of the *lean production* approach to car assembly (Womack et al. 1990; see also Beynon and Nichols 2006). But 'lean', as one of 'the world's most influential management ideas' is 'now widely promoted for use in public administration' (McCann *et al.* 2015), especially in the health care sector (Radnor *et al.* 2012).

Lean production

A combining, typically within the car industry, of teamworking with automated technologies. Workers are required both to initiate 'continual improvements' in quality and to ensure that every task is got 'right first time' and completed to a demanding 'just-in-time' schedule.

A 'lean' organisation has a tight managerial in which no time, resource or effort is allowed to be wasted. Yet workers are required to give a positive psychological commitment to this regime and to use their discretion enthusiastically within the spaces where this is allowed in order to 'benefit the customer'. On the basis of his detailed case study, Danford (1998a, 1998b) points to the contradiction between an increased level of labour exploitation through directly controlled teamworking and nurturing a committed and 'co-operative' workforce. This contradiction 'creates as many new potential conflicts and management problems as it resolves'. Yet, as Storey and Harrison (1999) showed, there is evidence of the adoption of 'world class manufacturing' practices enabling companies to become internationally competitive, with this sometimes leading to the 'degradation' of the worker experience and sometimes to its 'liberalisation' – the general direction followed being an outcome of a range of factors varying from labour market conditions, level of unionisation, organisational and technological factors and 'the underlying intent of management'. This suggests that lean production and similar operational management practices must be developed alongside HRM innovations. On the evidence of the first longitudinal study of the integration of operations management and HRM practices in British manufacturing, De Menezes *et al.* (2010) indeed show that such integration 'results in superior firm performance'. What gives this advantage, they suggest, is that these businesses are operating with a clear and integrated managerial philosophy, one which highlights 'the importance of continuous improvement and learning that is often allied to the lean production concept'.

In the USA, Milkman's (1997) study of a General Motors plant pointed to a tendency within 'new' production regimes towards a polarisation of skilling and experience within the workforce, with skilled male workers improving their position and production line workers experiencing a worsening. But, as Delbridge's (1998) British ethnography showed, whilst workers in these situations may not directly and overtly challenge heightened managerial controls, they nevertheless develop their own localised workplace controls as part of a low-key resistance to intensified labour exploitation. In a detailed study of changes at the Sochaux plant of Peugeot, Durand and Hatzfeld (2003) characterised the 'lean' innovations of ergonomic reform, tightened jobs times and devolution of worker responsibilities in terms of 'frugal modernisation', noting that, although workers emphasised continuity with the past, they nevertheless found that ergonomic changes did make work tasks lighter and that they were taking greater responsibility for quality. However, with tighter monitoring of their efforts, they struggled to find areas of relative autonomy which could give them scope for a degree of local informal bargaining with managers.

Sometimes accompanying moves towards lean production and sometimes completely independent of it, many organisations have undergone structural changes which have implications for both operations management and HRM. In their UK study, White *et al.* (2004) distinguished between two groups of organisational strategies. The first group included downsizing (reducing the workforce and increasing of the 'outsourcing' of work) and delayering (reducing the number of management grades – flattening the organisation to increase individual responsibility). Both of these tended to occur together but were independent of the strategies in the second group: high performance/high commitment ('various combinations of communications/participation, teamworking, skills/ development and incentives practices'); high-benefits strategy ('various combinations of both traditional fringe benefits and of family-friendly policies) and high-tech strategy (transforming administration and operations through extensive use of ICT). This second set of strategies tended to occur together. And what is especially interesting is that it was common for managements to pursue both the two groups of strategies, in spite of the fact that they might be seen as incompatible – as indeed they proved to be in the telecommunications factory case study we discussed earlier (in Snapshot 5.14).

The complexities and mixed messages that are apparent in all of this can be understood in part as reflecting the fact that employing organisations continuously face pressure for both the two main types of flexibility – flexibility for predictability and for adaptability. But there are other factors too – ones of a more society-wide nature. Some of these emerge in the attempt made by Gallie *et al.* (2004) to make sense of the fact that survey evidence shows a significant decline in task discretion in Britain in the 1990s – in spite of the fact that there was a rise in skill levels (which was indeed associated with high task discretion) and an increase in practices such as semi-autonomous teams, quality circles and consultative committees (which, again, produced higher levels of task discretion). To explain this, Gallie *et al.* (2004) point to 'macro type' factors rather than ones that are specific to individual organisations. In the private sector, there was growing international competitiveness, with particular pressure on delivery times – this pressure leading to 'marked intensification of work'. This intensification, together with increased monitoring of work activities made possible by more integrated computer systems, is likely to have 'narrowed the scope for initiative'. In the public sector, such an effect followed from government reforms and, in particular, the imposition of institutional targets. In addition to this, pressures for increased accountability and regulation may have helped account for a 'sharp decline in tasks discretion among those in professional and associate professional positions'.

Information and communication technologies and the 'call centre'

Computer-based information and communication technologies (ICTs) have the potential to modify significantly the ways in which we live and work. When they are utilised by managers, administrators and business people, certain basic characteristics of ICTs make them an ideal 'engine' for the future development of industrial capitalism and continuation of the advantages enjoyed by the more privileged sectors of societies. There is a fit between the basic dynamics of industrial capitalism and the potential that information technologies have in workplaces for reducing production costs; accelerating innovation in products and services and in the ways these are produced and delivered; increasing flexibility in production and service-provision methods.

LOOKING BACK <<<<<

Chapter 4 looked closely at changes and potential changes in work arising from developments in artificial intelligence and robotics.

Call centres have been an increasingly common form of knowledge-oriented workplaces. In call centres, employers seek a balance between the sort of discretion which is often associated with knowledge-based work (implying a need for *indirect* managerial controls) and machine-based work controls (typically associated with *direct* control regimes).

Call centre work

A type of work in which operators utilise computer terminals to process information relating to telephone calls which are made and/or received, these calls being mediated by various computer-based filtering, allocational, and monitoring devices.

The popular image of a call centre is one of a factory like room with people tied to the telephones and being subject to all-powerful electronic surveillance. Researchers have suggested that this is somewhat simplistic. A range of possibilities exists. The calls dealt with by these knowledge workers vary from ones that are relatively complex (therefore demanding discretion and a degree of indirect control) to calls which are routine, repetitive, simple and undemanding and can therefore be handled in a direct-control sweatshop manner. In their analysis of the broad rise of 'front-line' service work and their attention to work, ranging from call centre employment to highly knowledge-intensive professional jobs, in which workers have regular contact with actual or prospective customers, Frenkel *et al.* (1999) suggest that both theorists of knowledge-based work (Bell 1974) and ICT (Castells 1996) ignored the significant tendency of 'the rise of customer sovereignty in the context of a more competitive, globalised economy'. The implication of this trend for the work which people do is that the competitive importance to the employing enterprise of a high quality of interaction with customers necessarily pushes them towards an 'info-normative' type of control which emphasises worker discretion rather than direct or technical control. Their overall analysis is an optimistic one in which the combination of the growth of knowledge work, the use of ICTs and the emphasis on pleasing customers means that 'work is becoming more complex, in part because of customisation and in part because high labour costs and IT in combination are reducing the demand for lower-skilled jobs and increasing the demand for jobs with higher-level competences'.

Snapshot 6.5

Upgrading work in the Viewfields call centre

The Viewfields call centre business was an early entrant to the market and was established at a time of high unemployment in the town where it was located. The technology that was used made it easy for supervisors to check on the number of calls each operator was making. It was also easy for them to check that operators were following their scripts and were speaking politely to people. People who fell short were quickly replaced from the queue of people looking for employment. The management view was that, once a worker had 'mastered' a particular script, time should not be wasted on their learning a new one, simply for the sake of variety of experience. Recently, however, Viewfields started to find it difficult to recruit enough staff to keep the lines manned. There was growing dependence on part-time university student workers and these were increasingly resisting supervisors' attempts to tell them exactly what to do and how to do it. On top of this, Viewfields found several important clients were threatening to end their contracts because of the number of complaints they were receiving about Viewfields staff being brusque and off-hand when talking, on their behalf, to the clients' customers.

The managers realised that the technology they were using, and the need for standardised scripts, meant that they could overcome these difficulties by up-skilling the operators' jobs to make them more appealing to would-be recruits. This would also have the potential benefit of increasing worker satisfaction and thereby improving the quality of the work of the operators.

After first improving the workplace amenities like the restroom and building a new small gymnasium, it was decided to make a number of other changes that might significantly improve the work experience of Viewfields staff:
· Development opportunities were provided whereby staff could be trained to work with marketing colleagues to write scripts.
· A largely internal promotions policy was adopted with an emphasis on recruiting staff who had the potential to move upwards, ultimately up to the level of taking on the managing of their own client accounts.
· Operators were formed into teams and allowed not only to choose the person who would cover the development/monitoring role each week but also to organise their own cover for sick colleagues, altering their own shifts to make sure work requirements were covered.

This case demonstrates what is possible, but research suggests it is far from the norm, with Baldry *et al.* (2007) concluding from their research that call centre work typically involves direct controls and regimentation and follows Taylorist principles together with quantitative measures of performance. All of this is directed towards high productivity. However, the picture may be more complicated in the future as we see growing use of 'tele-health' call centres – a context where a higher degree of specialised professional knowledge discretion is likely to be required. This is noted by Russell (2008) who also reports that he has witnessed urban planners and trade union officers staffing call centres. As he comments, the relationships between call centres and 'the professional skills, identities and traditions associated with occupations such as nursing is going to be an intriguing one'. And it is made all the more intriguing by the potential role of the computerised – AI – systems – which are discussed in Chapter 4 and which may see professional workers of this type replaced by computerised systems which have absorbed professional knowledge and offer advice and information directly to users.

Culture management and worker subjectivity

Sociological attention to the cultural dimension of organisations has encouraged a managerial interest in developing 'strong' cultures that serve managerial interests. The theorising that encouraged this interest can be traced back to Selznick's (1949, 1957) contrast between the mechanical idea of an 'organisation' and the more culturally developed notion of an 'institution' (an idea which also influenced the institutional theorists discussed in Chapter 2). Organisations are set up to act as tools to meet certain purposes, Selznick argued, but a process of institutionalisation occurs whereby the organisation becomes a more responsive and adaptive social organism with an identity and a set of values. These integrate the organisation in such a way that it has significance for its members that is far greater than one of simply being involved in fulfilling the tasks for which it was originally designed. The management is centrally involved in moulding what Selznick calls the 'character' of the organisation. Although Selznick does not formally use the concept of 'culture', his thinking was taken up by the authors of one of the most widely read management books of all time, Peters and Waterman (1982), who argued that the American business organisations which they identified as outstanding or 'excellent' were characterised by several key features. These were not, as many might have expected, the rigorous use of techniques of organisational design, of financial planning, or of computerised control systems. Outstanding business success came, they argue, from reliance on simple structures, simple strategies, simple goals and simple communication.

The key to managing in a basically simple way in what are often large and potentially complex organisations is the use of a clear and 'tight' culture, Peters and Waterman insisted. The stronger was the culture, in which shared values would be communicated through 'rich tapestries of anecdote, myth and fairy tale', and the more it was directed towards the marketplace, the 'less need there was for policy manuals, organisation charts, or detailed procedures and rules'.

These ideas had a major impact upon management thinking, and it has become almost normal for the managements of the larger organisations in Britain and America to frame their restructuring activities in terms of 'changing culture' or 'managing through values'. Where close research on organisations adopting such approaches has emerged, the picture looks far more complex than the widely read prescriptive managerial texts would suggest, however. An ethnographic study of a case of attempted culture change showed how a 'discourse' of culture change, personal development and employee 'development' came to clash with alternative discourses which reflected corporate interests in cost controls and tight corporate control (Watson 2001a). The 'progressive' culture-based ideas became counter-productive as the expectations they created were undermined by corporate policies leading, for example, to regular redundancies among employees. These tensions clearly relate to differences of interest *within* an organisation's management, and McCabe (2000) illustrates from his case study the ways in which managers, whilst 'imbibing' new managerial discourses, nevertheless tend to slip back into an 'older language' of 'industrialism' which reflected their 'lived reality' – one of working within an organisation which, like all organisations, is 'replete with political intrigue, hierarchical divisions, inequality, power struggles and conflict'.

Parker's (2000) three case studies show the variety of ways in which managerial attempts to develop an organisational culture to which all employees can subscribe are undermined by the range of spatial, functional, generational and occupational divisions that manifest themselves in different ways in different organisations with, for example, doctors, managers and information technology specialists competing for control over new IT systems in a hospital and, in a foundry, tensions and distrust developing between progressive 'new engineers' and mass-production-oriented 'old engineers'.

In a further ethnographic study of an organisation attempting to 'mould' its culture and its employees, Kunda (1992) looked in detail at processes of 'normative control' through which attempts are made to win the deep commitment of technical workers to corporate goals and values. The author expresses strong concern about what he sees as managerial attempts to channel people's feelings, thoughts and ways of seeing the world. Yet he does show how individuals tend to balance an absorbing of some of this with a degree of personal distancing from the corporate embrace. Casey (1995) shows a degree of this too in her study of another American company which she calls Hephaestus, one which promoted an 'official discourse' defining an 'ideal Hephaestus person' who worked within 'values of diligence, dedication, loyalty, commitment and the ability to be a good team player, to be adaptive and flexible, and to be a good, somewhat conservative, citizen'. However, in spite of limited evidence of resistance and 'defence of self' among employees, Casey notes a 'homogeneity of view and values and a conformity of self-presentation' as the language practices and values 'become everyday parlance and employees act out the desired characteristics' so that 'most come to own these practices and roles of the ideal Hephaestus employee'.

Employers and managers engaging in these ways with issues of employees' self-identities and the values through which they judge the rights and wrongs of their daily lives has led some sociologists to raise value questions about such trends. To attempt to mould cultures – given that culture in its broad sense provides the roots of human morality, social-identity and existential security – is indeed to enter 'deep and dangerous waters' (Watson 2001a). The 'guiding aim and abiding concern' of what Willmott (1995) calls corporate culturism (and Parker (2000) calls culturalism) is to win the 'hearts and minds' of employees, and Willmott expresses deep anxiety about corporate attempts to 'colonise the affective domain' and to attempt to achieve 'the governance of the employee's soul'.

To talk of the employee's 'soul' is perhaps not as unrealistic as it might at first sound. The twenty-first century has seen increasing managerial efforts to bring 'spirituality' and a 'new age work ethic' into the workplace (Bell and Taylor 2003; Kamoche and Pinnington 2012; Saks 2011). This is not, however, a matter of encouraging spirituality for the general benefit of mankind. A study in Israel concluded that spiritual consultants were brought into the organisations studied by managers primarily to enhance productivity (Zaidman *et al.* 2009). The consultants emphasised the importance of individuals having 'awareness of his or her body, thoughts and feelings at the moment'. There was resistance to some of this but it was observed that the consultants' New Age ideas were taken up by employees who had been exposed to them in other contexts – this, Zaidman *et al.* (2009) suggest, 'reflecting the borderless nature of the field of New Age and possibly the 'longing' found in the mainstream for real experience'. This development can be related to what Fleming (2009) calls a 'new spirit of capitalism' and a growing managerial discourse of 'authenticity' which seeks to take over the once subversive idea of each person 'just being their self' in order to co-opt them into making enthusiastic corporate contributions.

LOOKING FORWARD >>>>>

Corporate attempts to shape employee identities will be returned to in Chapter 10 and the issue of employee resistance in Chapters 11 and 12.

Organisational identities

Managerial attempts to change organisational 'cultures' are clearly based upon an assumption that employees and others will be influenced in their behaviour by the conception which they have of the enterprise with which they are involved. This 'idea' that people have of any particular organisation can be conceptualised as a matter of *organisational identity* (Watson 2016). A literature has developed around this notion, and this continues to grow (Hatch and Shultz 2004; Pratt *et al.* 2016). A popular distinction used in that literature has been one between an internal 'organisational identity' and an external 'corporate identity'. However, a more useful way of conceptualising these matters is to treat internal and external as two aspects of an overall organisational identity (or set of identities), rather than as two separate things – as we see in the definition offered here.

Organisational identity

The understanding(s) of what an organisation 'is' or 'is like' among members of the various parties, inside and outside the organisation, who have dealings with that organisation. One element of this is the 'formal identity' manifested in the organisation's registered trading name(s) and legal status.

As the broad 'multiple constituency' thinking discussed earlier in the present chapter suggests, those in charge of work organisations face the problem of attracting people to use their services, work for them, trade with them and generally accept what they do as socially legitimate. An important managerial task is therefore that of creating a 'positive' organisational identity, an attractive 'corporate image' or a reputation as a 'good organisation to work for'. 'A good name' thus becomes important for every organisation and the considerable investment by modern corporations in public relations, advertising and the building of an employer brand. Gabriel *et al.* (2015) go as far as claiming that the growing influence of consumerism means that the contemporary manager is less likely to be a 'rational technician' and more likely to 'be preoccupied with the organizational brand, the customer experience, presentation and the management of meaning and emotion'.

Organisational identities emerge from the negotiated order of relationships between the various constituencies inside and outside the organisation upon which the organisation is dependent for its long-term existence. These identities are always in flux and are subject to conflicts of interest, contest, ambiguity and confusion. And any particular organisation may have an organisational identity that is clear, shared and relatively consistent across various constituencies. Equally, an organisation may be subject to a variety of different identities in the eyes of the different constituencies with which that organisation is concerned – some of these identities being relatively clear and some being relatively vague.

Organisational identities are not helpfully fully understood as the properties of organisations. Rather, they are elements of the socially constructed dimension of reality that exists in the cultural realm of social life. Individuals in the personal *identity work* which they necessarily do throughout their lives, in order to maintain a coherent sense of who and what they are, engage with these organisational identities, utilising them not just as prompts to action but also as resources for general social sensemaking and personal self-identity maintenance.

LOOKING FORWARD >>>>>

The notion of individual identity work is an important topic in Chapter 10, pp. 303–306.

All of this means that the managers of an organisation cannot simply construct an organisational name or identity unilaterally, consensually or permanently. As Rodrigues and Child (2008) show in the case of a Brazilian telecommunications company and its 'definition and redefinition' of corporate identity, a cyclical process occurs involving 'power relations, resource mobilisation and struggles for legitimacy'. Further, considerable rhetorical skills are required to produce what are often multiple organisational identities. This is demonstrated by Sillince and Brown's (2009) examination of the websites of forty-three constabularies and their attempts to achieve legitimacy with the variety of 'stakeholders' with which they deal.

Summary

Organisations, and the way they are continuously and inevitably changing, cannot be understood without locating them with the key dynamics of industrial capitalist societies. The 'mainspring' of these dynamics is one of technical and organisational innovation in a context of both the general pursuit of material human improvement across the world and the competitive activities of particular interest groups in that same world. Within this context, there have been a variety of innovations in the older and established economies of the world in which organisational managements, following a basic 'logic of corporate management' strive to establish and maintain a degree of control of employees and their activities, control which is nevertheless continually challenged by organisational members. 'Human resourcing' practices are central to these control attempts, and it is possible to see managers, in the light of preferences and organisational circumstances, adopting human resourcing policies and practices which lean towards either a 'high-commitment' or a 'low-commitment' ideal-type strategy. Associated with these two broad approaches to employment practices are two-ideal type approaches to achieving flexibility of operations: 'direct control' attempts, on the one hand, and indirect control attempts on the other. Associated with the latter style of managing organisations is a series of innovations such as teamworking, 'just-in-time' management, 'lean production', and computer-based automation provide a range of options for managers pursuing control and flexibility and the use of these is often associated with attempts to manage organisations through cultural manipulation and efforts to influence workers' 'subjectivities' and through efforts to manipulate organisational identities.

7 Occupations and the social organisation of work

Key issues

- To what extent does the occupational principle of the structuring of work survive alongside the organisational principle that has, in many respects, replaced it?
- What are the links between patterns of inequality and the occupational structures of societies?
- How are labour markets segmented and how does this segmentation relate to various forms of contingent and non-standard employment, to part-time and temporary work and to home and teleworking?
- What do we understand about 'portfolio' or 'boundaryless' careers?
- What kinds of work do people do which are outside the formal employment of people by work organisations?
- What patterns can be seen in inequalities between women and men, historically and in the contemporary world, and how can these patterns be explained?
- How does ethnic inequality connect to issues of work and its organisation?

The occupational principle of work structuring

There are two basic principles behind the way the work undertaken by people in modern societies is patterned. These principles are partly complementary and partly in a relationship of conflict and rivalry. They are:

- *The organisational principle of work structuring:* This has been the focus of the previous two chapters and involves the structuring of work on a bureaucratic, administrative or 'formal organisation' basis. Emphasis is on the ways in which work tasks are designed by the managerial agents of the owners of work organisations who then recruit, pay, co-ordinate and control the efforts of others to carry out tasks in a way which enables the organisation to continue into a future existence.

- *The occupational principle of work structuring:* The structuring of work on the basis of the type of work that people do. Emphasis is on the patterns which emerge when we concentrate on the ways in which specific work tasks are done. Here, we take as our starting point the carrying out of a specific type of work operation, say driving a lorry, cleaning a house, catching fish or running a business. We then concentrate on the social implications of the existence within society of groups of people regularly doing similar tasks.

The implications of the existence of occupational groupings arise at various levels, as we shall see in this chapter. Occupations have implications for the way a society as a whole is structured and for the way this structuring changes over time.

LOOKING BACK <<<<<

The importance of the shift from an emphasis on the *social division of labour* to a *technical division of labour* was emphasised in Chapter 4.

They also have implications for society in that occupational structures are closely related to patterns of structural inequality in class, status, gender and ethnic terms. Occupations have implications for the members of occupational groups, especially when there is the possibility of the people engaged in a particular occupation acting jointly or *collectively*, through trade union or 'professional' mobilisation, in order to defend or further shared interests. And there are implications for the individual engaged in a particular type of work and implications relating, for example, to how they enter that kind of work, learn how to do the tasks associated with it and advance their careers within their selected type of work activity.

It is important in defining an occupation to recognise that the notion is not simply a sociologist's conceptual tool of analysis but is also used by the people whom the sociologist studies. A working concept of occupation therefore has to take into account the fact that whether or not any given work activity is to be regarded as an occupation depends both on the decisions made by those doing the tasks and the inclination by the wider public to bestow such an identity on that type of work activity.

> ## Occupation
>
> Membership of an occupation involves engagement on a regular basis in a part or the whole of a range of work tasks which are identified under a particular heading or title by both those carrying out these tasks and by a wider public.

The concept of 'occupation' used here is wider than simply paid employment. Membership of an occupation may entail the total independence of a worker from an employer, as in the case of a freelance writer, say, and it may mean that there is no direct financial reward from the work. In this latter case, the individual would have to be supported by someone else. This would apply to a commercially unsuccessful poet or to a student for example.

Most people who carry out work tasks can be assigned to an occupation. But for many individuals, their location in a work organisation may be more salient than their occupational membership. In trying to learn where a stranger 'fits into society' we may ask either 'What do they do?' or 'Who do they work for?' Traditionally, we located people in society by their occupation – tinker, tailor, soldier, sailor – but with the growth of bureaucratised work organisations the specific tasks in which a person is engaged and the skills which go with it have become less relevant for many people than the organisation in which they are employed.

Snapshot 7.1

'She does something in the council offices'

A new neighbour moving into the street was being briefed by a long-standing resident about who was who in the street.

'So both you and your husband are teachers?'

'No, I'm a teacher but John is an accountant.'

'Oh I think that's similar to what Dave opposite you does. Anyway he has something to do with the financial side of things at Nuttlemans.'

'And his wife?'

'She's at Ferry's.'

'Doing what?'

'I don't know but I do know that her mum and dad were at Ferry's and she's been there since she left school'.

'Sandra's very nice. She goes out to work, I notice'.

'She does. She used to be just a housewife like me but now she does something in the council offices'.

In Snapshot 7.1, some people are identified in clear occupational terms as teachers, accountants or housewives whilst, for others, the organisational attachment is more pertinent; 'she's at Ferry's' or 'she does something in the council offices'. Often, however, a vestige of the occupational identification is retained within the organisational attachment, as in 'something to do with the financial side at Nuttlemans'. In spite of the everyday tendency often to focus on the organisational principles in locating people in the world of work, there are two special cases where the *study* of people's work has tended to concentrate on the occupational principle:

- Where the tasks associated with a job are particularly distinctive. This may be through their work having a degree of public visibility – as with police officers, teachers, or actors, say – or through their work being somewhat peculiar or deviant, as with prostitutes, undertakers, or criminals, say.
- Where the tasks involved in a certain kind of work are such that control over the carrying out of those tasks can be sought by members of the occupation itself at the expense of control by an employer, government or clients. These will tend to be highly skilled 'trades' or, more especially, the 'professions'.

The twentieth-century study of particular occupations by sociologists has tended to veer between a near obsession with high-status professionals and a fascination with various low-status or deviant work activities. The history of western occupations has, however, been very much one of the rise and fall of the degree of occupational self-control maintained by various groups. The occupational principle is perhaps most clearly seen in the occupational guilds which were at their height in the thirteenth century. It survived the growth of industrial capitalism and the new dominance of the organisational principle in the vestigial form of skilled trade unions, however. It has survived and indeed flourished in parts of the middle-class sphere of work in the guise of professionalism.

LOOKING FORWARD >>>>>

We will see the extent to which the notion of the profession, albeit a changing notion, is important in the contemporary world of work later in this chapter (pp. 261–270).

Occupational structure, class, status and inequality

In contrast to the term 'organisational structure', which refers to the internal patterning in work organisations, the concept of occupational structure is used by sociologists not to look at the shape of occupations themselves but to look at patterns of occupational activity at a societal level.

Occupational structure
The pattern in a society which is created by the distribution of the labour force across the range of existing types of work or occupation.

Sociological researchers often develop their own set of socioeconomic categories or classes to help in their investigations, one particularly influential scheme being the 'Goldthorpe class schema' (Goldthorpe 1987), which locates occupations in the class structure according to where people fit into the societal system of employment relations. Such principles were used by the sociologists to whom the UK government statistics office turned to devise a scheme for use in the first national census of the twenty-first century. This locates different occupational groups in a hierarchical classification according to criteria relating to the quality of the overall employment contract that members of any given occupation might expect to achieve – especially the working conditions, the prospects for future advancement and the degree of security of employment (Rose and O'Reilly 1997). The seven groupings ranged from higher managerial and professional occupations at the top of the hierarchy to 'routine' occupations at the other end.

This scheme was devised to take into account two main criteria: the role that people play in the broad occupational structure of society and the level of 'reward' or benefit that they receive for this contribution. The concept of class plays an important part in how sociologists theorise such issues and the concept links people's occupational position and their position in the overall societal structure of advantage.

Class
An individual's class position is a matter of the part which they play (or the person upon whom they are dependent plays) within the division of labour of a society and the implications which this has for their access to those experiences, goods and services which are scarce and valued in that society.

Weber recognised that alongside the objective aspect of social inequality, which can be understood as 'class' is a subjective aspect whereby people are located hierarchically in society in terms of prestige or status.

> ### Status
>
> That aspect of social inequality whereby different positions are awarded different degrees of prestige or honour.

People belong to both classes and 'status groups', membership of the latter giving a certain amount of socially estimated honour or prestige. In practice, says Weber, class and status positions tend to coincide, but he insists that this need not necessarily be the case and we can indeed see cases where some disjuncture occurs in the ethnic or religious status groupings that exist within societies. This is illustrated by the case of Henry Johnson in Snapshot 7.2 and his concern about his status or 'standing' in the town in which he lives a life which in economic and other ways would appear to be unequivocally middle class.

Snapshot 7.2

Henry's complaint

'As a successful black businessman I take a lot of pride in what I have achieved. In anyone's terms, you would think, I am a well-off, educated, middle-class member of society. I am sure when they analyse my census form they put me in a high-class position. But my sense of pride and achievement is regularly undermined by the way the other local business people seem to look down on me. I try to persuade myself that it is just a small town mentality and that I am an outsider who has moved up here from London. But I know it is not that. One of my business partners is Scottish, and although they make jokes about him being a foreigner, I know they respect him much more than they do me. As a black man, I simply don't have the standing that the others do.'

Class, then, whilst a key element in the 'stratification' of modern societies, has to be seen, as theorists of 'intersectionality' (Rodriguez *et al.* 2016) emphasise, in conjunction with and interlinked with other issues such as gender and ethnicity, and changes in patterns of inequality need to be understood not just in terms of technological and managerial changes, but also in terms of challenges to dominant interests that come from struggles by women, ethnic minorities and other socially excluded groups.

Intersectionality

The ways in which various categories of social difference – gender, ethnicity, class, nationality, sexuality and so on – intersect with each other in processes of identity-shaping, always within broader institutional patterns of power distribution, discrimination and inequality.

LOOKING FORWARD >>>>>

Gender and ethnicity are examined later in this chapter.

Henry Johnson's case illustrates the point that the 'economic' 'cannot be rigidly demarcated as an independent factor determining stratification position, since it is inextricably intertwined with social and cultural factors'.

A useful concept for examining matters of multiple influences on people's lives and identities is Bourdieu's notion of *habitus*, something which individuals 'absorb' from their upbringing and social context and which becomes almost a 'second nature'.

Habitus

Bourdieu's notion of a set of predispositions or inclinations to action which individuals develop and internalise over time in the light of their relationship to the power structure and culture of the society in which they live.

Snapshot 7.3

Angus, the posh wage slave

Yeah, it's interesting how people ask me, when the pub is quiet, 'What's your story then, Angus?'. I suppose this is inevitable. It is quite clear to everyone who comes in here that I am just a bar worker. But, somehow, they don't think this fits with the way I speak. I actually can't change the way I speak – any more than I could settle down in here at break time with a tabloid newspaper. My father was a big military man. No officer in his regiment – or officer's kid – would have survived if they had betrayed anything of a regional or lower-class accent. And, yes, I went to a posh boarding school. So the voice is, if you like, built in. But, in spite of the polish I received, I did not fit in at school. And once my family realised that I was uninterested in a military career, I was unpopular at home too. It's a long story, but I left school unqualified and, you might say, disinherited. Well no, that's not quite right. I did inherit a bit of money when my parents died; just enough to buy the flat that I still live in, across town. The flat is important, actually, because if you work in this trade, you get put out of work from time to time. Pubs are always closing or changing hands and, you know, you need to move on. Having the flat makes me feel less like the itinerant casual worker that I really am. I know that is the truth of my situation, in spite of the fact that I feel really settled in this pub. In fact, I go down well with a lot of the customers here. A lot of them are, like me, fans of real ale. A lot of them, like me, have beards. And, let's make no bones about it, a lot of them are pretty well educated. They enjoy talking to me. They appreciate my deep knowledge of good beer. They like to ask my advice on what to drink. So, what shall we say? Let's say my general demeanour keeps me in steady employment – for now anyway. I might be a bit posh for a pub worker, but I am just a pub worker. Yes, I am a posh wage slave, but I am a wage slave nonetheless, and I must not forget it.

One can clearly see the relevance of the concept of habitus to Angus's story in Snapshot 7.3. His family background has influenced his predisposition to speak in a particular way and to read certain newspapers. But these family circumstances are ones with close connections to the occupation of army officer. Such an occupation is an objective social reality as is the class position to which it is linked. Angus tells us quite a lot about his personal identity, but he is well aware that whatever 'subjectivity' he works with in making his way in life, he has a very clear current occupational location and lives in the objective class circumstance of an unqualified weekly paid employee working in an insecure labour market position. Valuable as this concept is when one is sociologically analysing people's lives and subjectivities, its power is undermined if – as tends to be the case – the objective categories or occupation and position in a class structure are excluded from analysis. To understand Angus's situation sociologically, then, we need to combine the style of analysis and the emphasis on subjectivity of the 'new' class analysis with attention to the objectively existing occupational and class structures within which he lives his life. As Crompton (2010) points out, just because people's consciousness of class and occupation is changing does not mean that class and occupation have, as phenomena existing beyond the individual, disappeared.

LOOKING BACK <<<<<

It was argued in Chapter 1 that a 'realist' position (recognising an objectively existing class structure in this case) can incorporate the 'interpretive principle'. Such a possibility is demonstrated by the present analysis of Angus's identity and class position.

Occupations in a changing class structure

We looked earlier at how social researchers relate occupational and class positions in modern societies. Sociologists have also attempted to understand the changes that are occurring in this relationship. Roberts (1977), for example, interpreted their study of British class imagery in the later decades of the twentieth century as showing that the class structure of Britain was fragmenting. And Marshall *et al.* (1988) argued that growing ambiguity, ambivalence and contradiction in people's class images were reflecting objective characteristics of an increasingly 'opaque' class structure. These authors followed Weber in identifying the operation of the 'capitalist market' as the primary mechanism determining class processes. Changing patterns of investment and division of labour meant that the ownership and control of capital was becoming more complex as family proprietorship gave way to pension funds, multi-national companies, cartels and the like. Also, the shedding of surplus labour during the recession which occurred prior to their study reinforced labour market segregation and in particular the boundary between those in relatively secure occupational or company careers and the unemployed and sub-employed. As a result of these trends – which are continuing apace in the twenty-first century – the owners and controllers of capital are less concrete and more distant, the occupational structure is more complex and manual/non-manual distinction is less salient than it was both sociologically and among the population at large.

These shifts have led various researchers to identify themselves with a 'cultural turn' in class analysis and to offer a 'new sociology of social class' (Reay 2005b), which focuses on people's identities, emotions and their subjective experiences of living in a particular class position. Savage *et al.* (2013), in association with the British Broadcasting Corporation and contacting 161,400 respondents via the internet, published the results of the 'largest survey ever of social class' (The Great British Class Survey). The key theorist used in the study is Bourdieu and, particularly, his model of three types of advantage-giving capital: economic capital (income and wealth); cultural capital (the appreciation and use of cultural goods and credentials associated with educational success); social capital (access to helpful social networks). The resulting seven-level 'new model of social class' recognises a wealthy elite, an established middle class, a technical middle class, a class of new affluent workers, a traditional working class, a class of (graduate) emergent service workers and a precariat – the latter being defined along the lines set out by Standing (2014) as a significant group characterised by high amounts of insecurity (and see later in this chapter, pp. 213–214).

With reference to this broad style of research, Hebson (2009) observes that it produces fascinating 'insights into how class is lived and represented' but is in danger of ignoring employment aspects of these subjectivities and underestimating the role that is played by workplace experiences. It seems, says Atkinson (2009), as if work is being replaced by 'culture' as 'the natural bedfellow of class'. This critique of cultural-and-class analysis has been developed and directly applied to the Savage *et al.* (2013) study. Mills (2014) argues that the study was little more than a 'data dredging exercise' with a typology being arbitrarily devised, without serious use of theory (in spite of the inspiring role of Bourdieu in the survey design).

Bradley (2014) argues that Savage *et al.*'s (2013) approach to class is 'gradational', rather than *relational*, as it has always been in the sociological 'Marxo-Weberian tradition' (with Marx identifying a relationship in which one class appropriates the wealth of the whole of society and Weber identifying market relations). Bradley offers her own scheme, one which identifies three (possibly four) classes, along with several 'class fractions'. There are three clear social classes. First, there is a highly wealthy and influential *elite* (with a sub-set of the super-rich). Second, there is a *middle class* in which the emphasis is on income rather than wealth. This has the class fractions of traditional professionals/senior managers; lower middle class people who are qualified but less well-paid and a possible 'middle-middle' of teachers, social workers, computer specialists and the like. Third, there is a *working class* of people who, as Marx and Weber defined them, have only their labour to sell. The class fractions here are those of a relatively affluent and aspirant upper-working class (including skilled workers and 'white van men'); a 'feminised middle grouping' of low-paid workers in retail, care and leisure services; and an unemployed or under-employed benefit-dependent group.

Bradley suggests that 'we may' treat the precariat as a separate class. This is a relatively heterogeneous group including 'armies of temps, cleaners, classroom assistants and hourly paid lecturers, call-centre workers, fruit-pickers, bar and restaurant staff'.

> ### Precariat
>
> A section of society, which might or might not be regarded as a social class, who have little economic, social or psychological security or predictability in their working lives and, hence, in their whole lives generally. The grouping is growing in size and range, to include not only members of what some termed an 'underclass' but also people, often with good educational credentials, who are pushed into artificial self-employment work, typically in digitally oriented work.

Contingent and non-standard employment

One of the main distinguishing features of an industrial capitalist society is that labour, or 'labour power', is treated as a commodity to be bought and sold on the market. This makes it vital to relate matters of occupational structure to the principles that underlie the operation of labour markets. It is also necessary to recognise the economic and political difficulties faced in industrialised societies generally that put pressures on how work is organised and how the overall division of labour is 'managed'.

When Fordist principles of organising employment practices, providing state welfare and developing economic policies were at their height in the middle period of the twentieth century (see Chapter 4), there was a tendency among governments to follow *corporatist* solutions to tensions arising over labour market inequalities and competitive actions of organised labour. This meant that important political decisions, especially with regard to the economy, were made by the state in close association with employers and trade unions. With the decline of Fordism and corporatist interventions there was a tendency towards labour market segmentation, towards the dualism of a primary and secondary labour market (Doeringer and Piore 1971; Goldthorpe 1984), or to a segmentation in which the primary labour market becomes further divided (Gordon *et al.* 1982).

> ### Labour market segmentation
>
> The effective division of an economy into different parts. In its early stages this tends to be dualistic, with a prosperous and stable core or primary sector of enterprises and jobs existing alongside a 'peripheral' or secondary sector which is relatively and systematically disadvantaged. The tendency is for this dualism to be followed by segmentation into further divisions.

Whereas corporatism dealt with the problems posed by major economic interest groups, and organised labour in particular, in an 'inclusionary' way – by involving them in forming and implementing economic policy – segmentation works on 'exclusionary' lines. Here, the increased power of organised interests is offset by the creating or expanding of groups of workers (and potential workers) who lack effective organisation or the potential to mobilise themselves – because, say, of their low educational resources, their gender or domestic situation or their ethnicity. This makes a labour force more susceptible to market forces and manipulation by employers and managers. And it produces the increasingly complex pattern of inequalities discussed earlier in this chapter.

In recognition of the need to go beyond a simple core/periphery distinction – a need that becomes particularly clear when the overall occupational pattern in society is examined – a distinction which is increasingly used is that between standard and non-standard (or 'contingent') employment.

Standard employment

Employment in which the contract between the employer and employee is understood to be one in which the employee is likely to stay with the employer over the long term at a particular location, putting in a working day and week which is normal for that industry and receiving regular pay and the protection of pension and sick pay benefits.

Non-standard/contingent employment

Employment in which contracts between employers and employees are short-term and unstable with the worker taking part-time, temporary and, sometimes, multiple jobs. The work is sometimes at home rather than in an organisationally located workplace with there being little by way of employment benefits.

The term 'contingent work' is often used for non-standard work, to recognise that the availability of short-term and unstable employment, in which there is a minimal attachment between employer and worker, is dependent or 'contingent' on employers' need for labour at a particular time. In the context of globalising trends, technological change and intense competition, employing organisations find themselves having both to contain their costs and maximise their flexibility. Their highly skilled 'standard employment' staff help achieve functional flexibility ('flexibility for long-term adaptability', p. 184). And numerical flexibility ('flexibility for short-term predictability, p. 184) is achieved by the use of various contingent labour resources: contract labour, part-time and temporary employment and 'zero hours contracts' (the latter being returned to in Chapter 10, pp. 312–315).

LOOKING BACK AND FORWARD <<<<< >>>>>

The circumstances which 'push' organisational managers sometimes towards what in Chapter 6 and Figure 6.1 are called 'low-commitment' and 'high-commitment' human resourcing practices are the same ones that influence each organisation's balance of standard and non-standard jobs.

The growth of non-standard work becomes relevant to issues of trade union representation which arise in Chapter 11.

The survival of the 'standard' job can be related to the pressures of tightening labour markets but it can also be related to the fact that the 'flexibility' which employers increasingly require is not just the type of flexibility for short-term predictability that might encourage an increase in non-standard employment. As we saw in Chapter 6, employers are also pressured to seek flexibility for long-term adaptability. This clearly fits better with secure and 'standard' employment arrangements as many employers recognise (McGovern *et al.* 2007). And it means that we have to be wary of pronouncements that the whole world of work is to shift towards one in which workers primarily work on short-term contracts in a computer-networked market place.

Nevertheless, the fullest analysis of the growth of non-standard and precarious work carried out by Kalleberg (2011, 2012), leads him to argue that 'polarized and precarious employment systems are not merely temporary features of the business cycle but represent structural transformations'. What he calls 'bad jobs' are no longer vestigial but a central component of US employment. Although the study focused on the USA, Kalleberg (2012) says all countries are under similar pressures 'in the light of more intense globalization, technological advances especially in information and communication technologies, greater mobility of capital and labor, new forms of organizational interdependence, and pressures that served to weaken unions'.

LOOKING FORWARD >>>>>

One of the most discussed types of employment contracts that might be seen epitomising new types of flexibility in labour markets is that of the 'zero hours' contract. These, and the possible consequences for people's lives, are examined in Chapter 10, pp. 312–315.

One outcome of these broad trends and also encouraged by changes in computer-based technologies is the emergence of the 'gig economy'.

Gig economy

Arrangements whereby independent workers contract with organisations and personal customers to fulfil short-term engagement via internet 'job sites', 'talent/professional/freelancing/web conferencing platforms' and remote-working apps.

Although press commentators and politicians tend to observe such trends as passengers hailing taxis via an 'app' and treat this as an indicator of a likely future, there is, as yet, no clear empirical evidence of a significant move towards a gig economy – which, it has to be stressed, does not mean that such developments will not become highly significant in the future. But whatever the extent of this particular trend, it generally means that the 'gig' workers are more likely to be based in their homes than in organisations' offices or workshops.

Home and remote work/teleworking

Associated with the notion of standard work or employment is the idea of people leaving their home each day to work for an employer in the workplace owned and managed by that employer. However, a growing proportion of workers in contemporary societies work in a home-based way without being formally employed by a single employer. In spite of surface similarities between such workers, it is vital not to regard people in this category as occupying a broadly similar occupational position. This is strikingly brought out by the comments made by Julian Redmile, a publican in a large village, as he talked about the various customers who used his public house in Snapshot 7.4.

It is clearly important not to lump together the various types of worker that Julian Redmile talks about. When we speak of 'homeworkers' we

Home workers in our village

'I get customers from across the spectrum of people in the village. Certain of them only come in here in the evenings and at the weekend. These are mainly the people who commute into one of the nearby cities to work for big employers there. The people who drop in during the day, for a pint or for a coffee, are interesting though. Only a minority of them work for the few local employers that we have. The others, in one sense or another work from home. And, I can tell you, there's all sorts in this category. Two or three of the women who do part-time bar work for me, for example, work at home during the day, assembling garments from sections which are delivered to their front door by a business which pays them by the piece. Then there's the bloke whose van is parked across the road at the moment. He's a painter and decorator whose 'office', as he calls it, is the back bedroom of his house. His paint store is the big shed in his garden. Very different from him is the man who you saw leaving a few minutes ago. He is a regional sales manager for a national company who co-ordinates sales workers from an office in his house. And the chap who was with him is a computer specialist who develops software. As I understand it, he develops these "applications" for just a couple of companies who he has long-term contracts with.'

need to distinguish between people who are working 'at home' or 'from home' for example, and, especially important, we need to distinguish between those who are self-employed in the sense of having a product or service to sell on the market and those who, although formally designated as 'self-employed' have, in effect, a waged work relationship with the businesses with which they are employed. Felstead and Jewson (2000) noted the increase in both what they call 'industrial homeworking' and 'teleworking' in the last quarter of the twentieth century, estimating that about a quarter of the British workforce was working at home for some or all of the time towards the end of the century, with this expected to increase to 50 per cent as the twenty-first century unfolded.

Many of those in the industrial homeworking category (the garment assemblers that Julian Redmile mentions, for example), and who are in a quasi-waged-based relationship with an organisation tend to have regular relationships with the businesses which bring work to their houses, lack the legal protection and benefits of the formally employed, yet still experience the pressure of deadlines, productivity rates, piece work systems, and fragmented work tasks. Such arrangements not only reinforce gender patterns of inequality (given the predominance of women homeworkers) but lower both labour and capital costs of employers who adopt such a labour strategy. Such organisations have an advantage over ones conventionally employing people, and these competitive pressures, in turn, reinforce the tendency to casualise the work of those they employ as in-workers.

The industrial type of homeworking can be seen as close to the 'outworking' tradition which existed before the Industrial Revolution and the spread of the factory system. However, the use of computers and information technology to enable people to work at home or from home introduces a new variant of the old theme with clerical and 'professional' workers increasingly engaging in 'teleworking', 'telecommuting' or 'networking', where computers are used to link the home and the client organisation.

Teleworking

Work which is carried out away from the location of an employer or work contractor using electronic information and computing technology in either or both (a) carrying out the work tasks (b) communicating with the employing or contracting organisation with regard to those tasks.

It would appear that teleworking involves a high proportion of people in 'senior' work, half of those identified at the turn of the century in the British Labour Force Survey (IES 2000) being managers or professionals. However, the technology is such that it would be as amenable to use by routine clerical workers as it is to those doing more complex tasks. Teleworking, again, is not a homogeneous occupational category. And it is extremely important to remember that with all kinds of homeworking, work is not an individual activity that can simply be switched from a structured and organised workplace to a domestic setting. The workplace, as Jackson and Van der Wielen (1998) point out, is 'not primarily a *physical* location but the locus of *collective endeavour*' and that, when telework has been introduced simply because it is technically feasible and economically desirable as a means of reducing office space and commuting costs, results have often been poor. With all types of homeworking, as Felstead and Jewson (2000) show, a great deal of what was formerly 'managerial' responsibility falls on the homeworkers themselves, and they can find it a considerable struggle to decide how and when to work, how to manage quality or health and safety standards and so on, as well as to maintain their relationship both with people in the organisations to which they relate and the other people living in the household (see also Phizacklea and Wolkowitz 1995; Feldstead *et al.* 2003). For people working from home, a process of adjustment has to occur, and in their examination of such processes, Tietze and Musson (2005) show that the 'relationship between home and work is recast'. However, they argue that this involves a process of 'mutual adjustment'. The logic of 'industrial production' does not come to permeate home life. Neither does the 'image of home' bring about a redefining of the nature of work.

Portfolio or 'boundaryless' careers

One way in which work might be 'non-standard' would be if those doing it held more than one job at the same time, or frequently moved from one job to another. But it was long ago recognised that certain individuals prefer not to confine their whole career to one employing organisation. W. Watson (1964), for example, identified the spiralist – a particular type of aspiring middle-class employee who moves 'upwards' in career by moving from organisation to organisation and locality to locality. This type of person would fit Gouldner's (1957) category of the cosmopolitan latent role holder, as opposed to a local latent role holder, a person who is more inclined to seek advancement through a single employing organisation. With the increasing pursuit of flexibility by employing organisations and the declining use of internal labour markets (Beynon 2002), it is argued that more and more people will build careers that take them beyond the boundaries of particular organisations or localities. Handy (1994) envisaged what he termed portfolio careers offering people opportunities for personal growth and enhanced choices in life. Individuals would combine a variety of work activities within their chosen bundle – some perhaps being primarily concerned with creating income, others aimed at achieving more extrinsic satisfactions.

Arthur and Rousseau (1996) argued that there was a general shift occurring from careers which are 'bounded' by relatively stable occupational and organisations structures to boundaryless careers where people move, over a lifetime, between occupations, organisations, localities and different types of work task. This is not said to be a move, however, to a state of 'career anarchy'. Instead, people with 'career capital', in the form of networks of contacts, a sense of self-assurance and a capacity to learn and develop new skills, are able creatively to 'enact' their careers by experimenting, improvising, adapting and then 'making sense' of their actions. Littleton *et al.* (2000) showed how this can work in practice with studies of workers in California's Silicon Valley and people working in the independent film-making industry. Arthur *et al.* (1999) examined the career history of seventy-five people working in jobs ranging from senior management to unskilled labouring in New Zealand to show that 84 per cent of these moved across jobs and localities in a way that could not be characterised as random. The authors demonstrated how individuals can be seen as experimenting and developing themselves as they move through these unplanned sequences, searching for novelty and fulfilment.

British evidence of people in portfolio work reporting a sense of freedom and feeling 'in control' in their work was produced by Cohen and Mallon (1999). But they present a more ambiguous overall picture in which a proportion of the people studied were anxious to reconstruct boundaries, rather than break out of them, for example by seeking long-term contracts with organisations. Research from labour economics on job stability is brought into this picture of complexity by Rodrigues and Guest (2010), this leading them to say that the evidence of 'the collapse of the traditional career model' is simply not supported by the evidence. The analysis here fits with the conclusions of King, Burke and Pemberton (2005) in their study of IT workers. The research led them to dispute the appropriateness of the term 'boundaryless' to describe independence from a single employer which provides a sense of liberation and freedom for workers. They show that the concept of boundary continues to be relevant in the light of their finding that the options facing these skilled 'new economy' workers are 'manifestly bounded by labour market intermediaries'. Employment agencies, for example, preferred 'known' candidates for jobs and were anxious to encourage 'shrewd human capital investments'. They viewed with suspicion highly career-mobile individuals when recruiting for permanent vacancies. A key factor in making 'boundaryless' careers work, however, is shown by Welch and Welch's (2015) study of international project work to be individuals' membership of career networks; their being involved in a 'community of practice' with other project workers.

Work outside employment

Self-employment

The idea of 'working for oneself' and being free of bosses at work is one that has long had appeal for many people in modern societies. To some extent, this is a tendency to reject a central characteristic of industrial capitalist societies.

> **LOOKING BACK <<<<<**
>
> The centrality of the institution of employment to industrial capitalism was explained in Chapter 4.

However, as we saw with home-based working, self-employment is a category which covers a range of possibilities, with some of these involving high levels of autonomy and others very little. Julian Redmile, the publican, is helpful here again, in Snapshot 7.5.

Snapshot 7.5

Self-employed people in our village

I think that you can see how much I enjoy this job. Much of this is to do with the interesting variety of people who come into the pub. But it is also because I am my own boss. I actually own this pub and, within the inevitable constraints of a bank manager who breathes down my neck all the time, I can more-or-less do things my own way. There are other publicans, however, who are pub managers and are completely dominated by their bosses. Some of these are employees. Others of them are technically self-employed but, given their contractual relationship with their pub company, are actually little freer than the employed managers. I know a number of people who left ordinary jobs, as you might call them, to run a pub and manage their own lives. Certainly some of these feel this to be the case, whether they are technically employed or self-employed. But others don't.

If I think about people in the village, you can see a similar pattern with them. At the one end of the spectrum there are a couple of owner-managers with quite large and flourishing businesses. That is the golden end of self-employment, you could say. But, having said that, one of them is always going on to me, after a few gins, about how with a big business like his 'your life is not your own'. I just tell him he has a great life, in every respect. But if that is the golden end of the spectrum, there are several self-employed building workers in the village who are at the crap end of the spectrum. These blokes, it seems to me, work exclusively for the other business owner who comes in here. I reckon he rips off these so-called self-employed blokes worse than he would be able to do if they were fully employed by him.

There are various ways in which people like building workers may be unreasonably exploited as a result of their being technically self-employed, especially in rural areas where elements of the 'deferential worker' survive (Newby 1977; Fletcher and Watson 2007). As Muehlberger (2007) points out, this kind of 'dependent self-employment' blurs the distinction between the 'employee' and the 'self-employed'; it allows firms to transfer fixed costs and entrepreneurial risk to the worker. But if we look at more 'professional' types of work, there is evidence that non-standard workers here (a proportion of whom are like to be technically self-employed) are disadvantaged in the workforce, compared to employed professionals (Hoque and Kirkpatrick 2003). Problems of this kind with both temporal and contractual non-standard work might be one factor influencing the fact that the proportion of self-employed workers in the UK tended to remain stable prior to the post–2008 recession, at around 10 per cent of the workforce (Edgell 2006). However, the number of self-employed rose significantly in the post–2008 recession and it can be argued that there has been 'simply not enough work around', with 'the possibility that some of the self-employed are closer to being self-unemployed' (Bell and Blanchflower 2013).

Paid work in the informal economy

When people are not formally employed or self-employed, they do not necessarily cease to engage in working activities that might ameliorate material aspects of their unemployed status. And people who are formally employed might choose to supplement their incomes by working informally in their 'spare' time, often avoiding declaring their income to the tax authorities. Both groups are sometimes said to be working in the informal economy (also known as the 'hidden', 'subterranean', 'submerged', 'shadow' or 'irregular' economy).

Paid work in the informal economy

Work, legal or illegal, which is done for gain but is not officially 'declared' for such purposes as taxation, social security or employment law compliance.

Paid work in the 'informal economy' is only one kind of 'informal work'. Williams (2004, 2007) uses the term 'paid informal exchange' and puts it alongside 'self-provisioning' (which includes domestic work to which we turn shortly) and 'unpaid community work' (which includes the voluntary work which we also consider later in this chapter). Yet the boundaries between these types of exchange are not sharp ones. Williams observes that, although paid informal exchange work is often 'market-like' and conducted for profit, some of it is 'conducted as paid favours for kin, friends and neighbours' this making it 'more akin to unpaid community work than market-like employment'. And interdependence often exists between these different activities (Williams and Nadin 2012).

In so far as these two types of work both exist, however, they are interdependent as well as separate. This is illustrated in Pahl's (1984) studies in the Isle of Sheppey, which showed that the benefits gained from the various kinds of informal economic activity occurring in this not untypical part of Britain accrued to those households in which there were already incomes from formal employment. This is clearly seen in 'self-provisioning' activities where the employed were much better able to brew their own beer or do their own decorating than the unemployed – who were less able to afford the materials. As in the formal business world, money is needed for investment before work is created, whether this be 'do-it-yourself' work or 'moonlighting' activities where tools, transport and raw materials are often needed to enable one to earn extra money 'on the side'. Williams and Windebank's (2003) intensive research showed that the more affluent homes were the ones most engaged in informal work activities. The key distinction, Williams (2007) suggests, is not between relatively formalised and informalised populations within societies. Instead it is between 'fully engaged (work busy)' groups who use *both* formal and informal labour to get work done, and relatively 'disengaged' groups amongst whom there is a lower level of both formal and informal work and, hence, 'a lesser ability to get necessary work completed'.

Domestic work

The separating of home and 'workplace' is a relatively recent historical development associated with the rise of industrialism. Nevertheless, work is still carried out in the home, as the evidence of most people's home lives readily demonstrates.

> ## Domestic labour
>
> Household tasks such as cooking, cleaning, shopping and looking after dependent young, old or sick members of the household.

The majority of full-time domestic workers are women who are located in the social division of labour with the title of 'housewife', and as Williams (1988) observed, the definition of 'domestic labour' which dominates the literature is one of the 'unpaid work undertaken by women in their own households'. Since this is not a paid or employee occupation and since housewives experience widely varying social and material conditions in line with the varying economic positions of their spouses, it is far more difficult to locate economically and sociologically than most occupations. It was therefore ground-breaking when Oakley (1974) analysed the work of housewives as if it were an occupation like any other. She reported three-quarters of her sample of women as dissatisfied with their role and noted its loneliness, its monotony, its repetitiveness, its long hours, its low status and the fact that tasks never seemed to be complete. Bonney and Reinach (1993), however, found a majority of houseworkers 'endorsing' the role. Women with young children experienced more of the negative features of the role than others. As these researchers say, their research stresses the need 'to appreciate the diverse, as well as the common, experiences of incumbents of the role of full-time houseworker'.

With the considerable increase in the proportion of women working outside the home which we noted earlier, it would be reasonable to expect that there would be a shift towards men and women sharing domestic tasks. Wheelock (1990), on the basis of a study in which the women were employed and the men were unemployed, suggested that the shifting pattern of paid work roles among men and women might indicate a trend towards a more egalitarian approach to domestic work. However, Morris (1988) reported her 'general impression . . . that within working-class culture there are strong feelings against male involvement in tasks commonly regarded to be essentially female'. Inevitably, the differing pictures emerging here are in part the outcome of different research designs. This was recognised by Warde and Hetherington (1993) who attempted in their investigation to produce evidence which could, as effectively as possible, be compared to material from the 1960s. This suggested that, with some qualification, 'gender stereotyping of specific work tasks and unequal contributions between men and women cannot have changed much in the last twenty years'. And Bond and Sales (2001) interpret survey evidence as showing that women carry a 'dual burden' of paid and unpaid work which 'disadvantages them in terms of employment, income and welfare'.

Such patterns appear to apply across social class boundaries. Edgell (1980) showed that the majority of the middle-class families he studied had a pattern of role segregation in which the wife 'typically performed a distinct range of domestic and child-rearing tasks considerably more often than the husband, and generally deferred to the husband's authority in the "more important" areas of decision-making'. The major influence on the pattern of role allocation was not the work or the family career cycles but the husband's orientation to paid work and the wife's orientation to domestic work. Again, the importance is demonstrated of the meaning which individuals attach to their work roles, whether these be employment or domestic. And this continues to apply, it would appear, when families are able to afford to employ domestic labour. The late 1980s in Britain saw a dramatic expansion in the use of waged domestic labour by high-income, dual-career households, according to Gregson and Lowe (1994a), whose research indicates that the employment of cleaners and nannies does not create a more egalitarian pattern of role allocation between men and women. What are emerging here are 'new domestic divisions of labour which involve just women' (Gregson and Lowe 1994b).

It remains to be seen how the activity of domestic labour, and how it is seen in society, will adjust to the increase in the numbers of 'house husband' domestic workers and the numbers of people brought into homes as paid domestic workers (Gregson and Lowe 1994a). Yet the evidence available so far is that whatever changes might be appearing are 'slow a-coming' with women continuing to 'perform a disproportionate amount of domestic and parenting work, even when they also undertake paid work' (Pilcher 2000).

Baxter (2000), on the basis of her Australian research evidence, suggests that it is helpful in trying to understand the 'slow pace of change' to look at women's 'subjective interpretations of the division of household tasks'. Although women in the study reported spending 24 hours per week on domestic work compared to men's reported 9 hours (and women spending twice as much time on childcare as men), 59 per cent of them said they felt this division to be a 'fair' one (compared to 68 per cent of men). And in almost all of the families in Beagan *et al.*'s (2008) study of 'foodwork' in three ethno-cultural groups in Canada the women 'held primary responsibility for foodwork', with no-one seeming to view this as unfair. Even when there is recognition of unfairness in the domestic division of labour, it does not necessarily follow that practices will change in the light of this evaluation. We see this in the case of Christopher and Christine Fellows in Snapshot 7.6.

Snapshot 7.6

Domestic work in Christine and Christopher Fellows' home

Christopher: I have to admit that I feel guilty about this, but home tasks are not shared equally between Chris and me. I didn't use to feel so bad about the situation when the children were small, Chris was working only part-time. I was building my career as a professional musician and Chris was there in the house when supper needed cooking, when the lawn needed mowing or the beds changing.

Christine: But I think the rot set in earlier than that, if you'll excuse the term, Chris. When we first lived together I should have insisted that you learned to cook. But, think about how it happened; it just seemed easier all round for me to prepare the food because I knew how to do it.

Christopher: And you seemed to do it so easily – and, of course, so well.

Christine: Be quiet, Chris. Flattery will not help you out here. My mother taught me to cook and yours didn't.

Christopher: So that's where the rot set in – with our mothers.

Christine: And their mothers, and their mothers before them. This might help explain things, Chris, but it doesn't excuse any of it. Anyway, I do all the household administration, don't I? And my mother didn't teach me about car and household insurance, taxation and all that.

Christopher: Yes, hands up. It has to be said that you are simply cleverer than me at these things, but I ought to get you to train me on these matters.

Christine: But this is where the problem now lies. We are both so busy in our careers that we don't have the time for us to sit down and for me to teach you to cook and do tax returns.

Christopher: I have been improving, though, haven't I? Although you've mowed the lawn more often than I have, it was me who made the new patio, wasn't it. And it was me who went along to the university open days last year when the twins were thinking about life after school. And I am sure you remember that I took complete charge of the cooking at our anniversary barbecue last weekend.

Christine: Don't make me angry, Christopher. You know damn well these are simply the exceptions that prove the rule.

Christopher: What rule?

Christine: The rule that I am the home person and do nearly everything in the home and family for you, whilst you, great master of the international musical world, simply deign to do a few symbolic 'big tasks', when it suits you.

As with all case studies, there are factors in the Fellows' family story which are particular to the specific situation; one of them is Chris's being a creative artist and the other a financial services expert, for example. But there are more widely applicable factors too: the fact that it was the female partner's mother who taught her child to cook and not the male partner's mother. Also, the tendency for male partners to take on mainly what Christine calls 'big tasks' has been noted by researchers. It was noted in a Swedish study, for example, that male partners tended to carry out bigger external and episodic jobs (like maintaining the car or clearing snow from around the house), whereas the women tended to cover the 'smaller' internal and repetitive jobs like cooking food, washing clothes or cleaning the house (Nordenmark and Nyman 2003). Just as with Christopher and his cooking at the anniversary barbecue, the men temporarily moved over into women's territory when it was a special occasion. And there may be a similar pattern suggested by Christopher's pride at attending university open days. Reay (2005a) in her study of parental involvement in children's school work observed that the bulk of 'home school work' was done by mothers – with fathers simply coming in to 'help' from time to time. And, again, the special occasion is important here: fathers, says Reay, tended to favour involvement in events like parents' evenings whilst 'hardly any' of the fathers studied 'got involved in the practical maintenance work that involved physical rather than mental labour, ironing school blouses or preparing packed lunches'. What, then, about the cases where women are higher paid than their partners? Lyonette and Crompton's (2015) research suggests whilst doing more than other men, such men still take a smaller share of domestic tasks than the women.

Voluntary work

A form of work which occurs outside the home but which nevertheless has a continuity with domestic work is that whereby people regularly visit a sick relative or elderly neighbour to carry out tasks which these individuals cannot do for themselves. This type of work or helping, say, to clean up one's street after a flood has an element of kin or community obligation to it. It is generally identified as *informal* voluntary work and it is distinguished from what might be seen as voluntary work proper, where the individual undertakes work in the absence of pressures from kin or community, typically through the auspices of a voluntary organisation. Such *formal* work, or 'volunteering', is given more attention than informal voluntary work, not only because it involves a greater element of 'the voluntary' but because it is increasingly seen alongside private and public sector provision as a 'third prong' of civil society which can be harnessed to 'meet welfare needs' (Williams 2007). In Snapshot 7.7, Pamela Wilby explains how she became involved in volunteering.

Voluntary work/volunteering

Unpaid involvement in organised work tasks which benefit members of society beyond (although possibly including) immediate relatives.

Edgell identifies the essence of formal voluntary work as its being unpaid and involving a 'gift in the sense that it reflects a sense of community' (Edgell 2006), and we can note that Pamela talks about reducing the amount of paid work she undertakes in order to *give* at least half a day a week to the voluntary organisation with which she is involved.

Pamela volunteers

My second child was hit and permanently injured by a car three years ago. This inevitably changed my life. But it was not just a matter of looking after the child in a different and more demanding way than what I had been used to with my first child, it made me feel that I wanted to do something to help other parents and children in similar situations, as well as myself and my child. I was fortunate to be in a professional family and was able to reduce my own working hours to enable me to give at least half a day every week to a charity in the city which both provides events and facilities for parents and children like my own and also lobbies the authorities for more measures to reduce road incidents which injure people (we refuse to call them 'accidents', by the way).

Pamela's case also illustrates an important point made by Taylor (2005), who argues that we must go beyond analysing people's psychological 'needs' in explaining people's engagement in voluntary work and connect any such psychological factors to their whole 'work trajectory' and, in particular, to 'their paid work and their economic and social position'. Voluntary work, like domestic work, Taylor points out, 'has to be supported economically' as it is, in this case, by Pamela's family having two, presumably relatively high, 'professional' incomes.

Women, men and work

In spite of past stereotypes in which men 'went out to work' whilst women did the 'housework', women have always played a major part in the employed workforces of industrial societies. A considerable increase in the extent of women in paid work came about over the past century yet, as Hakim's (1993, 2000) statistical analysis shows, there has been considerable continuity in the proportion of women in full-time work. She observes a decrease in both the proportion of women 'staying at home' and those pursuing full-time work careers as more and more part-time jobs have become available with the increasing flexibility of labour markets. By the closing years of the twentieth century, half of the workforce in Britain and other advanced industrial capitalist societies was female (Walby 1997; Crompton 1997) with married women, including those with children, forming a considerable proportion of this. In addition to increased employment flexibility leading to many more part-time jobs, disproportionately taken up by women, there has been growth in service jobs of the type with which women have traditionally been associated. This has been accompanied by the decline in manufacturing jobs, with which men have typically been associated, this not being unrelated to the increase in male unemployment – a situation that has seen a significant move away from the 'male breadwinner' pattern of family economy and the rise of the dual earning pattern. Bradley's (1999) study of the north east of England found two-thirds of the women covered reporting that their incomes were essential for the household and over a quarter assessing them as 'important'.

Despite this considerable change in the extent of work activities of women in advanced societies, patterns of occupational segregation have changed to a much lesser degree – men, broadly speaking, tending to do 'men's work' and women tending to do 'women's work'. And segregation is clearly present in developing economies as Caraway (2007) demonstrates in her study of manufacturing work in Indonesia. 'Men and women rarely do the same jobs', Caraway observes, even when they work in the same area of production. It was not abnormal for certain areas of production to be 'the exclusive preserve of one gender'.

Occupational segregation

A pattern of occupations in which some are predominantly male and others female. *Horizontal segregation* describes the tendency for male and female work to be separated into types of occupational activity whilst *vertical segregation* sees gender differentiation in who takes the higher level and who takes the lower level jobs within an occupation.

Although basic patterns of segregation have not changed, there has been significant change in certain high-status occupations such as law, accountancy and medicine – and to some extent management – with women's increased participation in higher education providing a new supply of qualified female workers (Walby 1997; Crompton 1997). However, when it comes to who fills the most senior posts in these occupational areas, we see the force of vertical segregation coming into play, with few women reaching the top jobs in the professional areas where they have increasingly played a part at the lower and middle levels (Wilson 1999). As Evetts (1996) observed, in scientific and engineering occupations, women's advancement faces the problem that senior positions within such occupations are likely to involve an emphasis on managerial work rather than strictly 'professional' activities. Such managerial work was very much defined as a masculine activity, with those women who did become managers still being identified as 'women managers' rather than simply as 'managers'. Bolton and Muzio (2008), after reviewing evidence of increased activity of women in the three 'professional' areas of law, teaching and management, conclude that the 'professional projects' of attaining and retaining professional status continue to be pursued as part of a 'masculine project of exploitation and control', one which 'represses, oppresses and subordinates the feminine'. In her study of the career experiences of British women civil engineers, Watts (2009) shows 'very few' women entering senior management posts. Those who do take on management roles have to assume 'male norms' and 'straddle a marginal territory that is bordered by exclusion and resistance'.

If we note the traditional association of women with the less pleasant and the more onerous work tasks in the home and we put this alongside the fact that men in employment are more or less in control of the better rewarded and higher status jobs, we can see why men might be expected to want to 'keep women in their place'. Research among male managers, for example, shows a tendency for men to 'work late' to demonstrate how committed and important they are to the company. This tendency has implications for the family lives too (Watson 2001a). The words of one of the managers in the study are reported in Snapshot 7.8.

Snapshot 7.8

Bed time stories

'Several of us were talking about this yesterday after the regional management meeting. 'Why are we hanging about here when we could be getting home a bit earlier than usual?' I asked the other blokes. Two of them, like me, had young children and all three of us admitted that we prefer to arrive home after the kids have been fed and bathed. It's nice to be able to see them before they go to sleep and to read their bedtime story to them, we agreed.'

'And you don't feel guilty about this?'

'To be honest, I think all three of us feel bad about it. We admitted to each other that it would probably be a good idea for us to get out of the managerial long-hours culture that we have in the business. But, whilst it lasts, we have got the benefit of a good excuse to get out of certain things at home.'

LOOKING BACK <<<<<

Snapshot 7.8 throws light on some of the factors behind the domestic role segregation that we considered when looking at domestic labour (pp. 224–228).

In a case study, Casey (1995) noted the importance to men, who wished to demonstrate their commitment to the organisation, of their cars being seen in the car park at the weekend and early in the morning, as well as in the evening. We can readily link this behavioural pattern to structural aspects of society if we remember that the people making the employment decisions within industrial capitalist societies are men – with many of these 'organisation men' showing 'extreme devotion to company and career', a commitment 'facilitated by the servicing work of secretaries and wives' (Roper 1994). And this servicing work includes emotional support given by wives and secretaries to help men maintain the appropriate masculine image of a character 'driven by intellect' rather than by emotion. Wacjman's study (1998) showed the difficulties faced by women in managerial careers who had to compete with men who were able to devote longer hours to work because they had supportive wives.

All of this contributes to the idea of a 'glass ceiling' existing in many organisations – one that encourages women to leave jobs for ones where a less male-dominated culture prevails (Marshall 1995). If women managers are also members of a minority ethnic group, it is more a concrete rather than a 'glass ceiling' upon which they find themselves hitting their heads (Davidson 1997).

Snapshot 7.9

Gendered roles and the microwave oven

- In the microwave factory, the female 'home economists' have different inputs from male designers, and indeed, a degree of tension exists between these groups.
- In the shops, women shop assistants sell functional 'white goods' like microwaves whilst the entertainment-oriented 'brown goods' (hi-fi's, etc.) are sold by male assistants, this being based on the alleged affinities of women and men salespersons to the gendered interests of the respective purchasers of these two types of product.
- In the home, there is the gender politics of food preparation in which men tend to make use of the oven but only within understandings that leave the main food-providing responsibilities to women.

The complex interplay between domestic identities and working patterns is not only seen at senior levels, it is important to note. Snapshot 7.9 reports a study which skilfully illustrates this point, is that of the development, manufacture, marketing and use of the microwave oven carried out by Cockburn and Ormrod (1993).

In spite of optimism in some circles that the growing use of computers in work would reduce or even remove gender inequalities in and around the workplace, studies show that this has had little impact. Woodfield (2000), for example, in her case study of a software company, shows how that company stressed the value of people having the right 'personality' and social skills, rather than straightforward technical skills. However, the vagueness of these criteria allowed senior men to promote other men and therefore continue to reproduce the traditional dominant type of male worker. And Brynin (2006) used data from across Europe to test whether the 'wage premium' which is conferred on workers by the use of computers benefits women enough to bring about 'equalisation through technology, or possibly even a female advantage'. She found no such 'across-the-board benefit' for women from the use of computers.

Managers are keen to recruit what Jenkins (1986) calls 'predictable manageable workers' thereby both creating and being influenced by general patterns of gender discrimination. Detailed case study research by Collinson *et al.* (1990) shows the considerable extent to which private sector managers, often in defiance of legal and organisational equal opportunities policies, blatantly excluded women from what they saw as 'men's jobs' and seemingly shamelessly utilised rationalisations for this which focused on the allegedly greater reliability and ability of men. Women's biology, their temperaments and their unreliability in the face of domestic commitments all rendered them less desirable for certain jobs – regardless of evidence which might have indicated to them otherwise. All of these assumptions about masculinity and femininity play their parts in the everyday interactions that occur in workplaces and help achieve what Collinson and Hearn (1996) call the 'gendering of organisations'. The discourses used both draw upon and contribute to the social construction of masculinities and femininities in the broadly gendered way in which the whole of work and social life is organised (Alvesson and Du Billing 1997).

Significant findings on gender roles have also emerged from research on those involved with small businesses. Scase and Goffee (1982) showed that wives of men who had established and were running such businesses tended to be economically, socially and psychologically subordinated to the needs of their husbands and that, without the largely unrecognised contributions of wives, many small businesses 'would not even get off the ground'. Not only do the wives contribute unpaid time and effort to the business, they are left to cope single-handedly with domestic work, often with limited financial resources, as their husband devotes himself to the fledgling business. And Baines and Wheelock (2000) show in their study of 'micro businesses' how spouses typically work together to run the enterprise but rarely do so on the basis of equality. At the other end of the scale, Mulholland (2003) closely studied seventy wealthy family businesses and found that the women in the family did indeed help create the wealth of these families, only to find later that their achievement had become appropriated and their inputs to the businesses marginalised by male members of the family. Mulholland observes the ways in which popular narratives about 'entrepreneurship' are used to support this marginalisation by continually linking entrepreneurship and masculinity. As Bruni *et al.* (2004) say, following their ethnographic study of Italian small businesses, the historical pattern whereby entrepreneurship is 'located in the symbolic universe of the male' continues to pertain.

Given that trade unions have increasing proportions of women in their memberships, we might expect them to be working significantly to change gender inequalities. Parker (2004) observes, however, that trade unions still tend to be dominated by men and remain male focused in their priorities. And this is in spite of the 'women's groups' which have been set up within unions to provide 'a collective space for women that helps them develop their strengths, advance their concerns and access empowering positions'. Parker sees a *transformative* potential in these groups, a potential to change the identities of trade unions rather than focusing on attempting either to compensate for the work-based inequalities between men or women or attempting to remove them. This potential is not however being realised.

The relationship between the work aspects and the domestic or personal aspects of the lives of men and women, and the way both of these play a part in how they shape their identities and make whatever choices are available to them, are complex and vary across class situations and occupational settings. A useful way of pulling many of these factors together is the total social organisation of labour (TSOL) concept developed by Glucksmann (1995, 2000, 2005).

LOOKING BACK <<<<<

Glucksmann's thinking was introduced early in Chapter 1 as part of the move to develop a 'new sociology of work'.

To understand gender aspects of social and employment change it is suggested that the starting point should not be one of focusing separately on the division of tasks in the different spheres of home and work, but of considering all the work done in a society whether it be paid, unpaid, permanent, casual, part-time, full-time, productive, 'reproductive' and whether it be carried out in domestic, organisational spheres, or wherever. Only when we adopt this position, and reject the automatic assumption of two 'separate spheres', will we come fully to understand the ways in which work meanings and personal identities are shaped – and the part that gender relations play in all of this.

Explaining patterns of gender inequality

To understand the differences between the work activities or experiences of women and men in society we have to recognise the interplay that occurs between factors that relate to the prevailing type of economic system and the more universal factors relating to relationships between men and women. To put it very simply, it could be said that the patterns currently prevailing in industrial capitalist societies serve both the interests of the employers as employers and the interests of men as men. The maintenance of women's relatively disadvantaged market position can be seen as functioning in three ways:

(1) It provides employers with a relatively cheap and malleable labour force.

(2) It reduces the number of potential competitors which aspiring males face in their work careers.

(3) It avoids attracting too many women away from the domestic setting which would either leave men without wives or would require them to take on the dirtier and more boring household tasks.

This kind of explanatory framework for looking at how the sexual division of labour operates in industrial capitalist societies usefully relates occupational patterns back to the wider pattern of inequality that prevails between the sexes in society at large. What it does not do, however, is to help us understand how male members of society came to achieve the kinds of advantage which it sees them having over women in the first place. To understand this is a much more challenging matter.

The first difficulty we have to overcome with regard to the problem of explanation is that of separating the particular pattern of male–female relations which exists in any one society or time from the more general patterns which run through all kinds of society. The importance of considering the particularities of the basic form of economic organisation, in ways like this, is effectively illustrated by the case of the !Kung people of Africa in Snapshot 7.10.

Underlying this kind of 'particular' process we have to find some general factor, or set of factors, which encouraged these tribes-people to adopt this type of sexual division of labour or encouraged the

Snapshot 7.10

Women and men of the !Kung

Draper (1975) observed that, as these people changed from a nomadic foraging type of economy to a more settled pattern in which the women engaged in agriculture and the men in herding, so could women be seen to lose the high degree of power and autonomy which they had held in the bush life. Whereas they had been mobile and independent workers in the bush, they were now less mobile and soon became tied to the home. There was an increase in domestic tasks to be done in the more settled existence and this became designated as the province of the women. The men, however, developed an 'aura of authority' and distanced themselves from the domestic world. In the place of the egalitarian pattern of childrearing followed in the bush came a more gender-differentiated pattern in which the lives of girls were more narrowly defined than those of the boys. The girls' world was to be the domestic one.

corresponding pattern to be followed historically in Europe with the growth of industrial capitalism. An important starting point for understanding these matters can be found in the observation of the anthropologist, Margaret Mead (1962), that a problem which faces all men, in all civilisations, is that of defining their role in a way which they feel is satisfactory to them. Women have a key role which is defined by nature: that of childbearing. Men, on the other hand, have to create a role for themselves through culture in order to differentiate themselves from women. It is almost as if men have to compensate for the fact that they have no natural role as significant as that of bearing children and therefore feel the need to give themselves prestige and status through cultural institutions which award them a superior status. Explanations of the tendency of males to want to assert dominance in most societies and in most social settings within any society can also be found in accounts of the psychology of childrearing. Chodorow (1978), for example, has argued that the social and psychological differences between men and women go back to the fact that male children, unlike female children, have to achieve their identity by breaking away from the mother who has nurtured them and by building an identity which is distinctive. This involves a rejection of feminine patterns of behaviour but also a fear of regressing to their earlier state. Masculinity has to be worked at and, as Chodorow says, because masculine identity is so 'elusive', it becomes important that certain activities are defined as masculine and superior. Control of these activities and 'the insistence that these realms are superior to the maternal world of youth, become crucial both to the definition of masculinity and to a particular boy's own masculine gender identity'.

It follows from this phenomenon that, although societies vary in the particular details of gender relations, there tends to be a general pattern whereby men take up certain occupational roles from which they exclude women – most typically roles in government, warfare and religion. And, typically associated with this, will be an awarding of high status to these exclusively male occupations and a tendency to downgrade the domestic tasks of women. These two tendencies are often linked by a 'superstructure of myths' (Pickford 1985), in which women's prime place in social life is seen as that of protecting, nurturing and fostering the growth of others and in which it is suggested that women's biology somehow makes them unfit to perform as, say, politicians, priests or generals. The concept of patriarchy is helpful here, this stressing the interrelating of the variety of aspects of relationships between men and women – paid work, domestic work, male sexuality, male violence, state power – and how they amount to a fundamental pattern of inequality (Walby 1986).

Patriarchy

The system of interrelated social structures and cultural practices through which men exploit women.

Cultural support and legitimation of patterns of sexual division of labour developed historically with the growth of certain 'patriarchal ideologies'. Hamilton (1978) noted the effect of Protestant thinking in giving 'unprecedented ideological importance' to the home and the family and in establishing the ideal for women of the faithful and supportive 'proper wife'. By the nineteenth century this had evolved into a powerful 'domestic ideology' which enabled working wives and mothers to be presented as unnatural and immoral (Hall 1992).

Ethnicity and inequality

When understanding inequality in industrial capitalist societies we have to look at the interrelated and cross-cutting factors of class, status, power, gender and ethnicity.

In the study of tendencies towards dualism and segmentation it has always been recognised that a major factor in their emergence was the availability to employers of migrant labour which could provide them with a flexible, tractable and generally quiescent source of labour supply (Doeringer and Piore 1971). Such migrants at certain times may

LOOKING BACK <<<<<

Ethnicity has played a part in two earlier parts of the present chapter. First, it was encountered in the consideration of social status and cultural factors in inequality, with the case of Henry Johnson illustrating some of the processes that occur (p. 209). Second, it was identified as a key factor in dualistic and segmented labour markets (p. 214).

be predominantly people of different skin colour and, at other times, may be from groups which are less visibly 'different'. The latter would have been the case in the past with European migration into the USA or, more recently, with the movement of eastern European workers into western European countries. And in all the varying circumstances in which ethnicity becomes influential in structuring and reproducing inequalities, there will always be an intertwining of economic and cultural factors – a mixing, for example, of people having limited capital in the sense of skills or knowledge and factors of racism and racial discrimination.

An influential line of thinking in the USA has highlighted economic factors in bringing about the patterns of economic hardship experienced by working class black people. The existence of racism and, for example, the tendency for employers to show preference for white workers over black ones, has been observed but judged by writers like Wilson (1987, 1996), to be less significant than the ways in which the decline of manufacturing industries in the north of the USA has disproportionately impacted on black working class employees, pushing them out of high-quality and well-paid manufacturing jobs into lower skilled and lower paid work in service industries. Carter (2003), however, in his study of ethnicity in British workplaces stresses the importance of processes of social exclusion and closure.

Social closure

The process whereby a group seeks to gain or defend its advantages over other groups by closing its ranks to those it defines as outsiders.

Carter (2003) utilises the Weberian concept of social closure to identify various ways in which dominant social groups are able to keep out members of groups which are ethnically different from them. They may use 'credentialist' criteria (stressing formal qualifications) or exercise sponsorship and patronage to favour individuals with an ethnicity similar to their own. And an important part is played in recruitment and occupational advancement by the informal networks from which culturally non-preferred workers and professionals are excluded. In a study of the ways in which minority ethnic workers are overrepresented in semi- and un-skilled work and amongst the unemployed in one British city, Mason (2003) stresses the importance of racism and discrimination, showing the various ways in which ethnic identities are constructed in the context of advantaged cultural groups working to maintain their advantage.

Summary

The occupational principle of work structuring has not been entirely overtaken by the organisational principle in modern societies. Especially significant is the close link that exists between occupational structures and inequalities of opportunity, reward, class, status, gender and ethnicity. In all of these areas the segmentation of labour markets is important as are the patterns of non-standard working. Part-time, temporary, home and teleworking play a part of the lives of many workers. And not all workers are employed by work organisations; many are self-employed, receiving pay for work in the 'informal economy' or are engaged in voluntary or domestic work.

Aspects of occupations: from managers to exotic dancers, artists to professionals and soldiers to investment bankers

Key issues

- Is there a management occupation?
- What is managerialism, and what are its consequences for organisations and society?
- How do supervisors, junior managers and team leaders fit into the occupational hierarchy?
- How helpful is it to speak of knowledge work and creative occupations?
- What is 'dirty work'?
- What role is played in working lives by patterns of occupational recruitment; occupational careers; occupational identities, cultures and ideologies; and occupational communities?
- What are 'professions'? To what extent can they be understood as outcomes of 'occupational strategies'; what part do they play in the shaping of societies?

The occupation of management and the ideology of managerialism

If we look at the occupational structure of a modern society, we will find a substantial number of workers who are designated as managers, whether these be people directing giant business corporations or individuals in charge of small shops or cafes. With regard to the latter category, Lloyd and Payne (2014) show that many shop managers are poorly rewarded and are 'highly constrained by the degree of centralized control wielded by head office'. This is far from the image that many people have of 'managers' as a person acting with relatively high personal discretion and enjoying high rewards.

However, given that the concept of occupation that is being used here involves 'engagement on a regular basis in a part or the whole of a range of work tasks which are identified under a particular heading or title by both those carrying out these tasks and by a wider public' (Chapter 6, p. 206), we can very reasonably talk of a managerial occupation, in spite of the heterogeneity of the activity. The designation of manager is used frequently and regularly across society and there is a definable type of tasks associated with the label: that of 'management'.

> ### Management
>
> Work tasks and ideas that are primarily concerned with directing various aspects of organisations rather than with carrying out the tasks that make up the main work of the organisation.

The 'rational-systems' style of popular thinking about organisations (Chapter 5, p. 136) treats managerial work as a science-like activity involving the design, control and maintenance of organisations as, in effect, big social *machines* established to fulfil 'organisational goals' (rather than to pursue any interests of their own). Managers are skilled and knowledgeable experts who apply rational and socially neutral knowledge and techniques.

> ### LOOKING BACK <<<<<
>
> The 'classic administrative principles' and 'scientific management' strands of thinking discussed in Chapter 5 (pp. 141–145) are early formal statements of the notion of the manager as a technical expert.

It is often said that these ideas were superseded by more social–science based investigations of the type reviewed as part of later strands of thinking in Chapter 5. However, although this may have happened in more scholarly or academic thinking about organisations and their management, rational–system thinking can be seen as having reached a greater height than ever in the form of the ideology of *managerialism*. This is central to dominant contemporary socio–political ideologies, much of the business education curriculum and a high proportion of business and management books.

> ## Managerialism
>
> A social and political ideology which treats most if not all social, political and cultural problems in contemporary societies as soluble by the application of managerial techniques and practices. Social problems and social welfare are *manageable* administrative-technical matters rather than matters open to political, ideological or value debate and democratic choice.

Originally the 'managerialism' term was used to refer to the type of society that Burnham (1945) identified in the 1940s, a society in which the people who manage or direct the corporations of modern societies take control away from the allegedly separate interest of those who own wealth. This analysis did not stand up to later empirical analysis (especially Zeitlin 1989), and it has become clear that family interests and broader 'constellations of interest' including banks, insurance companies and pension funds tend to ensure that the interests of owners generally take priority over those managers (Scott 1997). It is not unreasonable, nevertheless, to see managers as *agents* of the owners of capital. Research suggests that they seek ways of operating which recognise an affinity between their personal or group interests and the interests of those who employ them. This can be illustrated by Smith's (1990) study of middle managers in an American bank. A significant number of these managers clashed with the top management of the bank over organisational issues and implemented different measures from those that they were directed to take. Their defiance was not however anything to do with questioning basic corporate goals. Instead, their actions were 'shaped by an alternative sense of the corporate interest'. Watson (2001a) shows, similarly, how managers in a British company disputed the particular decisions and styles of their corporate headquarters on the grounds both of their own interests (including a desire to be more involved in strategic decisions) and those of the 'business as a whole'.

The modified use of the term managerialism to refer to what Klikauer (2013) calls a merging of management techniques with the belief that these techniques offer the best way to organise societies, retains the core idea that managerial practices are deeply implicated in global power relations, albeit without managers on their own coming to form a power elite. At first sight, managerialist principles might appear to be at odds with the increasingly globally-dominant *neoliberal* principles examined in Chapter 4 – given that managerialism calls for visible corporate managerial action rather than the working out of the 'invisible hand' of the market, the market being a key concept to neoliberals. However, if we look closely at the almost defining practice of neoliberal governments to move previously state-managed undertakings in fields of health, welfare, education and justice to privately owned enterprises, we readily see that those 'private' interests *manage* these enterprises using all the assumptions, techniques and practices developed by managers in the world of corporate business. Hence managerialism and neoliberalism go hand in hand with each other. And this consonance, in the view of many commentators, constitutes an undermining of democracy, if not of 'politics' itself.

As vitally important as these issues are, and as 'real' as managerialism is as an influence on everything that occurs within managerial work, we cannot directly read across from the claims that managerialist ideology makes about what managerial techniques can achieve to an understanding of the actual work which is done by people designated as managers. If we are going to understand such matters, we have to put aside the rational-systems perspective and apply what we earlier labelled an emergent-relational frame of reference (Chapter 5, p. 130). This is precisely what Tengblad (2012) does in his major overview of the work of managers, and his pulling together of twenty-one seminal studies (alongside thirteen empirical studies presented in his book) to create a 'practice-based theory of management'. To create a 'foundation' for such a theory, Tengblad derives ten 'theses' from existing knowledge of managerial work. Among these are the recognition that managerial work involves many unforeseen events, involves a hectic work pace and long working hours, is usually fragmented, is performed in an adaptive manner, is emotionally intense and involves substantial participation in informal activities.

In the earliest of the classic studies that Tengblad reviews, Carlson (1951) showed that a sample of managing directors were rarely alone and uninterrupted for periods long enough to engage in systematic analysis and thought. On the basis of a review of this kind of study, including a series of his own, Mintzberg (1973) argued that the manager's job is not one which 'breeds reflective planners'. Instead it produces 'adaptive information manipulators who favour a stimulus–response milieu'. Hence, managers gravitate towards the current, the specific and the well-defined and they prefer 'gossip, hearsay, speculation to routine reports'. Managerial work is thus seen as opportunistic, habitual and almost 'instinctual'. However, as the research of Kotter (1982) suggests, this may not reflect an inappropriate fondness for simply muddling-along but indicates a managerial recognition that their key concern has to be with developing and maintaining a network of relationships with other people in order to obtain the level of co-operation needed to get the job done. Close ethnographic examination of what happens day to day, month to month, in managerial work strongly suggests that managerial work is essentially social and political rather than fundamentally analytical (Watson 2001a).

Whilst detailed empirical research shows the daily activities of managers to be political in the sense of 'micropolitics' (Chapter 5), the earlier discussion of managerialism indicates that the managerial occupation is also deeply implicated in power relations at the societal and, indeed, global level. And, here, it is significant to note that managers at the various senior levels of corporations may, in effect, be splitting away in social class terms from the bulk of managerial workers. This can be inferred from their regular social mixing with leading politicians and their engaging with politics through government advisory roles or entry into, for example, the British House of Lords. It can also be inferred from the very high levels of material rewards such people gain from being in charge of businesses (often with little or no apparent connection existing between the performance level of their businesses and the levels of reward paid by the business, especially in the case of the payments made to business 'leaders' who are pushed out of or 'removed' from their roles). In the terms used in Chapter 7's discussion of pattern of social class, these very senior managers can be seen as members of the *elite* class whilst the bulk of managerial workers are to be located further down the class hierarchy.

LOOKING FORWARD >>>>>

The implications for this 'splitting off' of the upper echelons of the managerial hierarchy are returned to in Chapter 10 in an examination of the stress and anxiety aspects of managerial work.

A development which has been observed within managerial work in recent years has been the spread of internal consultants. As a result of their study of individuals with expertise in accounting, information technology or human resource management who are located within organisations' 'internal consulting units', Sturdy *et al.* (2015) propose the concept of the 'consultant manager', and they link this to a notion of a new *neo-bureaucratic management*.

LOOKING BACK <<<<<

Arguments against the identification of new 'post-bureaucratic' forms were set out in Chapter 5, pp. 149–151.

An alternative perspective on the development of internal consulting units is one which would examine the specificities of the work done by members of such units and to distinguish between those who are providing administrative or technical services to designated managers, particularly in the IT or routine accounting sphere, and those whose 'advice' to designated managers directly contributes to the broad shaping of the organisation – a type of work which, regardless of title or bureaucratic location, is managerial work. This is especially likely in the human resourcing sphere where, for many decades, personnel/HR managers have worked with a micropolitical rhetoric of their being 'advisory' when, in practice, their advice is such that 'line managers' ignore at their peril (Watson 1977).

Supervisors, 'first-line managers' and team leaders

Supervisors, 'foremen' and 'first-line managers' are an occupational group whose class and status location has often been seen as ambiguous. The industrial foreman emerged out of the role of the labour contractor or piecemaster in the late nineteenth and early twentieth centuries. Such an individual, says Littler (1982), would be 'the undisputed master of his own shop', yet the role was soon 'eroded' as incursions were made by various technical experts, inspectors and rate-fixers. This was followed by erosion by production engineers, personnel managers and the rest so that supervisors became classical industrial sociology's 'man in the middle' (Roethlisberger 1945) or the 'marginal man' of industry (Wray 1949).

LOOKING BACK <<<<<

Teamworking and lean production, both of which have significant implications for the role of the supervisor or first-line manager are examined in Chapter 6 (pp. 288–291 and pp. 192–194).

One might expect all this to have changed with the growth of team-working, a change in which control is allegedly moved downwards from supervisors to group members themselves. Yet comparative research in Britain, Germany and the USA suggests the change is not, as might be expected, predominantly one in which supervisors disappear from the scene. Instead, according to Mason (2000) such innovations as 'lean production' and teamworking have the potential to free supervisors from having to deal with the day-to-day details of the workplace and 'help to restore the influence of supervisors in strategic decision-making which was lost in the early transition from craft to mass production'. This could mean that first-line managers, as an occupational group, could be making a move upwards in hierarchical terms and are shaking off the ambiguity of the old foreman's 'man in the middle' position as they move upwards into 'management proper'. This is not the experience of Tom Shears in Snapshot 8.1.

Snapshot 8.1

Tom remembers an old song

I've been thinking of my Dad a lot since I got this team leader job and how he told me that when he was made a foreman, he jokingly sang,

'The working class can kick my arse,
I've got the foreman's job at last'.

As he fully expected, he was given something of a 'cold shoulder' by his former workmates. But in no way whatsoever, he insisted, was he now part of management, even though he does remember them at some point changing his job title from 'foreman' to 'supervisor' and telling him that he was now a 'first-line manager'. So, I wondered how all of this was going to play out for me when I accepted the team leader job here in the same company. It is certainly a different world but I don't think that what I do here on the shop-floor from day to day is really very different from what my father did. The bosses certainly don't involve me in any kind of business decisions. They tend, instead, to give me 'briefing sheets' about business and strategic matters and ask me to 'cascade it to the team'. In spite of this, I think I spend more time with the managers than my father did. They do consult me on operational aspects of changes they have in mind, and perhaps most significantly, they pull me upstairs to help them when they get bothered that we are not making our departmental targets.

The situation that Tom describes here fits into the pattern identified by Hales' (2005) systematic research on first-line managers. This suggests that there is no radical transformation in the work people do in this occupational category either downwards into team co-ordination or upwards into 'business management'. They retain the core supervisory role, located primarily at the operational level. Nevertheless, there has been a broadening of their role as their increasing accountability for 'operational fluidity' and, sometimes, for 'broader performance metrics' leads them to share responsibilities and accountabilities 'upwards' with managers rather than 'downwards' with team members. And a broad overview of subsequent research into the extent to which the spread of 'flatter hierarchies', generally understood as the ideal proposed by 'lean management' thinking, have come about concludes that when it comes to actual practices 'there is a lack of empirical support' for the removal of the supervisory level.

Knowledge, creative and cultural workers

It was observed in Chapter 4, when allegedly new types of 'information' or 'knowledge societies' were discussed, that speculation has been more to the fore than information about what was actually happening in occupational structures. This is not surprising, perhaps, given the vagueness of the concept of the knowledge worker. There is clearly no widely recognised occupation of knowledge work or everyday talk of a 'knowledge industry'. Instead, commentators tend to refer to a rather large and varied bundle of different occupations, all of which are involved in some way with knowledge and information rather than the producing of material goods or direct services to customers and clients. Thus we often see bundled together rather mundane 'IT' or clerical jobs in which 'data' is simply moved about with work undertaken by designers, scientists, librarians, researchers, engineers and programmers.

The poor definition of 'knowledge activities' which are 'uncritically identified with service activities and creativity of all types' has been a 'significant contributor to the collapse of the concept of the knowledge worker', argues Svarc (2016). We have thus been given a 'partial and simplistic view' of knowledge work (Brinkley *et al.* 2009). To improve this situation, Brinkley *et al.* carried out a large UK survey that focused on the tasks undertaken by workers, rather depending, as much research has done, on job titles or education levels. The researchers analysed the content of respondents' jobs in terms of the 'cognitive complexity' required for each task – 'the use of high-level "tacit" knowledge that resides in people's minds rather than being written down (or codified) in manuals, guides, lists and procedures'. Workers were then clustered into seven groups ranging from 'expert thinkers, innovators and leaders' (the most knowledge intensive groups) to 'assistants and clerks' (the least knowledge intensive).

The top group amounted to only 11 per cent of the workforce. So, in spite all the hyperbole, Brinkley *et al.* conclude that 'the reality is that even after 40 years of uninterrupted growth in knowledge based industries and occupations, such jobs account for only one in ten of those in work today'. Further, they suggest, on the basis of their research, knowledge workers 'are not spear-heading radical changes in the way we work'.

Another pair of occupational groupings which are often pointed to as playing an actual or potentially economically significant role in contemporary societies are those of jobs in the 'creative industries' and the 'cultural industries'. Sometimes the stress is on the way that members of a 'creative class' are transforming both work and consumption (Florida 2002), or may potentially do so in a radical or 'progressive' way (Banks 2007). At other times, the expressions 'creative' or 'cultural' worker seem to mean little different from 'knowledge worker', with occupations like architecture and design appearing both in lists of 'knowledge workers' and in the roll call of creative workers (Howkins 2001). A helpful attempt to tighten definitions has been that of Hesmondhalgh (2002) who writes about what he calls the 'core cultural industries'. These are to be recognised by the fact that they produce 'texts' and 'cultural artefacts' through forms of activity that are recognisably 'industrial'. Hence, we see in this core the occupations of print and digital publishing, video and computer game production, advertising and marketing, broadcasting, music writing and recording and film making.

Research is now beginning to tell us more about the tasks undertaken in these creative areas. Our understanding of occupational areas with an emphasis on 'the symbolic' rather than the material can be greatly enhanced by knowledge of how different jobs in this category vary in the degree of creativity, initiative and autonomy which they involve – in a parallel way to which Brinckley *et al.* earlier examined the cognitive dimension of the so-called knowledge workers. The tasks covered undertaken in the creative industries have the potential to provide workers with 'the pleasure of working with ideas', enjoying 'the complexity and challenge of original work', the 'opportunity for high commitment to quality products', as well as 'freedom from bureaucratic routines' which 'mitigates workers' feelings of discontent and of vulnerability to less than professional treatment' (Hesmondhalgh and Baker 2011). And whilst the makers of high-quality guitars may be subject to certain corporate controls and the pressures of markets, they are in the privileged position of being 'master craftspeople' with a sense of having some control of their market – one of 'elite musicians and wealthy buyers' (Dudley 2014).

The latter characteristic of creative industry work clearly relates to the managerial aspect of creative industries and connects to the observation of McKinlay and Smith (2009) that this management 'tends to be informal and intimate rather than formal or hierarchical'. However, one might query whether this more relaxed style of management applies as much to routine work as to the more obviously 'creative' tasks in any given creative industry; scene shifters in the theatre, say, or 'roadies' in the rock business. Valuable insight here is available in Siciliano's (2016) study of studio attendants which suggests that routine workers 'experience aesthetic pleasure vis-à-vis technology in ways similar to expressive cultural workers'. Siciliano argues that the technical artefacts reproduce the 'feel' of the work done by the 'expressive' cultural workers and that management exploit this tendency by placing these expressive technical artefacts throughout the workplace and encouraging their use during downtime. The combination of what one might call the 'pleasing technologies' of creative work with shrewd managerial practice means that routine workers in creative industries are typically willing to forgo the higher material rewards they might receive in another industry.

Dirty work and lowly occupations

In any society, there are various jobs which have a clear and often necessary function within the overall division of labour but which are seen by the public as 'dirty' – either in a literal way or figuratively in that the public regards them as somehow morally dubious. As a result of this cultural phenomenon, the work of people like mortuary attendants, sewerage workers, prison guards or even police or tax officers, can create problems for their members with regard to how they are received and accepted socially. Simpson *et al.* (2012) usefully define dirty work as 'tasks, occupations and roles that are likely to be perceived as disgusting or degrading' but it is perhaps more helpful to conceptualise the phenomenon in terms of its paradoxical nature: 'dirty' occupations play a part in servicing the social order generally approved of by the same people who often prefer to avert their eyes from such occupations – or from their members. And the same could be said of other pursuits of a more dubious or even illegal nature, with pornographers, prostitutes and 'exotic dancers' helping to cope with sexual tensions that might otherwise threaten the respectable institution of marriage.

Dirty work
An occupational activity which plays a necessary role in a society but which is regarded in some respects as morally doubtful.

Hughes and the Chicago school in the sociology of work who took the lead in analysing marginal or deviant occupations to illustrate principles applying to occupations in general, was introduced in Chapter 2 (pp. 47–49). This helps us see, as Hughes (1958) demonstrated, 'processes which are hidden in other occupations come more readily to view in these lowly ones'. Hence, the discussions later in this chapter of occupational recruitment and socialisation, occupational careers and occupational identity, culture and ideology pay central attention to 'dirty' occupations.

Many of the anxieties which arise for members of marginal occupations such as these may be seen as weaker versions of those which are experienced by people in more mainstream or 'respectable' occupations. It is not unknown, for example, for an estate agent, an undertaker or even an accountant to be as coy about their occupation in a social gathering as a lavatory cleaner or sewage farm worker. And even the greatly admired 'Samaritans' who counsel potentially suicidal people experience an element of being 'tainted' as a result of their contact with 'dirty emotions', strong emotions which are 'dirty' because they threaten preferred social orders (McMurray and Ward 2014).

Occupational recruitment and socialisation

At this point in the chapter, we move our analysis to the level of occupations themselves – looking at various characteristics which are shared, in different ways and to different extents by all or most occupations. And a logical starting point is to look at the processes whereby people enter an occupation and learn how to perform within it. These matters and especially the ways in which people 'learn the ropes' of particular occupations has been a key theme of writers in the interactionist tradition.

Becker *et al.* (1961), in a classic Chicago study of medical students, showed how groups facing common problems and situational pressures tend to develop certain common perspectives or 'modes of thought and action'. A peer group pressure on the individual's work orientation is thus created.

Occupational socialisation

The process whereby individuals learn about the norms, values, customs and beliefs associated with an occupation which they have joined so that they are able to act as a full member of that occupation.

Most people's work socialisation is not as specifically 'occupational' as that of medical students, however. A large proportion of people are recruited into work and trained by an employing organisation. Although this may emphasise a 'trade' or a type of 'professional work', it is much more likely to concentrate on the specific organisational tasks in which they will engage rather than on occupational characteristics of the work. The occupational principle nevertheless retains sufficient force for us to recognise the existence of various patterns of recruitment and socialisation which are essentially occupational rather than organisational.

Occupational recruitment

The typical processes and routes of entry followed by members of an occupation.

Certain occupations will restrict their entry in terms of the recruit's age. This often came about in the past through trade stipulations with regard to apprenticeships – something which served as a protection for members of that occupation by presenting a barrier to sudden or uncontrolled recruitment into the occupation. The stipulation of youth may also help with the problem of socialising new members of the occupation, not only in terms of learning skills but in order to aid the acquisition of appropriate attitudes and values. This is as likely to apply to a professionally oriented occupation as much as to a trade-based one. In some cases, the age requirement may relate to the physical attributes necessary in the occupation as would be the case with professional sportsmen, dancers, models, airline cabin crew ('air hostesses'! (Hochschild 1983).

Associated with age requirements may be certain educational or qualification barriers to occupational entry. This may be specific to the skills to be developed in the occupation – the requirement of some certification of mathematical ability in the case of engineering apprentices for example – or it may have far less specific functions. Dalton (1959), in his classic study of industrial managers, for example, pointed out that the 'total experience of going to college' may be more relevant to occupational success than the technical content of what is learned. The future executive learns, as a student, how to analyse their teacher's expectations and manoeuvres, how to utilise social contacts, how to cope with competition, meet deadlines, co-operate with others, cope with intangibles and ambiguities and make rapid adjustments to frequently encountered new personalities and situations. There equally may be a degree of occupational pre-socialisation in this sphere. This is suggested by Marceau's (1989) study which observed how common it was for her European business graduates to have been infused with business values and aspirations and inspired by the examples of their successful relatives. The majority of these graduates of a leading and prestigious European business school had fathers or grandfathers who had held senior business positions. More broadly, the connection between elite class backgrounds and entry to elite occupations has been widely and regularly demonstrated. Analysis of evidence from the Great British Class Survey (Chapter 7, pp. 212–213), for example, as used by Friedman *et al.* (2015) shows how 'traditional professions' such as law, medicine and finance are 'dominated by the children of higher managers and professionals'. There is wider recruitment by emerging high-status occupations, especially those involving IT. However, even when people without elite backgrounds successfully enter elite occupations they 'invariably fail to accumulate the same economic, cultural and social capital as those from privileged backgrounds'.

It is clear that a variety of patterns of occupational recruitment exist, ranging from the very formal to the very casual. The casual nature of the recruitment process is stressed, for example, in the case of striptease dancers by Skipper and McCaghy (1970). Occupational entry here is 'spontaneous, nonrational, fortuitous, and based on situational pressure and contingencies'. The appeal of monetary reward urged upon them by agents, friends and others encourages them to move on from work as singers, dancers, models and the like, to stripping. But the 'choices' made by strippers or lap-dancers must be set within the broader political economy of work and employment. As Hardy and Sanders (2015) point out, dancers enter the work 'to mitigate the precarious conditions of an unstable and weak job market' as well as declining real wages and lack of guaranteed career routes.

People may well 'end up' in an occupational setting simply because they have found no alternative. Gabriel (1988) showed this to be the case for most of the workers in his study of catering; they had 'an instrumental orientation thrust upon them by unrewarding jobs and the lack of alternatives due to the economic slump'. Few had systematically looked for alternatives; 'Age, lack of qualifications and training, poor command of the language, the chores of housekeeping and the need to look after children outside school hours, all compounded the feeling that "there is no alternative"'.

Once the typical pattern of recruitment to a given occupation has been noted attention can be turned towards the way in which people acquire occupationally relevant knowledge (Coffey and Atkinson 1994) and generally 'learn the ropes' (Geer *et al.* 1968) of the particular milieu which has been entered. Richman (1983) showed how traffic wardens only really learn the ropes once their formal training is over and they begin to collect 'a repository of information and collective wisdom' by means of an accumulation of 'stories from the street'. The more coherent and socially self-conscious the occupation the more likely is there to be an initiation ceremony at some turning point in this socialisation process, and the more pressing will be the need to learn the special language, formal and informal rules and attitudes of the group as well as the technical skills involved in the work. The informal rules, values and attitudes associated with an occupation are of great importance in helping the newcomer to adjust to the exigencies of the occupation that has been entered. Becker and Geer (1958), for example, observed the way in which the low status of the medical student within the hospital setting was adjusted to by the students through their suspension of the idealism with which they entered their training and its replacement by a relative cynicism which pervaded the student culture. The idealism which re-asserted itself later as the students moved closer to graduation and professional practice is consequently a more realistic one than had previously existed – an idealism which would not have helped the practitioner cope with difficulties to be confronted in the real world of medical practice.

A significant element of cynicism developed by the socialisation process is also suggested by Bryan's (1965) study of the 'apprenticeship' of call girls – an apprenticeship which has little to do with skills and is aimed at developing appropriate values and rules. Central to these values are those which stress the maximisation of gain for a minimum of effort and which evaluate people in general and men in particular as corrupt (the prostitute thus becoming defined as no more reprehensible than the public at large). Rules which follow from this include the regarding of each customer as a 'mark' and avoiding emotional involvement or pleasure with the client. In addition to learning relatively practical matters such as strategies to avoid violence (McKeganey and Barnard 1996), the prostitute learns to take on what Phoenix (1999) calls a 'prostitute identity' and see themselves as workers or 'rational-economic agents' as well as 'commodified bodies'. We see here a significant emotional element to the socialisation process, and this is also stressed in Hill's (1992) study of people becoming managers. This, she says, is 'both an intellectual and emotional exercise' with the managers being as 'desperate for help in managing the new position's emotions and stresses' as for help in solving business problems. Managers' interlinked personal and occupational identities are continually emergent and the 'managerial learning' that occurs once in a managerial occupation often relates back to learning experiences occurring throughout their earlier lives (Watson and Harris 1999). And it is vital to recognise that however powerful the processes of becoming a fully 'socialised' member of an occupation are, the individual has to retain their distinctive sense of self. Bennett's (2016) study of prison managers demonstrates the ways in which the individual 'becomes assimilated within the group whilst also maintaining a sense of individuality and self'.

Occupational careers

As was mentioned in our discussion of symbolic interactionism in Chapter 2, we can understand the way in which people achieve a sense of coherence in their working lives through the use of the idea of the 'subjective career'. However, the structural context which influences that processual self-view will be the objective career pattern provided by either an occupation or an organisation. These two are frequently related but, here, we are concerned with the occupational dimension.

Occupational career

The sequence of positions through which the member of an occupation typically passes during the part of their life which they spend in that occupation.

Different positions within an occupation generally involve different levels of prestige and give varying levels of reward of various other material and psychological kinds. We therefore tend to see careers in terms of the upward, downward or horizontal movement which they imply for the individual. It is commonplace to observe that many professional and administrative occupations provide career structures of a 'ladder' type; a series of positions of improving status and reward through which the successful individual can expect to move. But other occupations involve quite different career patterns. For many manual workers there may be little change in the work done over the whole of a working career and, although a certain status may accrue from 'seniority' in later years, it is just as likely that rewards may decrease as physical strength falls off. Strangleman (2004) points out that the 'railway careers' which developed through the nineteenth and into the twentieth centuries, with the role of the train-drivers at the peak, were a source of pride within the occupational culture but also operated as a self-disciplining device. Railway workers' expertise was not readily transferrable to other parts of the labour market.

It is an important part of the analysis of any given occupation to note just what shape the typical career, or variety of careers, may take. We may note, for example:

- the relative shortness of the typical career of the sportsperson, dancer, soldier or policeman;
- the insecurity of the typical career of the actor;
- the risks involved in certain business or 'entrepreneurial' careers.

These are all factors that seriously influence the orientation to work of the occupational member. Involvement in the occupation of lorry driver, for example, holds promise of advancement from initial shunting work to tramping and then to trunking but is later likely to return to the earlier lower-status shunting work (Hollowell 1968). Of course, any one occupation can offer more than one typical career pattern, depending on certain characteristics of the individual and various other career contingencies. The high-class call-girl, for instance, may progress to work as a madam, given the appropriate abilities and opportunities, or she may be reduced to the status of a street-walker – the difference between these two 'career grades' of prostitution being graphically illustrated by a prostitute interviewed by Terkel (1977) as equivalent to the distinction between an executive secretary and somebody in the typing pool. In the former role 'you really identify with your boss' whereas in the latter 'you're a body, you're hired labour, a set of hands on the typewriter. You have nothing to do with whoever is passing the work down to you. You do it as quickly as you can'.

Brewis and Linstead (2000b) note the variety of career patterns that sex workers can be seen to follow, varying from older prostitutes prolonging their business lives by offering 'domination' or sado-masochist specialisms, to street workers moving 'up' from street to parlour work, to a prostitute taking a business course to help her establish a business of her own. Whatever variety may exist in sex work, we cannot ignore the centrally important fact that such careers are highly precarious (Chapter 7, p. 214). And the same can be said of various other occupations. The case of jazz musicians is examined by Umney and Kretsos (2015) who show the way the way in which jazz musicians often deliberately prolong their time in precarious work in order to become 'established' within the occupation – often at the cost of becoming a parent or buying a house.

Occupational identity, culture and ideology

The three terms occupational identity, occupational culture and occupational ideology are often used interchangeably in the literature of the sociology of work and occupations. However, we can helpfully use the three terms to refer to different aspects of how occupations are *understood and evaluated*, both by their members and non-members.

Occupational identity, ideology and culture

Three dimensions of the way in which a particular type of work is understood and evaluated are:

(1) **Occupational identity**: The broad understanding in a society of what activities occur within a particular occupation and what contribution that occupation makes to society.

(2) **Occupational culture**: A more developed version of the publicly available occupational identity which is used *within* the occupation to provide ideas, values, norms, procedures and artefacts to shape occupational activities and enable members to value the work that they do.

(3) **Occupational ideology**: an expression of an occupational identity devised by an occupational group, or by its spokespersons, to legitimate the pursuit of the group members' common occupationally related interests.

This scheme could be applied to any given occupation to produce an analysis of a whole range of complexities and ambiguities which are likely to arise in the case of any particular occupation. To provide a simple example of how this might work we can take the case of a relatively straightforward occupation, that of soldiering.

The first thing to say about this illustrative case analysis is that it is highly contestable. This is inevitable, given that we have said, from the start, that these are three dimensions not just of understanding occupations but of *evaluating* them. This is most obvious, inevitably, in the case of the ideology dimension: these are statements designed to impress and gain support for the interests of the occupational members – at least as those who 'make the speeches' to the public choose to express matters. And a second caveat we have to make about studying occupational identities and cultures and how people are socialised into them is that we need to avoid what Leidner (2006) calls the 'risk of overstating the unity of cultures and their positive aspects'. This point is connected to

Snapshot 8.2

The occupation of soldiering

(1) **Occupational identity**: Soldiering is that work done on the part of a state in which arms and ammunition is deployed to further the interests of that state, either by the actual or the threatened use of violent force.

(2) **Occupational culture**: The wearing of uniforms, bearing of arms and the presentation of images of force, together with rigorous training and the suspension of individual identities, brings soldiers together into a highly disciplined and mutually supportive body of men and women who readily and, without question, obey the orders of their commanders.

(3) **Occupational ideology**: 'Our soldiers are among the finest, bravest and loyal men and women in the whole of society and every one of them would willingly lay down their lives if that were necessary for the defence of their country or for the pursuit of other legitimate interests of the state'.

the one about contestability. But it goes beyond it because, as Leidner expresses it, occupational cultures have a tendency to reproduce patterns of exclusion given that 'sexism, racism, and ethnocentrism flourish in many occupations, especially those with relatively strong cultures in which collective identities as members of the occupation overlap with collective identities based on gender, race and ethnicity'.

Occupational identities and cultures may function not just to exclude certain groups from entry into an occupation but to maintain a pattern of advantage and disadvantage within an occupation. Dick and Cassell (2004) show how male police officers strive to maintain an occupational identity which portrays policing as 'a complex array of activities, dominated by crimefighting' which is then used 'to justify the working practices that effectively bar women with young families from returning to full-time police work and, hence, from promotion opportunities that might have been theirs, had they served the requisite amount of time on the beat'. But in the same way occupational identities and communities may function divisively within an occupation, as in this case male-dominated policing, they can also be shaped to improve the lot of all members of an occupation, as Pringle (1989) argued was the case in her Australian study of the female dominated occupation of secretary. Pringle showed how the women she studied managed to move definitions of their occupational role away from that of the 'office wife' of the pre-1960s and 'sexy secretary' of the 1960s and 1970s towards some recognition of their being a member of the management team in their own right (and not as an appendage of a man). In achieving this redefinition of their work, these women were resisting a whole series of stereotypes and myths about their occupation which had been fairly prominent in popular culture for many decades.

Artists, on the other hand, are shown by Bain (2004) to have embraced certain myths about artistic work which have developed as part of the 'social construction of artistic identities' over the history of western art. They have, in effect, invented a history which has provided 'symbols of collective identification and a means of demarcating the contours of group membership'. Such occupational artistic identities inevitably function to support individuals' personal identity work (Chapter 9, pp. 303–306). And this identity work entails 'living in a certain way', as one of the musicians interviewed by Coulson (2012) puts it. This musician points out that no satisfaction can be gained from saying, 'I'm a musician' – one must actually be performing for audiences. And Simpson *et al.* (2014) show how butchers, especially in light of their competitive position *vis à vis* supermarket staff, can be seen working on a collective occupational identity which draws on notions of 'professionalism' (pp. 262–270), and makes reference to media images of celebrity chefs.

A powerful sense of occupational collective identification is shown to exist among investment bankers in Ho's (2009) participant–observer ethnographic study among workers on America's Wall Street ('the concentration of financial institutions and actor-networks – investment banks, pension and mutual funds, stock exchanges, hedge funds and private equity firms'). What brings these investment bankers together into what we might call an occupational culture is their sharing of a particular *habitus*. Habitus was defined earlier in this chapter, following Bourdieu, as a set of predispositions or inclinations to action which individuals develop and internalise over time in the light of their relationship to the power structure and culture of the society in which they live. Wall Street workers, says Ho, operate in a world of considerable insecurity. They are 'liquid employees' who are constantly liable to be 'downsized' out of their jobs. This insecurity is not experienced as a liability, however; it is treated as a challenge. The shared habitus is one of being among 'the best and brightest' products of elite families and universities for whom intense deal-making in an atmosphere of job insecurity (but with massive short-term incentives) is a sign of their smartness and superiority. The deals they 'push' are usually short-term transactions intended to boost stock prices and by 'pressuring corporations, bankers transfer their own models of employee liquidity onto corporate America'. This, says Ho, set the stage for the market crisis in the USA and beyond. The occupational or industrial culture of Wall Street investment bankers imposes 'its own organizational practices' onto corporations at large, together with all the associated insecurities and 'downsizings'.

LOOKING BACK <<<<<

Ho sets these trends in the context of the prioritising of share-holder value in the contemporary world. This was linked in Chapter 4 (p. 113) to the rise of neoliberalism and the financialisation of economies.

Turning away from particularly privileged workers to occupations whose members may feel a degree of discomfort about their marginality, it is apparent that occupational identities can become especially important. Fine (1996), in looking at kitchen workers, observed that occupational members can handle problematic issues that arise in their type of work by constructing from 'bundles' of relevant imagery occupational rhetorics which justify their activities. This concept is applied to management consultants by Kitay and Wright (2007). Such people have three problems to handle, 'legitimacy, efficiency and vulnerability' and the research suggests they handle these by developing occupational rhetorics which feature, depending on the circumstance, 'social roles' of professional, prophet, partner, business person or service worker. The problems which university contract researchers have centre on their low status within universities and the transient nature of their employment. Collinson (2004) shows two ways in which the staff handle such issues, as part of an occupational identity. First, they joke about how they are 'peripheral staff' or 'intellectual nomads'. But, second, they talk about the considerable knowledge and research skills that they are building up and they use these ideas as a 'valuable resource' to construct 'more positive occupational selves'. This issue of creating a positive evaluation of a marginal occupation is an especially significant one for members of 'dirty work occupations'.

LOOKING BACK AND FORWARD <<<<< >>>>>

Again, in the tradition of the Chicago sociologists, we are looking at a dirty or deviant occupation to develop insights which, in a less stark form, arise in more 'normal' occupations.

The whole issue of the protection of 'self', which we are considering here, arises again when we focus on issues of self-identity and work in Chapter 7 and 'resistance' in Chapter 12.

The work of veterinary technicians fits neatly into Hughes' notion of dirty work. Sanders (2010) shows how this job incorporates work activities that are 'physically disgusting, personally degrading, and undignified' in addition to 'gruelling emotional experiences that require workers to employ psychologically protective measures'. All of this is handled by a 'strong and supportive occupational culture' which highlights the technicians' love for animals and 'the part they can play in saving some who might otherwise be discarded'. By drawing on this cultural resource, individuals develop powerful commitments to the job and derive positive self-identities from it.

Prostitutes, another form of 'dirty work', face the problem of retaining self-respect and overcoming what O'Connell Davidson (1998) identifies as the denial of personhood implicit in a type of work that amounts to an 'eroticisation of social death'. Purely personal or psychological defence mechanisms would not be enough to handle this. They have to relate to wider societal norms because 'prostitutes and clients alike are socialised into a world where particular meanings are attached to human sexuality . . . a world in which it is widely held that the only legitimate sex is between men and women who love each other and that "money can't buy you love"' (O'Connell Davidson 1995). For this reason, occupational cultural devices need to be available to handle the sex worker's 'deviance' from these norms.

The legitimising function of certain aspects of the occupational culture upon which prostitutes typically draw is also illustrated in the ways in which prostitutes sometimes present themselves as skilled educators guiding people towards safe sex practices or as social workers providing services to disadvantaged clients (Brewis and Linstead 2000b). At the level of occupational identity, West and Austrin (2005) note that the sex and entertainment businesses are beginning to position commercial sex as 'normal business'. And whether or not such a contestable characterisation and evaluation of sex work becomes fully established in modern societies, it is clear that such a notion is found to be helpful to sex workers themselves with prostitutes, as Sanders' (2005) research suggests, developing a culture in which prostitutes manages their own and their clients' emotions in such a way that they 'feel they are selling a service, rather than themselves'. However, Hoang (2011) stresses that the expansion of sexual services is not only a global phenomenon but one in which the growing 'industry' involves multiple markets and produces class structures in the same way as other types of occupation: the industry is organised and stratified according to workers' differential access to economic, cultural, and bodily resources. Whilst this situation is one that the sociologist can reveal and analyse, it is vital to stress that to do this does not necessarily morally condone the selling of sexual services. A powerful argument against speaking of 'sex work' as a morally neutral category is put forward by Banyard (2016). And she argues that 'sexual consent is not a commodity, objectification and abuse are inherent to prostitution, and the sex trade poses a grave threat to the struggle for women's equality'. In the present volume, the term 'sex work' is used as an analytical category, and this use in no way implies any moral judgement. Such moral judgements are important and necessary across the world, and sociology can provide information and analyses to assist these important debates. It cannot, itself, offer moral evaluations.

Occupational communities

We can expect an occupational culture to be especially strong and to spill over into areas of members' lives outside the work sphere itself in occupations where the work and non-work lives of its members are closely related. This tends to be particularly the case with what some sociologists have described as *occupational communities*.

Occupational community

A form of local social organisation in which people's work and non-working lives are both closely identified with members of the occupation in which they work.

The notion of the occupational community was implicit in the analysis of Kerr and Siegal (1954) who suggested that the high propensity to strike of such groups as miners, longshoremen, sailors and loggers could be related to their living in an 'isolated mass'; the communities found in the 'coal patch, the ship, the waterfront district, the logging camp, the textile town' are all seen to have 'their own codes, myths, heroes and social standards'. Steel (2016) analyses similar types of social interaction which took place in the 1950s in the Finnish port towns of Helsinki and Kotka combining the concept of occupational community with the newer notion of *identity work* (Chapter 9, pp. 303–306).

Communities associated with coal mines, ports and forests have declined along with the decline of their associated industries. We might therefore decide that the very notion of the occupational community is one that can be abandoned. But Salaman (1974) suggested that the association between an occupation and a particular geographical location might be seen as just one type of occupational community. He identified that we might identify a second type of occupational community – one involving a 'whole occupation'. Such a notion was taken up by Filby (1987), after observing how an 'independence in relations with employers' is sustained by racing lads working in the Newmarket stables by a 'vibrant occupational culture'. In spite of 'disagreements, competition, divisions and contradictions' among the lads, 'the occupation of the racing lad provides a basis of a community of shared forms of discourse, understanding, experience and affectiveness'. Something similar is shown to exist among the workers in the public house hotels investigated by Sandiford and Seymour (2007). These workers fulfilled the key criteria of occupational community membership identified by Salaman; they built their lives around their work, made friends of their work colleagues and pursued work-based leisure interests.

The concept of occupational community may well increase its role within the sociology of work and organisation as an increasing proportion of the modern workforce become detached from employing organisations. Thus the occupational, as opposed to the organisational principle, may well be due for a renewal of interest in occupations and, indeed, occupational communities. Such a possibility is demonstrated by a study of video game developers where it is not 'the firm' but the occupational community that 'sustains and invigorates career identity and motivation, the attainment and maintenance of transferable skills, and the development of fruitful social networks' (Westar 2015).

Professionalisation, occupational strategies and role hybridity

The work that people do is bound up with the distribution of power and resources of society at large, as the present and previous chapters have shown. Most individuals are not in a position to defend or improve their location in the wider structure of advantage on their own. Some form of collective action to defend or further individuals' interests is inevitable. A variety of ways in which people attempt to control the extent of their autonomy in work will be discussed in Chapter 12, but our present concern is with the way the members of any identifiable occupation might form an association for such purposes by virtue of their membership of that occupation rather than on the basis of commonly experienced problems arising from their position as employees.

The trade union as an occupational association is of decreasing significance as former trade groups increasingly amalgamate to defend common interests as *employees* rather than as holders of specific skills and knowledge. The trade union strategy, traditionally associated with working-class values and interests, is essentially defensive. It is a coalition of interest arising from the recognition of a common problem of defending individuals' contractual relationships in a situation where the other party to that contract, the employer, tends to treat the rewards offered to employees as a cost to be minimised. But where the members of an occupation recognise in their skills, expertise or knowledge a potential basis for their own monopolistic control over their work they may look towards an alternative strategy; one which draws their eyes towards the traditionally middle-class symbol of professionalism. This, in contrast to the trade union strategy of seeking power through an amalgamation of occupational groups (following what Parkin, 1974, has called a 'solidaristic attempt at social closure'), is a move towards exclusivity, involving, in Weber's (1978) terms 'the closure of social and economic opportunities to outsiders'. It is the members of the occupational group, not a group of employees, who define who is an outsider.

Those occupations, like law and medicine, widely recognised as professions, can be seen as forms of work organisation which gave a place within industrial capitalism to people doing high-status work, whilst keeping them in part outside and above those processes which were bringing the work lives of so many people under the administrative control of employers.

> ### Professions
>
> Occupations which have been relatively successful in gaining high status and autonomy in certain societies on the basis of a claimed specialist expertise over which they have gained a degree of monopoly control.

It is not surprising that sociologists and social commentators over many decades have tended fairly straightforwardly to treat the profession as types of occupation and to differentiate between professions and 'non-professions'. But there has been a growing tendency within the 'burgeoning literature' on professional matters (Adams 2014), to move away from any such static emphasis towards a concern with occupational *processes* in which the concept, notion or symbol of professionalism is embraced by members of and spokespersons for various occupational groups to shape both the image of the occupation and occupational practices and arrangements. And one way in which this way of thinking can be further advanced is to make use of the concept of *institutional logics*, sets of values, rules, assumptions and practices associated with key institutions of a society which have been socially constructed over time and through which patterns of social organisation and human activity are shaped and given meaning.

LOOKING BACK <<<<<

The concept of institutional logic was introduced in Chapter 3, pp. 303–306.

The concept of institutional logics is fully compatible with the process-relational methodological principles set out with reference to organisations in Chapter 5 (pp. 63–65), and its close attention to any given society's institutions makes it especially fitted to performing the kind of international and comparative work which Adams (2014) argues is so necessary. Within a fully processual and institutionally oriented frame of reference occupations are regarded, like organisations, as *relational* phenomena – sets of relationships and associated understandings – and as *emergent* phenomena resulting from processes of exchange, negotiation, power, conflict and compromise in societies.

The institutional logic of professionalism

Control over work tasks which are important 'for society' and involve a body of theoretical knowledge and set of high-level skills is in the hands of a formal occupational association. This body oversees the supply of education and training, tests member competence and demands its members' compliance with a code of conduct. High rewards for members are justified by the occupation's primary altruistic service to society rather than by reference to economic or business criteria of success.

The development of this logic can be traced historically, in the UK particularly. The increasing influence of the work ethic in the developing industrial capitalist society in Britain meant that those upper-class practitioners in such areas as medicine, law and university teaching, who had formerly seen their efforts as gentlemanly pursuits rather than as labour, needed to redefine their position. We thus see the decline of what Elliot (1972) calls 'status professionalism' and the rise of occupational professionalism. Those who had previously been 'above' having an occupation (the upper class being in many ways a leisure class in principle if not always in practice), now embraced the occupational principle as a way of engaging in work without becoming contaminated by industrialism and commercialism. The ideology developed by such high-status groups existed beyond these specific occupations, however, being found among the military and senior civil servants and propagated in the universities and new public schools. This ideology of liberal education, public service and gentlemanly professionalism was elaborated, as Elliot (1972) stresses, in opposition to the growth of industrialism and commercialism: 'it incorporated such values as personal service, a dislike of competition, advertising and profit, a belief in the principle of payment in order to work rather than working for pay and in the superiority of the motive of service'.

The essence of the idea of a profession is *autonomy* – the maintenance of the control over work tasks by those doing these tasks. It should not be surprising therefore to find groups of people who operate within formal organisations or within other restricted settings looking to the traditional high-status 'free' professions to find ways of developing strategies to oppose control over them by others. The concern of so many sociologists with the occupational strategy of professionalisation is a justifiable one because it represents one of the major ways in which the prevailing mode of work organisation and control has been and will perhaps continue to be challenged. The possibilities of the occupational principle developing so as to reduce the conflicts and excesses of capitalism have been suggested by both classical and modern sociologists (Durkheim 2014; Halmos 1970). Crompton (1990) suggests a more nuanced view of these occupations as incorporating elements which 'reflect the contradictory tendencies underlying the division of labour' in modern societies. They are clearly involved in furthering the projects of 'dominant interests' in a capitalist market context. At the same time, they still express certain norms of what Merton and Gieryn (1982) termed *institutionalised altruism* in which 'experts and professionals have protected the weak as well as the strong, sought to restrain and moderate the excesses of the market'. Crompton (1990) relates this to the fact that market capitalism is 'simply not viable in its own terms'. Without accompanying norms of trust and reciprocity and the same defence of what Durkheim calls the 'non-contractual aspects of contract' the system would collapse. Consistently with this, Freidson (2001) argued that proponents of professionalism need to justify the considerable privilege that it offers those who embrace it, and suggests that this can be done by mediating between the state and private capital by sounding 'an effective third voice for choosing social policies that provide benefit to all'.

It is clear that in a society where the great majority of people work as employees rather than as independent fee-paid practitioners, any given group strategy – involving whatever mixture of self-interest and concern for others may be the case in particular circumstances – is likely to involve some mixture of elements from both the trade union and the professional ideal types of strategy. Hence we see the high-status medical profession using, from time to time, trade union tactics in its relations with the government which, in Britain, mediates between the professional and the client. Sociological analysis of occupations has often sought to identify the extent to which any given occupational group is able to act as an occupational collectivity, on the 'professionalisation' model. This has involved identifying the conditions which influence the capacity of any group to act in this way. Before we do this, however, we must clarify what we mean by the process of professionalisation.

Professionalisation

A process followed by certain occupations to increase its members' status, relative autonomy and rewards and influence through such activities as setting up a professional body to control entry and practice, establishing codes of conduct, making claims of an altruism and a key role in serving the community.

This process is clearly influenced by what we have conceptualised here as the institutional logic of professionalism. The connection between this and occupational strategies was suggested by Becker's (1971) classic analysis of what he termed the *symbol of professionalism*. Becker called this a 'folk concept' or image based on traditionally independent occupations like law and medicine and he argued that 'professions' are 'simply those occupations which have been fortunate enough in the politics of today's work world to gain and maintain possession of that honorific title'.

To acquire the professional label and the prestige and economic benefits associated with it, any given occupation (via its leaders or spokespersons) will, *to the degree to which its material situation allows it,* organise itself on a basis resembling the traditional elite occupations. An occupation following the professionalisation strategy will therefore tend to stress a claim to esoteric competence, the quality of which it will argue must be maintained for the sake of client and society, and will accordingly seek for its licensed members the exclusive right to do work in its sphere of competence whilst controlling who enters the work, how they are trained, how they perform their work tasks and how this performance is checked and evaluated. The fact that many occupations by their very nature can never approach the level of autonomy traditionally associated with lawyers and physicians does not prevent occupations as varied as industrial managers, estate agents and embalmers getting together and pursuing some elements of the professionalisation strategy.

LOOKING BACK <<<<<

We saw in Chapter 4 (pp. 118–119) the argument that the future of so-called professions might be radically threatened by changes in information technologies.

A view of professionalising processes as a form of occupational market strategy which seeks monopoly control over an area of activity so guaranteeing an advantaged position within the class structure was central to the influential analysis of Larson (1977). Larson (1990) subsequently said that her earlier work, in concentrating on Anglo-American cases, gave undue emphasis to the *market* aspect of professionalisation. In Britain and America, it may have been the distinctive 'inaction of the state' which prompted 'professional leaders to take the initiative in organising mechanisms of closure and protection around their fields'. Alternative processes of mobilisation around expert knowledge can occur in other circumstances. She argues, therefore, that we should move away from trying to develop a general theory of the professions and focus instead on the more important theme of 'the construction and social consequences of expert knowledge'. The concept of profession or professionalisation, however, is still pertinent, she argues, to the 'relatively high levels of formal education and relatively desirable positions and/or rewards in the social division of labour'. Education is thus the linking mechanism between occupational 'expertise' and social class advantage.

In spite of his 'defence' of professionalism as a force mediating between institutions of state and capital, Freidson (2001) identified professionalisation as a process of occupational closure and control, and he emphasises how attempts are made to 'institutionalise' specialist skill and expertise in occupational and organisational forms so that they become a resource to be used to the social and economic advantage of those engaged in the professionalisation strategy. Abbott (1988), however, attempted to change the direction of analysis away from professional structures and onto the work undertaken by professionals. He observes that there is a system of professions operating in any given society. Professions evolve through their interactions with each other; they compete with each other for jurisdiction over abstract knowledge. It is not control over technique which gives a group professional advantage (that can be delegated) but it is control over a 'knowledge system governed by abstractions' that allows members of an occupation to defend themselves from interlopers or 'seize new problems' (as medicine has seized alcoholism, according to Abbott). For his purposes, he says, motor mechanics would be a profession if they were able to develop a form of abstract knowledge about the repair of internal combustion engines. Were they to do this, they would assert their role within the 'competitive system' of professions and would take over or 'contain' what are currently sections of the engineering profession.

The value of this emphasis on competition between members of occupational groups for jurisdiction over abstract knowledge is that it brings together issues about the power and advantage of people's labour market position with the changing nature of knowledge, technology, markets and political contexts, with inequalities between professional groups being as important as inequalities across societies (Saks 2015). As global markets change, new technologies emerge and governments react to or attempt to shape these shifts, so certain groups within the division of labour will mobilise themselves to defend or further their interests. In all of this, the notions of 'profession' and 'professionalism' are likely to be powerful discursive resources that spokespersons of almost any expert-knowledge-related occupation are likely to deploy to protect and advance their shared interests. As Evetts (2006, 2016) suggests, a 'focus on the discourse of professionalism' offers a promising new direction for sociologists studying such occupational groups. The value of such an approach is illustrated by an analysis of the efforts made by what became the UK's Chartered Institute of Personnel and Development (CIPD) to gain – and later celebrate the gaining of – chartered 'professional' status through formal state recognition (in the form of the award of a royal charter). In presenting his organisation to the world as a 'profession', the main spokesman for the institute, its director general, showed considerable 'discursive ingenuity' (Watson 2002b).

Snapshot 8.3

Discursive ingenuity and the professional institute

The challenge faced by the director general of the UK human resource managers' professional association was one of managing to attach to the occupation all the kudos that comes from recognition as a 'profession', whilst avoiding the traditional image of 'the professional' as an independent and knowledgeable expert who distances themselves from 'trade' and from competitive business activities. The attachment of this latter image of 'professionalism' to the CIPD could be potentially disastrous for a body of people who are largely *employed* managers, a high proportion of whom work for competitive commercial organisations.

In celebrating the CIPD's new status, the director general could be seen to be pressing a whole series of emotionally and discursively positive 'buttons' that imply high occupational status, expert knowledge, social closure and national influence. He then, however, dropped into his text the phrase 'practical competence'. He was well aware of the danger of implying that these newly chartered human-resource management experts might be too remote or too intellectual. He therefore needed to stress that they are also 'practical'. But what about any anxiety over these managers losing sight of their commercial role? He firmly squashed any possible connotation of this 'new institute for a new millennium' being aloof from trade and profit making. He strongly emphasised the importance of members of the chartered institute being 'strategic' in their managerial roles. And what does this mean? It means 'taking advantage of uncertainty: looking for opportunities to wrong-foot competitors by transforming again and again the way things are done'. He is making it clear that there is no question of his members being above the rough and tumble of capitalist markets. He has abandoned the traditional image of professionals as people who disdain 'trade'. In the process of re-inventing his occupation, its spokesman-in-chief has ingeniously both drawn upon and reshaped existing discursive resources of 'professionalism'.

Research on how HR managers themselves see their occupation suggests that they are little attracted to the notion of an HR 'profession'. Wright (2008) shows that their preferred discourse is one which has 'recast' HR managers as 'business partners' and 'internal consultants'. The dynamic here, says Wright, is a 'deprofessionalising' one, with HR managers using the business partner discourse 'to appeal to senior managers as valued "servants of power"' – something completely at odds with the traditional ethos of a profession. In spite of this, it would appear that the power of the 'professional' label shows no sign of diminishing. Even 'competitive intelligence' consultants, whatever these might be, have 'jumped on the bandwagon' of 'professionalism' (Watson 2002a), and 'eco-auditors' are spoken of as an outcome of a 'new form of Euro-professionalisation' (Neal and Morgan 2000).

What unites all of these different occupational activities is the claim that they, or their spokespersons, make about their possession of expert knowledge. But different occupations providing this expert knowledge do so within different organisational frameworks. Hence, Muzio *et al.* (2007), having pulled together literature on the three 'expert' occupations of law, medicine and management consulting, identify three types of 'profession'. Law works on the classic model of a collegiate profession. Medicine is less collegiate because its practitioners are typically employees of large organisations. It operates therefore on an organisational profession model. The newer occupation, management consultancy, is even further away from the classic professional image, given its strong corporate involvement and its being very open to market forces. It is thus an entrepreneurial profession. If the notion of 'profession' is going to be retained in social science, then this typology is very helpful in dealing with the variety of occupational circumstances in which it may be relevant.

The concept of organisational professionalism is especially important given that, as Evetts (2016) puts it, 'both professionalism and organisations . . . are both changing as they co-exist and co-penetrate each other'. These processes of co-existence and inter-penetration persuade Evetts to embrace the concept of hybridity. Hybridity is not a matter of hybrid occupations emerging but of the development of what Waring (2014) calls 'hybrid professional–managerial roles'.

> ### Hybrid professional-managerial roles
>
> Positions within organisations usually found at the interface between an established professional group (like hospital doctors) and the wider organisation (a hospital or hospital group for example) in which 'professional' workers take on managerial or administrative tasks of co-ordinating professional/expert activities and organisational/ leadership ones.

Waring stresses that these roles are analytically significant, not only because they illustrate bridging between a professional group and its work context but also 'because they allow for the recombination and blurring of distinct professional and organisational modes of working'. The 'modes of working' perfectly fit the notion of institutional logics. Nurse-managers, doctor managers, university faculty deans, legal managing partners are all examples of people filling roles in which they have to manage the tensions between the professional institutional logic (with its emphasis on specialised expertise and occupational autonomy) and the bureaucratic-managerial institutional logic (with its emphasis on corporate purposes and 'top-to-bottom' control practices).

Summary

In analysing particular occupations, the sociologist may examine the distinctiveness of any given occupation's pattern of recruitment and socialisation, its career structure, its identity, culture and ideology and whether or not it is associated with an 'occupational community'. The sociologist of occupations will also examine occupational strategies which might be pursued, the strategy of 'professionalisation' continuing to be a particularly attractive option, one with considerable implications for how societies are shaped and changed.

9 Culture, work orientations and the experience of working

Key issues

- Does the meaning of work vary across historical periods and societies?
- How can we most usefully understand the processes whereby people enter particular types of work or occupation?
- What patterns are there in the ways in which people are or are not satisfied at work?
- What is the most helpful way of understanding the meanings which their work has for individual workers and for appreciating the way these meanings may change?
- What particular issues affect women workers when it comes to decisions about working?

Work, meaning and culture

Work is something we associate with human beings – unless we are thinking of animals that are given working roles by humans, as sheep dogs or dray horses, say. Yet all living creatures expend some kind of 'working' effort in the process of acting upon and taking from their environment whatever they need for survival. Human beings are no different from other animals in this general respect. Members of the human species are, however, different in three respects:

- They have devised an infinitely greater variety of ways of dealing with their material situation.
- They are unique in the extent to which they have divided up and allocated particular tasks to individuals and groups within the overall and general task of subsisting.

- They apply value-based judgements to the problem of maintaining life – distinguishing between 'good' and 'bad' or 'honourable' and 'dishonourable' ways of earning a living, for instance.

The human capacity to make choices on the basis of values means that neither the methods of work which human beings adopt nor the social organisation which accompanies it can be explained by reference to any clearly definable set of instincts. Human agency, choice, values and interpretations are essential factors to be appreciated in any examination of work forms and experiences.

Work is basic to the ways in which human beings deal with the problems arising from the scarcity of resources available in the environment. The scarcity of resources in the world influences the patterns of conflict and competition that arise between social groups. It follows from this that the social organisation of work will reflect the basic power relationships of any particular society. But patterns of social relationships do not relate to power structures alone. They are also closely connected to the patterns of meaning created within human cultures. And this means that the ways in which people think and feel about work will closely relate to their wider political and religious doctrines and to the culture of the society within which they live.

Culture
The system of meanings which are shared by members of a society, or other human grouping, and which define what is good and bad, right and wrong and what are the appropriate ways for members of that grouping to think and behave.

LOOKING FORWARD >>>>>

As we argue later (pp. 317–318), cultures also have to help people deal with basic human *angst*.

All cultures at the societal level have to deal with the same basic problems of human existence – of life, death, social obligation and so on – and they all give guidance on how to solve these problems. Cultures vary in the particular way these problems are tackled. And since the problems of how 'properly' to go about working and 'making a living' face all human groups, we would expect every society, through its culture, to have its distinctive way of making sense of the question of work and a distinctive set of values and priorities giving guidance on how its members should proceed with it. We can see some clear differences of emphasis historically by looking at the writings of individuals living in past societies. It is important to recognise, though, that this 'evidence' is typically that of members of social elites. This point is strongly made by Beard (2015) who notes that although Cicero and most of the Roman elite expressed disdain for wage labour and trade, the record to be found on the tombstones of 'ordinary' Romans make it clear that 'their job was the key to their identity' and often a matter of craft pride, however rough and demanding so much work clearly was. Bearing this in mind we can observe that:

- Ancient Greek thinkers regarded the most desirable and the only 'good' life as one of leisure. Work, in the sense of supplying the basic necessities of life, was a degrading activity which was to be allocated to the lowest groups within the social order and, especially, to slaves. Slavery was the social device which enabled the Greeks to maintain their view of work as something to be avoided by a full human being: what human beings 'shared with all other forms of animal life was not considered to be human' (Arendt 1959).
- Romans like Cicero tended to follow the Greek view, whilst Hebrew scholars expressed a view of work as unpleasant drudgery – which could nevertheless play a role of expiating sin and recovering a degree of spiritual dignity (Tilgher 1930).
- Early Christianity also modified the relatively extreme Greek view and recognised that work might make one healthy and divert one from sinful thoughts and habits. Leading thinkers of the Catholic Church, such as Aquinas, were influenced by the Greek view, but a doctrine emerged which gave a role for work in the Christian scheme of things as a penance arising from the fall and original sin. It also contributed to the virtue of obedience but was by no means seen as noble, rewarding or satisfying; 'Its very endlessness and tedium were spiritually valuable in that it contributed to Christian resignation' (Anthony 1977).
- The Reformation and the emergence of Protestant Christianity saw work coming to be treated positively within Western cultures. With Luther, we see the suggestion that work can itself be a way of serving God. This is the origin of the Western or Protestant work ethic.

LOOKING BACK <<<<<

The historical implications of this Protestant work ethic were discussed in Chapter 3 (pp. 89–91).

The key point is that the Protestant work ethic established the all-important idea that one's work was a 'calling' of equivalent value to that of a religious vocation – something which had previously involved a turning of one's back on the mundane and a movement 'upwards' towards virtue and other-worldliness. Where living a life of leisure, rather than working, had once been an indicator of prestige and a 'good life' it now became associated with failure and even disgrace.

> ### Work ethic
>
> A set of values which stresses the importance of work to the identity and sense of worth of the individual and which encourages an attitude of diligence, duty and a striving for success in the mind of the worker.

With the growth of modern industrial capitalism, we see the work ethic spreading further and wider with work becoming the essential prerequisite of personal and social advancement, of prestige, of virtue and of self-fulfilment. The modern pattern of working life in which 'jobs' and 'careers' are central to people's identities as well as sources of income is supported as the work ethic encourages people to seek and sustain involvement in this institutional pattern. Although in modern times the work ethic may not be formally underpinned by religious faith, it still has religious undertones. The ideas of a duty to work and to be dutiful in work are essentially moral and go deeper than our rational attachment to a particular way of making a living. As Max Weber (1965) put it, 'the idea of duty in one's calling prowls about in our lives like the ghost of dead religious beliefs'. It became apparent in the twentieth century that certain non-European cultures, especially in Asia, contained a strong element of a work ethic, suggesting that value systems other than those associated with Christianity have left a legacy corresponding the Protestant work ethic one.

It began to be suspected by some commentators in the latter half of the twentieth century that the 'work ethic' was losing its force. However, Rose (1985, 1988), in an analysis with continuing relevance to the second decade of the twenty-first century, rejected the thesis that the work ethic was being abandoned. He nevertheless argued that a process was under way whereby the more educated and highly trained were 'modifying the interpretation' of the work ethic whilst not 'repudiating it as a scheme of values'. A new pattern of work meanings was observed among the more educated and trained which contains elements of the traditional work ethic combined with a concern with self-fulfilment, the obtaining of 'just treatment' and the developing of 'more humanly rational economic organisation and technology'. This also involves an anti-authoritarianism in which people are systematically suspicious of those giving orders. The adoption of these 'post-bourgeois values' is likely to be encouraged, says Rose, by such structural changes as the growth of service work (where employers will experience a tension between wanting tight control and avoiding the danger of disaffected employees alienating clients) and the attraction to public service work of those more educated people who believe that they can here better follow a 'service ethic'. The new values are also supported by 'commercial hedonism' (taking the waiting out of wanting, as the advertisers put it) and, potentially, by the, as yet limited, re-negotiation of family and gender roles.

Wei Lei, made some comments to her university personal tutor which resonate with these observations in Snapshot 9.1.

Snapshot 9.1

Wei Lei reflects on 'working hard'

Now that we are in the final year of our degrees, I think most of us are working hard. We are simply being rational, I suppose you could say. We know that without hard work we won't get the careers that we want, and all the benefits that come with those. And, without hard work, we won't be free of petty bosses pushing us around in our future workplaces. But I have noticed that most of my friends, both the Chinese and European ones, are actually happier working hard at our studies than when we were concentrating on having a so-called 'good time' in the first year. I think this is something to do with our backgrounds. Although my family observed some of the old Chinese customs, I never saw them as religious. You could say, though, that hard work was their religion. Most of my friends would relate to this I think. We were actually saying, the other evening, that we tend to feel guilty if we are not working hard. At one level, yes, we are working hard to be able to have the goods and experiences that wealth can bring. But I am sure there is something at the deeper level as well; something as I said, that has to do with 'where we have come from' – and by this I don't mean China or London – it's something deeper than that.

Wei Lei is looking forward to a entering a work career and, sociologically, we can expect her post-university destination to result from a mixture of personal choices and structural circumstances.

Entering work

Choice and opportunity structures

A successful sociology is one that does full justice to the interplay between individual characteristics and initiatives on the one hand and structural factors and contingencies on the other. But in spite of the growing *sociological* emphasis on the interplay of agency and structure, there has been a tendency in much of the literature on how people enter work for a stress *either* on the individual's *choice* of occupation or on the *determining* influence of external factors. Much of the original literature on the so-called process of occupational choice was psychologically based and examines the way in which the individual develops and passes through a series of stages during which the self-concept grows as abilities, aptitudes and interests develop (Ginzberg *et al.* 1951; Super 1957). A sociological reaction to approaches which exaggerated the degree of free 'choice' which people have about the work they enter came with a stress on the ways in which, for many individuals, entry to work is a matter of fitting oneself into whatever jobs are available given the qualifications which one's class and educational background has enabled one to attain. Roberts (1975) argued that it is careers which tend to determine ambition rather than the other way round. Careers can be regarded as developing into patterns dictated by the opportunity structures to which individuals are exposed, first in education and subsequently in employment, whilst individuals' ambitions, in turn, can be treated as reflecting the influence of the structures through which they pass. In an attempt to do equal justice to both individual choice factors and structural circumstances, Layder *et al.* (1991) showed that 'structure and action are inextricably interwoven and should be given equal analytical weighting'. Their research on the transition from school to work shows that structural variables (ones over which they had no control) such as the social class of their parents, their sex and the local opportunity structure (measured by their place of residence and the level of unemployment at the time they entered the labour market) played a more significant role for people entering the middle and lower level jobs in the youth labour market than they did for those entering the higher levels. In the upper segments of the job market, it was found that 'the factors which individuals perceive as being a product of their own efforts and achievements are indeed the most significant factors in determining the level at which they enter the labour market'. Individuals here had a greater ability to control their circumstances through strategic activities of job search and behaviour informed by values and attitudes. Having

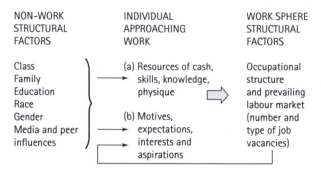

Figure 9.1 Factors influencing the individual's approach to work

said this, we need to look more closely at the particular influences of class, family and education.

To create a model which identifies the factors that influence how individuals approach work, we clearly must consider both objective and subjective factors. Objectively, the individual has certain resources such as cash, skills, knowledge or physique. Subjectively, the individual has certain motives, interests and expectations such as to make a living, achieve power or gain job satisfaction. Both of these sets of factors are, in turn, strongly influenced by structural factors. These are, on the one side, the structural settings of the individual's family, class, ethnic and educational background and, on the other side, the occupational structure and the prevailing job market. All these factors are interlinked as indicated in Figure 9.1 with the structure of opportunities acting as an influence alongside the various non-work influences on the individual's approach to work.

Class, family and educational influences

People do not enter the occupational structure with equal opportunities. Both the resources they take into the labour market and the aspirations they hold will be influenced by their class, family and educational background together with the way this affects their perception of themselves as members of a particular gender or an ethnic group or as male or female. Parental occupational and class background are likely to make a significant difference to the individual's life-chances both through the material advantages which can be given (providing books or computers in the home, for example) and through the kind of encouragement or discouragement which is provided. There are often direct pressures on a child's job preferences, with the parents either encouraging or discouraging them from entering work like their own or a desire to see a child succeed where a parent failed.

Snapshot 9.2

Three medical students talk about parental pressure

I am more or less happy being a medical student, I suppose. But I have to say that I don't think either my brother or I had much choice about this. Both our parents are doctors and it was simply taken for granted in the family that Lawrence and I would become doctors too. They are wonderful parents, and neither of us would have wanted to upset them by resisting our destinies.

That sounds frightening to me. My parents didn't push me in any particular direction. I must admit though that my Dad used to go on and on about my 'not ending up working in a shop, like me'.

Oh dear: parents! And I can give you a further variation on this theme. My mother, she's told me so often, was desperate to become a doctor. But she didn't make it. She now repeatedly tells me how pleased she is that I am living her dream.

Family networks, as well as parents, can play a significant role in individuals' work opportunities, not just in cases where middle-class parents have contacts which can provide entry to careers for their children but also where manual workers may 'sponsor' members of their own families in the organisation which employs them. Grieco (1987) showed how this can be helpful both to the employee, who gains support from family members both inside and outside work and is sustained in steady employment, and for employers, whose recruitment costs are kept low and who can look to employees' relatives to help train them and teach them to 'fit in'. Whipp (1990), in a study which shows the very significant role played by family networks in the British pottery industry, noted that potters frequently 'employed' their own relatives in subcontracting relationships. And in the Asian small businesses studied by Ram (1994), the employing of family members is shown to have:

- a practical rationale in which family labour is cheaper and easier to supervise, and
- an ideological rationale in which there was a concern to develop a 'family culture' for the organisation, one intended to promote trust and to align the goals of managers and employees (though what came about in practice was a form of 'negotiated paternalism', arising as family members resisted impositions).

LOOKING BACK <<<<<

All these matters of social class and occupational entry need to be seen in the broad context of class and occupational patterns, as discussed in Chapter 7, and in connection with processes of occupational recruitment in Chapter 8.

At the most general level, socialisation in the home and in society at large, especially through the images to be seen in the communication media, not only provides information about and evaluations of different occupations, it suggests what kind of work might be appropriate for members of each gender (Powell and Greenhaus 2010). And formal schooling operates alongside the general cultural and family socialisation processes. Devine (1992), for example, showed how the 'gendered' nature of subject choices within the education system 'accounts for the small number of women who embark on technical degree courses in pursuit of high-level careers in industry'. Even the ways in which certain school pupils resist authority at school was shown in a classic ethnography by Willis (1977), to be a form of preparation for the way those particular individuals will need to live with their subservient roles once they enter paid employment. The research on youth career entry carried out by Banks *et al.* (1992), is taken by the researchers to 'confirm the centrality of educational career in the reproduction of social inequality'.

The influence of class and family on individuals' entry and career advancement is seen in an especially bold way by research into (and public attention towards) the careers of British stage and screen actors. Using information from the Great British Class Survey (see p. 212), Friedman *et al.* (2015), show that actors with working-class backgrounds are significantly underrepresented within the profession. Further, the research indicates that even when those from working-class origins succeed in entering the occupation they do not have access to the same 'economic, cultural and social capital' as those from privileged backgrounds. And interview material reveals how these capitals shape the way actors can respond to occupational challenges. The researchers 'demonstrate the profound occupational advantages afforded to actors who can draw upon familial economic resources, legitimate embodied markers of class origin (such as Received Pronunciation) and a favourable typecasting'.

Work quality and satisfaction

Whatever it is that constitutes a 'good job', as Tilly and Tilly (1998) emphasised in a major overview of thinking, 'is hard to define' and can differ radically over 'time, place, culture and class'. Yet no research on job quality, it is pointed out, has found people giving priority to 'expressive values' over 'material measures of success'. In spite of this, there has been a long tradition in the psychological and the sociological study of work to focus on the expressive side of work involvement and, in particular, on people's 'satisfaction' with their work experiences. At first sight, we might expect this to be a very personal matter, varying from one unique human individual to another. However, satisfaction is not a totally individualistic notion. In any given society, there will be certain basic notions of what is desirable, and we can expect people with different degrees of access to these satisfactions at work to recognise this. Some indication of the distribution of these satisfactions can be derived if only in a very general way, by looking at the variations in response to questions about 'satisfaction' between people working in different settings.

In a classic review of a large body of early work satisfaction studies, Blauner (1964) found that four aspects of work emerged as significantly related to 'satisfaction': the importance or the relative prestige of the occupation; the degree of independence and control over the conditions of work (this covering the freedom from hierarchical control, the freedom to move about, the opportunity to vary the pace of work and allocate one's time); the extent to which social satisfactions are gained from working within an integrated group; and the degree to which people who work together share non-work activities – perhaps in something approaching an occupational community (Chapter 8, pp. 261–262). Additional factors were noted in a later review of work satisfaction surveys by Parker (1983), including opportunities to 'create something', 'use skill'; 'work wholeheartedly' and work together with people who 'know their job'.

All the factors connected to 'satisfaction' emerging in these studies relate to ones often characterised as intrinsic satisfactions in Figure 9.2 – that is, those relating to factors inherent in the work itself rather than the extrinsic rewards which may be obtained.

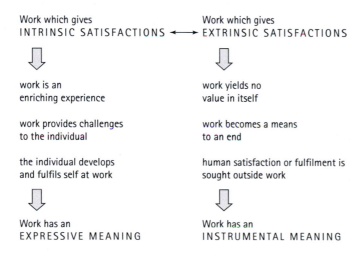

Figure 9.2 Intrinsic and extrinsic work satisfactions: a continuum

The relative importance to workers of intrinsic satisfactions has been related in classic industrial sociology thinking to the idea of *central life interests* (Dubin 1956). The more central a job is in a person's life, the more important intrinsic satisfactions would be to them. But, given the fact that certain jobs offer more possibilities of such satisfaction, it is not surprising that Dubin (1956), on the one hand, found that three out of four individuals in a large sample of *manual* workers, had central life interests outside their work whilst Orzack (1959), on the other hand, found that four out of five of the *professional* nurses whom he studied indicated a central life interest within their work. Cultural factors undoubtedly play a part in this. Hirschfield and Field (2000), for example, demonstrate a connection between people's work central-ity and their attachment to values associated with a Protestant work ethic, this suggesting that work centrality is tied into 'a person's value system and self-identity'. However, studies consistently show that there are occupational similarities in work meanings across different coun-tries, this implying that national cultural factors might be less influential than structural matters such as the market situation of the occupational activity (MOW Research Team 1987).

Issues that were once centrally utilised in the concept of satisfaction are often currently considered in terms of 'well-being'. The concept has not been used to a significant extent by sociologists, however. It is a tool more favoured by economists and, especially, by psychologists work-ing in the occupational safety and health sphere. Its primary focus is a *subjective* one (Pavot and Diener 2013). In more sociological work, the emphasis has shifted from the simple concept of 'satisfaction' towards a notion of the 'quality of work', and structural patterns (varying across societies) have been shown to be important. At a fairly simple level, higher levels of satisfaction are reported in smaller firms in the UK (Forth *et al.* 2006; Tsai *et al.* 2007). At an international level, a major study of work quality in France, Germany, Spain, Sweden and the UK examined five dimensions of the quality of work: job security, skill level, training opportunities, task discretion and work–family balance (Gallie 2007). The most significant factor influencing the differences across the selected societies was whether the *employment-welfare regime* which pre-vailed was *inclusive*, where all citizens share the same employment rights; *dualist*, where these rights are enjoyed by a privileged core of workers and *market*, where there is self-regulation by the market. Work qual-ity was shown to be highest where the inclusive employment regime operated. However, this did not apply to non-standard (temporary and part-time, see above, pp. 214–217) work – such workers appeared to be similarly disadvantaged across the five countries.

LOOKING FORWARD >>>>>

The nature of working relationships in small businesses is returned to in Chapter 11, p. 361.

We must always bear in mind that most of the 'data' about work satisfaction and some aspects of the 'quality of work' upon which generalisations tend to be made derive from the accounts given to researchers. The evidence is such, however, that at the very least we can take it that those in higher-level work expect more by way of intrinsic satisfactions than do those in more routine manual work. We might say that workers in routine jobs both find and seek satisfaction *in* work less than do those in managerial, professional or highly skilled work. But this does not mean that they are not satisfied *with* their job. The 'affluent' car workers in the classic study by Goldthorpe *et al.* (1968) appeared to be satisfied with jobs in which they achieved little or no intrinsic job satisfaction. They did not seek or expect such satisfactions.

LOOKING FORWARD >>>>>

To understand this research finding, these authors developed the concept of *orientation to work*, which was introduced in Chapter 2, and will be turned to later in the present chapter (pp. 287–290).

What has to be remembered, however, is that this finding does not mean that the employers of these men might not have improved the quality of their jobs through job redesign, which might have changed the work orientations of the workers, leading them both to increase their perceptions of job quality and their level of productivity. By the same token, workers with a work orientation which incorporated an expectation of high-quality work experience might well find that particular managerial changes precluding their continuing experience of high-quality employment – as we see in a study of older workers (p. 289).

Technology, work experience and alienation

Technology, for the majority of employees, is central to their work experience, and for many, it is something that is chosen and designed with its mode of use dictated by persons other than those applying it. In addition, these persons are frequently ones with higher status, higher levels of material rewards and, especially important, greater apparent autonomy in their own work experience than those directly applying the technology. Given cultural norms which encourage the valuing of personal autonomy, individuality and self-expression, we can see why technology is such a source of potential resentment, conflict and opposition in workplaces.

Industrial sociology in the 1960s paid considerable attention to the ways in which workers applying different types of technology were likely both to think and to act differently. Such an approach has been given the label of *technological implications*. Following this approach, investigators like Woodward (1965), Blauner (1964) and Sayles (1958) argued that workers' social relationships with each other, the quality of their work experience and their propensity to engage in conflict with management would be heavily dependent on technology. To make this clearer, let us compare a situation where the technology is a craft-based one with the very different technology used by an unskilled factory worker in Snapshot 9.3.

Technological implications thinking

The technology being used determines, or at least closely constrains, the way in which tasks are organised which, in turn, significantly influences the attitudes and behaviour of workers.

Snapshot 9.3

The meat worker and the stone mason compare their jobs

'I'll buy you another pint, Don, if you can tell me the difference between your job and mine. You keep telling us what a great job you have and you love going to work. I admit I don't enjoy my job, but I really want you to explain to me how you chipping away at lumps of stone every day in your dirty old workshop or up on the windy roof of the cathedral is really any different from me in my super-clean air conditioned factory chopping away at sheep and cow carcasses'.

'OK Mick: just two things. First, I work with mates I've known since we were lads. We trained together and we've always helped each other out at work. We go out together and several of us have even married our mates' sisters. You've met some of them here in the pub. But I've never seen you in here with any of your workmates'.

'No, I don't really know any of them. New people come and go. They're often gone before you've learned their names. There's no socialising in work or out of it'.

'And second, I am free to use my own judgement about how to do a carving, even when I've got to copy an old bit of the cathedral that needs to be replaced. Every job is, in some respect, different from what I did the day before. On top of that, there's no one looking over my shoulder as I work'.

'Fair enough. I've got to do exactly what the supervisor tells me. They know the most efficient way to chop up a beast. And I have to admit, a cow is a cow is a cow. And they make sure I take apart each cow the same way'.

'There you are, Mick. I'll have a pint of Mason's Ale. Thanks, mate'.

Snapshot 9.3 illustrates the fact that it is not the technology itself that operates on the individual. It is the opportunity which the technology allows for personal discretion and for the opportunity to socialise with others as well as the part it plays in the power relationships between the managers and the managed. Blauner's influential classic study, *Alienation and Freedom* (1964), attempted to bring together several of the major factors thought to influence work satisfactions and to relate those to work experience in different technological settings. He used the over-all concept of alienation to bring together those factors influencing satisfaction. These four 'dimensions of alienation', as he termed them, were *powerlessness*, or lack of opportunity for control; *meaninglessness* or lack of opportunity to feel a sense of purpose by linking one's job with the overall production process; *isolation* or an inability to relate closely to others at work; and *self-estrangement* or a lack of opportunity to achieve self-involvement or personal fulfilment at work. Looking at four industries, Blauner found that alienation was relatively low in the craft printing industry and the process chemical industry, higher in the machine-tending textile setting and highest on the car assembly line.

Alienation
A state of existence in which human beings are not fulfilling their humanity.

Blauner's thesis that 'alienation' varies with technology is open to the criticism that it trivialised Marx's much more powerful notion of alienation by conceptualising alienation in subjective terms. Also, the fragmenting of experience which Marx discusses is a much broader phe-nomenon than the one Blauner examined. It results from the capitalist organisation of work activity rather than the use of any particular technology within that context. The basic notion underlying the concept of alienation is one of 'separation' (Schacht 1970) and, in Marx's usage, various forms of 'separation' within human experience under capitalism are identified. Individuals

- become alienated or estranged from other people as relationships become merely calculative, self-interested and untrusting;
- become alienated from the product of their efforts since what is produced is expropriated from them and was not, anyway, conceived by the workers themselves to meet their own ends or needs;
- are alienated or separated from their own labour in that they do not derive the satisfactions or the delight that is possible in labour since that labour is forced upon them as a means of meeting other needs and because they put themselves under the control of other people in the work situation; and
- experience work as an alien thing which oppresses them.

Potentially, in the Marxian view, work could be a source of human fulfilment, and here we come to the essential element of Marx's notion of alienation: people can be alienated from themselves. Marx's conception of human nature is one in which it is assumed that people realise their essential nature, as a species, through productive work which is carried out for their own purposes and not under the control and exploitation of others. What this implies – and many users of the concept of alienation forget this – is that alienation is basically an objective state. Alienation is not necessarily reflected in felt job dissatisfaction or in frustration. A person may be very happy sitting at a desk in someone else's factory five days per week sorting pieces of paper which mean little to them, in return for a wage. This person is nevertheless alienated: they are not fulfilling themselves in the way they might be were they working under different conditions.

Although it can be argued that the concept of alienation is one that can be valuably, and indeed centrally, used in academic research (Shantz *et al.* 2012; Kalekin-Fishman and Langman 2015), more contemporary variants of the classic notion of alienation have been produced. One of these is Sennett's (1998) notion of the 'corrosion of character'. This emerges, Sennett argues, within the 'new capitalism' of flexibility, market domination, quick financial returns and impermanence. Under these conditions, and the associated corroding of loyalties, trust relations and mutual commitments in work contexts, people are no longer able to maintain a sense of character – a coherent personal narrative of who they are and where they have come from. This builds on a long-standing tradition in sociology that has concerned itself with the relationship between work and human 'dignity' (Hodson 2001; Sennett 2003; Strangleman 2006; Thompson and Newsome 2016), a notion which was implicit in the classic industrial sociology study in which Chinoy (1992, originally 1955), showed the extent of the gap between the ambitions for personal and family fulfilment instilled in American automobile workers and the realities of a class and employment system which denied the realisation of these ambitions.

> ### LOOKING FORWARD >>>>>
>
> A similar analysis to Chinoy's, and one which talks about indignities as well as unfulfilled ambitions, is discussed later in this chapter (p. 313) in connection with low-paid work in the USA and the UK.

Milkman, in noting the continuing relevance of the Chinoy's (1992) study half a century later, says such factory work 'remains deeply alienating' and adds that any 'reduction in the degradation of the labour process is counteracted by the continual fear of job loss' that pervades the major car producers. This research identifies the expectations which these American car workers had or have of work and recognises the distress that is caused when they are not met. However, it is important to note here that it was a failure to meet culturally supported expectations that created the problems and not the technology as such. Different expectations might lead to different experiences, as application of the important concept of work orientation has shown.

Work orientations: variations, dynamics and the negotiation of implicit contracts

> ### LOOKING BACK <<<<<
>
> We saw in Chapter 3 that the work orientation concept entered industrial sociology in the mid-1960s and that the perspective associated with it is one which, as its originators put it, takes the employee's own definition of the situation as an 'initial basis for the explanation of their social behaviour and relationships' (Goldthorpe *et al.* 1968).

A person's orientation to work is the meaning attached by people to their work which predisposes them to think and act in particular ways with regard to that work. Perhaps the greatest value of the work orientation notion for general discussions of 'work motivations' is that it overcomes the popular tendency to engage in 'either-or' types of debate about what people 'look for in their work'. So much everyday discussion of work attitudes and work motivation centres, in effect, upon the question of whether people generally are intrinsically or extrinsically oriented towards their work. It is frequently debated, for example, whether people 'go to work for the money' or 'are looking for job satisfaction'. Sometimes such discussions are about people in general and sometimes they are about a particular type of worker, or a particular individual. But this is too simplistic; the concept of work orientation goes beyond this and shows that the ways in which people approach their work typically includes mixtures of these basic inclinations whilst nevertheless containing specific leanings in one or other of these general directions. And the concept has been employed to help explain the factors, both individual and structural, which influence people's attitudes and behaviour with regard to their work. Orientations to work held by any particular individual will always be related to their particular stage in life and to their general circumstances at a particular time. We can thus provide a concept to 'operationalise' this insight: a concept of 'emergent life orientation' (Watson 2013b). These are biographical 'patterns' that emerge with the *identity work* processes that unfold over a person's lifetime.

Emergent life orientations

The meanings attached by people at a particular stage of their life to their personal and social circumstances, meanings which predispose them to act in particular ways with regard to the future, including their relationship to work and consumption.

LOOKING FORWARD >>>>>

The concept of *identity work* is examined closely in Chapter 10, pp. 303–306.

The expression about 'reinventing oneself' is rather interesting here and neatly captures two people's shift in both life orientation and work orientation. This particular case of 'reinvention' is a fairly 'cut and dried' one. Jim and Eileen were in a situation where their approach to life

Snapshot 9.4

Jim and Eileen shift their life orientation

Jim and Eileen had worked for many years for a large business which dominated their locality. They had similar orientations to their work as technical specialists: they took pleasure in the tasks they undertook and were happy with the respect they felt both the business and their colleagues gave them. They were equally happy with their salaries and their pension arrangements. But in their mid-fifties, they were horrified to find themselves made redundant as their employer closed the whole site in which they worked. They were unable to find any employment in the town in which they could use their skills and experience. After much reflection they decided to replace their large (and still mortgaged) house with a smaller one which was just affordable in their new circumstances. However, they felt unwilling to be, in Eileen's words, 'early retirees'. 'That did not feel like us', Jim said, 'And so, let's put it like this: we reinvented ourselves as self-employed flower growers and retailers'. Eileen observed: 'What had been our hobby now became our work and we started to come to terms with long working hours, a low income and rare holidays'.

and to work had to change as their jobs disappeared. And their age was an important factor in what they would do in their new situation. But what about older employees whose employment does not disappear but who find their work experiences and orientations changing as a result of changes made by employers in the face of increased competition, new technologies, restructured work, cost pressures and so on? White and Smeaton (2016), investigated changes of this kind over twenty years and showed that older employees – at all organisational levels – have experienced an increasingly negative orientation. The argument here is that older workers have 'more negative attitudes/ evaluations' than do younger employees. And this is not because they are worse affected but because 'they have lost more of what they expected to get'.

LOOKING FORWARD >>>>>

The broader issue of how employment experience has changed in different ways across Europe is discussed in Chapter 11.

What has happened, the authors suggest, is that the 'psychological contract' between the employers and the employees has been broken by the employers, leaving them with a worse 'deal' than they once had.

This takes us on to the concept of 'implicit contract' – something very similar to the notion of 'psychological contract' (Argyris 1960; Schein 1965, 1978).

The negotiation of implicit contracts in employment relations

If we concentrate on people who are engaged, in whatever way, by an employing organisation, the notion of work orientation can be linked to the notion of *implicit contract* – a concept that emerged at the same time as the work orientation one (Levinson *et al.* 1966), and is related to a concept that appeared in the very early days of industrial sociology: that of *effort bargain* (Behrend 1957; Baldamus 1961).

> ## Implicit contract
>
> The tacit agreement between an employed individual and an employing organisation about what the employee will 'put in' to the job and the rewards and benefits for which this will be exchanged.

The implicit employment contract is the largely tacit agreement made between the two parties with regard to what will be given by each and what each will take from the relationship. The employee's priorities, the resources which they take to the labour market and their personal circumstances all influence what kind of bargain they can make. The contract is formed as a result of 'various kinds of symbolic and actual events' which define what the employee will 'give in the way of effort and contribution in exchange for challenging or rewarding work, acceptable working conditions, organisational rewards in the form of pay and benefits, and an organisational future in the form of a promise of promotion or other forms of career advancement'. Schein (1978) says that this contract is 'psychological' in that the 'actual terms remain implicit; they are not written down anywhere'. However, 'the mutual expectations formed between the employee and the employer function like a contract in that if either party fails to meet the expectations, serious consequences will follow – demotivation, turnover, lack of advancement, or termination'. In Figure 9.3, we see the major elements that make up the implicit contract which can be seen to be at the core of every employment relationship.

Within the individual's personal priorities – conditioned as these are by personal resources brought to the labour market and by the knowledge and the reality of the jobs available – a certain degree of calculation

Figure 9.3   The individual's perceived implicit contract at the centre of their work orientation

is involved in the taking of any job. The individual will balance the likely personal costs in the shape of the amount of physical and mental effort to be expended, together with the likely deprivations of fatigue and the loss of freedom involved in accepting the instructions of others, against the available rewards. For certain employees, cash may be a priority; for others, there may be more concern with the career advancement possible in the future, whereas yet another person may be more interested in intrinsic job satisfaction, the status of a given job, the chance to control other people or simply the opportunity to fulfil personal values afforded by a job which, say, involves 'helping people'.

Whatever the individual's priority is, the various factors indicated in Figure 9.3 will have to be balanced against each other. The 'deal' that Mary Murray, in Snapshot 9.5, is making with the financial services firm she is joining clearly contains a number of factors which are implicit, rather than part of any written contract she may have signed. And she is trading off, in effect, what she is losing in leaving teaching with what she is gaining by moving into financial services. As a result of her, in effect, applying to her circumstances a calculating scheme, something like Figure 9.3, she has decided that the implicit contract or 'deal' she had with education has deteriorated sufficiently for her to make a move. And, in 'weighing things up' with regard to the new deal, she is again applying such a scheme.

The calculations that Mary Murray is making prior to changing to her new job will inevitably colour her experience in the work and whatever further decisions she makes. The implicit contracts we all

Mary's new job and new implicit contract

I spent a lot of time thinking about this change I am making: leaving school-teaching to sell financial services. I used to be happy with – what shall I call it? – yes, the *deal* I had with the education service. The money was reasonable, and I felt a lot of satisfaction in seeing children learn. Security was a big thing too, I felt. For all of that, I was happy to take the level of responsibility that you have being in charge of a classroom. I didn't find myself getting tired, and the Head Teacher left me more or less to my own devices. But, weighing things up, I am not so happy with the deal. The national curriculum imposes on me things I don't want to teach, so I have less control over the work. And, connected to this, I get less satisfaction. And I increasingly see friends in other careers making more money than me, and getting on faster in their careers. So I am leaving. The deal that I get with the new job is quite good. I have lost the security I had with the teaching, and I won't have the satisfaction of seeing children achieve. I will get a lot more money, I feel sure, but I am going to have to put in, so to speak, a lot more initiative than I have in the past. But I will be left free to do the job they way I think is best. I know I shall have to work hard to get the extra money. I reckon coming to terms with some of the more complicated products that I shall be selling in the future will take more mental effort than I have put into teaching for a long time.

make, prior to our entering any job or career orient our subsequent attitudes and work behaviours.

The implicit contract is never fixed, nor is it ever fully stable, and a key factor tending to threaten its stability is the push towards increased efficiency on the part of the employer (as, indeed, was the case in Mary Murray's teaching job). Those changes were the result of state efforts to change education. But many changes at work are made as part managerial efforts to improve worker 'motivation'. The attempts that managers frequently make to restructure work, redesign jobs and engineer organisational cultures can be understood in large part as attempts to *manipulate worker implicit contracts*.

LOOKING BACK <<<<<

The pressures to make changes in organisations and the various forms that these changes take were examined in Chapter 6.

The relationship between organisational managements and workers, unequal as the two parties typically are in terms of power and resources, is essentially one of *exchange* within the 'negotiated order' that is the

The managerial manipulation of worker implicit contracts

The attempts by managers to 'motivate' workers, not by 'meeting needs' as in classic motivation theory, but by negotiating with and persuading workers that a particular bundle of rewards that is on offer is a fair and reasonable return for the bundle of 'efforts' that the management is asking them to put in.

work organisation (Chapter 2, pp. 49–50). And how people behave or 'perform' in their employment situation is significantly influenced by how they perceive the 'employment deal' that is currently in existence between them and the organisation. Managers, in 'motivating' workers, structuring and restructuring their tasks or shaping and reshaping workplace 'values' are necessarily involved in complex processes of negotiation. They do not, however, necessarily straightforwardly and formally negotiate with workers what tasks they are to undertake or how much they are to be paid for doing those tasks. In effect, they negotiate over the basic 'realities' of the employment relationship.

Within the basic and unequal power balance of the employment relationship, managers work to establish, maintain and modify patterns of workplace relations and understandings. As part of this, the workers have to be persuaded that there is a fair and reasonable return for the efforts and initiatives that they are being asked to make, the risks to health and mental well-being they may need to take, and the degree of managerial authority over them that they accept. That 'return' will be a complex mix of monetary, psychological and social rewards. The mix of rewards will involve a certain amount of pay, a certain amount of security, a certain degree of opportunity for career advancement, a certain element of 'social standing' and so on. And managers will strive to ensure that this will be perceived by the employee as a fair balance with what is being asked of those employees by the employing organisation. Clive Dickenson in Snapshot 9.6 is an example of a manager consciously working to change the ways in which the 'deal' between the employer and the shop workers is perceived by the workers – to the benefit, as he sees it, of both the business and the staff.

Clive obviously feels good about what he is achieving. He is shaping relationships and manipulating implicit contracts in the way we would expect any manager to do. His efforts may be negatively judged as exploitive and manipulative. But what he is doing is what organisational leaders would probably wish their managers to do.

Snapshot 9.6

Clive goes for a 'win-win' in his supermarket store

An important part of my job as a manager is getting more work – and better quality of work – out of the staff I am in charge of. Typically when somebody starts working for us, they have a good idea from what they hear from people about us, as the second biggest supermarket in town. But, until recently, they did not expect, as part of the deal, to be given hours as flexible as the ones I have now brought in. Nor did they expect to be encouraged to develop relationships with the customers or to be consulted by me and the departmental managers about customer attitudes and expectations, the way the shop is organised or what changes I should press head-quarters to make in what we offer in the store. These are some of the things that I have been working on and, it would seem, the staff feel that their work is much more rewarding than it was. This is certainly suggested by the enthusiasm with which they have adopted my 'new ways' of doing things. I am getting really good advice from them which is improving the shop's business performance. And, guess what, both my labour turnover and my absence rates have improved enormously. It's a win-win – for the business and for the staff.

Patterns of work orientation and experience within the organisational hierarchy

LOOKING BACK <<<<<

The present analysis links this chapter's concern with *experiences* of inequality back to the *patterns* of inequality that were the subject of Chapter 7.

Because of the different resources that they take into the labour market, the quality of the implicit contract which a worker at a senior organisational level – occupying the associated middle- or upper-class position – makes is very different to the one that a worker at the bottom end of the organisational and class hierarchy can make.

The work orientations and work experiences of individuals are intimately related to the broad structural patterns of modern societies – patterns having interlinked corporate and societal dimensions:

- Those in the higher positions in the class structure, typically in managerial or professional positions, tend to have a relatively *diffuse implicit contract* which means, as Fox (1974) shows, that they will be required to use discretion in their work and experience a high-trust relationship with their superiors. The high trust which is put in this type of staff and the relatively high level of rewards (in the form of cash, status, opportunity for intrinsic satisfaction and career advancement offered) are reciprocated on the part of the employees with a willingness to comply with organisational requirements on their own initiative. The type of control to which they are submitted is *indirect* (Chapter 5, p. 180). Organisational norms are 'internalised' and individuals, in effect, control themselves (as well as their subordinates) on behalf of their superordinates.

- Those in lower class positions, typically in less skilled routine work, are more likely to experience a *restricted type of implicit contract*. The generally lower level of rewards is associated with what Fox (1974) describes as institutionalised low-trust relationships with superiors. Work tasks are much more closely prescribed and these are executed (their conception occurring elsewhere) on the basis of a contractual commitment which is specific rather than diffuse. This specificity is represented by there typically being an hourly or weekly wage as opposed to an annual salary, by the much tighter specification of what is required of them and, especially, by the lack of the inducement of potential career promotion. The control mechanism will tend to be of a *direct control* type – one tending to minimise worker responsibility and submitting workers to close supervision.

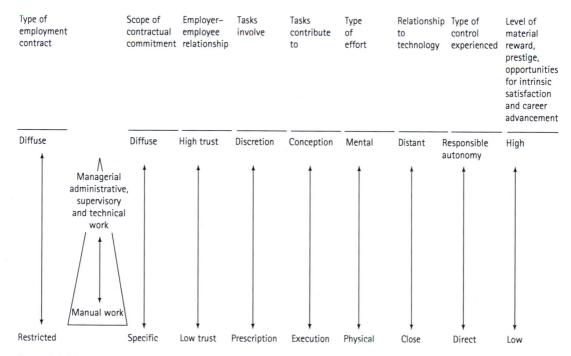

Type of employment contract		Scope of contractual commitment	Employer–employee relationship	Tasks involve	Tasks contribute to	Type of effort	Relationship to technology	Type of control experienced	Level of material reward, prestige, opportunities for intrinsic satisfaction and career advancement
Diffuse		Diffuse	High trust	Discretion	Conception	Mental	Distant	Responsible autonomy	High
	Managerial administrative, supervisory and technical work								
	Manual work								
Restricted		Specific	Low trust	Prescription	Execution	Physical	Close	Direct	Low

Figure 9.4 Two ideal types of relationship between individual and employing organisation (seen as two ends of various continuums related to the hierarchical structure of organisation)

The broad pattern here is represented in Figure 9.4. It shows general structural tendencies within which individuals each have their own unique experience of work and satisfaction.

Women's preferences, choices and work orientations

Although the economic dimension of paid work is likely to be a central factor in the working lives of most people, the orientation to work concept and the implicit contract model encourages us to be aware of the other factors which shape any given individual's approach to their work, in the light of their personal and family circumstances.

LOOKING BACK <<<<<

All the evidence examined in Chapter 7 points to the generally very different circumstances of women and men with regard to work.

The work orientations of women in paid employment are inevitably influenced by the implications of their gender and all that this implies for their life career. Detailed case and ethnographic studies carried out in the 1980s produced a subtle analysis of the variety of factors that play a significant part in the orientations of women at that time, alongside the obvious economic ones. Sharpe (1984), for example, suggested that it was the 'social characteristics' of working which gave most meaning to the jobs of the wives and mothers she interviewed and that this was especially the case after a period of not working. Pollert (1981) talked of the 'ray of light' provided in the factory she studied by the company of others for women with children who were experiencing the double burden of home and work. Cavendish (1982) added to this the point that her participant observation study of factory life gave her a feeling of being 'more rooted in social life', enabling her to become more outgoing and socially relaxed than she had previously been. On the basis of her sharing this life, 'it seemed only sensible to get married and benefit from the economics of scale of two wage packets'. To consider role reversal would have been 'economic suicide'.

Women's attitudes to work and family do not simply follow labour market opportunities and historical evidence shows that between the 1940s and 1965, attitudes 'changed independently of women's employment experience . . . that is, attitudes appeared to change before women's employment experience had grown' (Dex 1988). Subsequently, Dex argued, the structures of employment in Britain had been 'changing to accommodate to women's availability and attitudes towards work'. It is not a matter of women simply reacting to changes in demand: 'the fact that women are prepared to accept primary responsibility for child care, and then structure their employment participation around the availability of their husband to fill in the child care gaps, has its roots, in part, in attitudes'. Women's 'attitudes' cannot be separated from 'reflexive modernisation' trends in late modern societies for individuals generally to be concerned with expressing their identities and questioning traditional limitations on their desire to express or fulfil themselves (Beck *et al.* 1994). This was recognised by Hakim (2000), in her stress on the part played by choice or 'personal preference' in how women shape their lives. Structural circumstances are seen as freeing women to make such choices, these including the contraceptive and equal opportunities 'revolutions', the increase in white-collar work, the availability of jobs for secondary earners, as well as the cultural emphasis on personal preferences in lifestyles. As a result of these choices, three ideal type work–life preference groups are identified in contemporary European and American societies: *home-centred*, *work-centred*, *adaptive* – where women seek both to work and lead a full family life.

It was estimated by Hakim (2000) that around half of British and American women could be allocated to the adaptive category. However, her emphasis on choice and her desire to question the 'feminist myth' that part-time work is forced on women as a result of their domestic responsibilities (Hakim 1995), was controversial. Ginn *et al.* (1996) insist that the choices women make in these respects are often constrained ones, with the contentment they express explainable as an accommodation to their 'lack of alternatives and weak bargaining position', given the pressures of their domestic situation. Walsh's (1999) study of the work orientations of part-time working women showed more than half of her sample had made such constrained choices – choosing part-time work in order to cope with dependent children. Yet there was a significant proportion of women in the study who had chosen part-time work for a variety of 'lifestyle' reasons other than ones relating to domestic pressures. Casey and Alach (2004), in their study of women in non-standard, especially temporary, work show that, not only were these women undertaking such work out of preference but were doing this to practise their own 'self-styled, preferential arrangements' and to 'actively challenge' conventional economic assumptions of employment behaviour and traditional trajectories of women's lives. They were not making this preference in recognition of a primary commitment to family and domestic work or to conform to a 'secondary earner' status within the family. And an Australian study of women's aspirations and preferences (Johnstone and Lee 2016), leads the researchers to question the value of Hakim's Lifestyle Preference Theory, arguing that young Australian women's responses were 'best characterised by diversity and change' and that 'we cannot assume that young women have set ideas regarding what they want in later adult life or that their ideas will not change as their circumstances change'.

Using longitudinal data to test some of the contentions of the preference theory, Kan (2007) shows how 'women's employment careers are affected by both preferences and constraints'. This is perhaps not surprising but it underlines the importance of taking into account both 'agency' and 'structure' when trying to understand how and why women are balancing their working and home lives. And this must mean recognising the opportunity structures that women meet once they are in a particular kind of work. Evetts' (1996) study of women in science and engineering shows the importance of this in her analysis of the pattern of 'promotion accommodation' whereby women would opt out of their career for a period to have children and then accept as organisationally reasonable – gender-neutral that is – the consequential limits that this put on their career opportunities. Crompton and Harris (1998) showed something similar in the case of women doctors who 'satisficed', moderating that is, both their occupational and their family ambitions in order to reconcile the two. However, the researchers contrast this picture with the one they found with senior women in banking who had, unlike the women doctors, insisted on more sharing of domestic responsibilities with their spouses and refused to compromise their work careers. This finding is taken to show that occupations vary in the pressures they put on women to seek accommodations in their family relationships to avoid compromising occupational advancement.

A study of architects by Fowler and Wilson (2004), shows the considerable difficulties faced by women, and especially by mothers in this work. They infer that when markets are less localised and clients 'less forthcoming', as was the case here, the 'room for tolerance and nurture of those with young children becomes reduced'. The savagely competitive environment, for example, was seen as requiring tough masculine characteristics to impose time discipline on builders and others with whom the architects had to deal. In spite of this, the extent to which women workers will resist even the most oppressive atmosphere is indicated by Ngai's (2005) ethnographic study of women factory workers in China where the women energetically resisted the oppression coming from a combination of global capitalism, state socialism and familial patriarchy.

Summary

Work has had different meanings for people generally in different societies at different times in history. If we look at how societal meanings of work have changed over history we see that the 'work ethic' of modern societies is just one possibility. However, the particular meaning which work has for any given contemporary individual is likely to be strongly influenced by their family, class and educational background. Each individual makes their own work or occupational 'choices' to a certain degree, but these choices are made within the 'opportunity structures' in which people are socially located. Work can provide both intrinsic satisfactions (which come from 'the work itself') and extrinsic satisfactions (which come from the income or other rewards of work which are not directly connected to the actual tasks performed). The technology with which people work is always likely to influence the satisfaction that people gain from their work, but it does not determine it. It is better to look at the broad meaning which their work has for any particular individual; their orientation to work. At the core of a person's work orientation is a perceived 'effort bargain' or implicit contract with the employer – an understanding of the balance (or imbalance) between what the worker sees themselves 'putting into' their work and what they see themselves 'getting out' of it. These orientations and contracts are fragile and continually liable to change, whether this occurs, say, as a result of an individual's changed circumstances or as a result of a managerial initiative. What has traditionally been conceptualised as the managerial 'motivating' of workers can be more usefully conceptualised as a matter of managers manipulating the ways in which workers understand their implicit contract with the employer.

10 Identity, narrative and emotion in and out of work

Key issues

- How do we choose which set of underlying assumptions about the nature of human beings to apply to issues of work, identities, narratives, emotions and sexuality?
- What part does work play in people's identities and the ways in which individuals manage the identity issues that arise for them with regard to their work?
- How significant are narratives and stories in social life, and how do they relate to three levels of social life?
- What are the implications of 'zero hours' contracts for people generally and especially for those at the 'bottom of the heap'?
- What particular identity and meanings issues do managers find themselves faced with?
- What is the role of angst, emotions, aesthetics and sexuality in work-meaning processes?
- How does work affect people's lives outside of work?

Two sets of underlying assumptions about the nature of human beings

The set of assumptions about human individuals presented in Table 10.1 clearly parallels the set of assumptions about organisations which was explained in Chapter 5. Also, certain of these assumptions are implicit in much of Chapter 9 with the notion of emergence being most visible in the discussion of work orientations and people's *emergent life orientations* (p. 288). Chapter 9 emphasised that people bring their own meanings to their work and that these meanings or 'work orientations' may change over time, sometimes in quite significant ways. This insight powerfully

Table 10.1 An emergent-relational view of individuals contrasted with a rational-system view.

A rational-system view of individuals	An emergent-relational view of individuals
The individual is an *entity* which exists in its own terms with an essential or 'true' self.	Individuals are *relational* beings: their individuality only becomes possible as a result of relating to others.
The individual possesses a more-or-less fixed set of *personality* traits.	Individuals are always in a process of 'becoming': they have *emergent identities*.
The individual has various needs which create *motives* propelling them towards particular behaviours.	Individuals are *sensemaking* and *project-oriented* rather than need-led: in the light of how they interpret their situation they make *exchanges* with others to deal with their material and emotional circumstances.
The individual at work is capable of suppressing emotions so that their engagement in *rational analysis* and decision-making is unaffected by feelings and values.	Individuals are *simultaneously rational and emotional*: their feelings about the world and their reasoning capacities mutually influence each other.
The individual, regardless of the society in which they live, plays the role of worker, manager or whatever according to the logic of modern systems of employment and work organisation.	Individuals are cultural animals: they make sense of the world and their work activities in the light of the culture and values of the society and communities of which they are part.

challenges the conventional assumption that the human individual is a fixed entity with a given 'personality' that changes little over a lifetime.

Identity, self-identities and social-identities

Sociologists have increasingly recognised that people have *emergent identities* rather than fixed and relatively unchanging personalities. It has been argued by Giddens (1991) and Sennett (1998), that the nature of contemporary societies, with their encouragement of calculative and risk-taking orientations towards the world in which the individual takes responsibility for their own personal success, is putting more pressure than ever before on individuals to shape their own selves. The difference between these two influential authors, however, is that Giddens sees this situation as, on balance, 'creating expanding opportunities for

---

LOOKING BACK <<<<<

The post-structuralist notion of *subjectivity* (Chapter 3, pp. 79–81) has been significantly used to question the assumption that each person has an unchanging 'sovereign' or 'essential' self, as has the symbolic interactionist concept of *subjective career* (Chapter 3, p. 48) with its acknowledgement that people actively 'seek to achieve overall stability in their outward life and coherence in their inner world' (Collin 1986).

more people to exercise a degree of meaningful autonomy over their lives' whilst Sennett, more pessimistically, sees it as broadly 'corrosive of social bonds and personal meanings, producing an inability to act for the long term and making all social relations less sustainable' (Webb 2004).

The notion of 'identity' is an invaluable bridging concept between individual agency, choice and creation of self, on the one hand, and history, culture and social roles, on the other. It has also brought together researchers from 'disparate communities of scholars' (Brown 2009). However, there is a problem of terminology with the word 'identity'. It is frequently used in the social sciences, as in everyday discourse, to mean different things in different contexts. Thus, 'identity' is sometimes used to refer to people's notion of self ('he suffered an identity breakdown'), and at other times, it is used to refer to something much more cultural ('there is no real clarity about British identity'). And, beyond this, it can be treated as an administrative matter ('the case for identity cards'). A helpful way forward is suggested in Table 10.2. First, we conceptualise the broad notion of 'human identity' as the idea of who or what a particular person is, in relation to others. Identity defines in what ways any given individual is like other people and in which ways they differ from them. Second, we distinguish between three analytically separate but closely intertwined aspects of 'human identity': the internal *self-identity*, the external *social-identities* and personas (Watson 2008a, 2008b). *Self-identity* is the idea that each of us has about who we are. Whether this is more or less vague or more or less concise for any one of us, it is something that no one can live without. To be a sane and effective social actor, each individual must maintain a degree of coherence and consistency in their sense of who they are. Given that they are social or cultural animals, humans are not left to do this privately or 'in their own heads', so to speak. They do it with reference to the culture and the discourses around them. And especially significant within this culture is a variety of *social-identities* (mother, father, dentist, retired banker) which are, to various degrees, 'taken on board' by the individual through a mixture of choice and imposition. A persona is a matter of the way in which individuals present themselves to the world – in the light of both their self-identity and the social–identities that exist around them. As the word's origins suggest, a persona is a social mask, so to speak. It is quite common for a person to present themselves to others in the workplace as, say, a gregarious and ambitious individual whilst their home and family persona is of someone who is quiet, thoughtful and retiring. A different individual might 'play' this the opposite way round. And yet another might display the same persona in every aspect of their lives.

Table 10.2 Human identity, self-identity, social-identities and personas

<table>
<tr><td colspan="2" align="center">HUMAN IDENTITY
The notion of who or what a particular person is, in relation to others</td></tr>
<tr><td align="center">*Internal aspects* ← → </td><td align="center">*External aspects*</td></tr>
<tr><td>SELF-IDENTITY</td><td>SOCIAL-IDENTITIES</td></tr>
<tr><td>The individual's own notion of who and what they are</td><td>Cultural, discursive or institutional notions of who or what any individual might be</td></tr>
<tr><td></td><td>PERSONAS</td></tr>
<tr><td></td><td>The various public and private selves which the individual presents to people in the various circles in which they mix</td></tr>
</table>

Table 10.3 Five types of culturally available social-identity

Five types of culturally available social-identity

(1) Social-category social-identities: class, gender, nationality, ethnicity etc (upper class, female, Asian, Hindu, Scottish …)
(2) Formal-role social-identities: occupation, rank, citizenship etc (doctor, cleaner, captain, Spanish citizen)
(3) Local-organisational social-identities: an old-style Nottingham professor, a Boots pharmacist, a Rolls-Royce design engineer (there will be other versions of this: a local-community social-identity, for example: Ryland estate youths)
(4) Local-personal social-identities: characterisations which various others make of an individual, in the context of specific situations or events (life and soul of the office party, a good GuitarSpot customer, the branch-office clown …)
(5) Cultural-stereotype social-identities: a garrulous Frenchman, a boring accountant, a devoted mother

There is an enormous range of social–identities which a person may draw upon in forming their self-identities and shaping the persona or personas that they present to the world. Each social-identity has a multiplicity of variants and sub-categories available within any culture. Table 10.3 lists five major categories of social–identity and gives illustrations of each of these.

Identity work

In reality, self-identity and social-identities are intimately intertwined. We separate them for analytical purposes – to help us understand the ways in which people form, manage and, from time to time, repair their identities. The concept of *identity work* helps us do this (Sveningsson and Alvesson 2003; Watson 2008a). It brings together inward/internal self-reflection and outward/external engagement – through talk and action – with the five types of social-identity being pressed upon the individual or drawn upon by them as *discursive resources* to present a notion of 'who one is' to the individual and to others.

Identity work

The process whereby people strive to shape a relatively coherent and distinctive notion of personal self-identity and struggle to come to terms with and, within limits, to influence the various social-identities which pertain to them in the various milieux in which they live their lives.

In Snapshot 10.1, we witness Michael Waterbuck engaging in some identity work, as he reflects on who he is, in conversation with the researcher who is interviewing him. We should stress here that Michael is not simply 'reporting' to the researcher what is 'in his head'; he is actively working on his self-identity in talking about himself and his life. Identity-work is something that one does, directly or indirectly, in dialogue with 'others'. When we 'present' ourselves and display chosen personas to others we are also, to a certain degree, 'making' our 'self'.

Snapshot 10.1

Michael reflects on who he is

So, I see Michael that your life has changed enormously since you moved south. Do you have a sense that you are still the same person that you were before your marriage ended and you changed jobs?

You said you'd ask some difficult questions, and that is one. But, actually it is one that I have thought about quite a lot, probably because my mother keeps telling me I am still the 'lovely boy' I always was.

And what have you concluded?

I don't think I have come to a conclusion yet – and I know things will change further as I settle down here – but let me try and put some thoughts together for you. I think that would be helpful for me.

Thank you.

I used to be a happily married man. All my mates at work used to joke about that because I was always talking about Jeannie as if she was the best wife in the world. But I am now a bitterly divorced man. I am the useless husband and father whose wife ran off with an American airline pilot. I feel that bitterness almost like a physical pain inside me. And, this is the thing; I am only slowly making new friends down here because the people at work see me as this sad and bitter person. My former colleagues in the north saw me quite differently. Generally I was seen as one of the Stevensons' new-generation graduate managers, and in my own department, I was regarded as the good humoured and helpful elder brother figure who helped everybody in the office.

Go on.

Yes, I am a different person at work than I used to be.

But you are the boss, aren't you now?

Oh yes, I wasn't thinking about that, sorry. Uhm, let me think. If I were the bloke I used to be, before I became a regional manager, I would be a nicer, friendlier boss, than I am.

You don't think the job has changed you?

There is a lot more pressure in this office than there was up north. So perhaps that is making me into a sharp-tempered bastard, as well as the personal anger. Yes, that might be it.

Is that really what you are at work: a bad-tempered bastard boss?

Oh, I don't know. Actually, I am a bad-tempered bastard boss from up north.

What do you mean?

Before I moved down here, I never thought of myself as a northerner. But people are always going on about it. My secretary was probably being kind to me the other day when she said that people thought 'I wasn't so bad' and that my rather harsh manner was because I was a northerner.

What do you feel about being 'a northerner'?

It's rubbish. I can't stand those types who go about talking rudely and insensitively and then go, 'I can't help being a straight-talking northerner'.

You're saying that could be taken to imply that, deep down, you are a very polite and sensitive chap.

Ok, I'll settle for that. And [laughing loudly] can you tell me where to go for elocution lessons?

Because Michael Waterbuck is at something of a turning point in his life, he is likely to be more active an *identity worker* than most of us are when our lives are proceeding smoothly and we are not changing our jobs or our private lives. He is almost self-consciously explicit that he is working on both his notion of self-identity and social-identities to which he wishes to be associated through his persona, especially as a manager in his office. As discursive resources, he uses a variety of the 'social-identities' seen in Table 10.3. Michael uses:

- the *formal-role* social-identity of 'regional manager';
- the *local-organisational* social-identity of 'one of the Stevensons' new-generation graduate managers';
- the *local-personal* social-identity of 'bad-tempered boss';
- the *cultural-stereotype* social-identity of 'the bitter divorcee'; and
- the *social-category* social-identity of the 'northerner' (this perhaps having an element of the *cultural stereotype* social-identity too).

Whether we choose to understand the notion of 'a northerner' as a respectable social category or as a clichéd or stereotyped social–identity, it is an identity that Michael resists. As this conceptualisation of *identity work* recognises, people, within limits, try to influence the social–identities which might be attached to them.

Discursive resources are not simply 'drawn upon' by people to shape their identities. They are not picked off a menu of cultural offerings at the individual's whim. To repeat a phrase used earlier, they are also 'pressed upon' people. The social–identity of 'northerner' was pressed upon Michael Waterbuck, for example. Such pressures often take the form of powerful interests imposing identities upon the less powerful. The Foucauldian tradition (Chapter 3, pp. 79–81), emphasises that fact that discourse and power are deeply implicated in each other. One way in which this operates within work places was shown by Grey (1994), in his linking of a whole series of 'discursive and non-discursive practices' associated with accounting careers. The idea of an accounting career 'provides a meaning and a rationale for the otherwise disillusioning grind of accountancy training'. Regulation of behaviour is thus achieved in the form of a self-discipline which follows from trainees' acceptance of a 'discourse of career' – a discourse that supports a social–identity of 'the accountant' as well as the specific interests of the accounting firm in which the trainee is located. Sturdy (1992) combined this kind of insight with interactionist notions of the individual striving to achieve a sense of self, to throw light on the way the employers of the clerical workers he studied achieved the 'consent' of the workers to carry out managerial requirements. Collinson (1992) focused on the subjective experience of shop-floor employment and the role of gender and class elements in employees' subjectivities and how these are linked to patterns of both conformity and resistance in the workplace. He shows, for example, how 'manual workers' socially skilled and culturally embedded practices of resistance, compliance and consent' were 'heavily "saturated" with specific masculine subjectivities'. We will return to the notion of 'masculinity' shortly.

Narratives and the link between culture and identity

LOOKING BACK <<<<<

The role of different forms of narrative, myth, legend and so on were examined and illustrated in the consideration of organisational culture in Chapter 5, p. 135.

The social-identities we have just been looking at are part of the culture of a society or a part of a society. Culture, we might say, provides scripts with various 'character parts' which people might take on or be pushed into. This is to speak metaphorically, of course. But the metaphor is a powerful one because a vast amount of the cultural information to which we start relating, soon after birth, comes to us in a narrative form – through fairy tales, stories of our parents' childhood, films, television plays, newspaper stories, jokes, histories, biographies, gossip and so on. Not only this but we tend to learn about other people through the narratives that they offer us about themselves, just as we tend to give accounts of ourselves in narrative terms. We may provide a simple narrative, in the sense of a time-based sequence of events ('I was born in Australia but moved to the USA as a student, and I am now an accountant in Canada'). Alternatively we might present the type of more developed narrative that are worthy of the label of 'stories'. These accounts have more complex plots and involve a set of characters. We see such a story taking shape in the account of himself that Michael Waterbuck was presenting in Snapshot 10.1.

Narratives and stories

Narratives are accounts of events in the world that are organised in a time-related sequence.

Stories are more highly developed narratives: temporally sequenced accounts of events which unfold through plots involving the interplay of characters with interests, motives, emotions and moralities.

If we look closely at the identity work of any specific individual, or perhaps a group of closely associated individuals, it is helpful to observe the ways in which narratives come 'into play' in a way which relates to three 'levels'; the level of society and culture broadly; the level of the more local family, organisations or groups; the level of the individual's own experience and biographic identity work. Figure 10.1 sets this out graphically, effectively separating out narratives which relate to, first, the taken-for-granted 'realities' of whole cultures or societies (myths, grand narratives, histories, novels, dramas, characters from fiction and news broadcasting); second, to more specific or 'local' elements of society such as families, organisations, groups (organisational legends, family sagas, people's tales from their occupational experience); third, what individuals themselves have already created in terms of accounts of their own lives within processes of identity work (life stories, 'war stories' and

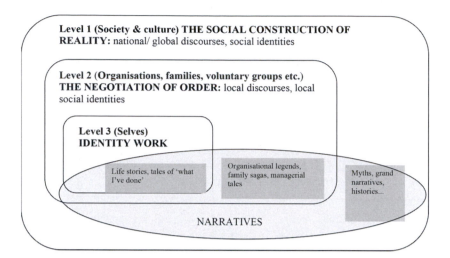

Figure 10.1 Narratives at three levels of social life

other accounts of 'what I have done in my life' or 'what was done to me in my life'.

The words of Jeremy Bentnall in Snapshot 10.2, spoken to the researcher investigating the backgrounds and careers of managers, show elements from all these levels in interplay.

Snapshot 10.2

Jeremy utilises narrative resources from three levels of social life

I generally tell people that I am an aeronautical engineer in spite of the fact that I worked on aero engines rather than aeroplanes as such. Having retired recently, I have been thinking about these things. When I was a boy, there were aeroplanes everywhere, it seemed. The Second World War was over, but the cold war meant that new aircraft from the nearby RAF test station were flying over our house all the time. We understood, rightly or wrongly, that our future would depend in part on the west having better planes than the Russians. I was conscious that all the tales in the adventure books that I used to read were shifting from tales of Spitfires and Hurricanes fighting Nazis to stories about brilliant inventions like vertical take-off and landing machines which would keep a Third World War at bay. As you might guess, I found myself identifying with the aircraft designers and engineers. If you heard all the big hero stuff that I got from my ex-Spitfire-pilot uncle, you might have expected me to aspire to being a pilot, in either the forces or in a test pilot role. But my parents were utterly against this, and my father's talk about what he called his personal 'bad war' strongly influenced me and shaped my university course and my eventual graduate apprenticeship in Royces. I must admit that I found the tales of the shop-floor and the design offices that the old hands in Royces told, day in and day out, gave me as many heroes to inspire me as had all of those tales of 'derring do' in the Battle of Britain. And, let me tell you, these inspirational characters included engineering managers as well as designers and brilliant shop floor blokes.

Narratives and stories link the human individual and their culture through the dual role of, first, providing 'inputs' to our identity-work and, second, providing 'outputs' in the form of the biographical narratives which we shape to help us make sense of who we are – both to ourselves and to others. Examination of a large and very detailed private autobiography by an engineering manager demonstrated the ways in which this individual both draws on the novels, poems and histories he read in his youth and produces tale after tale of life in the 'rough and tumble' of manufacturing industry (Watson 2009a). In the writing and in interviews with the researcher, Leonard Hilton is explicit about how he is trying to come to terms with his life and career both for his own peace of mind and so that his sons can know more of who their father is. He is a remarkably reflective and articulate individual, but his case illustrates something that applies to everyone. Every human being is both a user and a creator of stories. We return to this character in Chapter 12 (p. 381) to hear how a particular social–identity, that of the bully, plays a key role in his biography and his general personal sensemaking. Notions of masculinity inevitably arise in such a context.

Masculinity and identity

Throughout the narratives we encounter, from stories we hear about 'mummies and daddies' in childhood to films we watch and biographies of business leaders we might read in adulthood, we come across images – and social-identities – not just of what men and women are like but of what they perhaps should be like. Research has shown the particular significance in the context of work of notions of masculinity and how these relate to identity issues in the workplace (issues for women, of course, as much as for men). If one re-reads the interview transcript with Michael Waterbuck in Snapshot 10.1, for example, it is apparent that the concept of masculinity – without its actually being named – pervades his identity work.

As is illustrated in the study referred to earlier by Collinson, 'masculinity' is a powerful element of the social categorisation of men. It is a complex and shifting notion, however. Knights and McCabe (2001) demonstrate how a shifting discourse of masculinity operated in a financial services call centre, one in which the practices and the language of managers reflected the contradiction whereby a discourse stressing trust, teamwork and creativity simultaneously retained masculine notions of competition, control and conquest. These men are resisting a pressure to shift their identities towards a managerially instigated formal role of co-operative 'team-worker' to defend a more traditional social category identity of competitive male. Ways in which those allegedly subject to discursive identity-shaping pressures may resist them is also demonstrated by McDowell (2003), in her study of young men who might be expected to find their masculine identities threatened by the lack of the type of jobs traditionally associated with masculinity. She showed how they were active agents in the way they negotiated their identities and found their own rationales for the defence of their traditional masculinity. Something similar is shown by Simpson (2004), when she looks at men doing jobs traditionally associated with women; in effect they 'reconstruct the job' in a way which minimises its non-masculine associations.

A significant factor in the under-reporting to management of passenger anti-social behaviour, say Bishop *et al.* (2009), was the 'culture of masculinity' which was dominant in the bus company which they studied. The customer-facing *service* work that the male bus drivers were doing did not allow them to express traditional 'macho' values of 'strength, bravery and mastery'. In the light of this, they were reluctant, in effect, to show weakness by drawing the attention of 'superiors' to the trouble they encountered on their routes. They operated according to a 'central tenet of working-class masculinity': they preferred, they claimed, to 'stick up for themselves'.

Moulding human subjects and 'the enterprising self'

One very significant pressure on workers' and managers' self-identities is that coming from employers developing new forms of control in which attempts are made to 'mould the human subject', as Alvesson and Willmott (2002) put it, so that 'organisational control is accomplished through the self-positioning of employees within managerially inspired discourses about work and organisation with which they may become more or less identified and committed'. This can never be fully accomplished, these authors recognise, because such attempts are balanced by individuals with 'other elements of life history forged by a capacity to accomplish life projects out of various sources of influence and inspiration'. What has not been given detailed attention, however, according to Storey *et al.* (2005), are the outcomes of the identity work that organisational members do in terms of their personal self-identities. Our snapshot of Michael Waterbuck was an example of exactly this kind of analysis. And Storey *et al.* (2005) do something similar with the cultural workers they studied. These freelance and contract media workers were people whom one would expect to have absorbed to some extent the 'discourses of identity that are dominant currently with their industry' and, especially, the notion of the 'enterprising self'. The researchers concluded that workers variously 'incorporate, modify, or reject notions of enterprise in their reflexively organised narratives of self'.

This research questions the highly influential argument that a dominant or 'totalizing' notion of an 'enterprising self' (du Gay 1995) emerged in the latter part of the twentieth century as employers worked to establish what, in effect, was a new type of employee whose personalities were 'saturated with a culture of enterprise' (Cremin 2003). Fenwick (2002) came to similar conclusions on the basis of her study of women setting up and running their own businesses, arguing that 'entrepreneurism (sic) is not unitary' and that 'self-employed individuals negotiate multiple discourses and identities among which competitive individualism is not the most dominant'. And Bolton and Houlihan (2005) in their study of customer service demonstrate that the power of the 'discourse of enterprise and the cult of the customer' has been over-estimated. Generally speaking, detailed research supports the view expressed by Halford and Leonard (2006) that 'while generic discourses of enterprise, profession, gender or age may be important, they are received and interpreted in the particular and complex contexts that individuals move through in their everyday lives'. McCabe (2009) illustrates this argument when he reports how bank workers, whose employers endeavoured to 'reinvent employees as responsible, autonomous, self-regulating, customers-focused team players', could be seen as 'turning the discourse back on management' when they felt that the bank was not, in practice, allowing them to live up to the parts of the discourse which they felt were positive for their own work experience.

Identity tensions, ambiguities and occupational circumstances

If one is employed in an occupation that everybody understands, the matter of 'who one is' in the social world is somewhat less challenging for the individual than if their employment or occupational circumstances are ambiguous. Gotsi *et al.* (2010) argue that 'identity tensions' are especially common among creative workers. In their study of people working in new product design consultancies, they note a desire for people to see themselves 'as distinctive in their artistry, passion, and self-expression, nurturing an identity that energizes their innovative efforts'. But, at the same time, the pressures of market demands, budgets and deadlines encourages a more business-like identity 'that supports firm performance'. Particularly helpful to them in struggling with the tensions between these 'multiples identities' is the 'meta-identity' discursive resource of the 'practical artist'.

LOOKING BACK <<<<<

The creative and cultural industries were put in their occupational context in Chapter 8.

Another identity issue for workers in the creative or cultural industries is that of the precarious nature of their employment. Deuze (2007), for example, shows how media work is project-oriented, based on short-term contracts and is without clear working hours or a permanent work place. People therefore struggle to make sense of their careers and the relationship between their work and their non-working lives. And another problem which such workers face, say Costas and Kärreman (2016), is that of coping with a gap between expectations created by employers (who create discourses emphasising expertise, creativity, learning, autonomy and membership of an elite) and the realities of carrying out the tasks they are given. Workers may develop a 'bored self'. This is an 'arrested identity' which makes it possible for the individual to 'both hang on to the aspirational aspects of the identity suggested by company discourse while dealing with its disappointments'.

Zero hours contracts and work experience at the bottom of the heap

In Chapter 7, attention was paid to what are seen as the advantages and disadvantages of so-called portfolio of boundaryless careers. Perhaps inevitably, the crucial factor influencing the extent to which any given worker or type of worker can benefit from these trends in career patterning is that of the 'capital' that the individual takes into the labour market, in the sense mentioned earlier in this chapter. Research on people lacking such capital and having to work at the low wage end of modern labour markets suggests anything but a pattern of personal growth and fulfilment through experimentation and adaptation.

In an analysis reminiscent of the classic Chinoy (1992) study referred to previously, Ehrenreich writes about hearing throughout one's upbringing that hard work was the 'secret of success'. She comments, however, 'No one ever said that you could work hard – harder even than you ever thought possible – and still find yourself sinking ever deeper into poverty and debt'. If we needed to characterise a 'dead end job', Ehrenreich has done it for us – and for the millions of people who work in jobs like those that she sampled (Snapshot 10.3).

Toynbee did a similar study in the UK (Snapshot 10.4).

Snapshot 10.3

Humiliation and indignity at the bottom of the heap in the USA

Ehrenreich (2002) took several low-paid jobs in turn to discover first-hand what it is like to work in modern America as a care worker, cleaner, shop worker or waiter. The first thing she discovered was that none of these jobs was truly 'unskilled'. In each case, she had to 'master new terms, new tools, and new skills – from placing orders on restaurant computers to wielding the backpack vacuum cleaner'. But what Ehrenreich found 'surprised and offended' her most was the extent to which the worker's self-respect had to be surrendered in the face of a series of humiliations ranging from having one's purse searched or the 'routine indignity' of being tested for drugs. Workers were regularly 'kept in their place' by rules such as ones forbidding 'gossip', or even talking, and by little unexplained punishments such as having schedules or work assignments unilaterally changed.

Snapshot 10.4

Stress and hardship at the bottom of the heap in the UK

Toynbee (2002), in a British investigation similar to Ehrenreich's, powerfully illustrates the strains and the financial hardships of moving from one low-paid, low-status job to another. There was no question of 'moving seamlessly from one job to another with no unpaid gap', let alone seeking the personal fulfilments associated with 'portfolio' or 'boundaryless' careers. Toynbee observes that such conditions apply to the 'third of people' who have missed out on the considerable improvements in life circumstances experienced by the other two-thirds of the population, ones which have come about since the 1970s when she previously sampled a variety of manual jobs. Most of the poor in contemporary Britain, she comments, are 'now in work and working as I have described, ferociously hard, often at two or more jobs'.

The information and insights which Ehrenreich and Toynbee give us about low-paid work resulted from their personal immersion in that kind of work. Complementing this type of investigation, Biggs's (2015) interviews with individuals in a range of occupations provide an intensive examination of UK work experiences in the period following the 2008 debt crisis. The overall pattern revealed in the book *All Day Long* is one of considerable inequality in the ways people experience work. A high proportion of individuals had moved 'down' into less fulfilling work, with, for example, former coal miners making sandwiches for supermarkets and precision toolmakers running tanning salons. One of the women to whom Biggs talked was a care worker, in Gosforth, Newcastle upon Tyne, employed on a 'zero hours contract'.

Snapshot 10.5

Caring for the elderly on a zero hours contract

Rochelle Monte is mother of three children who, when interviewed by Biggs (2015), was working a 12-day fortnight (twelve days 'on' and two days 'off'). She was making half-hourly visits to deal with the very personal needs of frail elderly people. On Sundays, the hours were 7.30am until 10pm, and every working day, there was a constant rush to fit clients into the time available, with the care worker often managing little more than a packet of potato crisps for lunch – this ate whilst driving. Rochelle's employing organisation was owned by a private equity business, and its terms of appointment were expressed very clearly: 'Your employment with us is conditional on your agreement to work flexible hours or no hours, if the work is not available. . . . The company has no duty to provide any work at such times'.

Rochelle's is a clear example of the employment phenomenon of the zero hours contract.

Zero hours contract

An agreement between an employer and an employee that the employer may ask the employee to undertake work tasks as they require these tasks to be undertaken, but without there being any set minimum hours of work. In some cases, the worker is able to refuse work that is offered without the contract being terminated. In some cases, this is not possible.

Although this kind of contract has been heavily criticised, careful and systematic research by the Chartered Institute of Personnel and Development has revealed a more complex situation than many had assumed. A valuable and uncontroversial finding was that a quarter of British employers make use of zero hours contracts. However, much more controversial was the report's argument that 'while workers on these contracts may be less likely to feel involved at work and see fewer opportunities to develop and improve their skills than employees as a whole, they are also less likely to feel overloaded and under excessive pressure. The proportion of zero-hours contract and short-hours contract employees who say they are satisfied or very satisfied with their jobs – 65% and 67% respectively – is slightly higher than the proportion of employees as a whole (63%)'. It would seem that we have a situation here where we have to turn to the clichéd request for 'more research to be done'. And this would need to combine careful survey work with accounts of people involved in zero hours contracts. We need to know more about the circumstances in which such arrangements are acceptable to working individuals and ones in which they are not.

Managerial work, identities and experiences

It may be possible, as we saw earlier, to adopt an 'instrumental' orientation to work and lower the emotional involvement in it. This, however, is not so easily done for the worker in the professional or managerial sphere. The prior orientation to work of such people is likely to be quite different, and the absence of intrinsic satisfactions is likely to lead to a greater degree of dissatisfaction and felt deprivation than among working-class employees operating in settings at first sight far more potentially depriving. A picture consistent with this point was painted of the work orientations of British managers in a study by Scase and Goffee (1989). The people they called the 'reluctant managers' were the ones who were 'less than fully committed to their jobs and who have great reservations about giving priority to their work, their careers and, indeed, their employing organisations'. They were warier than they had been in the past about becoming completely 'psychologically immersed in their occupations'.

Similar pressures on the work of managers were observed in a study by Dopson and Stewart (1990), but they found different orientations from those observed by Scase and Goffee (1989), on the part of the managers they interviewed. In large part because they believed that they had greater control and responsibility in the 'flatter' managerial hierarchies than they had experienced in the older taller ones, they felt that their jobs had become more challenging and they 'enjoyed the additional responsibilities and variety of their work'. A third study of managerial work (Watson 2001a), suggested that either of these patterns of orientation is possible in different circumstances within the broad changes occurring in work organisations. The managers closely studied in one industrial organisation were shown to display a strong ambivalence towards their work. It was common within the firm for managers to say they felt rewarded by the opportunities presented in their immediate jobs to achieve tasks, to be 'in control' and to have the respect of the people they worked with. But they were increasingly 'becoming concerned about whether their energies were being directed towards the sort of overall business success' that would give them the security and involvement that they had once experienced.

LOOKING BACK <<<<<

An important background factor to these matters is the possibility that very senior managers are in a different – an elite – class category from the bulk of managerial workers. See Chapter 8, p. 244.

It would seem that in 'leading edge' companies that had 'downsized' there was an erosion of the old model of managerial employment, rather than a replacement of it (McGovern *et al.* 1998). There are fewer opportunities for upward promotion with sideways moves and 'managing your own career' being more the norm (with less employment security, especially for older managers). The picture painted by both the Watson and the McGovern studies is corroborated by a study of 251 middle managers in private and public sector corporations in the UK, USA and Japan (Hassard *et al.* 2009; McCann *et al.* 2010). A pattern was observed in which managers, at the same time as expressing pleasure in their work and commitment to their employer, reported that they were overworked in terms of both responsibilities and hours and were struggling with the stress arising from this. Some of these managers are receiving larger salaries than previously and are enjoying the experience of greater responsibility and more interesting work. However, this only partly mitigates against the tendency of the majority to feel overwhelmed with work pressure and to recognise that they cannot, within the flatter managerial hierarchies in which they operate, look forward to the rewards of promotion. There is a schism between top and middle managers and an expressed lack of fairness and recognition which, the authors comment, undermines 'collegiality' and a shared sense of goodwill.

In light of the changing situation of managers, and especially the so-called 'middle managers', it would appear, according to Wajcman and Martin's (2001) evidence, that younger managers are moving away from an orientation based on loyalty to the organisation to one emphasising individual career projects. This would fit with the argument of Harding *et al.* (2014), that middle managers move between 'contradictory subject positions that both conform with and resist normative managerial identities . . . middle managers are both controlled and controllers, and resisted and resisters'.

Men and women in these contradictory positions can be seen to draw upon a range of discourses to construct their self-identities and personas. Thomas and Linstead (2002) show middle managers struggling to avoid 'losing the plot' in the relatively blurred career situations they find themselves in. To provide legitimacy and to justify their existence they make use of various sets of discursive resources such as those of 'professionalism and expertise, gender, performance and commitment, and the public sector ethic'. In line with this analysis, Brocklehurst *et al.* (2009) note the reluctance of the managers they studied to use the title of 'manager'. This partly results, the researchers argue, from the overuse of the 'manager' title. But it also reflects the 'derogatory connotations of the term' which result from its associations with bureaucracy and inflexibility. These managers therefore sought 'justification for their status in alternative self-descriptions such as 'professional', 'entrepreneur' and 'project leader'. In the light of this kind of process, Martin (2005) goes as far as to suggest that a second managerial revolution is coming about. Managers created by the first revolution were able to base their career strategies on the possession of 'organisational assets' – capital which they possessed 'by virtue of their structural location in stable organisations'. But in the less stable and more flexible contemporary organisations this is less relevant and Martin shows how managers now rely more on 'reputational capital'; the image or 'cultural reputation of a manager's skills that inheres in their network of contacts'.

Anxiety and the human condition

One outcome of the growing interest in human subjectivity within the sociology of work and work organisations is the attention beginning to be paid to the anxieties, fears and emotions which are part of the human condition. The human being, in order to survive psychologically, has to overcome 'the precariousness of identity implicit in the unpredictability of social relations' (Knights and Willmott 1985). The world is potentially an utterly ambiguous place and, without the set of meanings that is supplied by human culture, people would be unable to cope. Without a sense of order or *nomos* (which comes from culture) the individual would become 'submerged in a world of disorder, senselessness and madness'

(Berger 1973). The anxiety or *existential angst*, which people can only handle with the help of culture, is more than a matter of specific fears. It has to be understood 'in relation to the overall security system the individual develops' as part of their self-identity (Giddens 1991). However, the human being is not a simple creature of its culture in the same way that other animals are creatures of their instincts. Cultures are constantly being made by people and each individual has their own interaction with – their own pattern of giving to and taking from – the cultures within which they live. This means that, for all of us, a sense of order and self-identity is constantly in the process of being won from the social environment in which we find ourselves. Angst is an ever-present condition which we, each and every one, have to handle. The work context is one of the key arenas in which we experience and learn to handle, more or less effectively, the angst which is inherent to the human condition.

Angst and managerial work

A study of managers in American corporations (Jackall 1988), suggested that managerial work of this kind is especially anxiety-making with managers constantly attempting to hide their daily fears, panics and anxieties behind a mask of self-control and amiability. Jackall shows his managers terrified by the unpredictability and capriciousness of their employment and work experience, a terror which they mask with a demeanour of enthusiasm. A different emphasis is to be found in a British study of managerial experience (Watson 2001a). Here anxiety is seen much more as the normal human condition but it is argued that the nature of managerial work and, especially, its expectation that the manager has to exert control over others (directly or indirectly) as well as over their own lives, can exacerbate this basic human condition. Managers having to face a 'double control problem' in this way leads them to seek comfort in managerial 'fads, fashions and flavour of the month' (Watson 1994), as well as encouraging them to engage in all kinds of ill-tempered behaviour, threats of violence, interpersonal rudeness as well as more benign joking behaviour. Most of the classic texts on management, Taylor's and Mayo's work most notably, portray managers as rational non-sentimental beings. This has been to deny the very humanity of those holding command roles in modern bureaucracies. Further, as Hay (2014) points out, the identity work which managers do is constrained by available social-identities of the manager. These make for 'an often uncomfortable and difficult process of becoming a manager where the individual struggles to live up to idealised notions of managerial work.

The rise of the stress discourse

An aspect of personal experience of work that relates to anxiety is that of 'stress'. The notion of stress and the popularity of its use is a historically recent phenomenon with what Newton (1995) calls 'the stress discourse' significantly coming to the fore in the 1970s and 1980s. At the heart of this discourse is a stretching of the simple and ancient notion of 'feeling distressed' to a near medical condition in which people's circumstances somehow render them incapable of performing in the way they would normally be expected to perform in those circumstances.

Stress
A sense of distress arising because of pressures experienced in certain social or economic circumstances that render the sufferer emotionally, and sometimes physically, incapable of continuing to behave in the ways expected of them in those circumstances.

The increasing attention to stress at work beginning in the latter quarter of the twentieth century has been linked with growing concern about the intensification of work together with increased job insecurity and longer working hours. However, this link is questioned by Wainwright and Calnan (2002) who, whilst accepting that work may currently be more demanding than it was in the recent past, question whether, when put in an historical context, contemporary work can be seen as the 'psychologically scarring' experience presented in the work-stress discourse. Just as Newton (1995) portrays the stress discourse as reducing the social to the biological, Wainwright and Calnan suggest that it takes emotional problems that could be seen as normal responses to everyday life and redefines them as symptoms of mental illness. They relate the rise of the stress discourse to the increasing popularity of psychotherapy and counselling and suggest that problems and conflicts at work that were once handled through collective industrial action or political changes are increasingly converted into individualised threats to worker health – issues to be dealt with by therapeutic intervention rather than by industrial or political action.

Emotions and feelings

Emotions and feelings
Feelings are sensations relating to a psychological state that are felt bodily. Emotions are the way these sensations are culturally interpreted.

When we talk of anxiety and stress, we are clearly dealing with aspects of human feelings and emotions – topics that sociological analysis has not tended to examine closely until recently. To make it easier to get a 'sociological purchase' on these matters, it is useful to conceptualise 'emotion' in cultural terms. We can apply this distinction between feelings and emotion in the situation where two shop workers, Kelly and Joan, find themselves, each in turn, having to deal with a difficult customer.

Snapshot 10.6

Kelly, Joan and the difficult customer

'I am glad that we don't get too many people like that coming into the shop. The man seemed to think it was my fault that we don't stock that product any more. I explained the situation to him as politely as I could but he just went on and on being completely obnoxious'.

'You must have felt awful'.

'Well, after several minutes of feeling quite calm I found my hands started to shake. Then I felt the heat in my neck and I knew very well that he would see my neck and face going redder and redder'.

'You were getting as angry as him, were you?'

'No, I think I was just embarrassed. I wanted to disappear from the face of the earth'.

'You weren't angry'.

'Well, perhaps I was. I was really beginning to take offence before he walked off over to you'.

'I suppose I was prepared for what was coming, as I saw him approaching me. So I stayed calm, like you, for quite some time. But when I realised he wasn't going to stop I decided to act as if he was making me cross. "Who do you think you are talking to?", I asked him. I put on this angry frown to try to get him to stop and think'.

'So you did get cross'.

'Well, actually, I started off just acting that way. I didn't actually feel angry inside. But as I rose to the part I think I did actually start to be genuinely angry'.

Kelly starts to feel agitated as she deals with the difficult customer, and she finds that her hands are beginning to shake and her skin reddens. Where 'emotion' comes into this is when she and Joan proceed to make sense of those feelings by drawing on discursive resources which are culturally available to them – relating them, as we hear, to 'anger', 'embarrassment' and 'taking offence'. However, we need to recognise that things do not always work in this order. We cannot say that emotions (the 'cultural' dimension of experiences) are always what follow feelings (the 'animal' dimension of the experience). In the case of Joan's experience, it would appear that a cultural awareness of the appropriateness of being angry in the face of rude behaviour triggered the physical sensations or 'feelings' that manifested themselves in this particular situation. This is similar to the not uncommon human experience where people force themselves to smile, when they are feeling unhappy, and find themselves, as a consequence of this action, actually feeling happier.

The rediscovery of feelings and emotions in the sociology of work and organisation is often connected to the influence of Max Weber and his ideal type of bureaucracy in which there is 'no place for love, hatred and all purely personal, irrational and emotional elements which escape calculation' (Weber 1978). But this should not be read as assuming that Weber wished to discourage attention to matters of irrationality or affectivity. His interest in these was 'submerged by twentieth-century rationalistic models of organisation' says Albrow (1994). Albrow (1997) argues that Weber was pointing out that the bureaucratic ethos does not attempt to exclude *per se* emotional elements from organisations – it is concerned only to exclude those 'which escape calculation'. This means, in effect, that emotions, feelings, sentiments and the like are harnessed to corporate ends in the ideal-type bureaucratised organisation.

LOOKING BACK <<<<<

This harnessing of 'sentiment' to business ends was central to the logic of Human Relations thinking (Chapter 2) where it was proposed that the managers should pay attention to the 'sentiments' of workers (like their desire to 'belong') and not allow these sentiments to undermine corporate purposes.

It is now recognised that emotions and feelings pervade every aspect of working and organisational lives. As Fineman (2003) puts it, emotions are not an 'optional extra, or incidental to "real" work' but are part of the 'warp and weft of work experiences and practices as people take into the workplace our loves, hates, anxieties, envies, excitement, disappointments and pride'. As Bericat (2015) points out '[a]n actor whose consciousness is limited to ideas or cognitions and lacking in social values or emotions is inconceivable'.

Emotional labour and emotion management

Emotional labour
An element of work activity in which the worker is required to display certain emotions in order to complete work tasks in the way required by an employer.

Issues of emotionality at work do not simply arise because 'people are people' and are therefore continually at the mercy of their feelings. Certain types of work formally require people to engage in what Hochschild (1983) calls *emotional labour*. Hochschild shows how the emotional labour required of airline flight attendants who were expected continually to wear the 'mask' of a smile when in the presence of passengers took its toll on these workers – whether they were those who complied zealously with the requirement or were those who handled it self-consciously as a form of 'acting'. There was always the danger of feelings of anger or irritation breaking through the facade of pleasure and happiness. Taylor (1998) draws a parallel between the emotional labour he observed among telephone sales agents, who were required to create an atmosphere of friendliness and intimacy with external customers, and the emotional labour that was required of production workers operating within a Total Quality Management regime which required them to treat 'internal customers' – organisational co-workers – in a similar manner.

There is a danger with analyses like this, however. The greatest one is that of creating an unrealistic division between a person's real or true self and their 'false' self (Theodosius 2008). As Bolton (2000, 2005) points out, the notion of 'emotional labour' can become overstretched and conceptually imprecise. Hochschild (1989) differentiated between two types of 'emotion management' that people engage in: the 'emotion work' that we all do in our private lives and 'emotional labour' that we do in a commercial context for a wage. But this tends to push aside the ways in which people at work engage with others emotionally in ways that are not directly tied into the formal job requirements. This most obviously occurs when people develop warm and supportive relationships with either co-workers or customers in the workplace out of personal choice – what Korczynski, 2003, calls 'communities of coping'). Bolton (2000) helps overcome this difficulty by developing four categories of emotion management:

- presentational, where emotions are handled according to general social rules;

- philanthropic, where emotional management is given as a gift;
- prescriptive, where emotional management occurs according to organisational or professional rules of conduct; and
- pecuniary, where emotional management is done for commercial gain.

Two of Bolton's categories, the prescriptive and the philanthropic, are used by Lewis (2005), in a special unit of a hospital (Snapshot 10.7). Notice here the important connection between emotions and gender. This is something that arises in many occupational circumstances as well as nursing and is an area in which we have to be careful of thinking stereotypically (Lewis and Simpson 2007).

Snapshot 10.7

Emotion management in a special care baby unit

Lewis (2005) draws three conclusions from her study of a special care unit for babies. First, she shows how nurses, whilst being subject to certain prescriptive norms and conventions, continuously exercise their own agency to decide which feelings rules they will draw upon. In handling a baby's illness, they tend to rely on prescriptive emotion management. But if a baby is shortly to die, they give extra support to parents, in line with philanthropic emotion management rules. Second, Lewis observed clashes – and a 'contested terrain' – between doctors, who preferred a 'masculinized' prescriptive-professional form of emotion management, and the 'feminized' philanthropic-gift form preferred by nurses. Third, Lewis noted how these clashes of approach led to 'off-stage' informal communities of coping in which nurses gave to each other the 'gift' of emotional support on a reciprocal basis. In this setting, nurses were able to 'drop their professional masks' and give vent to emotions which, formally, are regarded as undesirable – emotions like hurt, frustration, anger and grief.

Studies like those of Hochschild (1989) in the airline industry and Peccei and Rosenthal's (2000) in retailing and in call centres showed how employers sometimes set out to train and instruct workers in the expression of 'correct' emotions. But Bolton and Boyd (2003) found little evidence that the airline workers they studied actually internalised the emotional rules they were instructed to follow. And Seymour and Sandiford (2005), in their ethnographic study of a pub–restaurant chain, found that the management gave considerable autonomy to managers over such matters. The emotion management of the staff was influenced 'by emotion rules deriving from prior socialization processes and experiences, the wider organization, the unit manager, colleagues, customers, and self-regulation, rather than by explicit emotion rules acquired through training'.

The material shape of the workplace can also be a significant factor in the managing of potential emotional difficulties for workers. Hamilton and McCabe (2016), in their ethnographic study of the work of meat inspectors in chicken slaughterhouses, point out how the birds are 'de-animalized' to make the killing process 'emotionally neutral'. Especially important here is the zoning of the factory into discrete ante-mortem and post-mortem sections which 'compartmentalises' the killing process, rendering the technological arrangements as a 'production line' rather than a killing process; living chickens enter the process, and dismembered 'products' emerge at the other end.

We now turn to look at *aesthetic labour* and will consider the connections between this and emotional labour.

LOOKING FORWARD >>>>>

The way humour is used as part of an emotional management process by sex workers is examined in Chapter 12 (p. 376).

Aesthetic labour

An element of work activity in which the worker is required to display certain physical, body-related appearances or attributes in order to complete work tasks in the way required by an employer who believes that these attributes will appeal to customers or clients.

Aesthetic labour

The term 'aesthetic labour' was established as a result of researchers observing that employers were advertising for staff with attributes such as being 'well spoken', 'well presented' or even 'good looking' (Nickson *et al.* 2001). Such attributes, it was recognised, were ones which would be 'organizationally mobilized, developed and commodified' to attract and retain customers. The 'image' that workers present to others in work contexts has long been recognised as a factor in employment practices, in spheres varying from clerical and shop work to medicine and entertainment. Indeed, such matters were recognised by Hochschild (1983) in the original discussion of emotional labour. However, Witz *et al.* (2003) argue that attention to 'corporeal aspects' have been pushed into the background in emotional labour research, making it necessary to use the further concept of aesthetic labour in order to bring back to the foreground again the 'embodied character of service work' and to overcome the problem whereby 'current analyses are partial, myopically focused on employer attempts to recruit the right *attitudes* among workers...in order to affect the service encounter' (Warhurst and Nickson 2007, emphasis added). As Wolkowitz (2009) argues, attention to human physical attributes and the body must be a vital part of any sociology of work.

The new emphasis on aesthetic aspects of work has not gone without criticism. Entwistle and Wissinger (2006), for example, charge the proponents of the aesthetic labour notion with creating a reductive account of the aesthetic labourer as a 'cardboard cut-out' and aesthetic labour as 'superficial work on the body's surface'. In the course of studying the work of fashion models, these researchers argue that it is vital to give equal attention to the emotional aspect of aesthetic labour and the embodied dimension. The strength of this approach is suggested by Caitlin's comments on her work as a dancer (Snapshot 10.8), and it is taken further by Holla's (2016) study of fashion models. Holla emphasises that fashion models are caught up in a 'continuous process of aesthetic behaviour'. And, further, because models' private lives are strongly guided by 'professional imperatives', it can be argued that not only models' bodies but 'their entire selves are being colonized by an industry that is greed in nature'. It is clear, here, that the aesthetic and embodied aspects of this work cannot be pushed into the analytical background. It is also clear that the aesthetic or corporeal element of the performance cannot be separated from the emotional.

Snapshot 10.8

Caitlin's aesthetic and emotional labour

I know that I would never have got this job if I had not got a good body and, of course, a way of moving my body about which pleases audiences. But when I dance, I am not just pleasing the theatre managers or the audience. I am also doing something immensely important to me. I have dreamed of being a dancer since I was a small child. There is enormous pleasure in being able to live your dream in this way. But I also get a lot of pleasure from the physical experience of moving my body around the stage, relating to the music and the concept of each particular dance as well as to the audience. Having said that, I also have to say that I sometimes struggle emotionally with the problem of having to dress up and look happy on the stage when I am unhappy in my personal life or when I am not feeling well. And, if I am honest, I get quite worked up at times when I feel that the audience's eyes are more on another dancer than on me.

It is important to locate issues about both emotional labour and aesthetic labour within the overall relationship and the implicit contract between employers and workers. Bolton locates her analysis of emotional labour within the tradition of labour process analysis (LPA) and its concern with the full range of ways in which the labour activities of workers are exploited in the interests of 'capital' (see Brook 2009; Bolton 2009). And with regard to aesthetic labour, a study by Williams and Connell (2010) uses Bourdieu's concept of habitus to show how 'up-market' retailers with a 'cool' image attract middle-class workers into low-paid and insecure jobs which have few benefits or promotional opportunities by 'appealing to their consumer interests'. The 'worker-consumers' who staff these shop and engage in the aesthetic labour of 'looking good and sounding right' are attracted to the jobs, not because retail work in itself appeals to them, but because 'they are highly identified with the brands they sell'.

An illustration of the relevance of the 'sounding right' dimension of aesthetic labour is provided by Timming's (2016) study of the effects of foreign accents on American selection interviewers' perceptions of employability. The evidence suggests that the selectors actively discriminated in telephone-based job interviews against applicants speaking Chinese-, Mexican- and Indian-accented English. However, all three accents were rated higher in non-customer-facing jobs than in customer-facing jobs. But applicants speaking with British-accented English, especially men, 'fare as well as, and at times better than, native candidates who speak American English'.

LOOKING BACK <<<<<

Labour process analysis (LPA) is explained in Chapter 3, pp. 70–72, and the concept of *habitus* is covered in this chapter, p. 326.

Sexuality and the workplace

There are sexual dimensions to almost every aspect of organisational life, as Hearn and Parkin (1987) showed, even if these only become clearly manifest when formal complaints are made about sexual harassment (Hearn 2014), or where events occur such as the hospital 'works do' observed by these authors where open sexual acts occurred with couples making 'blatant use of the premises, both cubby holes and semi-public "back regions"'. Burrell (1984, 1992) pointed out how managements in organisations ranging from monasteries, prisons and ships at sea to factories and commercial organisations, attempt to repress sexual relations and expel them from the organisation into the 'home'. Yet people's notion of themselves as 'sexual beings' is a vital part of their identities, and Brewis and Linstead (2000b) argue that this influences the 'particular sense of organisation' that people experience in specific work circumstances. The sexual harassment discourse that one associates with attempts to avoid sexually abusive behaviour in organisations, for example, can come to reinforce such behaviour – by identifying men as predators and women as victims.

In spite of a managerial interest in suppressing sexuality in the workplace, managements may also collude in a degree of expression of sexuality as part of the delivery of what is not formally seen as a kind of sexual service. This is effectively shown in Filby's (1992) research in off-course betting shops where there is an 'elision . . . of emotional labour and sexuality'. Filby shows how a 'minority undercurrent' of the conversations which go on between staff and between staff and customers involve 'sexy chat' – speech acts 'which themselves are experienced as pleasurable as well as sometimes discomforting and hurtful'. Sexuality is also 'embodied in gaze, deportment and clothing, and sometimes more obviously in expressive physical encounters'. In the light of certain unspoken assumptions which exist about 'what men and women are and what male punters want' there is an extent, says Filby, to which 'these moments are related to the milieu of service delivery as implicitly constructed by management, a milieu which is envisaged as an aid to business'. Put more simply, the management is more than happy for customers to receive a little light sexual amusement. But this is always within certain norms. As Riach and Wilson (2014) say in the case of the pub workers they studied, 'what is distanced or perceived as possible only became apparent when practices or behaviours were "out of line"'. And, as Williams *et al.* (1999) observe, while service workers are sometimes paid to act in a 'sexy' manner or to engage in sexual innuendo with customers, in other jobs, in prisons or hospitals for example, 'mere rumours of sexual behaviour or desire can destroy a career'.

Work and non-working lives

The relationship between the work and non-work aspects of our lives is complex and two-way. At the highest level of generality, the two spheres interrelate to form a particular type of society, the industrial capitalist type in the present case. Work arrangements are located in the power structures and cultural understandings of the wider society with social class, family, education and other social structural factors having a major influence on individuals' prior orientation to work as well as on their socially conditioned predisposition to act and think in a certain way once in work.

Work and leisure

> ### Leisure
>
> Those activities which people pursue for pleasure and which are not a necessary part of their business, employment or domestic management obligations.

LOOKING FORWARD >>>>>

We should note that this definition does not preclude the possibility of people engaging in leisure within their formal working hours. Some of the activities considered in Chapter 12, and especially the engaging in humour could be seen as examples of 'leisure in work'.

Leisure is something we generally identify as 'not work'. It can be defined along such lines. Ways of taking leisure inevitably vary with personal taste. But they may also vary with different types of employment. The hours left free for leisure by different kinds of work and the money available to spend on leisure are factors which clearly relate work and leisure forms. However, other factors are also relevant and, to help indicate a pattern in these, Parker (1982), in an early study in this field, identified three types of relationship between work and leisure: extension, opposition and neutrality. These are illustrated in the conversation between two brothers and a sister in Snapshot 10.9. Heidi is a university lecturer, and a good proportion of her leisure can be seen as an *extension* of her work – something which tends to 'spillover' (Evans and Bartolemé 1980) into the rest of life. Will is a librarian, and his account of his leisure suggests an *oppositional* relationship with his work, whilst Evan, who is a local government office worker, manifests a *neutral* relationship between work and leisure. Nothing he says about his weekend plans appear to relate to his working week. This is quite different from his sister's and brother's accounts.

Snapshot 10.9

Heidi, Will and Evan and three relationships between work and leisure

Heidi: I can't join the family this weekend, I am afraid. I've just got out of the library this fascinating new book of poems that I'd really like to bring into my lecture on Monday. And on Sunday we have this reading group in the village which is meeting in the afternoon to discuss the novel that I introduced to the group. I'd be really sad missing their reactions to the book.

Will: I wish I could get as excited by all the horrible boring books that we have in the law library. The minute I get out of there on Friday I shall be down to the pub. A good bit of shouting and yelling at the football match on Saturday night will be good and, all week as I've crept quietly around the library, I've been looking forward to going out and getting totally smashed on Saturday night. But I will be at Mum's on Sunday for a good lunch and afternoon snooze.

Evan: I'll be there too. Gardening on Saturday, I think.

Work–life balance

Leisure is only one way in which time is spent away from the formal workplace. As was implied in the earlier definition of leisure, domestic management responsibilities can be understood as a form of work. We cannot simply talk of 'home' and 'work' as completely separate realms of existence, and once we attempt to get to grips with debates about achieving a 'balance' between work and other aspects of people's lives, we find that matters are much more complex than might be implied by public discussions of 'work–life balance' (a problematic term in itself, with its strange implication that work is one thing and 'life' another). In the light of a collection of research studies across Europe, it is observed that work–life balance is a complex phenomenon which involves interactions between cultural norms and policies, between state, employers and families as well as between men and women (Crompton *et al.* 2007; Warhurst *et al.* 2008). At the level of the work organisation, Mescher *et al.* (2010) note how employers use 'work–life balance support' as an HRM strategy to attract and retain talented employees. How significant this support is, in practice, is questionable. Kossek *et al.* (2010) argue that the initiatives taken within organisations are usual 'marginal' to general organisational practices and can have mixed consequences for individuals and organisations; whilst people may be better able to 'manage work and care-giving', they can 'increase work intensification and perpetuate stereotypes of ideal workers'.

In her influential book *The Time Bind* (2001), Hochschild argued that the type of work carried out in the home was becoming seen as less desirable than the work done in the workplace, the latter being both

LOOKING BACK <<<<<

Any discussion of the balance between working and non-working aspects of people's lives must consider the evidence on domestic labour and the domestic division of labour (Chapter 7, pp. 224–228) and on people working at home, and working from home (Chapter 6, pp. 217–220).

more economically and psychologically rewarding. A vicious circle was observed in Hochschild's research whereby people were opting to work longer in the formal workplace with the effect that home and family tasks seemed even more burdensome, this pushing people further into long working hours, at a significant cost to the quality of family life and, especially, the well-being of children. The public concern created by this study came on top of the effect of an earlier book by Schor (1991), which popularised the notion of the 'overworked American'. In Britain, worry about a poor 'work–life balance' with negative effects both on family life and workplace effectiveness was taken up by the government, and a government-sponsored study (DfEE 2000) pointed to a 'long hours culture' in which one in nine employees, many of these with children, were working more than a sixty-hour week, with two-thirds of men arguing that to shift to lower or part-time hours would undermine their career prospects. Having gathered statistical information about imbalances between work other parts of people's lives, Dex and Bond (2005) unsurprisingly identified as the main predictor of imbalance was working more than 48 hours per week, this followed equally (but at half the level of the long hours) by having caring responsibilities and being aged between 36 and 45. The policy implications of this evidence are simple and direct, with these authors suggesting that the overcoming of imbalance is primarily a matter of reducing long weekly working hours, especially in higher-grade occupations.

Gambles *et al.* (2006) warn against a 'myth of work–life balance' which suggests that there are relatively simple 'fixes' for current imbalances. The challenge of finding 'ways of working that support harmonisations of paid work and personal life in ways that will not harm workplace effectiveness' are considerable and must involve reconsideration of aspects of neoliberal capitalism, the 'lure of consumerism' and the general ways in which people 'connect with' each other in the modern world. Bloom (2016) goes as far as arguing that the idea of 'work–life balance' is a cultural fantasy which serves 'capitalist work and organisations' which, he says, always put a limit on 'life' through their requiring that 'live to work' rather than 'work to live'. People 'literally cannot go on subjectively "living" without capitalist work'.

It is important in all of this to avoid generalising too widely from evidence of what is being experienced by the sort of professional dual-earner couples with dependent children that writers like Hochschild focus upon. This view is supported by the research of Jacobs and Gerson (2004), who question the claim that there is a general pressure on people's time and that, instead, working time is becoming bifurcated with one segment of the labour market containing workers who are 'putting in more hours at work than ever before' whereas another segment 'are unable to find jobs that provide enough hours of work'. Research by Lee *et al.* (2007) tells us that whilst 22 per cent of workers in the world work more than 48 hours per week, there are many, largely part-time women workers, who struggle to find enough hours of work to make a reasonable living. In addition to this gender factor, Warren shows that there is a clear class pattern to work non-work imbalances, with the longest hours being worked by those in higher occupational hierarchy positions and, as most of the previous research indicated, that there is a particular problem where both the male and the female partners are pursuing high-level careers (Warren 2003). A particular, and interesting, finding from this research was that, although women were the main carers in all occupational groups where both partners worked, working-class men were more likely to share the breadwinner/caring role than were men in higher-status work.

Although it is vital to consider these wider patterns, it is necessary to balance this with attention to the complex psychological and symbolic processes by which people make sense of their time and manage multiple life domains. Nippert-Eng (1996) identified a continuum in the ways in which different people either 'integrate' or 'segment' the two 'life realms' of home and work (a 'segmenting' person might, for example, keep separate calendars for work and home activities, or keep work and home keys on separate key-rings, whilst an 'integrating' individual would use just the one calendar and the one key-ring). And if we look at behaviours in the workplace, D'Abate (2005) shows how we might see people allowing 'home and leisure realms [to] invade the work life realm' by engaging in home-oriented activities such as dealing with family or personal business matters from work, or engaging in leisure-related activities such as attending to demands of their friends or their sporting or entertainment activities whilst at work.

Unemployment

Although different governments, and the same governments at different times, define and measure unemployment in ways which suits their political purposes the experiences of being without a job, when a job is wanted and/or needed, are rarely positive. The experience of being unemployed in a society in which there is a work ethic which puts considerable value on being 'in a job', and where a reasonable level of income can only come for most people from employment, is likely to be both psychologically and materially distressing. There can be 'an experiential gap that can exasperate the jobless' in the face of 'the sheer force of the effect of no longer being creditworthy in a society that builds so many of its transactions, in one way or another, on cash' (Fineman 1987). Building on the much-cited study of unemployment in 1930 in Marienthal, (Jahoda *et al.* 1972), Jahoda (1982) concentrated on what people tend to lose, in addition to a source of income, when they become unemployed. A person's job:

- imposes a time structure on the day,
- enlarges the scope of social relations beyond the often emotionally charged ones of family and neighbours,
- gives them a feeling of purpose and achievement through task involvement in a group setting,
- assigns social status and clarifies personal identity, and
- requires one to engage in regular activity.

This emphasis on the 'human costs' of the loss of paid work, as opposed to the loss of the instrumental benefits of employment, has been highly influential. This is in spite of Jahoda's writing being framed by what Cole (2007) calls a tacit 'moral discourse of human nature as fundamentally a working or labouring nature'. Paid work is thus given too high a priority in how we think about human beings and about the society we live in.

A considerable variety of factors in addition to possible socio-psychological ones influence how unemployment is experienced. Both the financial impact and the impact on work identity and identity within the family tend to vary with the 'previous location within the labour market', for example (Ashton 1985). Workers who have been in routine and repetitive jobs can experience short-term unemployment as a relief, for instance, and housewives who also work full-time may be able to use their domestic responsibilities to 'impose a temporal structure on their daily activities' if they become unemployed.

A considerable amount of evidence has been collected to show that there is a significant connection between the experience of unemployment and both physical and mental ill health. In reviewing the evidence gathered by a series of studies, Gallie and Vogler (1994) showed that the unemployed suffer from a process of cumulative disadvantage and that their 'weak labour market position is accompanied not only by much greater financial difficulty, but by disadvantage in both health and hous-ing'. However, there are considerable differences in the way the 'welfare regimes' of different countries affect the experiences of the unemployed and, in addition to the level of support given by the state, factors such as the strength of family and community ties make a considerable differ-ence to the level of 'social exclusion' experienced by unemployed people (Gallie and Paugam 2000).

It is widely believed that it is the fall in income which has the greatest impact on people's mental health followed by the removal of the socio-psychological factors identified by Jahoda. Burchell (1994), however, places particular stress on insecurity as a generator of psychological stress. His research showed little difference between the levels of stress among the unemployed and among those experiencing high levels of insecurity within work. He further showed that unemployed people who enter a secure job show much greater improvement in psychological well-being than those taking up insecure jobs.

The evidence which we have from those cases where people appear to cope well with the experience of unemployment strongly indi-cates the importance of psychological factors and personal values. Warr (1987), for example, reported that the 'good copers' whom he studied all had financial difficulties but maintained high levels of emotional well-being. This was associated with 'considerable personal activity, driven by strongly held religious, social or political values'. Nordenmark and Strandh (1999) use Swedish evidence to demonstrate that relatively good mental well-being can be achieved if *both* economic and psychosocial needs are met by means other than employment. Miles (1984) found that the psychological well-being of the sample of more than a hundred unemployed men he studied was better where there was involvement in such activities as voluntary work, team sport or part-time education. But he added that the large majority of men failed to get very much access to experiences which would meet socio-psychological needs; the signs of 'adaptation to unemployment' were 'very limited'. This is supported by the evidence gathered by Gershuny (1994) which shows that, once they are unemployed, people have far fewer opportunities of experiencing social interactions than the employed. This applies to men more than women, however.

Based on their study of people's post-redundancy experience in the Welsh steel industry, Gardiner *et al.* (2009) argue that we will better understand the experiences of people losing their jobs if, in addition to structural constraints and enablers, we consider where any given indi-vidual is in their cycle of 'critical life events' and where they are located 'on the spectrum of career change experience'. To illustrate this point, the authors discuss case studies of individuals who experienced redundancy. Some, for example, were 'active career planners' who had planned and prepared for new careers prior to redundancy. Others were people at a 'careers cross-road', uncertain whether to invest in training for a career or simply to find 'a job'. And, on the evidence of four empirical studies, Dunn (2014) argues that many unemployed benefit claimants prefer living on state benefits to taking jobs which would increase their income, but which they find unattractive. Once again, we have to recognise the importance of looking at the circumstances of individuals and the meanings they attach to their particular experience within wider structural patterns.

Summary

A central concept in the previous chapter was that of work orientations. Work orientations need to be understood in relationship to people's *self-identities* and the *social-identities* and personas that are discursively available to them as they go about their personal *identity work*. Angst and emotion come into every kind of work, whether it be the unhappy experiences of people working in 'dead end jobs' or the relatively privileged work of managers. In an increasing proportion of jobs (especially service jobs) people are required to engage in *emotional labour* and, indeed, *aesthetic labour*. But people's emotions, experiences and satisfactions are not influenced by work in isolation. They are also shaped by the kind of 'balance' that they are able to create between their working and non-working lives.

11 Conflict, mobilisation and regulation at work

Key issues

- How can we most usefully conceptualise and analyse the wide range of conflicts and conflict behaviours which occur across the range of work situations?
- What is the relationship between conflicts and institutional (structural) tensions?
- How can the notion of *implicit contracts*, introduced in Chapter 9, be used to understand the emergence of grievances at work?
- In what ways do we see different interests being mobilised in workplaces and societies and what is the continuing role of trade unions and the institution of collective bargaining in these processes?

Conflict and co-operation at work

LOOKING BACK <<<<<

The need to give attention to both structural factors and the experiences and intentions of individuals was stressed in Chapter 1 (p. 8).

To do justice to the subtlety and the complexities of the phenomena which it studies, sociology has to take account of the interplay which occurs in social life between initiative and constraint. Structural patterns were emphasised in earlier chapters of this book on the nature of industrialised societies, on organisations and on occupations. The accounts given of these tendencies towards a patterning in work life were not, however, ones which *reified* these structures, giving them a concrete existence over and above the human efforts which create them. These structural tendencies are seen, rather, as the outcomes of various human processes of initiative, power–seeking, negotiation and conflict.

Conflict

Conflict occurs at two levels:
- *Conflict at the level of interests* exists where there is a difference between parties (employers and employees, say, or business owners and customers) over desired outcomes.
- *Conflict at the level of behaviour* comes about when parties seeking different outcomes either express their differences through such gestures as acting destructively or co-operating in a sullen or grudging manner.

The concept of *conflict* is one that is sometimes used with a structural emphasis, emphasising differences of interests between social parties. At other times, it refers to activities or behaviours. We can thus talk about conflict at the level of interests and conflict at the level of behaviour. Sociologically, conflicts exist and manifest themselves in the context of societal, occupational and organisational structures. These structures reflect in large part the greater success of some social groups compared to others in the securing of control over their own lives and over parts of the lives of others and hence in their gaining of access to scarce and generally desirable rewards. In Snapshot 11.1, Sandeep gives us some insight into these matters in the small personal story he tells about how he recognised first the conflict at the level of interests that exists between him and his friend and employer, Asif. But that conflict comes to the surface and apparent at the level of behaviour, when they fall out over Sandeep's salary and, for some months, each behaves awkwardly with the other.

Snapshot 11.1

Working for Asif

Working for Asif has been good a lot of the time. He's keen to be the boss of things and, frankly, I want to concentrate on my design work and not have to go out chasing business, as Asif does. So it's a good arrangement, especially given that we've been good friends since university.

My wife keeps pointing out to me, though, that in the final analysis I am his 'wage slave'; I am a big cost to the business, and it's in his interest to keep that cost as low as possible. And it's in my interest to get the best living I can – which, of course, puts up his costs. So, I have to concede to my wife, there is a sort of conflict of interest between us. But it's generally beneath the surface. We get on just fine, in spite of the fact that he's now becoming quite wealthy and is more respected in the community than I am. The only time things got bad between us was just after our second child was born. I really needed a better salary, and Asif told me that the business was struggling. This was the case, but I made up my mind that he was exaggerating this as an excuse for giving me a mean increase. So, I made sure I was late with a couple of projects, and I refused to work one weekend when we were struggling to finish a contract. He then refused to play golf with me and avoided me in the office. It was a month or two before we made friends again. But it was six months before he got me sorted out financially. The tensions were running quite high over that time, I can tell you.

Our illustration here is at the interpersonal level, but the differences between Asif and Sandeep can be seen as a microcosm of the wider employment world. The emphasis of this and the next chapter will be on various reactions to the efforts of the relatively powerful in the world of work to control and, inevitably – given the continuous dialectic which occurs between initiative and structuring – on the resulting institutionalisation of these reactions, giving us once again patterns or structures. This is not a matter of moving on to something different from the concerns of earlier chapters with occupational and organisational patterns as a matter of considering different aspects of the same things. Whereas, for example, the emphasis in our discussion of work organisations was on attempts of managerial interests to exert control over work and its products, we shall now give greater emphasis to the efforts and accommodations of the subordinate, the disadvantaged and the aspiring. The view from above, so to speak, will be complemented by the view from below. But efforts to control from above continue to play their part, as we see managerial efforts to manage conflict and to handle potentially rival challenges to control.

Industrial relations and the sociology of work and organisation

Part of the chapter will be concerned with the area of academic study which takes the title 'industrial relations'.

Industrial relations

The activities and institutions which jointly regulate the relationships between employers and groups of collectively organised employees.

The key institution here is that of *collective bargaining*, together with trade unions, employers' 'employee' relations departments, employers' associations and whatever kind of arrangement any given state might establish to assisting conciliation or arbitration. We consider collective bargaining and trade unions later in this chapter. What is clear, however, is that, as Ackers and Wilkinson (2008) put it, 'much of the world's working population are now well beyond the reach of joint regulation'. These commentators argue that academic 'industrial relations' (IR) must therefore reconstitute itself 'in dialogue with surrounding social science disciplines'. The sociology of work and industry is clearly of central importance here. It goes beyond the territory of traditional IR in two major ways. First, it sets specific conflicts and bargaining activities in the wider context of the structure and dynamics of the type of society in which they occur. Second, it looks to the opposite end of the spectrum to consider the unofficial, the informal and the relatively spontaneous activities of conflict, challenge and defence in workplaces.

Kelly (1998) importantly argued for a 'rethinking' of the subject of industrial relations consistent with the first of these more sociological emphases, expressing concern about traditional IR's tendency to avoid explicit theory construction and the difficulties of competing for attention with academic human resource management (HRM). Edwards (2005) subsequently called for more 'context-sensitive research', along with attachment to 'the programme of critical realism', to help academic IR make stronger links with social science thinking generally. In the same spirit, Ackers and Wilkinson (2008) suggested the way forward of linking with new institutionalist theory give a role to academic IR as the 'institutional analysis of the employment relationship'. Kaufman (2007) also called for a broad concern with employment relationships, arguing that this was the 'original' concern of IR scholars prior to the IR field risking its existence by adopting 'an overly narrow and union-centric perspective'.

Since the experience of work for the majority of people in industrial capitalist societies occurs in an employment relationship, employer–employee conflicts inevitably remain central to the concerns of the sociology of work and organisation. These conflicts are indeed the most

LOOKING BACK <<<<<

'HRM' as a facet of contemporary employment relationships was considered in Chapter 6 (pp. 178–193). Since the 1980s, a whole lot of academic posts, journals and books have come into being creating a new academic 'subject' of HRM.

Critical realism is introduced in Chapter 1, p. 24.

Institutional theory is introduced in Chapter 3, p. 66.

crucial ones, and they provide the context in which many other work conflicts occur. Edwards (1986) characterises the basic conflict of interests between capital and labour in terms of *structured antagonism*. Each side to the employment relationship 'depends on the other while also having divergent wants'. This means that 'conflict is intertwined with co-operation: the two are produced jointly within particular ways of organising labour processes'. However, employer–employee conflicts are by no means the only ones which occur, although the context for other divergences of interests will be the more basic patterns of 'structured antagonism'. Within this context, people at work not only come into conflict with their bosses and their subordinates but with their peers, their customers and their clients, as we shall see in Chapter 12.

For social life to proceed at work as in any other sphere, be it leisure activity or political life, there must be co-operation between people. Co-operation is not only vital for necessary tasks to be achieved; it also gives stability to daily life. The minimising or controlling of differences of interest between people required by it suggests some positive psychological significance for co-operative activity. Co-operation is comfortable, we might say. From this, it is not difficult to make the leap to the suggestion that co-operation is 'good' and conflict 'bad'. But co-operation and conflict cannot really be opposed in this way, either ethically or theoretically. Conflict and co-operation are omnipresent and inevitably co-existent in social life. Given the scarcity of humanly valued goods in the world and the competition which tends to follow in order to obtain access to these, we find that co-operation with one interest group may automatically imply conflict with another. Conflict-based activities are as much part of life therefore as 'co-operative' ones.

Conflict and co-operation are two sides of the same coin. Yet there is a common tendency in everyday thinking about social life to see examples of co-operation as healthy and conflicts as pathological. This no doubt relates back to the psychologically comforting overtones of the notion of co-operation. But it is none the less a nonsense. Co-operation cannot *of itself* be evaluated as good or healthy any more than can conflict *per se* be seen as bad or unhealthy. We can only judge it by the ends to which it is related. Co-operation with a murderer would be as widely deprecated, for example, as conflict with a rapist would be applauded. By the same token, to enter into conflict with one's employer (or one's employee) cannot of itself – without reference to the point at issue – be judged right or wrong, desirable or undesirable, healthy or unhealthy. Yet in our contemporary society such judgements do tend to be made. This probably results from ideological influences combined with the negative psychological overtones of the idea of 'conflict'. And such a tendency presents a major barrier to the understanding among academics and laymen alike of work conflicts and 'industrial relations' activity. For sociological analysis of these spheres to proceed, issue has to be taken with a formidable array of conventional wisdoms and everyday evaluative tendencies.

Analysing conflict at work: four frames of reference

Frames of reference

To come to terms with some of the difficulties of analysing issues of work conflict and to deal with the frequent confusions of description and prescription which characterise this field, it is helpful to look at the various frames of reference which are typically used in discussions of industrial relations issues. Following the approach of Fox (1973, 1974) and taking into account Budd and Bhave's (2008) extension of Fox's distinctions, we can identify four analytical frameworks which are available to us: the free market, the unitary, the pluralist and the radical. Each of these is based on key assumptions about work relations:

(1) *Free market* thinking assumes that employment relations are fundamentally matters of the buying and selling of services that are best handled by free-market bidding.
(2) The *unitary* framework assumes a fundamentally common interest between all of those operating in the workplace or in society at large.
(3) The *pluralist* view recognises a variety of interests but sees these as more or less balancing each other out in practice.
(4) The *radical/critical* perspective recognises the basic inequalities and power differentials characterising industrial capitalist society and relates work conflicts back to these structural patterns.

These four frames of reference are clearly rivals as tools for analysis. But our problem in evaluating them is made particularly complex by the fact that these three perspectives not only tend to describe the world differently but are frequently used to support arguments for how the world should or should not be. In other words, these analytical models also function as ideologies. Our consideration of these three approaches will primarily be concerned to judge their relative analytical utility.

Free market thinking

This is referred to as an 'egoist' theory of the employment relationship by Budd and Bhave (2008). It identifies employer interests as profit-maximisation and employee interests as ones of utility maximisation (survival and income), and its key belief is that 'freedom and individual self-interest yield optimal outcomes through free market transactions'. It is important to recognise the existence of this style of thinking in contemporary politics and society, and we must always acknowledge the 'buying and selling' aspect of employment relations. Nevertheless the lack of attention paid to the structures, cultures, meanings and work orientations which sociology shows to be so important to employment outcomes means that it has little to offer the sociology of work and organisation analytically. Echoes of it can, however, be heard in unitary thinking.

Unitary thinking

In what Fox characterised as the unitary frame of reference (1966, 1973), the employing organisation is treated as a community of interest. The management are the best qualified to decide how these common interests are to be pursued. Hence employee opposition is irrational and 'industrial action' on the part of the employee is generally misguided and frequently the outcome of the successful agitation of troublemakers or 'politically motivated' individuals. The ideological value of such a perspective to the owner or manager of the work organisation is clear to see; the employee who questions the authority of the manager can readily be compared to a disloyal family member or to a footballer who challenges the captain of his own team. In this way the employee challenge is rendered dishonourable or misguided.

At the national level, the unitary frame of reference makes much use of the concept of 'national interest', a notion which is popular with government representatives – whose task is not dissimilar at times to that of the manager in the work enterprise – in a way directly analogous to the industrial manager's talk of football teams, families and the like. The effectiveness of such appeals is questionable in practical terms. Nevertheless, some general legitimacy given to them in the culture at large is suggested by the resorting from time to time to criticisms of trade unions or groups of workers for 'holding the country to ransom'. As Fox (1973) pointed out, the unitary framework offers a variety of ways of questioning the legitimacy of trade union activities suggesting, alternatively, that unions are historical carryovers, no longer needed in an age of enlightened management; that they are outcomes of sectional greed; or that they are vehicles for subversive political interests.

There is no denying the sense behind the advocacy by leaders of enterprises or governments of 'team spirit' or community of interest. All leadership requires legitimacy, and this involves ideological utterances. Where such utterances become a threat to the understanding of what is the case is where prescription and description become confused. Managers or politicians are as likely to be misled as are the rest of us if they come to believe their own propaganda. To attempt to run an organisation or a government on the assumption that there are no fundamental conflicts of interest between employers and employees, producers and consumers and so on would be folly indeed. A recognition of this encouraged academics to adopt a 'pluralistic' frame of reference.

Pluralist analyses

Pluralism as both an ideology and an analytical perspective has been the subject of extensive debate among both political scientists and industrial relations analysts for half a century. At the level of the work organisation, this perspective recognises the existence within the enterprise of various different and indeed conflicting interests. However, these differences are ones that can be accommodated: the benefits of collaboration between these fairly evenly balanced interests are such that compromises can be achieved to enable collaborative activity to proceed – to the benefit of all parties. Employees do have to surrender autonomy at work and recognise certain managerial prerogatives. This should not be seen as unreasonable or as reflecting any basic inequality, since management has to accept corresponding constraints. These involve recognition of a right on the part of employees to organise themselves to 'loyally oppose' and bargain over rewards and procedures. In this view, trade unions and the mechanisms of collective bargaining are necessary for the 'managing' of the conflicts of interest which exist between employers and employed and whose existence it is naive and foolish to deny. At the national level, the state tends to be seen becoming involved as only one among the range of different stakeholders or as the protector of the public interest where that may be threatened by any one interest group becoming too powerful.

The pluralist frame of reference became almost an orthodoxy among British industrial relations experts in the 1960s, but for a variety of reasons, it became increasingly subject to critical scrutiny in the 1970s. This was largely as a result of its being found to be inadequate *sociologically*. As was pointed out by Fox, who became a leading critic of the pluralist perspective which he had once advocated, the pluralist framework offers a fairly appropriate set of working assumptions for those involved in the practical world of industry and politics, given that 'irrespective of personal philosophy, a working acceptance of the basic structure, objectives, and principles which characterise industry is usually a condition of being able to exert influence towards reform' (Fox 1973). Nevertheless, Fox argued, the radical alternative, as well as offering what Fox sees as a 'necessary stimulus and guide to the pursuit of more fundamental change', also has 'greater intellectual validity'.

Radical/critical perspectives

The sociological reaction to pluralist analyses of industrial conflict helped shape industrial sociology by providing a 'favourable context' for the new interest in labour processes which was to emerge (Brown 1992).

LOOKING BACK <<<<<

Labour process analysis is discussed in Chapter 3 (pp. 70–73).

The reaction to pluralism was based upon the recognition of various 'crucial limitations' of pluralist thinking (Brown 1983):

- Pluralist analyses fail to recognise the extent and persistence of 'marked inequalities of condition and opportunity' in society at large. This means that there is a playing down of the extent to which settlements ultimately rest on the power of some groups to impose outcomes on others in a society which lacks what Goldthorpe (1974) had called 'any principled basis for the distribution of income and wealth'.
- The extent to which the state has to become involved in industrial relations is underestimated.
- Too little attention is given to problems in the societal 'infrastructure' which is so diverse and differentiated that there is no basis for the growth of a formalised and centralised set of institutions for the regulation of industrial conflict.

It has been argued throughout the present book that a basic character-istic of sociological thinking is that it ultimately relates whatever it is studying back to the way society as a whole is organised. In light of this, it is not surprising that sociologists who have been sensitive to the struc-tured inequalities of modern societies baulked at industrial-relations analyses which might imply some degree of power equality between the various parties in industrial conflicts. However, some of the radical critics of pluralist thinking may have exaggerated the extent to which pluralists have assumed such equality. Radical analyses of industrial con-flict, in the sense of analyses which go beneath the surface phenomena to the underlying 'roots' of issues and stress the importance of basic inequalities, need not necessarily involve a rejection of pluralist *values*. Fox (1979) observed that one can argue that a country like Britain has deep social inequalities, and is not therefore adequately liberal and plu-ralist, whilst still believing in liberal pluralism as a means of action and a desirable goal. Because there is a tendency to question all forms of liberal pluralism within Marxism, as Fox pointed out, it may be helpful to use Crouch's (1982) distinction between Marxist analyses and radi-cal (or, more properly, 'radical pluralist') ones. This frame of reference can be judged as the one with the greatest utility for future sociological analysis on the grounds that it resonates most closely with what exist-ing sociological research and theorising has shown to be the case about 'how the world is'.

> ### A radical pluralist frame of reference
>
> A radical pluralist framework recognises the plurality of groups and interests in society (and welcomes social pluralism *in principle*) whilst observing the more basic patterns of power and inequality which tend to shape, as well as be shaped by, the plurality of groups and interests.

Institutional tensions and work conflicts

Identifying institutional tensions in social arrangements involves exam-ining how the various principles that underlie social organisation are inconsistent or clash with each other. Analysing institutional tensions helps us to locate internal tensions or strains which exist in how the social world is structured and which may lead to either collapse of social arrangements, on the one hand, or lead to social changes or adaptations on the other hand.

Institutional tensions

Tendencies within a social or organisational structure for different institutional logics to clash with each other in a way that, if not managed, may undermine that structure.

Marx's concept of contradiction, Chapter 3, which has some similarities to this notion, plays a key part in an analysis which has revolutionary implications for the whole capitalist mode of production. A concept of contradiction has been mobilised to a considerable extent in scholarly journals in recent times to cover a wide variety of different aspects of work and social organisation. This is demonstrated by McGovern (2014) who goes on to argue that the concept is too rarely rooted in a clear conceptual framework and that it would be an advantage to the sociology of work if there was 'a moratorium on further usage'. The much broader notion of institutional tensions might take its place, one might argue – as long as it is clearly rooted in an explicit broader conceptual framework – whether that be one from Weberian/institutional sociology or somewhere else.

LOOKING BACK <<<<<

The notion of tensions or clashes between institutional logics was closely examined in Chapter 3 (pp. 63–65) and examples of its deployment are seen throughout *Sociology, Work and Organisation*.

LOOKING BACK <<<<<

Durkheim's broader sociological contribution is examined in Chapter 2.

The basic idea of aspects of social organisation coming to clash with each other has played a part in sociology from early days. Durkheim's observation of industrial capitalism in action led him to an increasing awareness that persisting inequalities threatened the kind of social solidarity which he thought to be possible within the 'organic division of labour' which characterises modern economic life.

For economic life to be regulated there needed to be some kind of moral basis underlying it, otherwise anomie would prevail, but he could not see how such a 'normative order' could be achieved whilst inherited inequalities of opportunity and condition existed. Industrial capitalist society, with its basic class inequalities, has to impose order, and, to the extent that this is so, 'fundamental discontent and unrest persist if only in latent form' (Goldthorpe 1974). From his reading of Durkheim, Goldthorpe infers the futility of trying to bring lasting 'order' to industrial relations activity, on the lines advocated by pluralist thinkers, whilst major inequalities of wealth and opportunity persist in society at large.

Working at this 'whole societies' level, it is possible to draw together certain basic factors in the structure of industrial capitalist societies that give rise to conflicts in work. Industrial capitalist society involves the buying and selling of people's labour capacity. These transactions are not made on a basis of equality between the parties, however. Yet inequality itself does not create a problem. The threat to the stability of industrial capitalism arises from it in two indirect ways:

(1) Instability arises from the fact that industrial capitalism has been historically dependent on expressed values of social equality and of rewards based on achievement, values which conflict with the actual or effective distribution of rewards, and opportunities for advancement in society. This gap between claims and 'realities' is less likely to be visible during periods of economic growth and changing occupational structures than when growth slows down or stops. Inequalities of distribution, for example, are more likely to become contentious when there is a 'cake' of fixed size to share out, than when this cake is growing.

(2) Instability arises from the fact that, in a culture where individual freedom, choice, independence and autonomy are central values, the great majority of people in their work experience find themselves coming under the control and instruction of others to a degree which potentially clashes with cultural expectations.

LOOKING BACK <<<<<

This type of thinking might be seen as implicit in some of the concerns being expressed in the twenty-first century about the growing inequalities associated with emerging technologies. See Chapter 4.

Many of the conflicts which arise between employers and employees can be seen as paradoxical outcomes or unintended consequences of the actions and means which have been chosen by dominant interests themselves in the course of the history of industrial capitalism. Collective resistance to employers could not have arisen had not employers brought together employees in single workplaces, as Marx observed. Further, the instrumental and calculative approach to work of many employees about which employers tend to complain reflects the logic of employers' own policies as much as anything else: 'the first generation of factory workers were taught by their masters the importance of time; the second generation formed their short-time committees in the ten-hour movement; the third generation struck for overtime or time-and-a-half' (Thompson 1967). The low level of moral involvement of junior employees can also be seen as reflecting the very way their work is designed. If employees are given narrowly restricted tasks to do, are closely and often coercively supervised by 'superiors' and are treated as dehumanised factors of production, managements can expect little more than grudging compliance.

Low-trust management policies and control techniques are likely to be reciprocated with low-trust employee attitudes and behaviour. As Fox (1974) put it, 'low-trust industrial relations' result from this together with bargaining on a win–lose basis, attempts to bring the other side under closer prescription and control and a screening and distortion of communication between bargaining parties. Managements often recognise this danger and therefore attempt to build trust relationships. This reflects their involvement in the central contradiction that 'the function of labour control involves *both* the direction, surveillance and discipline of subordinates whose enthusiastic commitment to corporate objectives cannot be taken for granted; *and* the mobilisation of discretion, initiative and diligence which coercive supervision, far from guaranteeing, is likely to destroy'. But to build trust relations within employment is expensive and recognition of this takes them back to the pressure to substitute 'performance monitoring and control' for trust (Armstrong 1989). This, in turn, creates a tension: 'because trust is expensive there arises a contradiction between its indispensability and employers' economic interest in substituting for it'. Out of this contradiction, Armstrong sees arising a 'historical dynamic within capitalist organisations' whereby some managerial groups attempt to wrest from others a role in building trust on behalf of the employers for whom they are acting as agents. In this way, the specific type of 'micropolitical' rivalry between managerial groups is understood within the more structural dynamics of the basic employer–employee antagonism. This might be said, too, about what Currie *et al.* (2016) call the 'dynamics' of Human Resource Management (HRM).

LOOKING BACK <<<<<

'Micropolitical' conflicts are examined in Chapter 5 (pp. 158–165). HRM is discussed in Chapter 6 (pp. 178–183).

This broad type of analysis is fundamentally sociological. It not only questions the validity of many of the assumptions upon which the conventional pluralist frame of reference is based, it also inevitably takes issue with many of the simplistic and psychologistic common-sense beliefs which are held about industrial conflict. Such phenomena as strikes, restrictions of output, sabotage and managerial politics are understood sociologically not so much as the outcomes of greed, bloody-mindedness or envy but as partly logical reactions and initiatives of people living in a certain type of society and economy.

The basic reason, beyond general issues of 'human nature', why conflicts arise within the work institutions of industrial capitalist societies is that employers in effect 'use' employees for various purposes of their own whilst employees, in turn (though generally from a weaker position) use their employment for their own various purposes. For the employment relationship to exist at all, there is clearly a range of common interests, which provides the co-operative dimension to employment, whilst the remaining divergence of interests provides the considerable conflict dimension. Expressing this in institutional logic terms, we can say, that industrial capitalism is dependent on the three intertwined institutions of the employment and rational organisation of free labour (Watson and Watson 1999):

- the institution of *formally free labour* – labour which is not 'unfree' like that in slavery or serfdom and which, in principle, involves choices on the parts of workers about where and how they are going to work;
- the institution of *employment* whereby some people sell their capacity to work to others; and
- the institution of *rational organisation* which subjects work activities to processes of close calculation, a detailed division of labour, a bureaucratic hierarchical control structure.

Structural tension arises from the relationship between these three institutions, however. It is a tension between two logics or principles:

- the principle of *control* of human beings implicit in the institutions of employment and rational organisation, and
- the principles of *freedom and autonomy* implicit in the institution of formally free labour.

Within organisations, managers have to deal with the basic contradictory relationship between *controlling* workers and seeking their willing *commitment*. The basic tension between these two logics will mean, say Edwards and Wajcman (2005), that the pursuit of different managerial policies 'run across each other'. Thomas Toms, a union representative in a large machine shop, illustrates this in Snapshot 11.2.

Snapshot 11.2

Thomas watches the control-commitment pendulum swing back and forth

Management here move this way and then that way, and then back again, all the time. Earlier this year they came all heavy on the supervision side. They watched us like hawks and pushed instructions at us from morning until night. Then, last month, they seemed to realise that it was expensive having all these people on our backs all the time. And they also saw that none of us would take any sort of initiative when problems arose. So what did they do? They reduced the number of so-called team leaders and told the remaining ones to apply a 'lighter touch'. But I can see that the management is getting all jittery again. They are nervous about whether we are going to meet their weekly targets. I'll bet you that by the end of the year the pendulum will swing back again, and we'll be back under the supervisory thumb.

LOOKING BACK <<<<<

Related to these two 'logics' of control and commitment are the practices that were conceptualised as 'direct control' and 'indirect control' respectively in Chapter 6.

As Edwards and Wajcman put it, managers 'will be constantly juggling between [the] competing logics' of control and commitment. At the societal level, structures and institutions arise to regularise and cope with potentially disintegrative conflicts of interest. These institutions range from highly informal 'understandings' and accommodations in specific workplaces, to more formal collective bargaining arrangements, and to state involvements in employment relationships through methods as diverse as employment legislation, industrial policy and the placing of informal pressures on employers and trade unions. Although it is most often applied to institutions of collective bargaining, the notion of the institutionalising of conflict can usefully be applied to this very wide range of arrangements. All of these institutions function to help maintain and reproduce a particular type of social order that is associated with industrial capitalism. To locate the situation of the working individual to this broad structural context, it is helpful to return to focusing on the implicit contracts of people within employment relationships: effort bargains, fragile implicit contracts and the inevitability of grievances.

Effort bargains, fragile implicit contracts and the inevitability of grievances

LOOKING BACK <<<<<

Attention was drawn in Chapter 9 (p. 293) to the role of managerial initiatives in attempting to manipulate the implicit contract between the employing organisation and the worker to persuade the worker that the exchange occurring between the parties was a fair and reasonable one, thus 'motivating' the worker and getting his or her compliance with managerial requirements. It was emphasised, however, that these processes of exchange, negotiation and persuasion occur in a context of unequal power relationships.

There is always an underlying conflict of interests in work organisations, something that Sandeep's wife pointed out to him in Snapshot 11.1. This was emphasised in the classic analysis of Baldamus (1961), who pointed out that, 'As wages are costs to the firm, and the deprivations inherent in effort mean "costs" to the employee, the interests of management and wage earner are diametrically opposed'. This conflict of interests is manifested in the struggle which takes place to achieve 'wage disparity' in the favour of either the employer or the employee. In certain circumstances the employee may achieve an improvement in the amount of reward which they gain for a certain effort but, more typically in a capitalist economy, the tendency is towards disparity in the favour of the employer. This is:

- partly because employees have been socialised into accepting a certain level of work obligation 'as a duty', thus conceding some effort to the employer 'free of compensation', but
- probably more crucially, the employer, in the context of a capitalist market economy, simply cannot afford in the long run to concede wage disparity in the favour of employees. The capitalist context obliges the employer to intensify the work effort derived from the employee at a given cost.

Baldamus' concern with the ongoing conflict over what Behrend (1957) called the *effort bargain* tends to emphasise the material rewards available from work and concentrates on the factory shop floor situation.

The implicit contract, made up of a complex bundle of 'inputs' and 'rewards', is a fragile one, existing, as it does, in the context of the dynamic nature of the priorities of both work organisations and workers. The following framework, bringing together elements of our earlier analyses, sets this fragility in its broad sociological context and identifies how it makes inevitable the emergence of grievances in the workplace:

LOOKING BACK <<<<<

The concept of the implicit contract developed in Chapter 9 and represented in Table 9.2 broadens these insights to recognise that something similar to shop floor wage and effort bargaining goes on in all types of employment and over a wide range of issues, ranging from job satisfaction and social reward to matters of status and career potential.

(1) In a world where valued resources are scarce, people form coalitions of interest to help in the pursuit or defence of interests with regard to these resources.

(2) Over time, some groups win out over others in the competition for scarce resources and attempt to consolidate their advantage through their control of institutions and through the propagation of ideologies.

(3) Industrial capitalism emerged as 'bourgeois' groups which became successful in pursuing their interests in certain societies, but the advantages, which accrue from their use of such formally rational means as bureaucracy, technical division of labour, wage-labour, advanced technology and the rest, are constantly threatened. The threat comes not only from challenges on the part of less-privileged groups but also as a result of various contradictory tendencies in the industrial capitalist system itself.

(4) The relationship between the employer and the employee centres on an implicit contract. This is an agreement between unequal parties in which workers, in the light of their particular motives, expectations and interests, attempt to make the best deal possible, given their personal resources (skill, knowledge, physique, wealth, etc.). The bargain which is struck involves a certain relationship (in part explicit but largely, owing to its indeterminacy, implicit) between the employee inputs of effort, impairment and surrender of autonomy, and employee rewards of cash payment and fringe benefits, job satisfactions, social rewards, security, power status, and career potential.

(5) The bargain is essentially unstable, especially as a result of the market context in which it is made. Market viability on the part of the employer creates a constant pressure to minimise costs – this in turn leading to a pressure to either cut the rewards or increase the efforts of the worker – either way to the worker's disadvantage. However, workers are bound to defend themselves, especially since they buy goods and services on the same market. Paradoxically, the advertising and marketing efforts of employing organisations create

a pressure on their employees to increase, or at least hold stable, their rewards (employees and customers being ultimately the same people). The contradictory pressures operating on the employment relationship here are illustrated in Figure 11.1.

(6) To increase efficiency or market viability, employers introduce various organisational and technological changes (Chapter 5), but any such change, however minor it may seem, potentially invites opposition from employees whose implicit contracts may be seen to be threatened. This may be because of a tendency to reduce 'rewards' like job satisfaction or the opportunity to use craft skills, or because of a tendency to call for increased employee 'inputs' in the form of increased effort or a further reduction in the amount of autonomy which the employee has at work. Potential conflict, we can see, arises with practically any kind of managerial initiative in employment situations.

(7) Both to improve their market position and to defend themselves, employees tend to form various coalitions of interest to present the kind of group challenge which is necessary to have any effect in the face of the greater power of the employer (the exception here being where the individual worker has unique skills or knowledge on which the employer is dependent). Thus we get, within employing organisations, trade union organisation, 'professional' group mobilisation and 'informal' office and shop floor groupings. All of these present challenges to the managerial prerogative.

(8) In every workplace, there is a constantly negotiated and renegotiated agreement about what goes on and what rewards accrue. Only a fraction of the processes leading to this *negotiated order* (Chapter 2, pp. 49–50) is formal and much of the agreement is tacit. External conditions are never constant and therefore there are always threats to the stability of arrangements. The underlying conflicts of interest between employer and employee may become overt and apparent at any time and will tend to centre on two main issues: the amount of material rewards available to the employee and the extent of control over employees conceded to the employer.

(9) We can say that a grievance situation arises whenever a particular implicit contract is perceived to go out of balance. The grievance may lead to any of a range of worker reactions, from striking to absenteeism and from obstructive behaviour to resigning. A grievance can be settled or accommodated not only by a return to the prior status quo but by a rebalancing of the implicit contract in a new form; for example, an increase in cash being agreed to

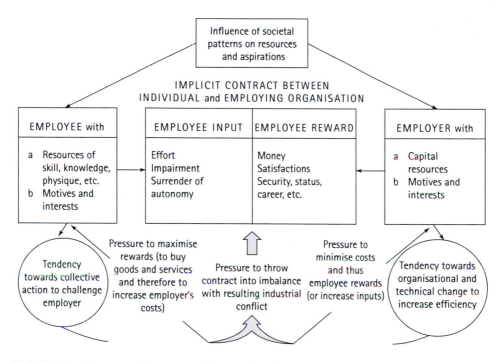

Figure 11.1 The implicit contract between employer and employee in its societal and economic context

compensate for a loss in autonomy resulting from an organisational or technical change.

Here we have a frame of reference which can be used to analyse conflict in the widest possible range of employment situations. Having established this framework we can now turn to the variety of ways in which people adjust and defend their interests and their very selves in their work situation.

The mobilisation of interests

Coalitions and interests

The typical worker in an industrial capitalist society, unless they have especially marketable personal skills or attributes, rarely has the capacity to defend themselves against attempts of employers to alter the balance of the implicit contract in the employer's favour – let alone improve the conditions or rewards of work. A concerted challenge coupled with the threat of a general withdrawal of effort can create such a possibility, however. We therefore see a general tendency within the world of work for groups to form around common interests and for collective action to be taken to defend or further those interests.

LOOKING BACK <<<<<

In the discussion of occupational strategies and cultures in Chapter 7, we saw how such mobilisation may occur around a common occupational interest, and particular attention was paid to the professionalisation process.

In the present chapter, we are concerned with situations where the common interest primarily arises, although not always exclusively, from the individuals' statuses as employees. Groups of employees located at all levels tend to form groups to defend or further their interests. Groups of employees, or their spokespersons, can be seen to make claims to professional status even when they are primarily managerial employees (Watson 2002b). And competing groups tend to exist within managements. However, it is at the lower levels, where autonomy and discretion is lower, that defensive groups are most necessary. It is here that we have traditionally seen the strategy of unionisation.

LOOKING BACK <<<<<

In our examination of 'micropolitics' in Chapter 5, we saw how managers form themselves into defensive cliques or assertive cabals, depending on how they perceive their career interests within the organisation.

Trade unions and collective bargaining

Early trade unions were only marginally related to industrial relations, as Hyman (2003) notes, originating as local societies of skilled workers operating as 'a social club, a local labour exchange, and an insurance society'. Yet as industrialisation proceeded, with employers becoming larger and more assertive, technologies changing, labour markets widening and occupational differences becoming blurred, they expanded, took on non-craft members and developed their structures to engage effectively in collective bargaining with employers.

Trade unions
Associations of employees formed to improve their ability to negotiate working conditions and rewards with employers and, sometimes, to represent common interests within the political sphere beyond the workplace.

Trade unions increased their significance in industrialising societies as the typical employment relationship changed from:

- a traditional one based on a *status contract*, a relatively diffuse master–servant relationship with an implication of longer-term mutual commitment, to
- one based on a *purposive contract* where 'the emphasis is on a transitory arrangement for limited and specific performances' (Fox 1974).

With the growing rationalisation of work organisations and the spread of low-discretion direct-control work tasks among white-collar groups unionism spread to groups higher and higher up the organisational and occupational hierarchy. The increasing application of what Baldamus (1961) called 'administrative instruments of effort intensification' on the part of employers later led to a shift from status to performance criteria and hence union-like initiatives among groups such as teachers and doctors (Eldridge 1975). Increasing stress on the cash nexus and the erosion of the 'moral obligations which are traditionally embedded in the idea of vocation' (Eldridge 1975), was reflected in the growth of the term 'instrumental collectivism' (Goldthorpe *et al.* 1968), and hence the spread of collective bargaining among non-working-class workers. There was still a social class dimension to these trends, however. One of the important factors in the expansion of white-collar trade unionism was 'the objective change in the class situation' of such workers (Crompton and Jones 1984). These resulted from pressures on labour costs which led to the rationalisation and deskilling of white-collar work and an accompanying decline in job security and in their conditions of employment relative to manual workers.

Given the low-trust type of economic exchange associated with this form of contract, collective defence of the employees' position becomes necessary. It would be wrong, however, to view the history of trade unionism simply in terms of necessary and inevitable reactions of a purely calculative kind. Trade unionism, particularly in Britain, has always been associated with the idea of a labour movement, something which has provided an ideology over and above the legitimation of sectional interests.

Labour movement

A coming together of such bodies as trade unions and associated political parties to represent the interests which employed people as a whole are believed to hold in common.

The political potential of trade unions, varying from vehicles of revolutionary potential in association with revolutionary political groups to acting more pragmatically to improve the welfare of working-class people, has been a matter of radical political debate from the time of Marx (Moses 1990). It is unlikely, however, that a political dimension to trade union activity can arise separately from a concern with the daily circumstances of people's employment situations. To mobilise people to act collectively, a fairly clear and direct link has to be established in their minds between the proposed political action and the specific circumstances of their lives that may be changed by that action. And the specific circumstances to which group leaders and their representatives typically have to look are connected with the implicit contract with the employer. To appeal to generalised ideal interests in the absence of a clear link between these and specific local advantage is unlikely to be effective given the essentially calculative ethos of the industrial capitalist workplace. British trade unions have generally been ambivalent towards politics and the law, and Hyman (2003) connects this, together with their going along with a system of labour law based on immunities as opposed to 'positive rights', to their experience of 'the anti-collectivist bias of the legal system' with the effect that 'laissez-faire was in this respect as resonant a slogan for trade unionists as for early British capitalists'. Freedom to engage in free collective bargaining has thus been a trade union priority.

Collective bargaining

A method of agreeing work conditions and rewards through a process of negotiation between employer representatives and the representatives of collectively organised employees.

The institution of collective bargaining did not arise solely as the result of pressures from employees. The organising of employees in trade unions in certain respects suited employers, not least because having an employee representative to negotiate for employees simplified the negotiating and communication channels which otherwise would have been necessary. This is not to suggest that employers always welcomed unionisation of employees – far from it. Union initiatives were only likely to be welcome to employers once the degree of organised employee opposition had reached a point where it was seen as needing to be contained and institutionalised. To a certain extent trade union leaders could be seen as 'managers of discontent' (Mills 1970; Watson 1988).

The historical rise of the shop steward movement has to be understood in the light of such tendencies. It was the joint creation of employees and managers and not something simply imposed on employers (Willman 1980). A similar pattern arose with regard to the institution of the closed shop, something which has now become of more historical than contemporary interest. This was an arrangement whereby work in a particular setting was exclusively carried out by members of a specified trade union. The closed shop – the demise of which came about as a result of state initiatives rather than employer ones – was something which managers encouraged to achieve 'order, cohesion, and a sense of authority in the workplace' (Taylor 1982).

When considering historical accounts such as these, it is vital to recognise that differences in national cultures and systems of political ideologies are important in understanding how trade unions and their members behave (Hodder and Edwards 2015). Fox (1985) showed how a series of features of British history lay behind the non-revolutionary nature of British trade unionism, for example. In addition to the role of a non-interventionist state, a period of economic growth and reluctance on the part of employers to engage in an all-out battle with trade unionism, there was an employer recognition of the part that 'respectable' trade unions could play as a safety valve for class conflict. On the employee side, the pre-industrial religious and political movements left a legacy of differentiated groupings that precluded the evolution of a general and united confrontational consciousness. Yet a low-trust adversarial approach to collective bargaining within enterprises did develop in Britain which Fox contrasts with the more consensual German approach, something which emerged from a different set of historical and cultural factors again.

In contemporary circumstances, it is a matter of debate whether British industrial relations are becoming Europeanised (with an emphasis on 'social partnership') or Americanised, an approach which 'embraces the continuing decline of unions and the assertion of a market-driven model' (Edwards 2003a). In an international study of the effects on the quality of work experience of economic downturn over the years 2006–2012, Gallie et al. (2004) conclude that the 'effects of economic crisis for intrinsic work quality' were less in Nordic countries and Germany compared to the UK as a result of their 'stronger systems of employee representation' in Europe and Scandinavia. This suggests that British employment relations are to be contrasted with those of Europe. And the American pattern, which provides a very different future for trade unions, has been closely examined by Rosenfeld (2014). The conclusion is a very negative one for trade unions, which are finding their influence both within employment itself and within society at large is in serious decline. Among the factors identified is the determination of leading business people to hold tight to executive control and he quotes a former Chief Executive Officer of a massive US retail business: 'We like driving the car and we're not going to give the steering wheel to anyone but us'. That business, we might note, owns and controls a major supermarket chain in Britain.

LOOKING FORWARD >>>>>

'Partnership agreements' are discussed later in this chapter.

Changing patterns of employer–union relations

In spite of international differences in patterns of employment relations, broad changes in the occupational structures and the social compositions of labour forces across the world in the latter part of the twentieth century were, Bean (1994) argues, 'largely detrimental to union organisation' and, in particular, 'the growth of new occupational groups with scarce skills' (leading to a preference for individual, rather than collective, labour market strategies) made it 'difficult for unions to recruit such workers, while the growing numbers of employees in private services with low-paid and insecure jobs' tended to 'lack the resources and cohesion to undertake collective action. British governments at this time were especially zealous in restricting the activities of trade unions, introducing a series of acts which, for example, first restricted and later removed all legal basis for closed shops, made secondary picketing illegal, made the sacking of strikers possible, required secret ballots before strikes and later for approval of political contributions, and required the regular re-election of main union leaders by secret ballot (see Daniels and McIlroy 2009). The government strategy was not so much to bear down directly on unions but to pass enabling legislation that would be implemented by employers, union members or even customers (Undy *et al.* 1996). The effect of all of these shifts was, in Fairbrother's (2000) terms, to leave the British trade union movement 'in a parlous state'. As Kelly (2005) commented, 'across the advanced capitalist world [unions] have lost members on an unprecedented scale, and it is now rare for them to organize more than a minority of the workforce'. And the loss of existing members is not the main explanation of this. Bryson and Gomez (2005) show that it is the reduced likelihood of people 'ever becoming a member', rather than the loss of existing members that is causing the decline in British trade union membership.

Accompanying the decline in union membership has been a decline in the occurrence of strikes. This occurred across most of western Europe in the last two decades of the twentieth century, but the decline has been steepest in Britain and has reached the lowest level since statistics were first collected in 1891 (Waddington 2003). This decline has resulted in part from the changing occupational structure (with traditionally 'strike-prone' industries declining) and in part from the changing balance of power (supported by state initiatives), and in part because the 'entrenched adversarialism' that once characterised certain sectors of the economy has been weakened with the 'resort to the strike' being seen as less 'natural' than it once was – this not necessarily meaning that the absence of strikes reflects the achievement of 'higher quality' industrial relations (Waddington 2003). Examination of a series of studies from across the world reveals that a range of variations on the basic strike notion is used. There is little evidence of an alternative having been discovered Gall (2013).

Changes in the 'power' of trade unions or the frequency of strikes have not resulted from a rush by employers to derecognise unions. Rather, managements have preferred simply to take advantage of the weakness of union representation in changing circumstances. Claydon (1989) observed that where there were attempts to *exclude* unions this was not part of any concerted anti-union movement but a matter of an 'extreme reflection of a much wider shift in the frontier of control *within* collective bargaining'. Millward *et al.* (2000) did not find significant evidence of employers actively derecognising unions noting that, instead, it was the persistently lower rate of recognition among new workplaces (and those that grew from being very small) that fuelled the continuing decline in the proportion of workplaces with recognition. This did not mean that employees were necessarily being denied a 'voice' in their workplaces but channels of communication changed a great deal, from ones involving trade unions and trade union representatives to 'channels where employees communicated directly with management, largely on occasions and on terms set by management themselves' (Millward *et al.* 2000). Legislative changes in the UK early in the twenty-first century nevertheless led to a significant rise in recognition agreements (Gall 2004). And the increasing use of a variety of channels for the expression of worker 'voice' is also apparent (Wilkinson *et al.* 2014), with initiatives by employers' Human Resources departments playing an important part, especially in areas like hotel and catering where a trade union presence has always been limited.

Alongside these changes, a shift in the relationship between trade unions and their members can be observed. This was seen as moving through three phases in Britain (Heery and Kelly 1994; Kelly and Heery 1994):

- Between the 1940s and the mid-1960s, a 'largely passive membership was serviced by a cadre of professional negotiators'.
- After the mid-1960s, this was partially displaced by a participative relationship in which 'the function of union officialdom was to facilitate self-serving and participation in decision-making by members'.
- From the mid-1980s, this organisational model gave way to a new servicing relationship in which members are viewed as reactive consumers whose needs must be researched and responded to using the techniques of strategic management.

A further shift then occurred, away from the *servicing* model, where members rely on union support and services from sources external to the workplace, to the *organising* model (Waddington 2003). This emphasises the role of local representatives and members, these being trained, guided and supported by the trade union (Gall 2003). There are significant variations in the organising model, however, as Simms and Holgate (2010) demonstrate in their review of the organising practices of three trade unions. Also the distinctions between the servicing and the organising models should not be exaggerated. Union leaders and full-time trade union officers are likely to mix both strategies as they continue to need to be sensitive to members' expectations and to the pragmatic circumstances in which they find themselves working (Watson, D.H. 1988). Heery *et al.* (2003) found the three approaches – servicing, organising and partnership – being used across trade unions, with each of them having potential, in different circumstances, for improving union representations. And Thursfield (2012) argues that union organisers are also adopting notions of managerial professionalism in which concepts like 'strategy, targets and efficiency prevail'. Turning to the readiness of workers to be mobilised. Cregan *et al.* (2009) identify two key factors which encourage this. First, there is the development of 'a group-based emotion' (as opposed to working in terms of calculative advantage) and, second, the presence of an element of 'transformational leadership' of the type seen in social movements.

An important development in employer–employee relations has been the partnership agreement.

Partnership agreements

Agreements between employers and trade unions to pursue mutual benefits within the employment relationship, especially so that managers gain greater labour flexibility and workers gain greater security and consultative involvement in management decisions.

Researchers have put forward evidence that many partnerships are employer-led and take advantage of trade union weaknesses, with the consequence that such arrangements disproportionately benefit managements (Stuart and Lucio 2005). Case study research in the aerospace industry was used by Danford *et al.* (2005) to support their view that the fundamental conflicts which exist between capital and labour render 'partnership' in employment relations unfeasible. Samuel (2007), however, argues that this kind of interpretation is sharply at odds with what empirical research more broadly indicates. His longitudinal case study research in the finance sector, for example, shows that some partnership agreements deliver mutual gains and endure. It is effective and sustainable where managers share decision-making with union representatives and allow genuine influence over decisions. Overall, say Bacon and Samuel (2009), on the basis of a UK survey of formal partnership arrangements, partnership agreements continue to be signed and tend to survive, especially in the public sector where they 'have emerged as a potentially important method of improving public service delivery'.

It is easy to assume that in smaller firms there will be a much greater degree of informality in employment relationships with the closeness of contacts between managers and workers making formalised collective bargaining unnecessary. Research over the years has shown that the potentially more 'intimate' and even family-like aspect of smaller enterprises does not avoid conflicts or preclude exploitative relationships (Holliday 1995), with external factors such as the influence of large firms over smaller ones pressuring managers to assert strong controls (Rainnie 1989) and patterns of internal relationships often involving continuous bargaining over shop floor activities (Ram 1994; Moule 1998). Given the considerable variety of different technologies and markets with which small firms are involved, it is possible to see a variety of different mixes of formal and informal employment relations practices across small firms in a way corresponding to what we might see in larger enterprises (Ram *et al.* 2001; Scase 2003; Edwards and Ram 2006; Atkinson 2008). In spite of this, when it comes to the quality of work experience in small firms, large scale survey material does suggest that there is still 'a good deal' in the argument that 'close working relationships between workers and managers 'produce mutual respect and even loyalty', 'where face-to-face relationships are the most intense, workers are most satisfied' (Tsai *et al.* 2007). What cannot be denied, on reviewing what research is available, is that 'the effects of partnership are ultimately complicated and uneven' (Butler and Tregaskis 2015).

Shop stewards and workplace representation

A major tension which has long existed within the trade union movement has been one between the need for large-scale representation across a wide constituency and the need for the defence of interests of individuals and groups in specific or 'domestic' work settings. It was this tension that can be understood as lying behind the growth of the shop steward movement in Britain during the First World War. This movement was motivated in part by radical and syndicalist ideals (Hinton 1973), but the later importance of the workplace representative or shop steward had a more pragmatic basis. The spread of payment-by-results schemes, the high demand for labour, the inappropriateness of the district (rather than plant-based) organisation of union branches and the decline of employer associations all contributed to the tendency for the workplace itself to become the point at which the implicit contract was to be protected or improved.

Shop steward/union workplace representatives

A worker representative and 'lay' trade union official who represents to management the interests of fellow employees who elect them as their workplace spokesperson.

Shop stewards can usefully be regarded as semi-formal workgroup representatives. This implies far more than their being a 'mouthpiece', however. It recognises the potential for them to articulate the common objective interests of the group, thereby creating subjective interests and willingness to mobilise. This equally may mean encouraging members to desist from immediate and spontaneous action as it might the opposite. Batstone *et al.* (1977) showed that the 'leader' type of steward, who tried actively to shape group activity, was more successful than the 'populist' steward who tended to follow group instructions. The stronger links of these 'leaders' with other stewards and the respect which they obtained from the management not only enabled the more effective defence of employee interests in the face of managerial control and the improvement in wages but also aided management by ensuring a greater predictability of shop floor. The behaviour and level of effectiveness of union representatives has changed over the decades, however. Darlington (1994) observed how the approach of stewards changed from being relatively *conflictual* in the 1970s to being more *consensual* in the 1980s. A range of factors influenced this but Darlington's case study research points to the importance of the management's approach to stewards and their tendency to switch back and forth between a 'hard-line approach' and a more co-operative 'soft line . . . aimed at incorporating them into accommodative relationships'. Although almost a quarter of a million workers in Britain were acting as workplace union representatives at the end of the twentieth century, shop stewards had become less effective in terms of outcomes than they previously were, often being 'ignored or sidelined by management' who are 'bypassing . . . shop stewards as communication channels to the workforce, and flouting . . . procedural presumptions of consultation or negotiation with trade union representatives before the implementation of change' (Terry 2003).

Summary

Conflict at work has two aspects to it. It exists where there is a clash of interests between different individuals or groups (between employers and workers, say), and it exists when those differences are translated into actions (when workers go on strike against employers, for example). Sociologists tend to see conflicts of both types as a normal part of organisational functioning and not as a pathological occurrence that comes about from time to time when normality 'breaks down'. Sociologists also tend to see conflict at work as a much broader phenomenon than one of 'industrial relations', with its focal concern with the collective organisation of workers and their collective bargaining with employers. This latter focus is nevertheless an important one and sociologists have debated the strengths and weaknesses of several different frames of reference which can be applied to industrial relations specifically or to work conflict more generally. But an important way of relating all these conflicts to social structural matters is to relate them to tendencies within social or organisational structures for certain principles on which those structures are based to clash with each other in a way which undermines those structures. But at the more surface level, at which both conflicts of interest and contradictions/institutional tensions manifest themselves, we see grievances arising whenever employer–employee 'implicit contracts', introduced in Chapter 9, become 'out of balance'. Once this occurs we tend to see interest groups mobilising themselves, and taking action. The institutions of industrial relations and collective bargaining have been of less significance in all industrial societies in recent times but innovations and adaptations continue to occur.

12 Resistance, mischief, humour and the defence of self

Key issues

- What kinds of expression of conflict, dissention, adjustment and resistance can we see if we look at everyday work activities across the whole range of work situations?

Resistance and complexity

When individuals take up a work role, they inevitably surrender a certain amount of autonomy. All workers, in effect, are *made use of* in some sense when they submit to the control of supervisors and managers in the work setting or the pressures put upon them by customers or clients. And whenever some human beings attempt to control or pressurise other human beings, the likelihood of, or perhaps the total certainty of, resistance arises. In Chapter 11, attention was paid to the relatively formal way in which structurally-based conflicts of interest manifest themselves in work settings and may be handled through institutionalised arrangements. We now concentrate on activities at the level of the workplace and the considerable variety of ways in which people, legitimately and illegitimately, adjust to the everyday circumstances in which they find themselves at work and the ways they resist, or otherwise deal with, being 'made use of' by employers, co-workers and customers – and even, with regard to employers, being 'disposed of'.

Organisational mischief

A concept that brings together the considerable variety of behaviours that arise in this context is that of 'organisational misbehaviour'. Vardi and Wiener (1996) defined this as 'any intentional action by members of organizations that violates core organizational and/or societal norms'. This conceptualisation, however, begs the question of whether these norms are official or unofficial ones.

> **LOOKING BACK <<<<<**
>
> The official/unofficial distinction is fully explained in Chapter 5.

We therefore need a conceptualisation that recognises the importance of the official/unofficial distinction when analysing organisational activities. We also need to recognise that these activities occur at all levels of organisations. Ackroyd and Thompson's (1999) overview of 'organisational misbehaviour' is limited to forms of resistance and adjustment of workers at lower organisational levels. In a later review, the same authors (Ackroyd and Thompson 2016) retain that focus, acknowledging that their lack of attention to managerial misbehaviour results from a lack of research evidence rather than anything else. Although 'worker' acts of misbehaviour or 'deviance' might generally be more visible than managerial ones, there is no reason why we should not expect even senior managers to pursue personal rather than corporate interests or to resist 'threats to self' coming from even more senior managers. It is quite possible for managers at the very top of corporations to act in ways both contrary to the official norms of the corporation and detrimental to the broader dominant interests served by the corporation. This is recognised with the concept of organisational mischief.

> ### Organisational mischief
>
> Activities occurring within the workplace that (a) according to the official structure, culture and rules of the organisation, 'should not happen' and (b) contain an element of challenge to the dominant modes of operating or to dominant interests in the organisation.

To understand many of the expressions of mischief that we are about to consider – from people making themselves absent from work or taking extended lunch breaks, to people sabotaging equipment, manipulating customers, bullying others or fiddling expenses – it is useful to take as a starting point the element of the implicit contract that requires people at work to surrender a degree of personal autonomy. This means that people have to put aside doing what it is that they might prefer to do (go to play golf rather than go to work, say, or slip cash into their own pockets rather than put it into the till). But it also means that they have to give up a degree of control over their very 'selves'. Sometimes having to take instructions from others may be a matter of minor irritation. But, at other times, it may be felt as a major attack on one's personal pride, or on the shared sense of honour of a working or occupational group. Karlsson (2012) treats 'organisational misbehaviour' as 'anything you consciously are, do and think at work that you are not supposed to be, do and think' and argues that it occurs as a result of an individual's deliberate attempt to defend their dignity.

The forms of 'mischief' to be considered in the present chapter, in one way or another, all involve a degree of resistance to the patterns of power in which people find themselves at work. This resistance may indeed prioritise the maintenance of individuals' sense of personal or occupational integrity. For example, in an ethnographic study of resistance to teamworking by technicians in a research and development laboratory (Thursfield 2015) it appeared that, although this resistance was 'oriented towards the interests of employees in their struggle for autonomy and personal fulfilment', it nevertheless operated, simultaneously 'in the interests of production'. This shows, Thursfield argues, that resistance does not have to be conceptualised as 'anti-work'; the technicians did not aim to disrupt or avoid work. They 'did their job well'. Although they refused to share knowledge with each other, refused to develop systems to support teamworking, refused to apply for the team leader roles and engaged in the collective ridiculing of the management's 'teamwork stories', little was done, in effect, to undermine 'the interests of the company'.

Actions when they are intended to defy, resist or undermine official authority or employer dominance may well have unintended consequences, just like actions pursued by management to further corporate aims. Acts of resistance may even strengthen sources of power or advantage that the 'deviant' was attempting to weaken. The act of misbehaviour committed by Frank Waters in Snapshot 12.1 illustrates this possibility in a striking manner. The general principle illustrated by this rather extreme example is something of which some organisational managements are well aware. This is illustrated by the 'counter-resistance' efforts of the consultancy firm studied by Kärreman and Alvesson (2010). One of these is a website in which people are encouraged to voice grievances and satirise the firm. Instead of this undermining the corporate ideology, 'the website satire and humour may add emotional resonance to otherwise cold and sterile corporate commandments'. It thus provides 'coping strategies instead of a radical questioning of the status quo'. Such efforts, alongside such practices as the careful vetting of individuals and the heavy emphasis on teams and work-groups created 'a context in which compliance is not only desirable: it is almost irresistible'. This kind of counter-resistance is similar to what Fleming (2009) calls 'designer resistance'. In this, organisations encourage employees to 'be themselves' and act in a cool and even cynical manner. The very fact that this 'resistance' is encouraged, we might say, means that it is contained.

LOOKING BACK <<<<<

The unintended consequences of managerial and bureaucratic practices were discussed in earlier discussions of Max Weber's thinking and in our examination of the nature of organisations.

Snapshot 12.1

Frank starts a fire

Frank Waters worked for a synthetic textiles company and he and his fellow workers found themselves becoming increasingly contemptuous of the owners and managers of the company. There were few other job opportunities open to them in the town and they regularly engaged in small acts of sabotage and minor theft from the business to relieve their frustrations. Frank, however, got so angry that one night he visited the factory in the middle of the night and set a fire going which completely burned down the factory. At first, the owners and managers were furious about what they were told by the fire service was clearly an act of arson. Later, they began to realise that this event was very much to their advantage. With the insurance money they invested in a much more modern factory with new machines and a much better layout. In addition to this, after six months close-down, they re-employed only the workers they were confident would be compliant, loyal and co-operative. Frank, and his close friends, found themselves replaced by such workers and the company went on to expand and to increase its profitability. Frank had got it very wrong.

Job control strategies and 'making out'

In Chapter 11, we considered the relatively formal way in which workers may 'mobilise' to protect their relative autonomy *vis-à-vis* management and defend their implicit contract with an employer by joining trade unions and acting collectively within the formal institution of collective bargaining. Another form of mobilising is the adoption by groups of workers of *job control strategies* or what employers might prefer to call 'restrictive practices'. A particularly significant activity here, given the constant pressure on employers to rationalise their methods and improve their efficiency, is the tendency of non-managers to resist managerially instigated changes.

'Resistance to change' on the part of lower status employees is frequently regarded as a kind of neurotic behaviour or an irrational conservatism. In practice, it is often highly rational. This only becomes clear once we recognise that any change in work organisation, payment scheme, technology or whatever, contains a potential threat to the implicit contract between employer and employee. Unless the employee can clearly see that there is not going to be a disparity in the favour of the employer (and a consequent loss to the employee), the safest thing to do is to resist the change. The charge of irrationality often arises, however, because managers make the judgement (in the spirit of unitary thinking that we considered in Chapter 11 that workers are failing to see that the changes will benefit the employees as well as the employer. In the low-trust atmosphere which characterises so much of contemporary employment relations, it is most unlikely that employees will 'take the management's word for it'. If employees have any kind of countervailing power at all they are likely to draw on it and insist on negotiating over any managerially initiated change which may threaten their current implicit contract. In an ethnographic case study in which a serious dispute almost occurred over management's attempt to stop factory workers making tea on the shop floor, it became apparent that this seemingly trivial concern was anything but trivial to the foundry workers concerned (Watson 1982). The workforce treated the management's intention to interfere with established break-time practices as a very serious infringement of their general autonomy. The workers' implicit contract was threatened by the management's apparent intention to increase the sphere in which it exerted control over employee behaviour. As many employees explicitly stated, this was a matter of principle. Ultimately this issue was conceded by the company, and a number of other fairly costly concessions had to be made in the course of negotiations before union co-operation with the introduction of changes was secured. The whole shop floor strategy was based on a sensible, rational and wisely sceptical approach to defending the existing implicit contracts of employees.

One form of job control strategy which has received a great deal of attention over the years has been the practice of work-groups who are paid on an incentive scheme to restrict their output to a level which they find acceptable. Over a hundred years ago, Taylor called this 'systematic soldiering' and treated it as an abuse which scientific management would remove. In their interpretation of this kind of behaviour in the Bank Wiring Room at the Hawthorne plant, the Human Relations investigators did not stress the rationality of the fixing of a norm of a 'fair day's work' and the defence of this norm by the sanctioning of 'ratebuster' and 'chiseller' behaviour (going above and below the norm, respectively). Instead, they interpreted the phenomenon in terms of an assumed social need and the necessary defence of a psychologically supportive group social system.

LOOKING BACK <<<<<

'Taylorism' or 'scientific management' and 'human relations' thinking are explained in Chapter 2.

Subsequent studies of the way incentive schemes are 'fiddled', especially those of Roy (1952, 1953, 1954) and Lupton (1963) laid emphasis on the rationality behind them. Lupton argued that the 'systematic manipulation of the incentive scheme' was an effective form of worker control over the job environment. The 'fiddle' not only gives a measure of control over the relationship between effort and reward but protects the workers against the effects of management shortcomings, defends them against rate cuttings and helps stabilise earnings. The widely followed practices of 'cross booking' and 'banking' of work helps hide high bonuses when these are earned and enables workers to carry over and spread earnings. This activity of 'making out', in American terminology, can also give workers an opportunity for self-expression and the enjoyment of an '"exciting game" played against the clock on the wall, a "game" in which the elements of control provided by the application of knowledge, skill, ingenuity, speed and stamina heightened interest and lent to the exhilaration of "winning" feelings of "accomplishment"' (Roy 1952). Burawoy (1979) who found himself doing research in the same factory that Roy had studied years earlier, observes however, that in developing these strategies of seeming independence, the workers were also accommodating to the established pattern of power and ownership in the factory, a pattern in which they were the relative losers – in political economy terms, they were 'manufacturing their own consent'.

Accommodation, subjectivity and values

To talk about people defending their sense of self in the face of more powerful 'others' is not to assume that each individual has a fixed 'self' which is wholly separate from its structural context. Self-identities 'are always in process' and power 'provides the conditions of possibility' for the self-formation of identities, 'a process involving perpetual tension between power and resistance or subjectivity and identity' (Jermier *et al.* 1994). Accommodation to managerial requirements is thus always partial and the concept of subjectivity is helpful in understanding why.

LOOKING BACK <<<<<

The idea of 'subjectivity' was introduced in Chapter 3 and later connected to the concept of 'self-identity' in Chapter 10.

In their research on work under a Total Quality Management regime (Chapter 6, p. 187), Knights and McCabe (2000) applied a notion of subjectivity as 'the way in which individuals interpret and understand their circumstances [which is] bound up with the sense they have of themselves'. They concluded that however hard consultants and managers search for a 'perfect' technology for controlling labour, 'even in the most oppressive regimes, there will be spaces and opportunities for escape and perhaps even a bit of misbehaviour'.

An individual's self-identity involves them in holding values and beliefs which will always differ in part from those implicit in the 'subjectivities' which are pressed upon them in the discourses current in their employment setting. This is illustrated by O'Connell Davidson's (1994) research in a newly privatised public utility. Clerical workers' resistance to changes being made by the management to emphasise profitability at the expense of service to the public, as these employees saw it, related to the 'subjective state' of these workers and this, says O'Connell Davidson, was not simply shaped by their immediate work situation but also by 'their commitment to supplying a socially useful service'. Similarly, opposition to corporate policies by managers in ZTC was shown to be related not just to a sectional interest in keeping open the plant in which these managers worked but also to personal values and notions of personal integrity – these often being articulated in terms of 'the sort of person I am' (Watson 1996b).

Withdrawal, instrumentalism and the management of boredom

One of the most direct ways of reacting to the deprivations of a given work situation is to leave the job. Indeed, levels of 'labour turnover' in employing organisations are often taken to be useful indicators of the level of conflict within that organisation. It was shown in a classic study of navvies, for example, that 'jacking suddenly and for little or no reason was regarded as a demonstration of freedom and independence of the employer' (Sykes 1969). The importance of the idea of 'jacking' in the navvies' occupational ideology reflects the men's strong desire to feel and be seen as being independent of any particular employer and as indicating a basic hostility to employers in general.

The same grievances or dissatisfactions to which people react by leaving their job may equally take the form of absence from work or the collective application of formal sanctions. Even accidents may reflect industrial discontent (Nichols 1997). But care has to be taken in regarding different manifestations of conflict as straightforward alternatives for employees. Edwards and Scullion (1982) stressed that the different forms of conflict behaviour which they studied, ranging from absenteeism to strikes and effort bargaining, have to be understood in the context of the specific work control structures of which they are a part. They show, for example, how the absenteeism among a set of women workers was acceptable to their management. These same managers, however, would have found a similar level among male workers – who were much more directly and intensely controlled than the women – far less acceptable. Absenteeism itself is not an issue; the issue is what it means given the control structure context in which it occurs. As Turnbull and Sapsford (1992) observed in the case of the British docks, where there is a considerable conflict across the workplace 'frontier of control' then absenteeism is especially likely to be an 'expression of industrial conflict' rather than a matter of separate individuals choosing to take time off without reference to wider norms of that workplace. Here, absenteeism is more a social than an individual act as is seen elsewhere where there exists a 'subculture' of absenteeism (Edwards and Whitson 1989). Although such a 'subculture' may be detrimental to organisational performance, it can also be beneficial or 'functional' to an employing organisation through helping to handle potential problems that might arise from, say, employee exhaustion. This was the case in a call-centre studied by Deery et al. (2010). There was acceptance of high levels of absenteeism by workers and management alike. This shows, say the researchers, that 'a supportive co-worker absence culture and team leader absence permissiveness can lessen the effects of job demands on emotional exhaustion and improve worker wellbeing'.

One very significant way in which the employee may come to terms with work deprivations is by taking his or her identity not so much from the occupation but from their home life. Thus, for the 'instrumental privatised worker' (Chapter 9, p. 252), it is the non-work life which forms the central life interest. Work deprivations are coped with by their being rationalised as necessary means to other ends. Here, for instance, we find workers accounting for their acceptance of the negative aspects of work by pointing to the way that their income is enabling them to give their children a better 'start in life'. In addition to or as alternatives to deriving vicarious satisfactions from children's advancement people may daydream at work about the material goods or the holidays which their work enables them to buy and this may be extended into fantasising about the delights of, say, winning the national lottery. Another form of 'disengagement' is that labelled Svejkism (after the hero of the novel *The Good Soldier, Svejk* by Jaroslav Hasek, 1973) by Fleming and Sewell (2002). Here, the workers act at a surface level as if they are supportive of an organisation's official norms and of managerial authority whilst, without this being observed by the authorities, they 'shirk', 'drag their feet' and engage in minor acts of sedition which are intended to impress fellow workers. Dave Scrimshaw in Snapshot 12.2, was a past master at a 'scrimshanking version' of this – one in which ironic deference is theatrically expressed to authority figures, for the entertainment of workmates.

Snapshot 12.2

Scrimshaw scrimshanks

We used to think that the word 'scrimshank' was named after Dave Scrimshaw. Perhaps his name encouraged him in his youth to develop his scrimshanking skills or perhaps the name was just a coincidence. Anyway, you should have seen him operate. When the warehouse boss used to come down to tell us that, say, a new delivery of breakfast cereals would soon be arriving, he would look delighted and ask questions like, 'And which cereal is it arriving today, Mr Cooper?' And, then, 'Oh yes Mr Cooper, I think that one has to be handled with special care, so we'll go very gently'. And then, when the boss had gone and the lorry arrived, he would conspicuously throw or kick the boxes all over the warehouse. And then he'd engage in some other wheeze to impress the lads. One of his favourite tricks was to construct for himself a little sleeping 'den' between the piled up boxes. And, yes, he'd then make a display of climbing into this space 'for a nice rest'. We'd then hear this snoring coming from his hiding place – whether he was sleeping or pretending to sleep, we never knew. But you can be damn sure of one thing – the boss never caught him being anything but the hardest working and most conscientious worker of us all.

In their discussion of what they call the 'hidden injuries of class', Sennett and Cobb (1977) argued that for people to accept a circumstance whereby they are constantly given orders by others they may have to adjust by viewing themselves in a self-disparaging way and even by feeling secretly ashamed of what they are. Purcell (1982) suggested that a key reaction of the women factory workers whom she studied to such 'hidden injuries' was one of fatalism. This was manifested in their daily interest in horoscopes, fortune-telling and superstitions. She argued that this is stronger among women than among men. Women at work, as in their biological and domestic lives, have to adjust to 'things happening to them' more than do men. Gossip, among men as much as among women, can play a role in encouraging fatalism with it sometimes acting as a medium of 'emotional ventilation' (Ribeiro and Blakely 1995). However, gossip may function in different ways in different circumstances, sometimes simply helping to alleviate boredom, sometimes helping workers adjust to insecurities and anxieties arising in the workplace (Noon and Delbridge 1993) and, at other times, especially when there is considerable change and disruption, heightening anxieties and insecurities (Tebbut and Marchington 1997).

Although social evaluations of what is 'boring' in any given context will influence perceptions, boredom is very much an individual matter and is perhaps best understood as an emotional or affective state (Loukidou *et al.* 2009). The simplest expedient for handling such an affective state is probably for the individual to allow themselves to be 'drawn along' by the technology which they are operating – what Baldamus (1961) called 'traction'. Delbridge (1998) reports his participant observer experience of assembly-line work coming to 'hypnotising him so that he almost became entranced by it on occasions'. Nevertheless, a typical work shift represents a long period of time for the manual worker to pass in this way. For long periods of unchallenging work to be psychologically manageable, the experience has to be structured and broken down into manageable components. This type of structuring is illustrated in Roy's (1952) classic participant observation study of a group of machine operators who alleviated the monotony of their daily routine by creating games and rituals within the work-group and by devising a series of work-breaks: coffee time, peach time, banana time, window time, and so on. An alternative strategy is for workers to devise ways of imposing their own pacing on even the most mechanically paced of jobs. On the car assembly line, for example, the individuals may work 'back up the line' to 'build a bank' (by completing operations before the car reaches their station on the line) and hence buy time for themselves (Walker and Guest 1952).

One broad type of 'withdrawal' from work tasks is the engagement in *empty labour* or 'private activities at work' (Paulsen 2013, 2015).

Empty labour

Activities engaged in by workers that involve withdrawal from tasks which they are formally engaged to undertake in the workplace; such activities range from groups of people playing cards on a nightshift to individuals linking to the internet for personal purposes ('cyberloafing') when they believe they are unobserved or ignored (a 'blind eye' being turned) by work supervisors.

These are activities that are ones which, yet again, might in certain circumstances be regarded as a form of 'resistance' to managerial control and in other circumstances be regarded as helpful to managers – when they function as a convenient way of handling slack periods in the cycle of work.

The playing of music in the workplace is often understood as a way in which people's potential boredom is handled. This is undoubtedly the case. But the sociologist would inevitably want to put such a phenomenon in a wider social context. This is done by Korczynski (2014) whose ethnographic study in a blinds-making factory led him to point out that listening to music is not simply an individualistic matter. There is also 'social listening' and he observes the ways in which the factory workers used the music to making meanings. The enthusiastic reception of the playing of the Animals' song 'We've got to get out of this place' can clearly be seen as a gesture of resistance, albeit a symbolic one. The fact that worker attachment to this song was expressed regardless of ethnicity, age or gender suggests to Korczynski that the shared class position of the workers was an important element in the meaning that was attached to it.

Humour and play at work

Joking and humour is more than a peripheral or incidental aspect of work activities and cultures. As Westwood and Rhodes put it, 'humour and comedy are pervasive, entrenched and highly meaningful aspects of human experience and that they are as significant in organisational and work contexts as they are in any other domain of human activity'. Humour has even been suggested as providing a possible methodology for sociology (Watson 2015). And the terms *humour* and *comedy* cover a wide variety of activities.

> ## Workplace humour
>
> All forms of communication occurring in the work situation which create within people feelings of amusement and a predisposition to express that emotion through laughter.

At its simplest, workplace humour is a way of inserting a degree of fun or leisure into the working day. However, it has functions that go beyond this and a parallel can be drawn between joking at work and behaviour patterns noted by anthropologists in other settings. The classic discussion of the so-called joking relationship in social life is that of Radcliffe-Brown (1965). He points out how playful antagonism and teasing may help individuals in a potentially conflictful situation to accommodate to each other thus enabling them to co-operate and interact successfully. Such relationships are typically seen to develop in families between new spouses and their various 'in-laws'. In an early contribution to the literature on humour in work settings, Bradney (1957) showed how such relationships and associated humorous behaviour developed between sales assistants in a London department store. It was in the interest of each assistant to increase her own sales, something which put her in conflict with colleagues. To avoid hostility and strain, joking was regularly resorted to. For example, a new assistant seen to be working too hard and seriously was told by an old hand 'You want to sell up the shop today, don't you?' Bradney notes that this was said 'in a friendly joking manner even though it did conceal a reprimand'.

The two-sided nature of much humour and what we might call 'workplace play' was noted by Applebaum (1981) in his study of construction workers, and he observed that 'kidding and horseplay' simultaneously channel hostility and elicit feelings of friendship and solidarity. This corresponds to the suggestion in Boland and Hoffman's (1983) machine-shop study that humour and workplace play serve a dual function – helping people accept a structure whilst avoiding their surrender of self. Thus, jokes are played on new members to teach them their 'place', but later jokes are allowed which reverse this 'place' – building them up again. Humour and play thus help maintain an organisational culture. Again, activities implying subversion and resistance help existing structures reproduce themselves. The apparent 'usurpation of work' has both 'functional and dysfunctional aspects (Sørensen and Spoelstra 2011). Or, as Linstead (1985) says, humour has the capacity both to 'resist a dominant formulation and also to accommodate to it'.

The variety of functions and effects of humour in the workplace is illustrated in Snapshot 12.3 by Sanders' (2004) study of sex workers.

Humour among sex workers

Sanders saw humour being used by the sex workers she studied as part of an emotional management process which made it possible for them 'to act under one disguise with clients' while reserving their 'true' selves for their private, domestic lives.

Humour was also used as part of a 'conscious business strategy' designed to please the clients and encourage them to return in the future. They adopted the stereotypical image of the 'happy hooker' and joked and bantered with the clients to help speed along the 'passive' business transaction and gain the maximum profit for a minimum time and emotional input.

In large saunas where there was high staff turnover, humour played an important solidarity function. 'Raillery, jesting and comedy about clients, men and society's hypocritical views on prostitution create in-group cohesion in a short space of time'. This also helped new workers to learn quickly about the work, and its risks, from others.

There was also a managerial use of humour in this context. When workers broke the rules (smoking cannabis on the premises, shirking cleaning duties, for example), informal warnings were given in a jokingly mocking manner. A manager was heard telling a worker to get on with some vacuum cleaning because 'there are more from where you come'. But this heavy threat was lightened somewhat with 'You might impress the punters darling, but you certainly don't impress me with your fancy nails'.

LOOKING BACK <<<<<

Emotion management, more broadly, is examined in Chapter 10 (pp. 322–324).

Taylor and Bain (2003) stress the potential for humour to undermine managerial authority, showing in two call centre case studies how 'humour and joking contributed to the development of attitudes standing in sharp contrast to managerial values and priorities'. At the same time as managers and supervisors may be the targets of worker humour, they frequently use it themselves to achieve their purposes. Far from sabotaging organisational purposes, humour can be 'instrumental in pursuing it' (Barsoux 1993). Managers, says Barsoux, sometimes use humour 'as a sword to influence and persuade, to motivate and unite, to say the unspeakable and to facilitate change', and sometimes 'as a shield, to deflect criticism, to cope with failure, to defuse tension and to make their working lives more bearable'. Humour is increasingly used as a deliberate and formal managerial device. To revitalise the damaged corporate cultures that resulted from the downsizing and fragmentation of organisations in the late twentieth century, say Deal and Kennedy (1999), managers can be seen 'putting the fun back into work' in such places as the airline where employees were rewarded for introducing joking into their working practices.

In the workplace the dominant mode of making sense of events is what Mulkay (1988) calls the 'serious mode'. Subordinate to this, but always likely to break through it, is a 'humorous mode', and Barsoux (1993) shows how the 'serious, structured, rational side of business provides a poignant backdrop' for humour. Humour is born out of incongruity and a key incongruity in organisations is that between this serious side of life and the 'pettiness, chaos, fallibility and uncertainty of any human endeavour'. We often laugh at work, then, as we attempt to come to terms with the contrast between the earnestness of the tasks we are meant to undertake and our human shortcomings. Laughter helps us 'cope emotionally with that which could frighten us into madness: the fragility of our identities and the contingency of our social locations' (Watson 2001a).

Much of the workplace joking which goes on can hardly be seen as riotously funny, and the humour indulged in by Roy's subjects (1952) in his classic 'banana time' article is funny only in its pathos. One of the men's standard themes, for example, was to ask each other 'how many times did you go poom-poom last night?' The perfunctory nature of much workplace communication was recognised by Meissner (1976) who portrayed workplace humour as a rather alienated form of activity in itself, as opposed to a brave resistance to alienation. Such a suggestion is clearly made when he claims that the kind of obscene joking frequently observed among female manual workers is participated in more 'as a matter of defence against male presumption and dominance than for fun'. If it is at all funny, he notes, it is only in a 'self-destructive sense'.

In contrast to this, Willis (1977), in an influential ethnographic study, emphasised the ways in which manual workers 'thread through the dead experience of work a living culture which is far from a simple reflex of defeat'. He notes how in the shop floor situation and in the classroom situation of boys destined for the shop floor there is the same kind of informal groupings with the same counter-cultural 'complex of chauvinism, toughness and machismo'. He argued that the attempts of 'the lads' to control their own routines and life spaces at school parallel their fathers' informal control strategies at work. He also noted continuities between the attitudes to conformists and informers ('earoles' and 'grassers') in both situations as well as their common 'distinctive form of language and highly intimidating humour', where many of the verbal exchanges which occur are 'pisstakes', 'kiddings' or 'windups'. The way in which the working-class counter-culture can be seen as a reaction to middle-class culture is illustrated by the fact that the shopfloor 'abounds with apocryphal stories about the idiocy of purely theoretical knowledge'. A story is told, for example, of the book enthusiast who sent away for a book which he has yet to read – it arrived in a wooden box which he is unable to open.

The multiple purposes which humour may serve in the manual work situation is illustrated by Collinson's (1992) factory study which highlighted 'three aspects of the joking culture', first, as a medium to help develop 'collective solidarity to resist boredom, the organisational status system and managerial control'; second, to reinforce the central values of 'working class masculinity' so that workers were 'required to show a willingness, for example, to give and take a joke, to swear, to be dismissive of women, white-collar workers and managers' and to retain their domestic authority; and third, to control those perceived to be 'not pulling their weight'. But, as we saw earlier, humour is equally a concern of managers in organisations, and Collinson (2002) observes that in so far as humour is becoming involved in both resistance and control it is 'becoming incorporated into the contested terrain that is the contemporary workplace'. Collinson sees two historical and contemporary managerial strategies towards humour: a strategy of humour suppression and a strategy of humour manufacture.

LOOKING BACK <<<<<

These two humour strategies fit closely with the two broader managerial strategies of *direct control* or *responsible autonomy* or 'indirect control' (Chapter 6).

Put simply, organisational managers might choose to pursue worker compliance by stopping those workers joking and fooling about at work or, alternatively, they might choose to invite workers to joke and fool about with the managers – as long, of course, as those humorous activities contribute to the long-term success of the corporation. The complexities and, indeed, ambiguities of the part that humour plays in manager–worker negotiations of order is especially clearly brought out in close studies of small firms. Humour is closely but ambiguously involved in maintaining the informality of employment relations that typically characterises small organisations by 'downplaying status differences and indicating a sense of personal closeness' (Mallet and Wapshott 2012). Playing down the differences in the standing of owner-managers and that of their employees is, however, only that of 'masking' – and the mask is always at the risk of slipping off, especially when owner-managers start to introduce organisational changes.

Sexual harassment and bullying

Sexual harassment
Unwanted and offensive expressions of sexual interest in a person or persons through words, gesture or touch.

The harassment or informal persecution of people at work is the last thing we might think of as funny. Yet studies show that sexual harassment, in particular, is often connected by its perpetrators with 'having a laugh' or 'just joking' (Wise and Stanley 1987). Sexual harassment may be perpetrated on men or women by people of the same or a different sex and it involves the expression of a sexual interest which may take either an apparently complimentary or an insulting form. Although men at work do experience sexual harassment (Lee 2000), the dominant form of the phenomenon is that in which men harass women and a key characteristic of such harassment at work is its treatment of women as primarily sexual beings rather than full persons (Pringle 1989) who can be treated in a derogatory and undermining fashion and, in effect, can be excluded from full participation in a male dominated workplace culture where men 'routinely act in concert' to 'mobilise masculinities at work' (Martin 2001).

Sexually harassing practices create considerable barriers to the movement of women into areas of work which were previously the preserve of men or into previously male dominated levels of authority in workplaces. The study by Collinson and Collinson (1996) of women in insurance sales showed how the 'exercise of gendered power by men' eventually led to the 're-exclusion of women' from this area of employment that women were beginning to penetrate. Women were harassed by managers, colleagues and clients and not only were these practices rationalised as 'rites of passage' or 'normalised' with comments to the effect that it was all 'a bit of fun', they involved blaming the victims for their own persecution – this giving harassment a 'vicious, self-justifying logic' whereby 'its reproduction was rationalised on the grounds that it already existed'. Women who cannot 'take the jokes' that men make are deemed unfit to work amongst those men.

Ethnographic research has an especially significant role in helping to 'illuminate the complex and occasionally interactive nature of harassment' which other studies have not covered (Chamberlain *et al.* 2008). The complex ways in which women deal with men's sexual conduct towards them at work are particularly well demonstrated by Denissen's (2010) ethnographic study in the building trade. This trade has a work culture which involves a range of sexual conduct including 'pornography, foul language, and sexualized stares, comments, gestures, pictures, and jokes'. Although the women had an awareness of sexual harassment law and workplace policies they actively interpreted sexual activities before reacting to them. They did this by taking into account not just legal definitions but such factors as 'the potential for harm, their co-worker's intentions, and the surrounding work climate'. Consequently they treated certain actions as not 'crossing the line', these including foul language, pornography, sexualised talk about other women, sexualised jokes, teasing and playing around (such as walking behind a tradeswoman with a pipe as a phallus). Denissen argues that these actions are not defined as sexual harassment 'because they are not personalized or because they occur within work relations that are seen as accepting and respectful'. In spite of this, 'research consistently demonstrates that, like other forms of sexual violence, individuals who experience workplace sexual harassment suffer significant psychological, health- and job-related consequences' (McDonald 2012).

Bullying at work

Repeated actions towards people at work which have the effect of humiliating and mentally distressing them.

Bullying at work (sometimes called 'mobbing') may well contain a sexual element but it can be seen as a broader phenomenon. As with sexual harassment bullying behaviour is something that must be related to the employee expectations which prevail in any given work setting as to whether certain actions are to be judged as 'bullying' or not. As Parzefall and Salin (2010) point out, 'different behaviours may be perceived as bullying in different organizational contexts, occupations and countries'. This is not to argue, however, that, as these authors put it, 'bullying is completely in the eye of the beholder'. Although it does not provide a completely unambiguous indicator of the crossing line for bullying, the definition provided earlier in this chapter recognises that bullying is an activity that has a deleterious psychological effect on those bullied, leading, as Martocci (2015) puts it, to the 'social destruction of self'. A characteristic of bullying that is commonly recognised by researchers is the victim's 'difficulty in defending themselves', this implying, as Branch *et al.* (2013) point out, the presence of an imbalance of power between the parties, whether this be a matter of formal or informal power.

Most people's first awareness of bullying occurs at school. As Vega and Comer (2005) say, 'Bullying is a pattern of destructive and deliberate demeaning of coworkers or subordinates that reminds one of the activities of the "schoolyard bully"'. In an private autobiographical account of his life from birth to his retirement from a senior management post, Leonard Hilton draws direct parallels between the bullies he met in his school playground, the lower and middle management bullies he saw bullying people once he went into industry and the senior managers bullying middle managers in the later part of his career (Watson 2009a). He shows how the techniques he developed as a schoolboy to deal with bullies were vitally helpful to him in his working and managerial career.

Although bullying in workplaces may be carried out on workers by co-workers, it is generally 'associated with differences in power and status' and it is 'superiors' who are the main culprits, with work organisations more likely to be sites of bullying when their culture incorporates 'an exaggerated emphasis on winning, greed, privilege, power and management by fear' Fineman (2003). Sometimes, organisations whose employment management (HR) practices are at what we characterised in Chapter 6 (p. 180) as the low-trust low-commitment end of the continuum, have been characterised as 'bullying organizations' and, as Hoel and Beale (2006) point out, the employment relations context must always be taken into account when examining workplace bullying. We must add to this the observation that harassment and bullying is not only perpetrated by organisational members upon each other. It is also liable to enter the worker–client relationship in service work. Workers in restaurants and hotels, in particular, are made vulnerable to abuse by customers, given the quasi-servant role they have to play and given the fact that this is often a matter of women providing service to men (Hall 1993; Guiffre and Williams 1994; Leidner 1993; Guerrier and Adib 2000).

Given the damage and distress that can be imposed upon people who are bullied at work, there is perhaps an inevitable tendency to regard bullying in psychological and individualistic ways. After noting that a psychological perspective dominated early research on bullying, Berlingieri (2015) argues that continuing research must locate workplace bullying 'within a framework of where power cannot be separated from social dimensions within and outside the workplace'. A powerful example of research following this emphasis is provided by Soylu and

Sheehy-Skeffington (2015), who report a study of intergroup bullying of members of low-status groups in Turkey. People who were interviewed spoke of bullying acts 'used to get rid of unwanted personnel' in order to avoid severance pay and of the removal of supporters of a former government from positions of political and economic influence. More fundamentally, bullying functioned as part of 'working towards the dominance of the sociocultural worldview of one political group over another'.

Cheating, fiddling and breaking things

The counter-cultures which grow up in work settings in part represent a challenge and an opposition to dominant interests and values, but in the end these cultures often enable the less privileged simply to adjust to their lack of freedom and privilege at work. To this extent they provide an integrative mechanism within work organisations.

LOOKING BACK <<<<<

Again we need to remember that organisations are constituted by the interplay between official and unofficial practices of participants and remind ourselves of the point made earlier in the present chapter that (unofficial) acts of organisational mischief can have unintended consequences as readily as can (official) managerial initiatives.

If we look at the type of pilfering and fiddling which Mars and Nicod (1984) observed among hotel waiters, it is clear that the money made – which is seen unofficially as 'a part of wages' – is a form of theft from the employer. Yet we need to bear in mind that these losses by theft may constitute very reasonable 'costs' from the employers' point of view. This is not only because they enable wage rates to be kept low but also because they constitute a form of reward which is not conducive to official negotiation. Because of this, unionisation is unlikely. By maintaining a particularly individualistic form of activity, the potential for collective organisation and opposition to managerial control is effectively reduced. Ditton's (1977) participant study of bread salesmen also showed how illegal gains can become part of the implicit contract of the employee. Here it is the money 'fiddled' from customers which makes up the wage and Ditton (1974) interpreted the way 'the firm's entry and training procedures are explicitly geared to teaching recruits how to rob the customer regularly and invisibly' as indicating how the fiddle helps solve certain managerial problems.

The officially deviant behaviour in these cases is very much tied into the implicit contract between the individual and the employer. In other cases the illegal activity may be more clearly group-based, as happens in the case of dockers (Mars 1974). Here the illegal activity and its control contribute to group solidarity, which may indeed contribute to its oppositional potential. Yet it is also likely, given the particular technology involved, to increase their technical efficiency, and hence the meeting of official goals. The social functions of illegal activity in the workplace were strongly emphasised by Henry (1978), who argues that the general trading in pilfered goods which goes on in many workplaces and which constitutes a 'hidden economy' involves deals which 'often have less to do with the material worth of the goods and more to do with fulfilling the expectations and moral obligations of the friendly relationship'. To obtain for a colleague something which 'fell off the back of a lorry' is as much to 'do a favour' for that colleague as it is to make money, we might say. The extent and variety of workplace fiddles is enormous (Snapshot 12.4).

Snapshot 12.4

Hawks, donkeys, wolves and vultures

In a survey by Mars (1982) fiddling is shown to be 'woven into the fabrics of people's lives' but in ways which vary with their occupation:

- Hawks are the entrepreneurs and professionals.
- Donkeys are those highly constrained by rules at the cashier's desk or beside a machine.
- Wolves operate in packs in places like the docks.
- Vultures operate in highly individualistic and competitive ways as befits their work as we see, for example, with travelling sales representatives.

Mars' typology is described as a seminal work by Thornthwaite and McGraw (2012) and they stress its continuing value, whilst noting that the 'occupational categories of workplace crime are now more blurred, with some jobs and fiddles spanning categories'. Although, technology has changed the nature of fiddling, they observe, 'new forms have emerged as old ones have disappeared'.

Workplace fiddles represent activities designed primarily to benefit individuals and groups at work. They may or may not threaten the dominant interests in the work organisation but, if they do, this is not their key purpose. With sabotage, however, such a purpose is more central.

> ### Sabotage
>
> The deliberate disruption of work flows within an organisation or the undermining of the conditions whereby dominant management purposes are readily achieved.

Destructive physical workplace behaviour is perhaps the most obvious form of sabotage. Such acts should not, however, be seen as meaningless.

Snapshot 12.5

Three types and levels of sabotage

Taylor and Walton (1971) identified three types of physical sabotage, each with a different degree of immediate disruptive intent:

- Attempts to reduce tension and frustration – for example, the ship builders who, about to be sacked on completion of a ship, got drunk and smashed the royal suite.
- Attempts to facilitate or ease the work process – for example, 'tapping' nuts into place in aircraft assembly.
- Attempts to assert control – for example, the 'collective bargaining by riot' indulged in by the Luddites.

Thus, even literally destructive behaviour can be seen as a part of the process whereby realities are negotiated, interests are defended, and the problems of 'getting through' the day at work are coped with. The most apparently senseless acts of vandalism have a rationale – a rationale which can only be appreciated as long as we note not only the conflicts but also the element of reciprocity between employer and employee expectations which develops in many 'low-trust' employment situations. This reciprocity is illustrated in the comments of a former shop steward in a car industry press shop who suggested that workers tend to feel that if they are treated like children they can act like children and hence behave irresponsibly (Brown 1977). Sabotage should not be associated with low-status work alone and may take forms other than that of engaging in physical destruction. Where managers and technocrats find themselves subjected to the types of control normally associated with manual workers, LaNuez and Jermier (1994) observe that we may find them: letting machines break down; allowing quality to fall; withholding critical information; revealing information to competitors; denigrating the product; speaking negatively about the organisation to employees;

falsifying data; engaging in actual physical destruction; for example, destroying information. LaNuez and Jermier suggest five macro-level forces which can lead to this: mergers and organisational restructuring; increased use of monitoring and other control strategies; technological changes that have replaced highly skilled with less skilled labour; deskilling and deprofessionalisation; displacement due to technological obsolescence.

Although the tendency is to think of sabotage as a matter of breaking rather than making things, the concept applies very significantly to service work. Lee and Ok (2014) suggest that 'retaliatory actions, altering the speed of service, playing pranks, and expressing frustration or aggression to customers' are examples of service sabotage and they argue that a significant majority of workers in the hotel industry report involvement in such activities. Individuals' motives vary from 'the benign, to the recalcitrant, to the, significantly less common, malicious' (Harris and Ogbonna 2012).

Helpful as it is to look at individual workers' motives for sabotaging services, to understand this, as well as fiddling and cheating sociologically, we clearly need to locate it in the social structure and culture of the setting in which it occurs. Quinney (1963) made this point when he showed how the level of prescription violations committed by retail pharmacists depended on the way the individual deals with a particular 'role conflict' built into the occupation; that between an orientation to professional values on the one hand and business values on the other. In effect, the extent to which those activities which are labelled 'deviant' are ultimately oppositional in society at large is questionable. 'Fiddling' can be seen as sharing many features with business and legitimate commerce itself and, like selling, it can be said to epitomise the 'capitalist spirit' (Ditton 1977). In the jargon of the deviance theorists, much workplace deviance is sub-cultural rather than contra-cultural: it reflects dominant values and norms as much as or more than it opposes them.

Rule manipulation

Supervisors and managers are necessarily implicated in many of the manifestations of conflict at work that we have considered here. Conflict and co-operation are two sides of the same coin and, at all levels, the breaking of official rules designed to help achieve official goals may, paradoxically, be necessary to meet these goals.

Writers who have used the insights of ethnomethodology in studying organisations have questioned the common assumption that rules determine behaviour. It is argued, instead, that individuals frequently

LOOKING BACK <<<<<

In Chapter 5, p. 165, we saw how supervisors operate an 'indulgency pattern' whereby rule-breaking is connived at to achieve employee co-operation, and we noted how bureaucratic procedures are sometimes broken or modified to get the job done.

Ethnomethodology was introduced in Chapter 2.

use rules as *resources* or as means to be employed in dealing with whatever situations arise and have to be coped with. Thus, Bittner (1967) shows how the police officers operating on skid-row do not simply enforce the law – even when they invoke it. Instead they 'merely use it as a resource to solve certain pressing practical problems in keeping the peace'. Zimmerman (1973) has shown how reception personnel in a public assistance organisation similarly draw on official rules and procedures to explain or justify the way they happen to cope with the day-to-day pressures and circumstances of their jobs. People cope with the conflicts and contradictions of their work situation through what Zimmerman (1973) calls 'the practicalities of rule use'. This is illustrated in Manning's (1977) discussion of the contradiction between:

- the 'myth' of police work, which sees it as controlling crime, and
- 'the reality' in which they maintain order (often without invoking the law) and help out people in trouble.

In the end, street-based police officers have to use their discretion and decide how they should apply general rules to particular situations. In this way, the individual working police officer finds a source of relative freedom from control by superiors. The 'fractional bargaining' indulged in by industrial supervisors (Kuhn 1961) and the condoning of prisoner rule-breaking by warders (Morris and Morris 1973) can be seen in a similar light.

Service work and defence of self

Given the strong cultural value put upon independence, autonomy and self-expression, problems are as likely to arise for many of those in work which involves taking instructions from customers or clients as they are for people who take orders from bosses.

LOOKING BACK <<<<<

The strategies used by prostitutes to maintain their self-respect were noted earlier (Chapters 8 and Chapter 9).

Korczynski (2009) talks here of a worker/customer/management triangle and raises the question of how the 'alienation' in service workers' relationship with customers relates to their alienation from their employers and managers. If service workers come to regard the customer as the primary alienating figure within their jobs, this may 'reorder the ways in which class conflict around the labour process is played out'; specifically, 'spontaneous, individualized conflict may be played out against the customer as the party who is experienced as the prime alienating figure rather than against the more distant management figure who plays such a central role in structuring the worker-customer relationship'. Also, the more potentially demeaning the service provided by the service worker, the greater is likely to be the tendency for contempt for the client to become an element of the particular work culture. Hence we get a variety of depersonalising titles used for the client: the 'mark', 'john', 'patsy', 'trick' or 'punter'. In all of these is an implication of naïveté on the part of the client. This implies superiority on the part of the worker, one which compensates for his or her superficial subservience.

Labelling of clients is not simply a mechanism used by service workers to maintain their self-respect in the face of implied servant status. The refining of the labelling process and the development of typologies of clients can play a useful technical role and help the individual cope with the exigencies of the job. Taxi drivers, for instance, find that their livelihood depends on how accurately they can 'size up' the ability of potential customers to pay. Hence, as Davis (1959) observes, they may utilise a typology of customers which ranges from the generously-tipping 'sport' through the 'blowhard', the 'businessman' and the 'live ones' to the 'stiffs' who give no tips and are passionately disliked. Correspondingly, Spradley and Mann (1975) describe the complex typology of customers used by cocktail waitresses (jocks, animals, regulars, bitches, annies, zoos, pigs, johnnies etc.) and note how, in particular, the most potentially antagonistic relationship which exists within the bar, that between waitresses and female customers, is reflected in the way 'bitches' almost become a synonym for 'women'. (We see something very similar in Snapshot 12.6.)

Every service occupation has its own types of 'awkward customer' and develops techniques to deal with them, whether it be the handing out of large quantities of low-value coins in the change of the shop assistant's over-choosy customer, or the adoption of ludicrously jargon-ridden language by the car-mechanic dealing with a know-all motorist. Sanctions play an important role in the achieving of client control; an integral element of service work, as Richman observes in noting how busmen tended to train their passengers into 'the correct attitude'

Customer labelling in the fish and chip shop

I remember when I worked in the fish and chip shop that it used to bother us a bit that we were slaving away over the hot fat, serving the punters, when most of the people who called into the shop were either on their way home from work, didn't work at all or were heading home after a good night on the beer. One of the ways we cheered ourselves up about this was to make sure that we labelled every customer with one kind of insulting label or another. I remember three of these. The FOBs were 'fat overeating slobs'. The TLTCs were 'too lazy to cook'. And the SUBS were people we thought were 'soaking up the beer'.

(1969) and how traffic wardens (later 'civil enforcement offices') accrue to themselves or lose honour through the 'street bargains' which they make with motorists (1983). The warden who bargains successfully with the motorist transforms them into a 'client', 'instilling a sense of social responsibility' towards the warden's purposes which gives legitimacy to the warden's activity. And ride operators at Disneyland have a variety of ways of punishing customers who offend them, including adjusting their seat belts so tight that the customer doubles over with pain (van Maanen 1991). Practices like this should not be seen, however, simply as acts of resistance against customers. They also represent a degree of protest against managerial control, in so far as the employing organisation is not one whose managers are likely to appreciate their workers hurting their customers. But, in a contrasting situation, Lankshear *et al.* (2001) observed call centre workers resisting managerial controls and applying their 'own definitions of professionalism and good performance' in order to give the customers better treatment than directly following managerial dictates would allow. Such are the complexities of the relationships and patterns of conflict and co-operation to be seen within the negotiated orders of all workplaces.

Summary

Alongside whatever organised 'industrial actions' still occur, there continues to occur a considerable variety of both group and individual actions of adjustment, resistance and organisational mischief. These can be seen across all types of work organisation and occupation and they range from daydreaming, joking, bullying, cheating, sabotaging, stealing and name-calling. And it is not a straightforward matter as to whether any one of these conflict-oriented actions hinders or helps corporate or managerial interests. The sociologist has to examine every kind of organisational action, whether it is taken by managers or workers, with recognition that, like everything else in societies and social life, the outcomes of human initiatives never straightforwardly fulfil the purposes for which they were chosen.

Concept guide and glossary

The main concepts used throughout the text are presented here together with a number of other sociological terms that the reader may come across in this and in other sociological works. The subject index can be used to link most entries to the main text.

Action research A form of combined research and consultancy in which the client receives help with problem-solving whilst the researcher/consultant is able to contribute the knowledge gained in the process to the academic community.

Aesthetic labour An element of work activity in which the worker is required to display certain physical, body-related appearances or attributes in order to complete work tasks in the way required by an employer who believes that these attributes will appeal to customers or clients.

Alienation A state of existence in which human beings are not fulfilling their humanity.

Ambiguity See also **Uncertainty**. A state in which the meaning of a situation or an event is unclear or confused and is therefore open to a variety of interpretations.

Anomie A form of social breakdown in which the norms that would otherwise prevail in a given situation cease to operate.

Artefacts Objects that have been created by human hands. They often play a symbolic role within organisational cultures as well as fulfilling a practical function. A worker's uniform is an artefact that plays both a practical and a symbolic role, for example.

Authority Power which has been 'legitimised' or made acceptable to those subject to it.

Automation The application of machinery which is controlled and co-ordinated by computerised programmes to tasks previously done by direct human effort.

Bounded rationality   See **Rationality, bounded.**

Bourgeoisie   A Marxian category which includes all of those in a capitalist society whose ownership of capital enables them to subsist without selling their labour power (their capacity to work). The term is sometimes used in a more general way to refer to a 'middle class'.

Bullying at work   Repeated actions towards people at work which have the effect of humiliating and mentally distressing them.

Bureaucracy   The control and co-ordination of work tasks through a hierarchy of appropriately qualified office holders, whose authority derives from their expertise and who rationally devise a system of rules and procedures that are calculated to provide the most appropriate means of achieving specified ends.

Business process re-engineering (BPR)   The restructuring of an organisation to focus on business processes rather than on business functions. Advanced management control information technologies are used together with teamworking and employee 'empowerment'.

Call centre work   Work in which operators utilise computer terminals to process information relating to telephone calls which are made and/or received, these calls being mediated by various computer-based filtering, allocational and monitoring devices.

Capitalism   See **Industrial capitalism.**

Capitalist labour process   The design, control and monitoring of work tasks and activities by managers acting as agents of the capital owning class to extract surplus value from the labour activity of employees.

Career   A sequence of social positions filled by a person throughout their life or through an aspect of their life such as their involvement in work.

Class   An individual's class position is a matter of the part which they play (or the person upon whom they are dependent plays) within the division of labour of a society and the implications which this has for their access to those experiences, goods and services which are scarce and valued in that society.

Class consciousness   A state of awareness of their common interests and situation by the members of an objectively existing social class.

Classical administrative principles   Universally applicable rules of organisational design – structural and cultural – widely taught and applied, especially in the first half of the twentieth century.

Closed shop   An arrangement whereby work in a particular setting is exclusively carried out by members of a specified trade union. Pre-entry closed shops required workers to be union members before they could be recruited whereas the new worker could join the union after entering the job in the case of the post-entry closed shop.

Closure, social   The process whereby a group seeks to gain or defend its advantages over other groups by closing its ranks to those it defines as outsiders.

Collective bargaining   A method of agreeing work conditions and rewards through a process of negotiation between employer representatives and the representatives of collectively organised employees.

Community   Often used to mean more or less the same as 'society'. The word generally implies a smaller entity than does 'society', however. The essence of the idea of community is that people feel strongly aware of belonging to it and accept its traditions. It is small-scale and intimate and is characterised by face-to-face relationships.

Concepts   Working definitions that are chosen or devised for use in scientific analysis. They are the way scientists define their terms for the purpose of a specific investigation. They therefore differ from dictionary definitions – these tending to have a more general and therefore much less precise applicability.

Conflict   A phenomenon that occurs at two levels. Conflict *at the level of interests* exists where there is a difference between different parties (employers and employees, say, or workers and customers) over desired outcomes; and conflict *at the level of behaviour* comes about when parties seeking different outcomes either directly clash over those differences and engage in open dispute or indirectly express their differences through such gestures as acting destructively or co-operating in a sullen or grudging manner.

Conjugal roles   The parts played in the household by husbands and wives.

Contingencies   In organisation theory: those circumstances which influence the ways in which organisations are structured. Examples are the size of the organisation, the nature of the technology used or the state of the organisation's environment.

Contradictions   Tendencies within a social or organisational structure for certain principles on which that structure is based to clash with each other in a way that undermines that structure.

Convergence thesis   Societies which industrialise become increasingly alike in their social, political and cultural characteristics as well as their work organisations.

Co-operatives, worker   Work enterprises jointly owned and controlled by those who work in them.

Corporatism   A political system in which major decisions, especially with regard to the economy, are made by the state in close association with employer, trade union and other pressure group organisations.

Cultural capital   The various linguistic and social competences derived from and certificated by the education system and manifested in a certain manner, ethos, knowhow and set of aspirations.

Culture The system of meanings which are shared by members of a society, organisation or other human grouping, and which define what is good and bad, right and wrong and what are the appropriate ways for members of that grouping to think and behave.

Deskilling An approach to the redesign of jobs which involves a lowering of the skill levels required from those filling the job than had previously been the case.

Determinism A way of thinking in which the causal factors behind whatever is being considered are seen to lie outside of human agency.

Deviance The failure, deliberate or otherwise, of people to comply with the rules, standards or norms of any group, organisation or society in which they are involved.

Dialectic The interplay between two potential opposites which leads to a third possibility. For example, the interplay between individual initiative and social constraint (which are often seen as opposing phenomena) can be seen as leading to a third phenomenon – 'society'.

Differentiation The process in which a society or an organisation is divided into specialised parts which contribute to the functioning of the whole.

Direct and indirect management control attempts Managers, in striving to achieve control over people's work efforts, may lean towards the adoption of either direct or indirect controls. *Direct controls* involve close supervision and monitoring of activities, tight rules, highly prescribed procedures, centralised structures, low-commitment culture, low-trust culture, adversarial culture and a tightly bureaucratic structure and culture. And *indirect controls* involve the 'empowering' or giving task discretion to workers, loose rules, flexible procedures, decentralised structures, high-commitment culture, high-trust culture, an emphasis on the mutuality of interests and a loosely bureaucratic structure and culture.

Dirty work An occupational activity which plays a necessary role in a society but which is regarded in some respects as morally doubtful.

Discourses Sets of concepts, statements, terms and expressions which constitute ways of talking or writing about a particular aspect of life, thus framing the way people understand and act with respect to those areas of existence.

Division of labour The allocation of work tasks to various groups or categories of individual. The **social division of labour** is the allocation of work tasks at the level of society, typically into trades and occupations; and the **technical division of labour** is task specialisation within an occupation or broad work task.

Domestic labour   Household tasks such as cooking, cleaning, shopping and looking after dependent young, old or sick members of the household.

Dominant coalition   The grouping of individuals within an organisation who effectively have greater influence over events than any other grouping.

Dualism   The effective division of an economy into two major parts; typically a prosperous and stable 'core' sector of enterprises and jobs and a 'peripheral' sector which is relatively and systematically disadvantaged.

Effort bargain   See **Implicit contract**.

Embourgeoisement   The adoption by working-class people of the attitudes and lifestyle of middle-class groups.

Emergent life orientations   The meanings attached by people at a particular stage of their life to their personal and social circumstances; meanings which predispose them to act in particular ways with regard to the future, including their relationship to work and consumption.

Emotional labour   An element of work activity in which the worker is required to display certain emotions in order to complete work tasks in the way required by an employer.

Emotions   Feelings are sensations relating to a psychological state that are felt bodily and emotions are the way these sensations are culturally interpreted.

Empirical enquiry   That part of social science activity which involves observation, experiment or other forms of data collection as opposed to the conceptual, theoretical and interpretative work.

Empty labour   Activities engaged in by workers that involve withdrawal from tasks which they are formally engaged to undertake in the workplace; such activities range from groups of people playing cards on a nightshift to individuals linking to the internet for personal purposes ('cyberloafing') when they believe they are unobserved or ignored (a 'blind eye' being turned) by work supervisors.

Enacted environment   Organisational environments exist for members of organisations by virtue of the interpretations they make of what is occurring 'outside' the organisation and the way their own actions influence or shape those occurrences.

Entrepreneurial action   The making of adventurous, creative or innovative exchanges (or 'deals') between the entrepreneurial actor's home 'enterprise' and other parties with which the enterprise trades.

Ethnography   A style of social science writing which draws upon the writer's close observation of and involvement with people in a particular social setting and relates the words spoken and the practices observed or experienced to the overall cultural framework within which they occurred.

Ethnomethodology   The study of how ordinary members of society in their everyday lives make the world meaningful by achieving a sense of 'taken-for-grantedness'.

Financialisation   A process whereby financial institutions come to dominate economic activity with increasing emphasis on the trading of financial assets (shares, bonds, options, mortgages and other debts) as opposed to the exchange of goods and services produced in the traditional economy.

Flexibility for long-term adaptability   The ability to make rapid and effective innovations through the use of job designs and employment policies that encourage people to use their discretion, innovate and work in new ways for the sake of the organisation – as circumstances require. This fits with *indirect control* managerial practices.

Flexibility for short-term predictability   The ability to make rapid changes through the use of job designs and employment policies that allow staff to be easily recruited and trained or easily laid off – as circumstances require. This fits with *direct control* managerial practices.

Flexible firm   A pattern of employment in which an organisation divides its workforce into *core* elements who are given security and high rewards in return for a willingness to adapt, innovate and take on new skills, and *peripheral* elements who are given more specific tasks and less commitment of continuing employment and skill enhancement.

Flexible specialisation   An approach to employment and work organisation which offers customised products to diversified markets, building trusting and co-operative relationships both with employees, who use advanced technologies in a craft way, and other organisations within a business district and its associated community.

Fordism   A pattern of industrial organisation and employment policy in which (a) mass production techniques and an associated deskilling of jobs is combined with (b) treatment of employees which recognises that workers are also consumers whose earning power and consumption attitudes – as well as their workplace efficiency – affect the success of the enterprise.

Function   An action or an institution has a function within a social system if it contributes towards the maintenance or adaptation of that system. A 'dysfunction' exists when the effect is one 'harmful' to that system.

Functionalism   An approach within sociology which explains aspects of societies or organisations in terms of the contribution they make to the functioning of that society or organisation as a whole.

Gig economy   Arrangements whereby independent workers contract with organisations and personal customers to fulfil short-term engagement via internet 'job sites', 'talent/professional/freelancing/web conferencing platforms' and remote-working apps.

Globalisation   A trend in which the economic, political and cultural activities of people in different countries increasingly influence each other and become interdependent.

Habitus   Bourdieu's notion of a set of predispositions or inclinations to action which individuals develop and internalise over time in the light of their relationship to the power structure and culture of the society in which they live.

Harassment   See **Sexual harassment**.

High-performance work systems   High discretion, skill and collaborative problem-solving is applied in a team-oriented way and is rewarded with relatively high pay, security and the provision of high-quality training.

Human relations   The term is used by sociologists almost exclusively to refer to a 'school' of industrial sociology and to managerial styles which follow its general recommendations. The school is that associated with the Hawthorne experiments carried out in the pre-war years in America. Its emphasis is on the ways in which the 'social needs' of workers are met or are not met in the work situation.

Human Resource Management (HRM)   The managerial utilisation of the efforts, knowledge, capabilities and committed behaviours which people contribute to work organisations as part of an employment exchange (or more temporary contractual arrangement) to bring about the completion of work tasks in a way which enables the organisation to continue into the future.

The HRM expression is sometimes used in a generic way (as above) to refer to all managerial activities that are concerned with employment (or 'personnel') aspects of work organisations. But it is also used to refer to one particular style of employment management, that involving a 'high-commitment human resourcing strategy'. In such strategies, employers seek a close and psychologically involving relationship with workers; they build opportunities for personal development into people's careers; people's employment is expected to continue over a longer-term period, potentially covering a variety of different types of work, and workers are given discretion about how tasks are carried out. To complicate matters further, the HRM term is also used to refer to the study of employment management activities (giving us university departments, professors and journals of HRM).

Humour See **Workplace humour**.

Hybrid professional–managerial roles Positions within organisations usually found at the interface between an established professional group (like hospital doctors) and the wider organisation (a hospital or hospital group for example) in which 'professional' workers take on managerial or administrative tasks of coordinating professional/expert activities and organisational/leadership ones.

Ideal type A model of a phenomenon or a situation which extracts its essential or 'pure' elements. It represents what the item or institution (capitalism, bureaucracy, instrumental work orientation, for example) would look like if it existed in a pure form.

Identity The conception which each individual develops, in relation to others, of who and what they are. There are two components of the idea of human identity: *self-identity* being an individual's own notion of who and what they are; and *social-identities;* cultural or discursive notions of who or what any individual might be.

Identity work The process whereby people strive to shape a relatively coherent and distinctive notion of personal self-identity and struggle to come to terms with and, within limits, to influence the various social-identities which pertain to them in the various milieux in which they live their lives.

Ideology/group ideology A set of ideas which are located within a particular social group and which fulfils functions for that group. It helps defend, justify and further the interests of the group with which it is associated.

Implicit contract The tacit agreement between an employed individual and an employing organisation about what the employee will 'put in' to their job and the rewards and benefits for which this will be exchanged.

Incorporation The process of directing the political and economic activities of groups who may threaten a social order or system so that they operate within that order instead of threatening it. This is often associated with the 'institutionalising' of conflict.

Indulgency pattern The ignoring of selected rule infringements by supervisors in return for those being supervised allowing supervisors to call for co-operation in matters which, strictly speaking, they could refuse.

Industrial capitalism A form of society in which privately owned large-scale and/or complex technologies are widely applied (with state support) to the pursuit of economic efficiency on a basis whereby the capacity for work of the members of some groups is sold to or otherwise acquired by profit-seeking social groups who control and organise it in such a way that the latter groups maintain relative advantage with regard to those resources which are scarce and generally socially valued.

Industrial relations   The activities and institutions which jointly regulate relationships between employers and groups of collectively organised employees.

Informal economy   An area of economic exchange in which work, legal or illegal, is done for gain but is not officially 'declared' for such purposes as taxation.

Informating work   ICTs can 'record' and hence can 'play back' or make visible the processes behind the operations that were once deep in the minds of the people doing that work.

Information and Communication Technologies (ICTs)   The combination of microelectronic and computing technologies with telecommunications to manipulate human information.

Institution, social   A regularly occurring and therefore normal pattern of actions and relationships.

Institutional entrepreneurs   Individuals with significant resources and interests who can stand back from existing institutional arrangements in order to create new institutional patterns or change existing ones.

Institutional logics   The sets of values, rules, assumptions and practices associated with key institutions of a society (such as family, the market, politics, religion, bureaucratic administration) which have been socially constructed over time and through which patterns of social organisation and human activity are shaped and given meaning.

Institutional tensions   Tendencies within a social or organisational structure for different institutional logics to clash with each other in a way that, if not managed, may undermine that structure.

Instrumentalism   An orientation to work which treats it as a means towards ends other than ones to do with work itself. It typically involves a primary concern with the money to be earned.

Interpretivism and the interpretive principle   Interpretiv*ism*/ construction*ism*/constructiv*ism* works on the assumption that there are no social realities beyond the processes whereby people observe and 'socially construct' the world. This is a non-realist position. However, realists may incorporate the interpretive principle into their realism, recognising that interpretive or social construction processes *play a part* in bringing about a social world which then has a reality of its own.

Intersectionality   The ways in which various categories of social difference – gender, ethnicity, class, nationality, sexuality and so on – intersect with each other in processes of identity-shaping, always within broader institutional patterns of power distribution, discrimination and inequality.

Jargon, work related   Language use and terms that are peculiar to a specific organisational, occupational or technical context.

Job design   The shaping of particular jobs, especially with regard to how narrow or broad the tasks associated with those jobs are and the extent to which jobholders exercise discretion in carrying out those tasks.

Job enrichment   The expansion of the scope of jobs by such means as the re-integration of maintenance or inspection tasks; an extension of the work cycle; an increased degree of delegation of decision-making by job holders.

Just-in-time (JIT) production processes   A way of organising production processes so that no buffer stocks are held in the factory, with materials and components only being delivered immediately before they are required.

Labour market, internal   The creation by an employer of a stable and well-rewarded labour force through a policy of internal promotion and training.

Labour market segmentation   The effective division of an economy into different parts. In its early stages this tends to be dualistic, with a prosperous and stable core or primary sector of enterprises and jobs existing alongside a 'peripheral' or secondary sector which is relatively and systematically disadvantaged. The tendency is for this dualism to be followed by segmentation into further divisions.

Labour movement   A coming together of such bodies as trade unions and associated political parties to represent the interests which employed people as a whole are believed to hold in common.

Labour process   See **Capitalist labour process**.

Lean production   A combining of teamworking with automated technologies. Workers are required both to initiate 'continual improvements' in quality and to ensure that every task is got 'right first time' and completed to a demanding 'just-in-time' schedule.

Legends, organisational   Narratives about events that might or might not have happened in the organisation's past, which have a sense of wonder about them and which point to activities that the listener is encouraged to admire or deplore.

Leisure   Those activities which people pursue for pleasure and which are not a necessary part of their business, employment or domestic management obligations.

Life–chances   The ability to gain access to scarce and valued goods and services such as a home, food and education.

Logic of corporate management   The logic of corporate management is one of shaping exchange relationships to satisfy the demands of the various constituencies, inside and outside the organisation, so that continued support in terms of resources such as labour, custom, investment, supplies and legal approval is obtained and the organisation enabled to survive into the long term.

Management   Work tasks and ideas that are primarily concerned with directing various aspects of organisations rather than with carrying out the tasks that make up the main work of the organisation.

Managerial manipulation of worker implicit contracts   The attempts by managers to 'motivate' workers not by 'meeting needs' as in classic 'motivation theory' but by negotiating with and persuading workers that a particular bundle of rewards that is on offer is a fair and reasonable return for the bundle of 'efforts' that the management is asking them to put in.

Managerialism   A social and political ideology which treats most if not all social, political and cultural problems in contemporary societies as soluble by the application of managerial techniques and practices. Social problems and social welfare are *manageable* administrative-technical matters rather than political, ideological or value matters.

Managerialist thesis   The claim that the people who manage or 'direct' the corporations of modern societies have taken control away from those allegedly separate interests who own wealth.

Methodology   A term often misused to refer to research techniques and which, properly, refers to the philosophical issues raised by the attempt to investigate the world scientifically and, in particular, issues relating to the assumptions that researchers make about the nature of societies, organisation and individuals.

Micropolitics   The political processes that occur within organisations as individuals, groups and organisational 'sub-units' compete for access to scarce and valued material and symbolic resources.

Mobility, social   The movement of people between different positions in the pattern of inequality of any society. It may be intra-generational (the individual changes their position within their own life career) or inter-generational (where the individual moves into a position which differs from that of their parents). Movement may be upwards or downwards.

Models   Analytical schemes which simplify reality by selecting certain phenomena and suggesting particular relationships between them.

Modernism   An approach to dealing with the world based on the application of rational and scientific analysis to social, political, economic and industrial institutions in the belief that this can lead to greater human control over the world and thus bring about general progress in the condition of humankind.

Myths, organisational   Narratives about events that are unlikely ever to have happened but which illustrate some important 'truth' about life in the organisation.

Narratives and stories   Narratives are accounts of events in the world which are organised in a time-related sequence. Stories are a more highly developed form of narrative: they are temporally sequenced accounts of events which unfold through plots involving the interplay of characters with interests, motives, emotions and moralities.

Negotiated order   The pattern of activities which emerge over time as an outcome of the interplay of the various interests, understandings, reactions and initiatives of the individuals and groups involved in an organisation.

Non-standard/contingent employment   Employment in which contracts between employers and employees are short term and unstable with the worker taking part-time, temporary and, sometimes, multiple jobs. The work is sometimes at home rather than in an organisationally located workplace with there being little by way of employment benefits.

Norm, social   Part of the underlying pattern of social life – the standards to which people are expected to conform or the rules of conduct whose infringement may result in sanctions intended to encourage conformity.

Occupation   Membership of an occupation involves engagement on a regular basis in a part or the whole of a range of work tasks which are identified under a particular heading or title by both those carrying out these tasks and by a wider public.

Occupational career   The sequence of positions through which the member of an occupation typically passes during the part of their life which they spend in that occupation.

Occupational community   A form of local social organisation in which people's work and non-working lives are both closely identified with members of the occupation in which they work.

Occupational culture   A more developed version of the publicly available occupational identity (next entry) which is used within the occupation to provide ideas, values, norms, procedures and artefacts to shape occupational activities and enable members to value the work that they do.

Occupational identity The broad understanding in a society of what activities occur within a particular occupation and what contribution that occupation makes to society.

Occupational ideology an expression of an occupational identity (above entry) devised by an occupational group, or by its spokespersons, to legitimate the pursuit of the group members' common occupationally related interests.

Occupational recruitment The typical processes and routes of entry followed by members of an occupation.

Occupational segregation A pattern of occupations in which some are predominantly male and others female. *Horizontal segregation* describes the tendency for male and female work to be separated into types of occupational activity, whilst *vertical segregation* sees gender differentiation in who takes the higher level and who takes the lower level jobs within an occupation.

Occupational socialisation The process whereby individuals learn about the norms, values, customs and beliefs associated with an occupation which they have joined so that they are able to act as a full member of that occupation.

Occupational structure The pattern in a society which is created by the distribution of the labour force across the range of existing types of work or occupation.

Official and unofficial aspects of organisations *Official* aspects of organisations are the rules, values and activities that are part of the formally managerial-sanctioned policies and procedures. *Unofficial* aspects are the rules, values and activities that people at all levels in the organisation develop but which do not have formal managerial sanction.

Official control apparatus of an organisation The set of roles, rules, structures, value statements, cultural symbols, rituals and procedures managerially designed to co-ordinate and control work activities.

Organisation man A male executive employee whose whole life is moulded by the corporation for whom he works.

Organisational culture The set of meanings and values shared by members of an organisation that defines the appropriate ways for people to think and behave with regard to the organisation.

Organisational identities The understanding(s) of what an organisation 'is' or 'is like' among members of the various parties, inside and outside the organisation, who have dealings with that organisation. One element of this is the 'formal identity' manifested in the organisation's registered trading name(s) and legal status.

Organisational mischief Activities occurring within the workplace that (a) according to the official structure, culture and rules of the organisation, 'should not happen' and (b) contain an element of challenge to the dominant modes of operating or to dominant interests in the organisation.

Organisational principle of work structuring Work is patterned at the outcome of institutional arrangements in which some people conceive of and design work and then recruit, pay, co-ordinate and control the efforts of other people to complete work tasks.

Organisational structure The regular or persisting patterns of action that give shape and a degree of predictability to an organisation.

Organisations See **Work organisations**.

Orientation to work The meaning attached by individuals to their work which predisposes them to think and act in particular ways with regard to that work.

Paradigm A 'model' in the very broadest sense in science which includes basic ideas about how investigations should proceed as well as what assumptions are to be made about the relationships between phenomena.

Paradox of consequences The tendency for the means chosen to achieve ends in social life to undermine or defeat those ends.

Paradox of organising The tendency for the means adopted by organisational officials/managers to achieve particular goals to fail to achieve these goals since these 'means' involve human beings who have goals of their own which may not be congruent with those of the managers.

Participative observation A research practice in which the investigator gets 'close to the action' by joining the group or organisation being studied – as either a full or partial member – and both participating in and observing activities, as well as asking questions, taking part in conversations and reading relevant documents.

Patriarchy The system of interrelated social structures and cultural practices through which men exploit women.

Pluralism Social scientific perspectives which emphasise the multiplicity of interest groups within societies or organisations. It is often, unreasonably, used to refer to what is properly seen as just one type of pluralist perspective – that in which the various interest groupings in society are seen as being more or less equally powerful. See also **Radical pluralist frame of reference**.

Political economy Social scientific approaches which emphasise the power dimensions of social life and how these, together with the ways in which production is organised, influence whatever particular phenomena are being considered.

Population ecology   A type of organisation theory which concentrates on how organisations adapt and evolve in order to survive within the general population of organisations of which they are a part.

Portfolio or **boundaryless careers**   A pattern of working in which the individual does not enter an employment relationship with a single work organisation but is engaged by a variety of different organisations or clients, each for a segment of their working time.

Positivism   The term is generally used to refer to a position which sees social science and the natural or physical sciences as equivalent and therefore as amenable to the same basic kind of investigative procedure. It sees the social world as an objective reality external to those who study it and seeks explanations in the form of general theories or *covering laws* which can be used to make predictions. For some, the essence of the positivism is the idea of social science as a means of predicting and therefore the controlling of social institutions and events.

Post-Fordism   A pattern of industrial organisation and employment policy in which skilled and trusted labour is used continuously to develop and customise products for small markets.

Post-industrial society   A type of economically advanced social order in which the centrally important resource is knowledge, service work has largely replaced manufacturing employment, and knowledge-based occupations play a privileged role.

Postmodernism   An approach to the world which rejects attempts to build systematic explanations of history and human activity and which, instead, concentrates on the ways in which human beings go about 'inventing' their worlds, especially through language and cultural innovation.

Postmodernity   An alleged state into which the world is moving which departs from the key organising principles of modernity.

Power   The capacity of an individual or group to affect the outcome of any situation so that access is achieved to whatever resources are scarce and desired within a society or part of a society.

Pragmatism   A school of philosophy originally developed by Charles Peirce, William James and John Dewey, which treats reality as the circumstances with which people have to come to terms in order to cope in the world. Knowledge which is created about 'how the world works' in different spheres of human life can only ever be relatively 'true'. The truth of knowledge is judged by the extent to which it informs people's attempts to pursue their various projects in the sphere of life to which the knowledge relates.

Precariat A section of society, which might or might not be regarded as a social class, who have little economic, social or psychological security or predictability in their working lives and, hence, in their whole lives generally. The grouping is growing in size and range, to include not only members of what some termed an 'underclass' but also people, often with good educational credentials, who are pushed into artificial self-employment work, typically in digitally oriented work.

Problematic, A This is similar to a paradigm (p. 403) but the term emphasises the role of certain problems or issues which give a focus to the process of selecting phenomena to concentrate on. A problematic is thus a set of linked concepts focusing on particular problems or issues.

Productive co-operation The achievement, in the light of the tendency of people involved in organisations to have their own projects, interests and priorities, of a degree of working together that ensures that tasks carried out in the organisation's name are fulfilled to sufficient a level to enable the organisation to continue in existence.

Professionalisation A process followed by certain occupations to increase its members' status, relative autonomy and rewards and influence through such activities as setting up a professional body to control entry and practice, establishing codes of conduct, making claims of altruism and a key role in serving the community.

Professions Occupations which have been relatively successful in gaining high status and autonomy in certain societies on the basis of a claimed specialist expertise over which they have gained a degree of monopoly control.

Proletariat This category, in the basic Marxian scheme, includes all of those who lack sufficient capital upon which they can subsist and who, therefore, are forced to 'sell their labour power' (capacity to work) on the market.

Psychologism A tendency to explain social behaviour solely in terms of the psychological characteristics of individuals.

Radical pluralist frame of reference Such a perspective recognises the plurality of groups and interests in society (and welcomes social pluralism *in principle*) whilst observing the more basic patterns of power and inequality which tend to shape, as well as be shaped by, the plurality of groups and interests.

Rationalisation A trend in social change whereby traditional or magical criteria of action are replaced by technical, calculative or scientific criteria.

Rationality and change The criterion of rationality involves submitting decisions and actions to constant calculative scrutiny and produces a continuous drive towards change.

Rationality, bounded Human reasoning and decision-making is restricted in its scope by the fact that human beings have both perceptual and information-processing limits.

Rationality, instrumental The calculated choice of appropriate means to achieve specific ends.

Realism, social scientific The assumption that social reality exists independently of how people observe and make sense of it.

Reification/personification An error in which an abstraction is treated as a 'thing' or a living person. The error is committed, for example, when one talks of 'society' or an 'organisation' *doing* something – or *making* people act in certain ways.

Resistance See **Organisational mischief**.

Responsible autonomy An approach to the design of work tasks which gives discretion to those doing the work on the understanding that they will choose to accept the managerial trust put in them and perform the tasks in accordance with managerial priorities. It can be contrasted with 'direct controls'. See **Direct and indirect management control attempts**.

Restructuring of work The changing patterns of work experience, organisational and occupational activity both resulting from and contributing to economic, political and cultural changes unfolding across the world.

Rites, organisational Rituals that are relatively formally (though not necessarily officially) organised and pre-planned.

Rituals, organisational Patterns of behaviour that regularly occur in particular circumstances or at particular times in an organisation.

Role, social People are said to be playing a role in social life whenever they act in a situation according to well-defined expectations.

Sabotage The deliberate disruption of work flows within an organisation or the undermining of the conditions whereby dominant management purposes are readily achieved.

Sagas, organisational Narratives with a series of events that are said to have unfolded over time and which constitute an important part of the organisation's history.

Science A formal, systematic and precise approach to building up a body of knowledge and theory which is rigorous in examining propositions about the social world in the light of available evidence. Sociology is a science because it makes generalisations as systematically as possible in the light of available evidence.

Scientific management An approach to workplace organisation and job design associated with F. W. Taylor which is based on the principle of giving as much initiative about how tasks are done as possible to managerial experts who define precisely how each detailed aspect of every job is to be carried out.

Self-actualisation　'To become more and more what one is, to become everything that one is capable of becoming' (Maslow 1943).

Semi-autonomous work-groups　A work-group or 'team' in which individual jobs are grouped to focus work activities on an overall 'whole task', with group members being fully trained and equipped so that they can be given discretion over how the task is completed.

Sexual harassment　Unwanted and offensive expressions of sexual interest in a person or persons through words, gesture or touch.

Shop steward/union workplace representative　A worker representative and 'lay' trade union official who represents to management the interests of fellow employees who elect them as their workplace spokesperson.

Social construction of reality　The process in which people, through cultural interaction, give meaning to the world – a world that may well exist beyond language but which can only be known and communicated by people through language-based processes of cultural interpretation and sensemaking.

Socialisation　The process whereby individuals learn about the norms, values, customs and beliefs of a group, occupation, organisation or society.

Society　The broad pattern of social, economic, cultural and political relationships within which people lead their lives, typically but not exclusively in the modern world, as members of the same nation state.

Sociology　The study of the relationships which develop between human beings as they organise themselves and are organised by others in societies and how these patterns influence and are influenced by the actions and interactions of people and how they make sense of their lives and identities.

Socio-technical systems　An approach to work design in which the technical and the social/psychological aspects of the overall workplace are given equal weight and are designed at the same time to *take each other into account.*

Standard employment　Employment in which the contract between the employer and employee is understood to be one in which the employee is likely to stay with the employer over the long term at a particular location, putting in a working day and week which is normal for that industry and receiving regular pay and the protection of pension and sick pay benefits. See also **Non-standard employment**.

State   That set of institutions which, in a modern society, typically includes government, parliament, civil service, educational and welfare apparatuses, the police, military and judiciary.

Status, social   That aspect of social inequality whereby different positions are awarded different degrees of prestige or honour.

Stratification, social   The patterns underlying the inequalities which exist between people in a society and form 'layers' on the basis of such factors as class or status.

Stress   A sense of distress arising because of pressures experienced in certain social or economic circumstances that render the sufferer emotionally, and sometimes physically, incapable of continuing to behave in the ways expected of them in those circumstances.

Strike   The collective withdrawal from work of a group of employees to exert pressure on the employer over any issue in which the two sides have a difference.

Structuration   Ongoing processes in which individual initiatives are interwoven into the patterns of human interaction which sometimes constrain and sometimes enable those initiatives.

Subjective career   The way an individual understands or makes sense of the way they have moved or are moving through various social positions or stages in the course of their life, or part of their life.

Subjectivity   The notion that individuals are continually developing, in the light of the discourses surrounding them, of who they are and how they fit into the social world.

Symbol   Any act, word, sound or object acts as a symbol when it stands for 'something else' that is not visible, audible or tangible.

Symbolic interactionism   The study of social interaction which focuses on how people develop their concept of *self* through processes of communication in which symbols such as words, gestures and dress allow people to understand the expectations of others.

Systems thinking   A way of viewing social entities such as societies or organisations as if they were self-regulating bodies exchanging energy and matter with their environment in order to survive.

Taylorism   See **Scientific management**.

Teamworking   A form of group-based work activity in which a degree of discretion is left to group members, acting in a co–operative manner, about how they perform the tasks allocated to them.

Technological implications   A way of thinking about technology which sees it as determining, or at least closely constraining, the way in which tasks are organised with this, in turn, significantly influencing the attitudes and behaviour of workers.

Technology The tools, machines and control devices used to carry out tasks and the principles, techniques and reasoning which accompanies them.

Teleworking Work which is carried out away from the location of an employer or work contractor using electronic information and computing technology in either or both (a) carrying out the work tasks (b) communicating with the employing or contracting organisation with regard to those tasks.

Theories Systematic generalisations about 'how the world works' resulting from the application of scientific procedures.

Total Quality Management (TQM) An approach to the production of goods and services in which employees at all levels focus on 'satisfying customers', use statistical and other techniques to monitor their work and seek continuous improvement in the processes used and the quality of what is produced.

Trade unions Associations of employees formed to improve their ability to negotiate working conditions and rewards with employers and, sometimes, to represent common interests within the political sphere beyond the workplace.

Trust relations *High-trust* relations are said to exist in an organisation when employees and managers both feel able to take it for granted that broad mutual expectations established between them will be met and continue to be met, without the need closely to specify those expectations or to monitor their fulfilment. When this is lacking, *low-trust* relations are said to prevail.

Uncertainty See also **Ambiguity**. A state in which the understanding of a future situation or event is unclear or confused and is therefore open to a variety of interpretations.

Values Notions of what is good and bad, right and wrong, within a society or a part of a society.

Virtual or networked organisations Sets of work arrangements in which those undertaking tasks carried out under a corporate name largely relate to each other through electronic communications rather than through face-to-face interaction.

Work The carrying out of tasks which enable people to *make a living* within the social and economic context in which they are located.

Work design See also **Job design; Job enrichment**. General principles about how narrow or broad the tasks associated with jobs should be and the extent to which jobholders should use discretion in carrying out those tasks.

Work ethic A set of values which stresses the importance of work to the identity and sense of worth of the individual and which encourages an attitude of diligence, duty and a striving for success in the mind of the worker.

Work organisations   Social and technical arrangements and under-standings in which a number of people come together in a formalised and contractual relationship where the actions of some are directed by others towards the achievement of work tasks carried out in the organisation's name.

Work orientation   See **Orientation to work**.

Workplace humour   All forms of communication occurring in the work situation which create within people feelings of amusement and a predisposition to express that emotion through laughter.

Bibliography

Abell, P. and Reyniers, D. (2000) 'Review article: on the failure of social theory', *British Journal of Sociology*, 51: 739–750.

Abott, A. (1988) *The System of Professions: An Essay on the Division of Expert Labour*, Chicago: University of Chicago Press.

Ackers, P. and Wilkinson, A. (2008) 'Industrial relations and the social sciences', in P. Blyton, N. Bacon, J. Fiorito and E. Heery (eds), *The Sage Handbook of Industrial Relations*, London: Sage: 53–68.

Ackroyd, S. and Fleetwood, S. (2000) *Realist Perspectives on Management and Organisations*, London: Routledge.

Ackroyd, S. and Thompson, P. (1999) *Organisational Misbehaviour*, London: Sage.

Ackroyd, S. and Thompson, P. (2016) 'Unruly subjects: misbehaviour in the workplace', in S. Edgell, H. Gottfried, and W. Granter (eds), *The Sage Handbook of the Sociology of Work and Employment*, London: Sage: 185–204.

Ackroyd, S., Batt, R., Thompson, P. and Tolbert, P. (eds) (2005) *The Oxford Handbook of Work and Organization*, Oxford: Oxford University Press.

Adams, T.L. (2014) 'Sociology of professions: international divergences and research directions', *Work, Employment and Society*, 29(1): 154–165.

Aglietta, M. (1979) *A Theory of Capitalist Regulation: The U.S. Experience*, London: New Left Books.

Ailon-Souday, G. and Kunda, G. (2003) 'The local selves of global workers: the social construction of national identity in the face of organizational globalization', *Organization Studies*, 24(7): 1073–1096.

Albrow, M. (1970) *Bureaucracy*, London: Macmillan.

Albrow, M. (1994) 'Accounting for organisational feeling', in L.J. Ray and M. Reed (eds), *Organizing Modernity: New Weberian Perspectives on Work*, London: Routledge: 98–121.

Albrow, M. (1997) *Do Organisations Have Feelings?*, London: Routledge.

Aldrich, H.E. (2011) *An Evolutionary Approach to Entrepreneurship*, Cheltenham: Edward Elgar.

Allen, J. and du Gay, P. (1994) 'Industry and the rest: the economic identity of services', *Work, Economy and Society*, 8: 255–271.

Alvesson, M. and Du Billing, Y. (1997) *Understanding Gender and Organizations*, London: Sage.

Alvesson, M. and Karreman, D. (2000) 'Varieties of discourse: on the study of organizations through discourse', *Human Relations*, 53: 1125–1149.

Alvesson, M. and Thompson, P. (2005) 'Post-bureaucracy?', in S. Ackroyd, R. Batt, P. Thompson, and P. Tolbert (eds), *The Oxford Handbook of Work and Organization* Oxford: Oxford University Press: 485–507.

Alvesson, M. and Willmott, H. (2002) 'Identity regulation as organizational control: producing the appropriate individual', *Journal of Management Studies*, 39: 619–644.

Amoore, L. (2002) *Globalisation Contested: An International Political Economy of Work*, Manchester: Manchester University Press.

Anthony, P.D. (1977) *The Ideology of Work*, London: Tavistock.

Applebaum, E., Bailey, T., Berg, P. and Lalleberg, A.L. (2000) *Manufacturing Advantage: Why High Performance Work Systems Pay Off*, Ithaca, NY: Cornell University Press.

Applebaum, H.A. (1981) *Royal Blue: The Culture of Construction Workers*, New York: Holt, Rinehart and Winston.

Arendt, H. (1959) *The Human Condition*, New York: Doubleday.

Argyris, C. (1960) *Understanding Organizational Behaviour*, Homewood, IL: Dorsey Press.

Armstrong, P. (1986) 'Management control strategies and interprofessional competition: the case of accountancy and personnel management', in D. Knights and H. Willmott (eds), *Managing the Labour Process*, Aldershot: Gower: 19–43.

Armstrong, P. (1989) 'Management, labour process and agency', *Work, Employment and Society*, 3: 307–322.

Armstrong, P. (1993) 'Professional knowledge and social mobility: postwar changes in the knowledge-base of management accounting', *Work, Economy and Society*, 7: 1–21.

Arthur, M., Inkson, K. and Pringle, J. (1999) *The New Careers: Individual Action and Economic Change*, London: Sage.

Arthur, M.B. and Rousseau, D.M. (eds) (1996) *The Boundaryless Career: New Employment Principle for a New Organisational Era*, New York: Oxford University Press.

Ashforth, B.E., Pratt, M.G., Ravasi, D. and Schultz, M. (eds) (2016) *The Oxford Handbook of Organizational Identity*, Oxford: Oxford University Press.

Ashton, D.N. (1985) *Unemployment under Capitalism: The Sociology of British and American Labour*, Brighton: Wheatsheaf.

Atkinson, A.B. (2015*) Inequality: What Can Be Done?* Cambridge, MA: Harvard University Press.

Atkinson, C. (2008) 'An exploration of small firm psychological contracts', *Work, Employment and Society,* 22(3): 447–465.

Atkinson, P. and Housley, W. (2003) *Interactionism*, London: Sage.

Atkinson, W. (2009) 'Rethinking the work-class nexus: theoretical foundations for recent trends', *Sociology,* 43(5): 896–912.

Autor, D.H. (2015) 'Why are there still so many jobs? The history and future of workplace automation', *Journal of Economic Perspectives*, 29(3): 3–30.

Bacon, N. and Samuel, P. (2009) 'Partnership agreement adoption and survival in the British private and public sectors', *Work, Employment and Society,* 23(2): 231–248.

Bacon, N., Wright, M., Demina, N., Bruining, H. and Boselie, P. (2008) 'The effects of private equity and buy-outs on HRM in the UK and the Netherlands', *Human Relations,* 61(10): 1399–1433.

Bagguley, P., Mark-Lawson, J., Shapiro, D. and Urry, J. (1990) *Restructuring: Place, Class and Gender*, London: Sage.

Bain, A. (2004) 'Constructing an artistic identity', *Work, Employment and Society,* 19(l): 25–46.

Baines, S. and Wheelock, J. (2000) 'Work and employment in small businesses: perpetuating and challenging gender traditions', *Gender, Work and Organization*, 5: 45–55.

Baldamus, W. (1961) *Efficiency and Effort*, London: Tavistock.

Baldry, C., Bain, P., Taylor, P., Hyman, J., Scholarios, D., Marks, A., Watson, A., Gilbert, K., Gall, G. and Bunzel, D. (2007) *The Meaning of Work in the New Economy*, Basingstoke: Palgrave Macmillan.

Ball, S.J. (2003) *Class Strategies and the Education Market: The Middle Classes and Social Advantage*, London: Routledge.

Bank of America Merrill Lynch (2015) 'Creative disruption', available at http://textlab.io/doc/1553458/creative-disruption-bank-of-america-merrill-lynch

Banks, M. (2007) *The Politics of Cultural Work*, Basingstoke: Palgrave Macmillan.

Banyard, K. (2016) *Pimp State: Sex, Money and the Future of Equality*, London: Faber and Faber.

Baritz, L. (1960) *The Servants of Power*, New York: Wiley.

Barley, S.R. (2010) 'Building an institutionalist field to corral a government: a case to set an agenda for *Organisation Studies*', *Organisation Studies* 31:777–805.

Barnard, C.I. (1938) *The Functions of the Executive*, Cambridge, MA: Harvard University Press.

Barsoux, J-L. (1993) *Funny Business: Humour, Management and the Business Culture*, London: Cassell.

Batstone, E., Boraston, I. and Frenkel, S. (1977) *Shop Stewards in Action*, Oxford: Blackwell.

Batt, R. (2000) 'Strategic segmentation in front-line services', *International Journal of Human Resource Management*, 11(3): 540–561.

Batt, R., Thompson, R. and Tolbert, P. (eds) (2006) *The Oxford Handbook of Work and Organization,* Oxford: Oxford University Press: 115–137.

Baum, J.A.C. and Shipilov, V. (2006) 'Ecological approaches to organizations' in S.R. Clegg, C. Hardy, T.B. Lawrence and W.R. Nord (eds), *The Sage Handbook of Organization Studies* (2nd edn), London: Sage: 55–110.

Baumann, Z. (2005) *Liquid Life*, Cambridge: Polity.

Baumann, Z. (2007) *Liquid Times: Living in an Age of Uncertainty*, Cambridge: Polity.

Baumann, Z. and May, T. (2001) *Thinking Sociologically*, Oxford: Blackwell.

Baxter, J. (2000) 'The joys and justice of housework', *Sociology*, 34: 609–631.

Beagan, B., Chapman, G.E., D'Syla, A. and Basset, B.R. (2008) '"It's just easier for me to do it": rationalizing the family division of foodwork', *Sociology*, 42(4): 653–671.

Bean, R. (1994) *Comparative Industrial Relations*, London: Routledge.

Beard, M. (2015) *S.P.Q.R.: A History of Ancient Rome*, London: Profile Books.

Beck, U. (2000) *The Brave New World of Work*, Cambridge: Polity.

Beck, U., Giddens, A. and Lash, S. (1994) *Reflexive Modernization: Politics, Tradition and Aesthetics in the Modern Social Order*, Cambridge: Polity.

Becker, H.S. (1971) 'The nature of a profession', in H.S. Becker (ed), *Sociological Work: Method and Substance*, London: Allen Lane: 298–300.

Becker, H.S. and Geer, B. (1958) 'The fate of idealism in a medical school', *American Sociological Review*, 23: 55–110.

Becker, H.S., Geer, B., Hughes, E.C. and Strauss, A.L. (1961) *Boys in White*, Chicago: University of Chicago Press.

Beer, M. and Spector, B. (1985) 'Corporatewide transformations in human resource management', in R.E. Walton and R.R. Lawrence (eds), *Human Resource Management: Trends and Challenges*, Boston: Harvard Business School Press: 219–253.

Behrend, H. (1957) 'The effort bargain', *International Labor Relations Review*, 10: 503–515.

Beirne, M. (2008) 'Idealism and the applied relevance of research on employee participation', *Work, Employment and Society*, 22(4): 675–693.

Beirne, M. (2013) *Rhetoric and the Politics of Workplace Innovation*, Cheltenham: Edward Elgar.

Bell, D. (1976) *The Cultural Contradictions of Capitalism*, London: Heinemann.

Bell, D. (1974) *The Coming of Post-Industrial Society*, London: Heinemann.

Bell, D.N.F. and Blanchflower, D.G. (2013) 'Unemployment in the UK revisited', *National Institute Economic Review* 224(1): F8–F22.

Bell, E. and Taylor, S. (2003) 'The elevation of work: pastoral power and the new age work ethic', *Organization*, 10: 329–349.

Bendix, R. (1963) *Work and Authority in Industry*, New York: Harper and Row.

Bendix, R. (1965) *Max Weber: A Sociological Portrait*, London: Methuen.

Bennett, J. (2016) *The Working Lives of Prison Managers*, Basingstoke: Palgrave Macmillan.

Berger, P.L. (1973) *The Social Reality of Religion*, London: Penguin.

Berger, P.L. and Luckmann, T. (1971) *The Social Construction of Reality*, Harmondsworth: Penguin.

Bericat, E. (2015) 'The sociology of emotions: four decades of progress', *Current Sociology* 64(3): 491–513.

Berlingieri, A. (2015) 'Workplace bullying: exploring an emerging framework', *Work, Employment & Society*, 29(2): 342–353.

Best, S. and Kellner, D. (1991) *Postmodern Theory: Critical Interrogations*, London: Guilford Press.

Beynon, H. (1984) *Working for Ford* (2nd edn), Harmondsworth: Penguin.

Beynon, H. (1992) 'The end of the industrial worker?', in N. Abercrombie and A. Warde (eds), *Social Change in Contemporary Britain*, Cambridge: Polity.

Beynon, H. and Nichols, T. (eds) (2006) *The Fordism of Ford and Modern Management: Fordism and Post-Fordism, Vols. I and II*, Cheltenham: Edward Elgar.

Beynon, H. (2002) *Managing Employment Change: The New Realities of Work*, Oxford: Oxford University Press.

Bhaskar, R. (1989) *Reclaiming Reality*, London: Verso.

Biggs, J. (2015) *All Day Long: A Portrait of Britain at Work*, London: Serpent's Tail.

Bishop, S. and Waring, J. (2016) 'Becoming hybrid: the negotiated order on the front line of public-private partnerships', *Human Relations*, 69(10): 1937–1958.

Bishop, V., Cassell, C. and Hoel, H. (2009) 'Preserving masculinity in service work: an exploration of the underreporting of customer anti-social behaviour', *Human Relations*, 62(1): 5–25.

Bittner, E. (1965) 'The concept of organization', *Social Research*, 32: 239–255.

Bittner, E. (1967) 'The police on skid row: a study of peace keeping', *American Sociological Review*, 32(5): 699–715.

Blau, P.M. (1963) *The Dynamics of Bureaucracy*, Chicago: University of Chicago Press.

Blauner, R. (1964) *Alienation and Freedom*, Chicago: University of Chicago Press.

Bloom, P. (2016) 'Work as the contemporary limit of life: Capitalism, the death drive, and the lethal fantasy of 'work–life balance', *Organization,* 23(4): 588–606.

Bobbit, P. (2002) *The Shield of Achilles: War, Law and Course of History*, London: Allen Lane.

Boland, R.J. and Hoffman, R. (1983) 'Humor in a machine shop: an interpretation of symbolic action', in L.R. Pondy, P. Frost, G. Morgan and T. Dandridge (eds), *Organizational Symbolism*, Greenwich, CT: JAI Press: 187–198.

Bolton, S. and Boyd, C. (2003) 'Trolley dolly or skilled emotion manager? Moving on from Hochschild's Managed Heart', *Work, Employment and Society*, 17(2): 289–308.

Bolton, S. and Houlihan, M. (2005) 'The (mis)representation of customer service', *Work, Employment and Society,* 19(4): 685–703.

Bolton, S. and Muzio, D. (2008) 'The paradoxical processes of feminization in the professions: the case of established, aspiring and semi-professions', *Work, Employment and Society,* 22(2): 281–299.

Bolton, S.C. (2000) 'Emotion here, emotion there, emotional organisations everywhere', *Critical Perspectives on Accounting*, 11: 155–171.

Bolton, S.C. (2005) *Emotion Management in the Workplace*, Basingstoke: Palgrave.

Bolton, S.C. (2009) 'Getting to the heart of emotional labour: a reply to Brook', *Work, Employment and Society,* 23(3): 549–560.

Bond, S. and Sales, J. (2001) 'Household work in the UK: an analysis of the British Household Panel Survey 1994', *Work, Employment and Society*, 15: 233–250.

Bonney, N. and Reinach, E. (1993) 'Housework reconsidered: the Oakley thesis twenty years later', *Work, Employment and Society*, 7: 615–617.

Boreham, P., Parker, R., Thompson, P. and Hall, R. (2008) *New Technology @ Work*, London: Routledge.

Boudens, C.J. (2005) 'The story of work: a narrative analysis workplace emotion', *Organization,* 26(9): 1285–1306.

Boxall, P. (2007) 'The goals of HRM', in P. Boxall, J. Purcell, and P. Wright (eds), *The Oxford Handbook of Human Resource Management*, Oxford: Oxford University Press: 48–67.

Boxall, P., Ang, S.H. and Bartram, T. (2011) 'Analysing the "black box" of HRM: uncovering HR goals, mediators and outcomes in a standardised service environment' *Journal of Management Studies,* 48(7): 1504–1532.

Boyer, R. (1988) *The Search for Labour Market Flexibility*, Oxford: Clarendon.

Bradley, H. (2014) 'Class descriptors or class relations? Thoughts towards a critique of Savage et al', *Sociology,* 48(3): 429–436.

Bradley, H. (1999) *Gender and Power in the Workplace: Analysing the Impact of Economic Change*, Basingstoke: Macmillan.

Bradney, P. (1957) 'The joking relationship in industry', *Human Relations,* 10: 179–187.

Branch, S., Ramsay, S. and Barker, M. (2013) 'Workplace bullying, mobbing and general harassment: a review', *International Journal of Management Reviews*, 15(3): 280–299.

Bratton, J. and Gold, J. (2015) 'Towards Critical Human Resource Management Education: a sociological imagination approach', *Work, Employment and Society*, 29(3): 496–507.

Braverman, H. (1974) *Labor and Monopoly Capital*, New York: Monthly Review Press.

Brewis, J. and Linstead, S. (2000a) '"The worst thing is the screwing": context and career in sex work', *Gender, Work and Organization*, 7: 168–180.

Brewis, J. and Linstead, S. (2000b) *Sex, Work and Sex Work: Eroticizing Organization?*, London: Routledge.

Bridges, W. (1995) *Jobshift: How to Prosper in a Workplace Without Jobs*, London: Brealey.

Brinkley, I., Fauth, R., Mahdon, M. and Theodoropoulou, S. (2009) *Knowledge Workers and Knowledge Work*, London: The Work Foundation.

Brocklehurst, M., Grey, C. and Sturdy, A. (2009) 'Management: the work that dares not speak its name', *Management Learning* 41(1) 7–19.

Brook, P. (2009) 'In critical defence of 'emotional labour': refuting Bolton's critique of Hochschild's concept', *Work, Employment and Society,* 23(3): 531–548.

Brown, A.D. (2009) 'Organizational Identity', in S.R. Clegg and C.L. Cooper, *The Sage Handbook of Organizational Behaviour, Vol 2 Macro Approaches*, London: Sage: 175–191.

Brown, G. (1977) *Sabotage*, Nottingham: Spokesman Books.

Brown, P. and Hesketh, A. (2004) *The Mismanagement of Talent*, Oxford: Oxford University Press.

Brown, R.K. (1983) 'From Donovan to where? Interpretations of industrial relations in Britain since 1968', in A. Stewart (ed), *Contemporary Britain*, London: Routledge & Kegan Paul: 439–461.

Brown, R.K. (1992) *Understanding Industrial Organisation*, London: Routledge.

Brown, R. K. (1997) 'The changing practices of work', in R.K. Brown (ed), *The Changing Shape of Work*, London, Macmillan: 20–53.

Bruni, A., Gherardi, S. and Poggio, B. (2004) 'Doing gender, doing entrepreneurship: an ethnographic account of intertwined practices', *Gender, Work and Organization* 11(4): 406–429.

Bryan, J.H. (1965) 'Apprenticeships in prostitution', *Social Problems*, 12: 287–297.

Bryman, A. (2004) *The Disneyization of Society*, London: Sage.

Brynin, M. (2006) 'Gender, technology and jobs', *The British Journal of Sociology,* 57(3): 437–453.

Bryson, A. and Gomez, R. (2005) 'Why have workers stopped joining unions? The rise in never-membership in Britain', *British Journal of Industrial Relations,* 43(1): 67–92.

Buchanan, D. and Badham, R. (1999) *Power, Politics, and Organizational Change: Winning the Turf Game*, London: Sage.

Buchanan, D.A. (2000) 'An eager and enduring embrace: the ongoing rediscovery of teamworking as a management idea', in S. Procter and F. Mueller (eds), *Teamworking*, Basingstoke: Macmillan: 25–42.

Budd, J.W. and Bhave, D. (2008) 'Values, ideologies, and frames of reference in industrial relations', in P. Blyton, N. Bacon, J. Fiorito and E. Heery (eds), *The Sage Handbook of Industrial Relations*, London: Sage: 92–112.

Buhlungu, S. (2009) 'The decline of labor studies and the democratic transition', *Work and Occupations*, 36: 145–161.

Burawoy, M. (1979) *Manufacturing Consent*, Chicago: University of Chicago Press.

Burawoy, M. (1985) *The Politics of Production*, London: Verso.

Burawoy, M. (2014) (ed), 'Precarious engagements: combat in the realm of public sociology', *Current Sociology Monograph 1*: 62(2).

Burchell, B. (1994) 'The effects of labour market position, job insecurity and unemployment on psychological health', in D. Gallie, C. Marsh and C. Vogler (eds), *Social Change and the Experience of Unemployment*, Oxford: Oxford University Press.

Burchell, B., Ladipo D. and Wilkinson F. (2001) *Job Insecurity and Work Intensification*, London: Routledge.

Burnham, J. (1945) *The Managerial Revolution*, Harmondsworth: Penguin.

Burns, T. (1954) 'The directions of activity and communication in a departmental executive group', *Human Relations*, 7: 73–97.

Burns, T. (1955) 'The reference of conduct in small groups: cliques and cabals in occupational milieux', *Human Relations*, 8: 467–486.

Burns, T. (1961) 'Micropolitics: mechanisms of institutional change', *Administrative Science Quarterly*, 6: 257–281.

Burns, T. (1962) 'The sociology of industry', in T. Welford, M. Argyle, D. Glass and J. Morris (eds), *Society: Problems and Methods of Study*, London: Routledge and Kegan Paul: 185–215.

Burns, T. (1977) *The BBC: Public Institution and Private World*, London: Macmillan.

Burns, T. and Stalker, G. (1994) *The Management of Innovation* (2nd edn), Oxford: Oxford University Press.

Burrell, G. (1984) 'Sex and organisational analysis', *Organisation Studies*, 5: 97–118.

Burrell, G. (1992) 'The organisation of pleasure', in M. Alvesson and H. Willmott (eds), *Critical Management Studies*, London: Sage: 66–89.

Butler, P. and Tregaskis, O. (2015) 'Workplace partnership and legitimacy: a multi-layered analysis of the shop steward experience', *Work, Employment and Society*, 29(6): 895–911.

Callaghan, G. and Thompson, P. (2002) 'We recruit attitude: the selection and shaping of routine call centre labour', *Journal of Management Studies*, 39(20): 233–254.

Caraway, T.L. (2007) *Assembling Women: The Feminization of Global Manufacturing*, Ithaca, NY: Cornell University Press.

Carey, A. (1967) 'The Hawthorne Studies: a radical criticism', *American Sociological Review*, 32: 403–416.

Carlson, C. (1951) *Executive Behavior*, Stockholm: Strombergs.

Carroll, G.R. (ed) (1988) *Ecological Models of Organisations*, Cambridge, MA: Ballinger.

Carter, J. (2003) *Ethnicity, Exclusion and the Workplace*, Basingstoke: Palgrave Macmillan.

Carter, M. J. and Fuller, C. (2016) 'Symbols, meaning, and action: the past, present, and future of symbolic interactionism', *Current Sociology*, 2016: 1–31.

Cascio, W.F. (2002) 'The virtual organization', in C.L. Cooper and R.J. Burke (eds), *The New World of Work: Challenges and Opportunities*, Oxford: Blackwell.

Casey, C. (1995) *Work, Self and Society: After Industrialism*, London: Routledge.

Casey, C. and Alach, P. (2004) '"Just a temp?": women, temporary employment and lifestyle', *Work, Employment and Society,* 18(3): 459–480.

Castells, M. (1996) *The Information Age: Economy, Society and Culture, Vol. I: The Rise of the Network Society*, Oxford: Blackwell.

Castells, M. (1997) *The Information Age: Economy, Society and Culture, Vol. II: The Power of Identity*, Oxford: Blackwell.

Castells, M. (1998) *The Information Age: Economy, Society and Culture, Vol. III: End of Millennium*, Oxford: Blackwell.

Castells, M. (2000) 'Materials for an exploratory theory of the networked society', *British Journal of Sociology*, 51: 5–24.

Cavendish, R. (1982) *Women on the Line*, London: Routledge and Kegan Paul.

Chamberlain, L.J., Crowley, M., Tope, D. and Hodson, R. (2008) 'Sexual harassment in organizational context', *Work and Occupations,* 35(3): 262–295.

Chia, R. (2003) 'Organization theory as a postmodern science', in H. Tsoukas and C. Knudsen (eds), *The Oxford Handbook of Organization Theory: Meta-Theoretical Perspectives*, Oxford: Oxford University Press: 113–162.

Child, J. (1972) 'Organisational structure, environment and performance', *Sociology*, 6: 2–22.

Child, J. (1997) 'Strategic choice in the analysis of action, structure, organizations and environment: retrospect and prospect', *Organization Studies*, 18(1): 43–76.

Child, J. (2005) *Organization: Contemporary Principles and Practice*, Oxford: Blackwell.

Child, J. and Smith, C. (1987) 'The context and process of organisational transformation', *Journal of Management Studies*, 24: 565–593.

Chinoy, E. (1992) *Automobile Workers and the American Dream* (2nd edn), Urbana and Chicago: University of Illinois Press.

Chodorow, N. (1978) *The Reproduction of Mothering: Psychoanalysis and the Sociology of Gender*, Berkeley: University of California Press.

Chugh, S. and Hancock, P. (2009) 'Networks of aestheticization: the architecture, artefacts and embodiment of hairdressing salons', *Work, Employment and Society,* 23(3): 460–476.

CIPD (2015) *Zero-Hours and Short-Hours Contracts in the UK: Employer and Employee Perspectives*, London: Chartered Institute of Personnel and Development Policy report.

Clark, I. (2009) 'Owners and managers: disconnecting managerial capitalism? Understanding the private–equity business model', *Work, Employment and Society,* 23(4): 775–786.

Claydon, T. (1989) 'Union derecognition in Britain in the 1980s', *British Journal of Industrial Relations*, 27: 214–223.

Clegg, S.R. and Carter, C. (2009) 'Globalization and organizational behaviour', in S.R. Clegg and C.L. Cooper (eds), *The Sage Handbook of Organizational Behaviour*, Vol. 2: *Macro Approaches*, London: Sage.

Clegg, S.R., Courpasson, D. and Phillips, N. (2006) *Power and Organizations,* London: Sage.

Coates, R.V. and Pellegrin, R.J. (1957) 'Executives and supervisors: informal factors in differential bureaucratic promotion', *Administrative Science Quarterly*, 2: 299–315.

Cockburn, C. and Ormrod, S. (1993) *Gender and Technology in the Making*, London: Sage.

Coffey, A. and Atkinson, P. (eds) (1994) *Occupational Socialisation and Working Lives*, Aldershot: Ashgate.

Coffey, D. (2006) *The Myth of Japanese Efficiency: The World Car Industry in a Globalizing Age*, Cheltenham: Edward Elgar.

Cohen, L. and Mallon, M.N. (1999) 'The transition from organisational employment to portfolio work: perceptions of "boundarylessness"', *Work, Employment and Society*, 13: 329–352.

Cohen, M.D., March, J.G. and Olsen, J.P. (1972) 'A garbage can model of organisational choice', *Administrative Science Quarterly*, 17: 1–25.

Cole, M. (2007) 'Re-thinking unemployment: a challenge to the legacy of Jahoda *et al*', *Sociology*, 41(6): 1133–1149.

Collin, A. (1986) 'Career development: the significance of subjective career', *Personnel Review*, 15: 22–28.

Collinson, D., Knights, D. and Collinson, M. (1990) *Managing to Discriminate*, London: Routledge.

Collinson, D.L. (1992) *Managing the Shopfloor*, Berlin: de Gruyter.

Collinson, D.L. (2002) 'Managing humour', *Journal of Management Studies*, 39: 269–288.

Collinson, J.A. (2004) 'Occupational identity on the edge: social science contract researchers in higher education', *Sociology*, 38(2): 313–329.

Collinson, D.L. and Hearn, J. (1996) *Men as Managers, Managers as Men*, London: Sage.

Collinson, M. and Collinson, D.L. (1996) '"It's only dick": the sexual harassment of women managers in insurance sales', *Work, Employment and Society*, 10: 29–56.

Collinson, M., Edwards, M. and Rees, C. (1997) *Involving Employees in Total Quality Management*, London: Department of Trade and Industry.

Costas, J. and Kärreman, D. (2016) 'The bored self in knowledge work', *Human Relations*, 69(1): 61–83.

Coulson, C. (2012) 'Collaborating in a competitive world: musicians working lives and understandings of entrepreneurship, *Work, Employment and Society,* 26: 246.

Courpasson, D. and Clegg, S. (2006) 'Dissolving the iron cages? Tocqueville, Michels, bureaucracy and the perpetuation of elite power', *Organization*, 13(3): 319–343.

Cregan, C., Bartram, T. and Stanton, P. (2009) 'Union organizing as a mobilizing strategy: the impact of social identity and transformational leadership on the collectivism of union members', *British Journal of Industrial Relations,* 47(4): 701–722.

Cremin, C.S. (2003) 'Self-starters, can-doers and mobile phoneys: situations vacant column and the personality culture in employment', *Sociological Review,* 51(1): 109–128.

CRESC (2009) *An Alternative Report on Banking Reform,* Manchester: Centre for Research on Socio-Cultural Change, University of Manchester.

Crompton, R. (1990) 'Professions in the current context', *Work, Employment and Society,* Additional Special Issue: 'The 1980's: a decade of change?': 147–166.

Crompton, R. (1997) *Women and Work in Modern Britain,* Oxford: Oxford University Press.

Crompton, R. (2010) 'Class and employment', *Work, Employment and Society,* 24(1): 9–26.

Crompton, R. and Harris, F. (1998) 'Gender relations and employment: the impact of occupation', *Work, Employment and Society,* 12: 297–315.

Crompton, R. and Jones, G. (1984) *White-Collar Proletariat: Deskilling and Gender in Clerical Work,* London: Macmillan.

Crompton, R., Lewis, S. and Lyonette, C. (2007) *Women, Men, Work and Family in Europe,* Basingstoke: Palgrave Macmillan.

Crouch, C. (1982) *Trade Unions: The Logic of Collective Action,* Glasgow: Fontana.

Crozier, M. (1964) *The Bureaucratic Phenomenon,* London: Tavistock.

Cullen, D. (1997) 'Maslow, monkeys and motivation theory', *Organization,* 4: 355–373.

Currie, D., Gormley, T., Roche, B. and Teague, P. (2016) 'The management of workplace conflict: contrasting pathways in the HRM literature', *International Journal of Management Reviews.* DOI: 10.1111/ijmr.12107.

Currie, G. and Spyridonidis, D. (2016) 'Interpretation of multiples institutional logics on the ground: actors' position, their agency and situational constraints in professionalized contexts', *Organization Studies,* 37(1): 77–97.

Cyert, R.M. and March, J.G. (1963) *A Behavioural Theory of the Firm,* Englewood Cliffs, NJ: Prentice-Hall.

D'Abate, C.P. (2005) 'Working hard or hardly working: a study of individuals engaging in personal business on the job' *Human Relations,* 58(8): 1009–1032.

Dahler-Larsen, P. (1994) 'Corporate culture and morality: Durkheim inspired reflections on the limits of corporate culture', *Journal of Management Studies,* 31: 1–18.

Dallyn, S., Marinetto, M. and Cederström, C. (2015) 'The academic as public intellectual: examining public engagement in the profession-alised academy', *Sociology*, 49(6): 1031–1046.

Dalton, M. (1951) 'Informal factors in career achievement', *American Journal of Sociology*, 56.

Dalton, M. (1959) *Men Who Manage*, New York: Wiley.

Danford, A. (1998a) *Japanese Management Techniques and British Workers*, London: Mansell.

Danford, A. (1998b) 'Teamworking and labour regulation in the auto-components industry', *Work, Employment and Society*, 12: 409–443.

Danford, A., Richardson, M., Stewart, P., Tailby, S. and Upchurch, M. (2005) *Partnership and the High Performance Workplace: Work and Employment Relations in the Aerospace Industry*, Basingstoke: Palgrave Macmillan.

Daniels, G. and McIlroy, J. (2009) *Trade Unions in a Neoliberal World*, London: Routledge.

Dant, T. (1999) *Material Culture in the Social World*, Buckingham: Open University Press.

Darlington, R. (1994) *The Dynamics of Workplace Unionism: Shop Stewards' Organisation in Three Merseyside Plants*, London: Mansell.

Davidson, M.J. (1997) *The Black and Ethnic Minority Woman Manager: Cracking the Concrete Ceiling*, London: Paul Chapman.

Davis, F. (1959) 'The cabdriver and his fare', *American Journal of Sociology*, 65: 158–165.

Davis, L.E. and Taylor, J. (1979) *The Design of Jobs* (2nd edn), Santa Monica, CA: Goodyear.

Day, R.A. and Day, J.V. (1977) 'A review of the current state of negotiated order theory: an appreciation and a critique', *Sociological Quarterly*, 18: 126–142.

de Menezes, L.M., Wood, S. and Gelade, G. (2010), 'The integration of human resource and operation management practices and its link with performance: a longitudinal latent class study'. *Journal of Operations Management*, 28(6): 255–471.

Deal, T.E. and Kennedy, A.A. (1982) *Corporate Cultures: The Rites and Rituals of Corporate Life*, Reading, MA: Addison-Wesley.

Debrah, Y.A. and Smith, I.G. (eds) (2002) *Globalization, Employment and the Workplace: Diverse Impacts*, London: Routledge.

Deery, S., Iverson, R.D. and Walsh, J.T. (2010) 'Coping strategies in call centres: work intensity and the role of co-workers and supervisors', *British Journal of Industrial Relations*, 48(1): 181–200.

Delarue, A., Van Hootegem, G., Procter, S. and Burridge, M. (2008) 'Teamworking and organizational performance: a review of survey-based research', *International Journal of Management Reviews*, 10(2): 127–148.

Delbridge, R. (1998) *Life on the Line in Contemporary Manufacturing: The Workplace Experience of Lean Production and the 'Japanese' Model*, Oxford: Oxford University Press.

Delbridge, R. and Edwards, T. (2008) 'Challenging conventions: roles and processes during non-isomorphic institutional change', *Human Relations,* 61(3): 299–325.

Delbridge, R. and Ezzamel, M. (2005) 'The strength of difference: contemporary conceptions of control', *Organization,* 12(5): 603–618.

Deloitte (2015) 'From brawn to brains: the impact of technology on jobs in the UK', available at http://www2.deloitte.com/uk/en/pages/growth/articles/from-brawn-to-brains--the-impact-of-technology-on-jobs-in-the-uk.html

Deloitte LLP, Osborne, M. and Frey, C.B. (2014) *Agiletown: The Relentless March of Technology and London's Response*, London: Deloitte.

Denissen, A.M. (2010) 'Crossing the line: how women in the building trades interpret and respond to sexual conduct at work', *Journal of Contemporary Ethnography* 39(3): 297–327.

Desai, M. (2002) *Marx's Revenge*, London: Verso.

Deuze, M. (2007) *Media Work*, Cambridge: Polity Press.

Devine, F. (1992) 'Gender segregation in the science and engineering professions: a case of continuity and change', *Work, Employment and Society,* 6: 557–575.

Dex, S. (1988) *Women's Attitude towards Work*, London: Macmillan.

Dex, S. and Bond, S. (2005) 'Measuring work-life balance and its covariates', *Work, Employment and Society,* 19(3): 627–637.

DfEE (2000) *Work–Life Balance 2000*, London: Department for Education and Employment.

Dick, P. and Cassell, C. (2004) 'The position of policewomen: a discourse analytic study', *Work, Employment And Society,* 18(1): 51–72.

DiMaggio, P.J. (1988) 'Interest and agency in institutional theory', in L. Zucker (ed), *Research on Institutional Patterns and Organizations: Culture and Environment*, Cambridge, MA: Ballinger: 3–22.

DiMaggio, P.J. and Powell, W.W. (1983) 'The iron cage revisited: institutional isomorphism and collective rationality in organizational fields', *American Sociological Review* 48: 147–160.

Ditton, J. (1974) 'The fiddling salesman', *New Society*, 28 November, 535–537.

Ditton, J. (1977) *Part-time Crime*, London: Macmillan.

Dobbin, F. (2009) 'How Durkheim's theory of meaning-making influenced organizational sociology', in P.S. Adler (ed), *Sociology and Organization Studies*, Oxford: Oxford University Press: 200–222.

Doeringer, P.B. and Piore, M.J. (1971) *Internal Labor Markets and Manpower Analysis*, Lexington, MA: D.C. Heath.

Donaldson, L. (1996) *For Positivist Organization Theory*, London: Sage.

Donati, P. (2011) *Relational Sociology: A New Paradigm for the Social Sciences*, New York: Routledge.

Dopson, S. and Stewart, R. (1990) 'What is happening to middle management?', *British Journal of Management*, 1: 3–16.

Dorado, S. (2005) 'Institutional entrepreneurship: partaking and convening', *Organization Studies*, 26: 385–414.

Dore, R. (2008) 'Financialization of the global economy', *Industrial and Corporate Change* 17(6): 1097–1112.

Draper, P. (1975), '!Kung women: contrasts in sexual egalitarianism in foraging and sedentary contexts', in R.R. Reiter (ed), *Towards an Anthropology of Women*, New York: Monthly Review Press: 77–109.

Drori, G.S., Meyer, J.W. and Hwang, H. (2006) *Globalisation and Organization: World Society and Organizational Change*, Oxford: Oxford University Press.

Drucker, P. (1992) *Managing for the Future: The 1990s and Beyond*, Hemel Hempstead: Butterworth Heinemann.

Drucker, P.F. (1968) *The Age of Discontinuity: Guidelines to Our Changing Society*. London: Transaction.

du Gay, P. (1995) *Consumption and Identity at Work*, London: Sage.

du Gay, P. (2000) *In Praise of Bureaucracy: Weber, Organization, Ethics*, London: Sage.

du Gay, P. (ed) (2005) *The Values of Bureaucracy*, Oxford: Oxford University Press.

Dubin, R. (1956) 'Industrial workers' worlds: a study of the central life interests of industrial workers', *Social Problems*, 3: 131–142.

Dudley, K.M. (2014) *Guitar Makers: The Endurance of Artisanal Values in North America*, Chicago: University of Chicago Press.

Dunn, S. (2014) *Rethinking Unemployment and the Work Ethic: Beyond the 'Quasi Titmuss' Paradigm*, Basingstoke: Palgrave Macmillan.

Durand J-P. and Nicolas Hatzfeld, N. (2003) *Living Labour: Life on the Line at Peugeot France,* (transl. D. Roberts), Basingstoke: Palgrave Macmillan.

Durkheim, E. (1982) *The Rules of the Sociological Method*, New York Free Press.

Durkheim, E. (2014) *The Division of Labour in Society*, Basingstoke: Palgrave Macmillan.

Edgell, S. (1980) *Middle Class Couples*, London: Allen and Unwin.

Edgell, S. (2006) *The Sociology of Work: Continuity and Change in Paid and Unpaid Work*, London: Sage.

Edwards, P. (1986) *Conflict at Work*, Oxford: Blackwell.

Edwards, P. (1990) 'Understanding conflict in the labour process: the logic and autonomy of struggle', in D. Knights and H. Willmott (eds), *Labour Process Theory*, London: Macmillan: 125–152.

Edwards, P. (2003a) 'The employment relationship and the field of industrial relations', in P. Edwards (ed), *Industrial Relations: Theory and Practice* (2nd edn), Oxford: Blackwell: 1–36.

Edwards, P. (ed) (2003b) *Industrial Relations: Theory and Practice* (2nd edn), Oxford: Blackwell.

Edwards, P. (2005) 'The challenging but promising future of industrial relations: developing theory and method in context-sensitive research', *Industrial Relations Journal*, 36(4): 264–282.

Edwards, P. and Ram, M. (2006) 'Surviving on the margins of the economy: working relationships in small, low-wage firms', *Journal of Management Studies*, 43(4): 894–916.

Edwards, P. and Wacjman, J. (2005) *The Politics of Working Life*, Oxford: Oxford University Press.

Edwards, P.K. and Scullion, H. (1982) *The Social Organisation of Industrial Conflict*, Oxford: Blackwell.

Edwards, P.K. and Whitson, C. (1989) 'Industrial discipline, the control of attendance and the subordination of labour', *Work, Employment and Society*, 3: 1–28.

Ehrenreich, B. (2002) *Nickel and Dimed*, London: Granta Books.

Eldridge, J.E.T. (1971) 'Weber's approach to the study of industrial workers', in A. Sahay (ed), *Max Weber and Modern Sociology*, London: Routledge and Kegan Paul: 97–111.

Eldridge, J.E.T. (1975) 'Industrial relations and industrial capitalism', in G. Esland (ed.) *Employment in Britain*, Oxford: Blackwell.

Eldridge, J.E.T. (2009) 'Industrial sociology in the UK: reminiscences and reflections', *Sociology*, 43(5): 829–845.

Eldridge, J.E.T., Cressey, P. and MacInnes, J. (1991) *Industrial Sociology and Economic Crisis*, Hemel Hempstead: Harvester Wheatsheaf.

Elliot, P. (1972) *The Sociology of the Professions*, London: Macmillan.

Elliot, P. (1973) 'Professional ideology and social situation', *Sociological Review*, 21.

Emirbayer, M. (1997) 'Manifesto for a relational sociology', *American Journal of Sociology*, 103 (2): 281–317.

Emirbayer, M. and Johnson, V. (2009) 'Bourdieu and organizational analysis', *Theory and Society*, 37(1): 1–44.

Entwistle, J. and Wissinger, E. (2006) 'Keeping up appearances: aesthetic labour in the fashion modelling industries of London and New York', *The Sociological Review*, 54(4): 774–794.

Evans, M. (2007) *A Short History of Society: The Making of the Modern World*, Maidenhead: Open University Press, McGraw-Hill.

Evans, P. and Bartolemé, F. (1980) *Must Success Cost So Much?* London: Grant McIntyre.

Evetts, J. (1996) *Gender and Career in Science and Engineering*, London: Taylor and Francis.

Evetts, J. (2006) 'Short note: the sociology of professional groups – new directions', *Current Sociology*, 54(1), 133–143.

Evetts, J. (2016) 'Hybrid organizations and hybrid professionalism: changes, continuities and challenges in professional work', in A. Wilkinson, D. Hislop, and C. Coupland (eds), *Perspectives on Contemporary Professional Work: Challenges and Experiences*, Cheltenham: Edward Elgar: 16–34.

Ezzy, D. (1997) 'Subjectivity and the labour process: conceptualising "good work"', *Sociology*, 31: 427–444.

Fairbrother, P. (2000) *Trade Unions at the Crossroads*, London: Mansell.

Fairclough, N. (2005) 'Discourse analysis in organization studies: the case for critical realism', *Organization Studies*, 26(6): 915–939.

Farrell, C. and Morris, J. (2003) 'The "neo-bureaucratic" state: professionals, managers in schools, general practices and social work', *Organization*, 10(1): 129–156.

Fayol, H. (1949, orig. 1916) *General and Industrial Management* (transl. C. Stores), London: Pitman.

Felstead, A. and Jewson, N. (2000) *In Work, At Home: Towards an Understanding of Homeworking*, London: Routledge.

Feldstead, A. Jewson, N. and Walters, S. (2003) 'Managerial control of employees working at home', *British Journal of Industrial Relations*, 41(2): 241–264.

Fenwick T.J. (2002) 'Transgressive desires: new enterprising selves in the new capitalism' *Work, Employment and Society,* 16(4): 703–723.

Filby, M.P. (1987) 'The Newmarket racing lad: tradition and change in a marginal occupation', *Work, Employment and Society*, 1: 205–224.

Filby, M.P. (1992) '"The figures, the personality and the bums": service work and sexuality', *Work, Employment and Society*, 6: 23–42.

Fine, G. (1996) *Kitchens: The Culture of Restaurant Work*, Berkeley, CA: University of California Press.

Fineman, S. (ed.) (1987) *Unemployment: Personal and Social Consequences*, London: Tavistock.

Fineman, S. (2003) *Understanding Emotion at Work*, London: Sage.

Finlay, W. and Coverdill, J.E. (2002) *Headhunters: Matchmaking in the Labor Market*, Ithaca, NY: ILR Press.

Finn, R. (2008) 'The language of teamwork: reproducing professional divisions in the operating theatre', *Human Relations,* 61(1): 103–130.

Fleming, P. (2009) *Authenticity and the Cultural Politics of Work: New Forms of Informal Control*, Oxford: Oxford University Press.

Fleming, P. and Sewell, G. (2002) 'Looking for the Good Soldier, Svejk: alternative modalities of resistance in the contemporary workplace', *Work, Employment and Society*, 36(4): 857–873.

Fletcher, D.E. and Watson, T.J. (2007) 'Voice, silence and the business of construction', *Organization*, 14(2): 155–174.

Fletcher, R. (1971) *The Making of Sociology, Vol. 1*, London: Joseph.

Florida, R. (2002) *The Rise of the Creative Class and How It's Transforming Work, Leisure and Everyday Life*, New York: Basic Books.

Forth, J., Bewley, H. and Bryson, A. (2006) *Small and Medium-Sized Enterprises: Findings from the 2004 Workplace Employment Relations Survey*, London: Department of Trade and Industry.

Foucault, M. (1980) *Power/Knowledge: Selected Interviews and Other Writings*, Brighton: Harvester.

Fowler, B. and Wilson, F. (2004) 'Women architects and their discontents', *Sociology*, 38(1): 101–119.

Fox, A. (1966) *Industrial Sociology and Industrial Relations*, London: HMSO.

Fox, A. (1973) 'Industrial relations: a social critique of pluralist ideology', in J. Child (ed), *Man and Organisation*, London: Allen and Unwin: 185–233.

Fox, A. (1974) *Beyond Contract: Work, Power and Trust Relations*, London: Faber.

Fox, A. (1979) 'A note on industrial relations pluralism', *Sociology*, 13: 105–109.

Fox, A. (1985) *History and Heritage: The Social Origins of the British Industrial Relations System*, London: Allen and Unwin.

Freidson, E. (2001) *Professionalism: The Third Logic*, Cambridge: Polity.

Frenkel, S.J., Korczynski, M., Shire, K.A. and Tam, M. (1999) *On the Front Line: Organization of Work in the Information Economy*, Ithaca and London: Cornell University Press.

Freund, J. (1972) *The Sociology of Max Weber*, Harmondsworth: Penguin.

Frey, C.B. and Osborne, M.A. (2013) *The Future of Employment: How Susceptible Are Jobs to Computerisation?*, available at http://www.nigel-todman.com/The_Future_of_Employment.pdf

Friedland, R. and Alford, R. (1991) 'Bringing society back in: symbols, practices, and institutional contradictions', in W.W. Powell and P. J. DiMaggio (eds), *The New Institutionalism in Organizational Analysis*, Chicago, IL: University of Chicago Press, 232–263.

Friedman, A.L. (1977) *Industry and Labour*, London: Macmillan.

Friedman, A.L. (2004) 'Strawmanning and labour process analysis', *Work, Employment and Society*, 38(3): 573–591.

Friedman, S. (2016) 'Like Skydiving without a parachute': how class origin shapes occupational trajectories in British acting', *Sociology*, 50(3): 1–19.

Friedman, S., Laurison, D. and Miles, A. (2015) 'Breaking the "class ceiling"? Social mobility into British elite occupations', *The Sociological Review*, 63(2): 259–289.

Gabriel, Y. (1988) *Working Lives in Catering*, London: Routledge.

Gabriel, Y., Korcznski, M. and Rieder, K. (2015) 'Organizations and their consumers: bridging work and consumption', *Organization*, 22(5): 629–643.

Gall, G. (2003) *Union Organizing*, London: Routledge.

Gall, G. (2004) 'Trade union recognition in Britain, 1995–2002: turning a corner?', *Industrial Relations Journal*, 35(3): 249–270.

Gall, G. (2013) *New Forms and Expressions of Conflict at Work*, Berlin: Springer.

Gallagher, D.G. (2002) 'Contingent work contracts: practice and theory', in C.L. Cooper and R.J. Burke (eds), *The New World of Work: Challenges and Opportunities*, Oxford: Blackwell: 115–136.

Gallie, D. (ed) (2007) *Employment Regimes and the Quality of Work*, Oxford: Oxford University Press.

Gallie, D. and Paugam, S. (eds) (2000) *Welfare Regimes and the Experience of Unemployment in Europe*, Oxford: Oxford University Press.

Gallie, D., Felstead, A. and Green, F. (2004) 'Changing patterns of task discretion in Britain', *Work, Economy and Society*, 18(2): 243–266.

Gallie, D., Felstead, A., Green, F. and Inanc, H. (2014) 'The quality of work in Britain over the economic crisis', *International Review of Sociology*, 24(2): 207–224.

Gamble, A. (2009) *The Spectre at the Feast: Capitalist Crisis and the Politics of Recession*, Houndmills: Palgrave Macmillan.

Gambles, R., Lewis, S. and Rapoport, R. (2006) *The Myth of Work-Life Balance: The Challenge of Our Time for Men, Women and Societies*, Chichester: Wiley.

Gane, N. (2014) 'Sociology and neoliberalism: a missing history', *Sociology,* 48(6): 1092–1106.

Gardiner, J., Stuart, M., MacKenzie, R., Forde, C., Greenwood, I. and Perret, R. (2009) 'Redundancy as a critical life event: moving on from the Welsh steel industry through career change' *Work, Employment and Society,* 23(4): 727–746.

Geary, J.F. and Dobbins, A. (2001) 'Teamworking: a new dynamic in the pursuit of management control', *Human Resource Management Journal*, 11: 3–23.

Geer, B., Haas, J., Vivona, C., Miller, S.I., Woods, C. and Becker, H.S.

(1968) 'Learning the ropes', in J. Deutscher and J. Thompson (eds), *Among the People*, New York: Basic Books: 209–233.

Gergen, K.J. (1992) 'Organisation theory in a postmodern era', in M. Reed and M. Hughes (eds), *Rethinking Organisation*, London: Sage: 207–226.

Gershuny, J. (1978) *After Industrial Society*, London: Macmillan.

Gershuny, J. (1994) 'The psychological consequences of unemployment: an assessment of the Jahoda thesis', in D. Gallie, C. Marsh, and C. Vogler (eds), *Social Change and the Experience of Unemployment*, Oxford: Oxford University Press: 213–230.

Gershuny, J. (2000) *Changing Times, Work and Leisure in Postindustrial Society*, Oxford: Oxford University Press.

Giddens, A. (1971) *Capitalism and Modern Social Theory*, Cambridge: Cambridge University Press.

Giddens, A. (1991) *Modernity and Self-Identity: Self and Society in the Modern Age*, Cambridge: Polity Press.

Gillespie, R. (1991) *Manufacturing Knowledge: A History of the Hawthorne Experiments*, Cambridge: Cambridge University Press.

Ginn, J., Arber, S., Brannen, J., Dale, A., Dex, S., Elias, P., Moss, C., Pahl, J., Roberts, C. and Rubery, J. (1996) 'Feminist fallacies: a reply to Hakim on women's employment', *British Journal of Sociology*, 47: 167–174.

Ginzberg, E.J., Sinzberg, S., Axelrad, S. and Herma, J.L. (1951) *Occupational Choice*, New York: Columbia University Press.

Glucksmann, M. (1995) 'Why "work"? Gender and the "total social organisation of labour"', *Gender, Work and Organisation*, 2: 63–75.

Glucksmann, M. (2000) *Cottons and Casuals: The Gendered Organisation of Labour in Time and Space*, Durham. NC: Sociology Press.

Glucksmann, M. (2005) 'Shifting boundaries and interconnections: extending the "total social organisation of labour"', in L. Pettinger, J. Parry, R. Taylor and M. Glucksmann, (eds), *A New Sociology of Work?* Oxford: Blackwell/Sociological Review.

Goffman, E. (1961) *Asylums*, Harmondsworth: Penguin.

Golding, P. (2000) 'Forthcoming features: information and communications technologies and the sociology of the future', *Sociology*, 34: 165–184.

Goldthorpe, J.H. (1974) 'Industrial relations in Great Britain: a critique of reformism', *Politics and Society*, 4: 419–452.

Goldthorpe, J.H. (1984) 'The end of convergence: corporatist and dualist tendencies in modern western societies', in J.H Goldthorpe (ed), *Order and Conflict in Contemporary Capitalism*, Oxford: Clarendon Press: 315–343.

Goldthorpe, J.H. (1987) *Social Mobility and Class Structure in Modern Britain* (2nd edn), Oxford: Clarendon Press.

Goldthorpe, J.H. (1995) 'The service class revisited', in T. Butler and M. Savage (eds), *Social Change and the Middle Classes*, London: UCL Press: 313–329.

Goldthorpe, J.H., Lockwood, D., Bechhofer, F. and Platt, J. (1968) *The Affluent Worker: Industrial Attitudes and Behaviour*, Cambridge: Cambridge University Press.

Gordon, D.M., Edwards, R, and Reich, M. (1982) *Segmented Work, Divided Workers*, Cambridge: Cambridge University Press.

Gorz, A. (1999) *Reclaiming Work: Beyond the Wage-Based Society*, Cambridge: Polity.

Gotsi, M., Andriopoulis, C., Lewis, M.W. and Ingram, A.E. (2010) 'Managing creatives: paradoxical approaches to identity regulation', *Human Relations, 63*(6): 781–805.

Gouldner, A.W. (1955) 'Metaphysical pathos and the theory of bureaucracy', *American Political Science Review* 49: 496–507.

Gouldner, A.W. (1957) 'Cosmopolitans and locals', *Administrative Science Quarterly*, 2: 281–306.

Gouldner, A.W. (1964) *Patterns of Industrial Bureaucracy*, New York: Free Press.

Gouldner, A.W. (1971) *The Coming Crisis of Western Sociology*, London: Heinemann.

Grant, D., Hardy, C., Oswick, C. and Putnam, L. (eds) (2004a) *The Sage Handbook of Organizational Discourse*, London: Sage.

Grant, D., Hardy, C., Oswick, C. and Putnam, L. (2004b) 'Introduction' in D. Grant, C. Hardy, C. Oswick, and L. Putnam, (eds.) *The Sage Handbook of Organizational Discourse*, London: Sage.

Gray, J. (1998) *False Dawn: The Delusions of Global Capitalism*, London: Granta Books.

Greener, I. (2009) 'Entrepreneurship and institution-building in the case of childminding', *Work, Employment and Society*, 23(2): 299–325.

Gregson, N. and Lowe, M. (1994a) *Servicing the Middle Classes: Waged Domestic Labour in Britain in the 1980s and 1990s*, London: Routledge.

Gregson, N. and Lowe, M. (1994b) 'Waged domestic labour and the renegotiation of the domestic division of labour within dual career households', *Sociology*, 28: 55–78.

Grieco, M. (1987) *Keeping It in the Family: Social Networks and Employment Chance*, London: Tavistock.

Grey, C. (1994) 'Career as a project of the self and labour process discipline', *Sociology*, 28: 479–497.

Grint, K. and Woolgar, S. (1997) *The Machine at Work: Technology, Work and Organisation*, Cambridge: Polity Press.

Grugulis, I., Willmott, H. and Knights, D. (2001) The Labor Process Debate – *International Studies of Management and Organization*, 30: 3–11.

Guerrier, Y. and Adib, A.S. (2000) '"No, we don't provide that service": the harassment of hotel employees by customers', *Work, Employment and Society*, 14: 689–705.

Guest, D. (1991) 'Personnel management: the end of an orthodoxy', *British Journal of Industrial Relations*, 29: 149–176.

Guiffre, P. and Williams, C. (1994) 'Boundary lines: labelling sexual harassment in restaurants', *Gender and Society*, 8: 374–401.

Gulick, L. and Urwick, L. (1937) *Papers on the Science of Administration*, New York: Columbia University Press.

Habermas, J. (1987*) Lectures on the Philosophical Discourse of Modernity*, Cambridge, MA: MIT Press.

Hakim, C. (1993) 'The myth of rising female employment', *Work, Employment and Society*, 7: 97–120.

Hakim, C. (1995) 'Five feminist myths about women's employment', *British Journal of Sociology*, 46: 429–455.

Hakim, C. (2000) *Work-lifestyle Choices in the 21st Century: Preference Theory*, Oxford: Oxford University Press.

Haldane, A. (2015) 'Labour's share', available at www.bankofengland. co.uk/publications/Pages/speeches/default.aspx

Hales, C. (2002) 'Bureaucracy-lite and continuities in managerial work' *British Journal of Management*, 13: 51–66.

Hales, C. (2005) 'Rooted in supervision, branching into management: continuity and change in the role of first-line manager', *Journal of Management Studies,* 42(3): 471–506.

Halford, S. and Leonard, P. (2006) 'Place, space and time: contextualizing workplace subjectivities', *Organization Studies,* 27(5): 657–676.

Hall, C. (1992) 'The early formation of Victorian domestic ideology', in C. Hall (ed), *White, Male and Middle Class: Explorations in Feminism and History*, Oxford: Polity: 75–93.

Hall, E. (1993) 'Smiling, deferring and flirting: doing gender by giving "good service"', *Work and Occupations*, 20: 452–471.

Halmos, P. (1970) *The Personal Service Society*, London: Constable.

Hamilton, L. and McCabe, D. (2016): '"It's just a job": Understanding emotion work, de-animalization and the compartmentalization of organized animal slaughter', *Organization,* 23(3): 330–350.

Hamilton, R. (1978) *The Liberation of Women*, London: Allen and Unwin.

Hancock, P. and Tyler, M. (2001) *Work, Postmodernism and Organization: A Critical Introduction*, London: Sage.

Handy, C. (1994) *The Empty Raincoat: Making Sense of the Future*, London: Hutchinson.

Hannan, M. and Freeman, J. (1989) *Organizational Ecology*, Cambridge, MA: Harvard University Press.

Harding, N., Lee, H. and Ford, J. (2014) 'Who is "the middle manager"?', *Human Relations*, 67(10): 1213–1237.

Hardy, K. and Sanders, T. (2015) 'The political economy of "lap dancing": contested careers and women's work in the stripping industry', *Work, Employment and Society*, 29(1): 119–136.

Hargraves, O. (2014) *It's Been Said Before: A Guide to the Use and Abuse of Clichés*, Oxford: Oxford University Press.

Harley, B. (2001) 'Team membership and the experience of work in Britain: an analysis of the WERS98 data', *Work, Employment and Society*, 15: 721–742.

Harris, L.C. and Ogbonna, E. (2012) 'Motives for service sabotage: an empirical study of front-line workers', *The Service Industries Journal*, 32(13): 2027–2046.

Hassard, J. and Parker, M. (eds) (1993) *Postmodernism and Organizations*, London: Sage.

Hassard, J., McCann, L. and Morris, J. (2009) *Managing in the Modern Corporation: The Intensification of Managerial Work in the USA, UK and Japan*, Cambridge: Cambridge University Press.

Hatch, M.J. and Cunliffe, A.L. (2006) *Organization Theory: Modern, Symbolic and Postmodern Perspectives*, Oxford: Oxford University Press.

Hatch, M.J. and Shultz, M. (eds) (2004) *Organizational Identity*, Oxford: Oxford University Press.

Hatt, P.K. (1950) 'Occupations and social stratification', *American Journal of Sociology*, 55: 533–543.

Hay, A. (2014) '"I don't know what I am doing!": Surfacing struggles of managerial identity work', *Management Learning*, 45(5): 509–524.

Haywood, C. and Mac an Ghaill, M. (2003) *Men and Masculinities*, Buckingham: Open University Press.

Hearn, J. (2014) 'Sexualities, organizations and organization sexualities: Future scenarios and the impact of socio-technologies (a transnational perspective from the global 'north')', *Organization*, 21(3): 400–420.

Hearn, J. and Parkin, W. (1987) *'Sex' at 'Work': The Power and Paradox of Organisation Sexuality*, Brighton: Wheatsheaf.

Heath, C., Knoblauch, H. and Luff, P. (2000) 'Technology and social interaction: the emergence of "workplace studies"', *British Journal of Sociology*, 51: 299–320.

Hebson, G. (2009) 'Renewing class analysis in studies of the workplace', *Sociology*, 43(1): 27–44.

Heery, E. and Kelly, J. (1994) 'Professional, participative and managerial unionism: an interpretation of change in trade unions', *Work, Employment and Society*, 8: 1–22.

Heery, E., Sims, M., Delbridge, R., Salmon, J. and Simpson, D. (2003) 'Trade union recruitment policy in Britain: form and effects', in Gall, G. (ed), *Union Organizing: campaigning for union recognition*, London: Routledge: 56–78.

Held, D., McGrew, A., Goldblatt, D. and Perraton, J. (1999) *Global Transformations*, Cambridge: Polity.

Hendry, C. and Pettigrew, A. (1990) 'Human resource management: an agenda for the 1990s' *International Journal of Human Resource Management,* 1(1): 17–43.

Henry, S. (1978) *The Hidden Economy*, London: Robertson.

Herman, A. (2001) *The Scottish Enlightenment: The Scots' Invention of the Modern World*, London: Fourth Estate.

Hernes, T. and Maitlis, S. (eds) (2010) *Perspectives on Process Organization Studies: Process, Sensemaking & Organizing*, Oxford University Press: New York, 2010.

Herzberg, F. (1966) *Work and the Nature of Man*, Cleveland, OH: World Publishing Company.

Hesmondhalgh, D. (2002), *The Cultural Industries*, London: Sage.

Hesmondhalgh, D. and Baker, S. (2011) *Creative Labour: Media Work in Three Cultural Industries*, London: Routledge.

Hickson, D.J. (1999) 'Politics permeate', in R.H. Rosenfeld and D.C. Wilson, *Managing Organizations* (2nd edn), London: McGraw-Hill.

Hickson, D.J., Hinings, C.R., Lee, C.A., Schneck, R.E. and Pennings, J.M. (1971) 'A strategic contingencies theory of intra-organisational power', *Administrative Science Quarterly*, 16: 216–229.

Hill, C. (1974) *Change and Continuity in Seventeenth Century England*, London: Weidenfeld and Nicolson.

Hill, L.A. (1992) *Becoming a Manager: Mastery of a New Identity*, Boston, MA: Harvard Business School.

Hill, S. (1988) *The Tragedy of Technology*, London: Pluto.

Hillman, A.J., Withers, M.C. and Collins, B.J. (2009) 'Resource dependence theory: a review', *Journal of Management*; 35: 1404–1427.

Hinton, J. (1973) *The First Shop Stewards' Movement*, London: Allen and Unwin.

Hirsch, P. Fiss, P.C. and Hoel-Green, A. (2009) 'A Durkheimian approach to globalization', in P.S. Adler (ed), *Sociology and Organization Studies*, Oxford, Oxford University Press: 223–245.

Hirst, P. and Thompson, G. (1996) *Globalization in Question*, Cambridge: Polity Press.

Hirst, P. and Zeitlin, J. (1991) 'Flexible specialisation versus Post-Fordism: theory, evidence and policy implications', *Economy and Society*, 20: 1–55.

Ho, K. (2009) *Liquidated: An Ethnography of Wall Street*, Durham: Duke University Press.

Hoang, K.K. (2011) '"She's Not a Low-Class Dirty Girl!": Sex Work, in Ho Chi Minh City, Vietnam', *Journal of Contemporary Ethnography*, 40(4): 367–396.

Hobsbawm, E.J. (1969) *Industry and Empire*, Harmondsworth: Penguin.

Hochschild, A.R. (1983) *The Managed Heart: The Commercialisation of Human Feeling*, Berkeley: University of California Press.

Hochschild, A.R. (1989) *The Second Shift*, New York: Avon Books.

Hochschild, A.R. (2001) *The Time Bind: When Work Becomes Home and Home Becomes Work* (2nd edn), New York: Owl Books.

Hodder, A. and Edwards, P. (eds) (2015) 'The essence of trade unions: understanding identity, ideology and purpose'. *Work, Employment & Society*, 29(5): 843–854.

Hodson, R. (2001) *Dignity at Work*, Cambridge: Cambridge University.

Hodson, R. (2010) 'Work group effort and rewards: the roles of organizational and social power as context', *Organization Studies*, 31: 894–916.

Hoel, H. and Beale, D. (2006) 'Workplace bullying, psychological perspectives and industrial relations: towards a contextualized and interdisciplinary approach' *British Journal of Industrial Relations*, 44(2): 239–262.

Holla, S. (2016) 'Justifying aesthetic labor: how fashion models enact coherent selves', *Journal of Contemporary Ethnography* 45(4): 474–500.

Holliday, R. (1995) *Investigating Small Firms: Nice Work?*, London: Routledge.

Hollowell, P.G. (1968) *The Lorry Driver*, London: Routledge and Kegan Paul.

Hookway, N. (2015) 'Moral decline sociology: the legacy of Durkheim', *Journal of Sociology*, 52(2): 271–284.

Hoque, K. and Kirkpatrick, I. (2003) 'Non-standard employment in the management and professional workforce: training, consultation and gender implications', *Work, Employment and Society*, 17(4): 667–689.

Hoskin, K. (1998) 'Examining accounts and accounting for management', in A. McKinlay and K. Starkey (eds), *Foucault, Management and Organization Theory: From Panopticon to Technologies of Self*, London: Sage: 93–110.

Houlihan, M. (2002) 'Tensions and variations in call centre management strategies', *Human Resource Management Journal* 12(4): 67–85.

Howkins, J. (2001), *The Creative Economy: How People Make Money from Ideas*, Harmondsworth: Penguin.

Hughes, E.C. (1937) 'Institutional office and the person', *American Journal of Sociology*, 43: 404–413.

Hughes, E.C. (1958) *Men and Their Work*, New York: Free Press.

Hutton, W. (2015) *How Good We Can Be*? London: Little, Brown.

Hyman, R. (1989) *The Political Economy of Industrial Relations*, London: Macmillan.

Hyman, R. (2003) 'The historical evolution of British industrial relations', in P. Edwards, (ed), *Industrial Relations: Theory and Practice* (2nd edn), Oxford: Blackwell: 37–57.

IES (2000) *Labour Force Survey*, Brighton: Institute for Employment Studies.

Jackall, R. (1988) *Moral Mazes: The World of Corporate Managers*, New York: Oxford University Press.

Jackson, P.J. and Van der Wielen, J.M. (1998) *Teleworking: New International Perspectives from Telecommuting to the Virtual Organisation*, London: Routledge.

Jacobs, J.A. and Gerson, K. (2004) The *Time Divide: Work, Family, and Gender Inequality*, Cambridge, MA: Harvard University Press.

Jacobs, J.A. and Gerson, K. (2001) 'Overworked individuals or overworked families', *Work and Occupations*, 28: 40–63.

Jacoby, S.M. (2004) *The Embedded Corporation: Corporate Governance and Employment Relations in Japan and the US*, Princeton, NJ: Princeton University Press.

Jacques, R. (1996) *Manufacturing the Employee*, London: Sage.

Jacques, R. (1999) 'Developing a tactical approach to engaging with "strategic" HRM', *Organization,* 6(2): 199–222.

Jahoda, M. (1982) *Employment and Unemployment: A Social Psychological Analysis*, Cambridge: Cambridge University Press.

Jahoda, M., Lazarsfeld, P.F. and Zeisel, H. (2002, originally 1972) *Marienthal: The Sociography of an Unemployed Community*, London: Transaction.

Janssens, M. and Steyaert, C. (2009) 'HRM and performance: a plea for reflexivity in HRM studies', *Journal of Management Studies*, 46(1): 143–155.

Jaros, S.J. (2001) 'Labor process theory: a commentary on the debate', *International Studies of Management and Organization*, 30: 25–39.

Jenkins, R. (1986) *Racism and Recruitment: Managers, Organisations and Equality in the Labour Market*, Cambridge: Cambridge University Press.

Jermier, J., Knights, D. and Nord, W.R. (eds) (1994) *Resistance and Power in Organisations*, London: Routledge.

Jessop, R. (2002) *The Future of the Capitalist State,* Cambridge: Polity.

Johnson, P. and Duberley, J. (2000) *Understanding Management Research,* London: Sage.

Johnstone, M. and Lee, C. (2016) 'Lifestyle preference theory: no match for young Australian women', *Journal of Sociology,* 52(2): 249–265.

Kalekin-Fishman, D. and Langman, L. (2015) 'Alienation: the critique that refuses to disappear', *Current Sociology Review,* 63(6): 916–933.

Kalleberg, A.L. (2000) 'Nonstandard employment relations: part-time, temporary and contract work', *Annual Review of Sociology,* 26: 341–365.

Kalleberg, A.L. (2011) *Good Jobs, Bad Jobs: The Rise of Polarized and Precarious Employment Systems in the United States, 1970s–2000s,* New York: Russell Sate Foundation.

Kalleberg, A.L. (2012) 'Job quality and precarious work: clarifications, controversies and challenges', *Work and Occupations,* 39(4) 427–448.

Kallinikos, J. (2004) 'The social foundations of the bureaucratic order', *Organization,* 11(1): 13–36.

Kamoche, K. and Pinnington, A.H. (2012) 'Managing people 'spiritually': a Bourdieusian critique', *Work, Employment and Society,* 26(3): 497–513.

Kan, M.Y. (2007) 'Work orientation and wives' employment careers: an evaluation of Hakim's preference theory', *Work and Occupations,* 34: 430–462.

Karlsson, J.C. (2012) *Organizational Misbehaviour in the Workplace: Narratives of Dignity and Resistance,* Basingstoke: Palgrave Macmillan.

Kaufman, B.A. (2007) 'The development of HRM in historical and international perspective', in Boxall, P., Purcell, J. and Wright, P. (eds), *The Oxford Handbook of Human Resource Management,* Oxford: Oxford University Press.

Kelly, J. (1998) *Rethinking Industrial Relations: Mobilization, Collectivism and Long Waves,* London: Routledge.

Kelly, J. (2005) 'Labor movements and mobilization', in S. Ackroyd, R. Batt, P. Thompson, and P. Tolbert, (eds), *The Oxford Handbook of Work and Organization,* Oxford: Oxford University Press: 283–304.

Kelly, J. and Heery, E. (1994) *Working for the Union: British Trade Union Officers,* Cambridge: Cambridge University Press.

Kenney, M. and Florida, R. (1993) *Beyond Mass Production: The Japanese System and Its Transfer to the US,* New York: Oxford University Press.

Kerr, C. and Siegal, A.J. (1954) 'The inter-industry propensity to strike', in A. Kornhauser, R. Dubin and A.M. Ross (eds), *Industrial Conflict,* New York: McGraw-Hill: 189–212.

King, Z., Burke, S. and Pemberton, J. (2005) 'The "bounded" career: an empirical study of human capital, career mobility and employment outcomes in a mediated labour market', *Human Relations,* 58(1): 981–1008.

Kirton, G. (2006) 'Alternative and parallel career paths for women: the case of trade union participation', *Work, Employment and Society,* 20(1): 47–65.

Kitay, J. and Wright, C. (2007) 'From prophets to profits: the occupational rhetoric of management consultants', *Human Relations,* 60(11): 1613–1640.

Klein, L. (2005) *Working across the Gap: The Practice of Social Science in Organizations,* London: Karnac.

Klikauer, T. (2013) *Managerialism: A Critique of an Ideology,* Basingstoke, Palgrave Macmillan.

Knights, D. and McCabe, D. (1998) '"What *happens* when the phone goes wild?": staff stress and spaces for escape in a BPR telephone banking work regime', *Journal of Management Studies,* 35: 163–195.

Knights, D. and McCabe, D. (2000) '"Ain't Misbehavin"? Opportunities for resistance under new forms of "quality" management', *Sociology,* 34: 421–436.

Knights, D. and McCabe, D. (2001) '"A different world": shifting masculinities in the transition to call centres', *Organization,* 8: 619–645.

Knights, D. and McCabe, D. (2003) 'Governing through teamwork: reconstituting subjectivity in a call centre', *Journal of Management Studies,* 40(7): 1587–1619.

Knights, D. and McCabe, D. (2016) '"The 'missing masses' of resistance": an ethnographic understanding of a workplace dispute', *British Journal of Management,* 27(3): 534–549.

Knights, D. and Willmott, H. (1985) 'Power and identity in theory and practice', *Sociological Review,* 33: 22–46.

Knights, D. and Willmott, H. (eds) (1989) *Labour Process Theory,* London: Macmillan.

Korczynski, M. (2002) *Human Resource Management in Service Work,* Basingstoke: Palgrave.

Korczynski, M. (2003) 'Communities of coping: collective emotional labour in service work', *Organization,* 10(1): 55–79.

Korczynski, M. (2004) 'Back-office service work: bureaucracy challenged?', *Work, Employment and Society,* 18(1): 97–114.

Korczynski, M. (2014) *Songs of the Factory: Pop Music, Culture and Resistance,* Ithaca, NY: Cornell University Press.

Korczynski, M. and Ott, U. (2004) 'When production and consumption meet: cultural contradictions and the enchanting myth of customer sovereignty', *Journal of Management Studies,* 41(4): 575–600.

Korczynski, M., Hodson, R. and Edwards, P. (eds), (2005) *Social Theory at Work*, Oxford: Oxford University Press.

Korczynski, M., Pickering, M. and Robertson, E. (2013) *Rhythms of Labour: Music at Work in Britain*, Cambridge: Cambridge University Press.

Kossek, E.E., Lewis, S. and Hammer, L.B. (2010) 'Work-life initiatives and organizational change: overcoming mixed messages to move from the margin to the mainstream', *Human Relations,* 63(1): 3–19.

Kostera, M. (2014) *Occupy Management: Inspirations and Ideas for Self-Organization and Self-Management*, London: Routledge.

Kotter, J.P. (1982) *The General Managers*, New York: Free Press.

Krippner, G.R. (2005) 'The financialization of the American economy', *Socio-Economic Review* 3(2): 173–208.

Kuhn, J.W. (1961) *Bargaining in Grievance Settlement*, Columbia University Press.

Kumar, K. (1978) *Prophecy and Progress*, Harmondsworth: Penguin.

Kumar, K. (1996) *From Post-industrial to Post-Modern Society*, Oxford: Blackwell.

Kunda, G. (1992) *Engineering Culture: Control and Commitment in a High-tech Corporation*, Philadelphia: Temple University Press.

Landsberger, H.A. (1958) *Hawthorne Revisited*, Ithaca, NY: Columbia University Press.

Lane, D. (2007) 'Post-state socialism: a diversity of capitalisms?', in D. Lane and M. Myant (eds), *Varieties of Capitalism in Post-Communist Countries*, Basingstoke: Palgrave Macmillan 13–39.

Lankshear, G., Cook, P., Mason, D., Coates, S. and Button, G. (2001) 'Call centre employees' responses to electronic monitoring: some research findings', *Work, Employment and Society*, 15: 595–605.

LaNuez, D. and Jermier, J. (1994) 'Sabotage by managers and techno-crats', in J. Jermier, D. Knights and W.R. Nord (eds), *Resistance and Power in Organisations*, London: Routledge.

Larson, M.S. (1977) *The Rise of Professionalism: A Sociological Analysis*, Berkeley: University of California Press.

Larson, M.S. (1990) 'On the matter of experts and professionals, or how impossible it is to leave nothing unsaid', in M. Burrage and R. Torstendahl (eds), *The Formation of Professions*, London: Sage: 24–50.

Lash, S. and Urry, J. (1987) *The End of Organised Capitalism*, Cambridge: Polity.

Latour, B. (1993) *We Have Never Been Modern*, Brighton: Harvester Wheatsheaf.

Latour, B. (2005) *Reassembling the Social*, Oxford: Oxford University Press.

Lawrence, P.R. and Lorsch, J.W. (1967) *Organisation and Environment*, Cambridge, MA: Harvard University Press.

Lawrence, T., Suddaby, R. and Leca, B. (2011) 'Institutional work: refocusing institutional studies of organization', *Journal of Management Inquiry* 20(1): 52–58.

Layder, D., Ashton, D. and Sung, J. (1991) 'The empirical correlates of action and structure: the transition from school to work', *Sociology*, 25: 447–464.

Leadbeatter, C. (2000) *Living on Thin Air: The New Economy*, London: Viking.

Leca. B. and Naccache, P. (2006) 'A critical realist approach to institutional entrepreneurship', *Organization,* 13(5): 627–651.

Lee, D. (2000) 'Hegemonic masculinity and male feminisation: the sexual harassment of men at work', *Journal of Gender Studies*, 9: 141–155.

Lee, J.J. and Ok, C.M. (2014) 'Understanding hotel employees' service sabotage: emotional labor perspective based on conservation of resources theory', *International Journal of Hospitality Management*, 36:176–187.

Lee, S., McCann, D. and Messenger, J.C. (2007) *Working Time around the World: Trends in Working Hours, Laws and Policies in a Global Comparative Perspective*, London: Routledge.

Legge, K. (1995) *Human Resource Management: Rhetorics and Realities*, Basingstoke: Macmillan.

Leidner, R. (1993) *Fast Food Fast Talk: Service Work and the Routinization of Everyday Life*, Berkeley: University of California Press.

Leidner, R. (2006) 'Identity and work', in M. Korczynski, R. Hodson, and P. Edwards, (eds), *Social Theory at Work*, Oxford: Oxford University Press.

Levinson, H., Price, C., Munder, K. and Solley, C. (1966) *Men, Management and Mental Health*, Cambridge, MA: Harvard University Press.

Lewis, P. (2005) 'Suppression or expression: an exploration of emotion management in a special care baby unit', *Work, Economy and Society*, 19(3): 565–581.

Lewis, P. and Simpson, R. (eds) (2007) *Gendering Emotions in Organisations*, Basingstoke: Palgrave Macmillan.

Likert, R. (1967) *The Human Organisation*, New York: McGraw-Hill.

Lincoln, J. and Guillot, D. (2006) 'A Durkheimian view of organizational culture', in M. Korczynski, R. Hodson, and P.K. Edwards (eds), *Social Theory at Work*, Oxford: Oxford University Press: 88–120.

Linstead, S. (1985) 'Jokers wild: the importance of humour in the maintenance of organisational culture', *Sociological Review*, 33: 741–767.

Lipietz, A. (1987) *Miracles and Mirages: The Crisis in Global Fordism*, London: Verso.

Littler, C. (1982) *The Development of the Labour Process in Capitalist Societies*, London: Heinemann.

Littleton, S.M., Arthur, M.B. and Rousseau, D.M. (2000) 'The future of boundaryless careers', in A. Collin and R.A. Young (eds), *The Future of Career*, Cambridge: Cambridge University Press: 101–114.

Llewellyn, N. and Hindmarsh, J. (eds) (2010) *Organisation, Interaction and Practice*, Cambridge: Cambridge University Press.

Lloyd, C. and Payne, J. (2014) '"It's all hands-on, even for management": managerial work in the UK café sector', *Human Relations,* 67(4): 465–488.

Lomi, A. and Harrison R.J. (2012) 'The garbage can model of organizational choice: looking forward at forty', *Research in Organizations, vol. 36,* Bingley, UK: Emerald Books, 3–17.

Loukidou, L., Loan-Clarke, J. and Daniels, K. (2009) 'Boredom in the workplace: more than monotonous tasks', *International Journal of Management Reviews* 11(4): 381–405.

Luff, P., Hindmarsh, L. and Heath, C. (eds) (2000) *Workplace Studies: Recovering Work Practice and Information System Design*, Cambridge: Cambridge University Press.

Lupton, T. (1963) *On the Shopfloor*, Oxford: Pergamon.

Lyonette, C. and Crompton, R. (2015) 'Sharing the load? Partners' relative earnings and the division of domestic labour', *Work, Employment and Society*, 29(1): 23–40.

Lyotard, J.-F. (1984) *The Postmodern Condition*, Manchester: Manchester University Press.

Mallett, O. and Wapshott, R. (2014) 'Informality and employment relationships in small firms: humour, ambiguity and straight-talking', *British Journal of Management*, 25(1): 118–132.

Mangham, I.L. and Pye, A. (1991) *The Doing of Management*, Oxford: Blackwell.

Manning, P.K. (1977) *Police Work: The Social Organisation of Policing*, Cambridge, MA: MIT Press.

Marceau, J. (1989) *A Family Business? The Making of an International Business Elite*, Cambridge: Cambridge University Press.

March, J.G. and Olsen, J.P. (1976) *Ambiguity and Choice in Organisations*, Oslo: Universitetsforlagtt.

Marchington, M., Grimshaw, D., Rubery, J. and Willmott, H. (eds) (2004) *Fragmenting Work: Blurring Boundaries and Disordering Hierarchies*, Oxford: Oxford University Press.

Marens, R. (2009) 'It's not just for communists any more: Marxian political economy and organizational theory', in P.S. Adler (ed), *Sociology and Organization Studies*, Oxford: Oxford University Press: 92–117.

Marglin, S. (1974) 'What do bosses do?: the origins and functions of hierarchy in capitalist production', *Review of Radical Political Economics*, 6: 60–112.

Mars, G. (1974) 'Dock pilferage', in P. Rock and M. McIntosh (eds), *Deviance and Control*, London: Tavistock: 209–228.

Mars, G. (1982) *Cheats at Work*, London: Allen and Unwin.

Mars, G. and Nicod, M. (1984) *The World of Waiters*, London: Allen and Unwin.

Marshall, G., Newby, H., Rose, D. and Vogler, C. (1988) *Social Class in Modern Britain*, London: Hutchinson.

Marshall, J. (1995) *Women Managers Moving On*, London: Routledge.

Martin, B. (2005) 'Managers after the era of organizational restructuring: towards a second managerial revolution' *Work, Employment and Society,* 1 9(4): 747–760.

Martin, P.Y. (2001) '"Mobilising masculinities": women's experiences of men at work', *Organization*, 8: 587–618.

Martin, R. (2008) 'Post-socialist segmented capitalism: the case of Hungary: developing business systems theory', *Human Relations*, 61(1): 131–159.

Martocci, L. (2015) *Bullying: The Social Destruction of Self*, Philadelphia, PA: Temple.

Maslow, A. (1943) 'A theory of human motivation', *Psychological Development*, 50: 370–396.

Maslow, A. (1954) *Motivation and Personality*, New York: Harper and Row.

Mason, D. (ed) (2003) *Explaining Ethnic Differences: Changing Patterns of Disadvantage in Britain,* Bristol: The Policy Press.

Mason, G. (2000) 'Production supervisors in Britain, Germany and the United States: back from the dead again?', *Work, Employment and Society*, 14: 625–645.

Matthewman, S. and Hoey, D. (2006) 'What happened to postmodernism?', *Sociology,* 40(3): 529–547.

Mayo, E. (1933) *The Human Problems of an Industrial Civilisation*, New York: Macmillan.

Mazzucato, M. (2013) *The Entrepreneurial State: Debunking Public vs. Private Sector Myths*, London: Anthem Press.

McAuley, J., Duberley, J. and Johnson, P. (2007) *Organization Theory: Challenges and Perspectives*, Harlow: FT Prentice-Hall.

McCabe, D. (2000) 'Factory innovations and management machinations: the productive and repressive relations of power', *Journal of Management Studies*, 37: 931–953.

McCabe, D. (2007) *Power at Work: How Employees Reproduce the Corporate Machine*, London: Routledge.

McCabe, D. (2009) 'Enterprise contested: betwixt and between the discourses of career and enterprise in a UK bank', *Human Relations*, 62(10): 1551–1579.

McCann, L., Hassard, J. and Morris, J. (2010) 'Restructuring managerial labour in the USA, the UK and Japan: challenging the salience of 'varieties of capitalism', *British Journal of Industrial Relations*, 48(2): 347–374.

McCann, L., Hassard, J.S., Granter, E. and Hyde, P.J. (2015) 'Casting the lean spell: the promotion, dilution and erosion of lean management in the NHS', *Human Relations*, 68(10): 1557–1577.

McDonald, P. (2012) 'Workplace sexual harassment 30 years on: a review of the literature', *International Journal of Management Reviews*, 14(1): 1–17.

McDowell, L. (2003) *Redundant Masculinities? Employment Change and White Working Class Youth*, Oxford: Blackwell.

McGovern, P. (2014) 'Contradictions at work: a critical review', *Sociology*, 48(1): 20–37.

McGovern, P., Hope-Hailey, V. and Stiles, P. (1998) 'The managerial career after downsizing: case studies from the "leading edge"', *Work, Employment and Society*, 12: 457–477.

McGovern, P., Mills, C. and White, M. (2007) *Market, Class and Employment*, Oxford: Oxford University Press.

McGregor, D.C. (1960) *The Human Side of Enterprise*, New York: McGraw-Hill.

McKeganey, N. and Barnard, M. (1996) *Sex Work on the Streets: Prostitutes and Their Clients*, Buckingham: Open University Press.

McKenzie, D. and Wajcman, J. (1985) *The Social Shaping of Technology*, Milton Keynes: Open University Press.

McKinlay, A. and Smith, C. (2009) *Creative Labour: Working in the Creative Industries*, Basingstoke: Palgrave Macmillan.

McKinlay, A. and Starkey, K. (eds) (1998) *Foucault, Management and Organization Theory*: From Panopticon to Technologies of Self, London: Sage.

McLennan, G. (2003) 'Sociology's Complexity', *Sociology*, 37(3): 547–564.

McMurray, R. and Ward, J. (2014) '"Why would you want to do that?": defining emotional dirty work' *Human Relations*, 67(9): 1123–1143.

Mead, G.H. (1962) *Mind, Self and Society*, Chicago: University of Chicago Press.

Mead, M. (1962) *Male and Female*, Harmondsworth: Penguin.

Meissner, M. (1976) 'The language of work', in R. Dubin (ed), *The Handbook of Work, Organisation and Society*, Chicago: Rand-McNally.

Merton, R.K. (1957) 'Bureaucratic structure and personality', in *Social Theory and Social Structure*, New York: Free Press: 195–206.

Merton, R.K. (1982) *Social Research and the Practicing Professions*, Cambridge, MA: Abt Books.

Merton, R.K. and Gieryn, T. F. (1982) 'Institutionalized altruism: the case of the professions', in R.K. Merton (ed), *Social Research and the Practicing Professions*, Cambridge, MA: Abt Books: 109–134.

Mescher, S., Benschop, Y. and Doorewaard, H. (2010) 'Representations of work-life balance support', *Human Relations*, 63(1): 21–39.

Meyer, J. and Rowan, B. (1977) 'Institutionalised organisations: formal structure and myth and ceremony', *American Journal of Sociology*, 83: 340–363.

Miles, I. (1984) 'Work, well-being and unemployment', in P. Marstrand (ed), *New Technology and the Future of Work Skills*, London: Pinter.

Miles, S. (2001) *Social Theory in the Real World*, London: Sage.

Milkman, R. (1997) *Farewell to the Factory: Auto Workers in the Late Twentieth Century*, Berkeley: University of California Press.

Miller, P. and O'Leary, T. (1987) 'Accounting and the deconstruction of the governable person', *Accounting, Organizations and Society*, 12: 235–265.

Miller, S.L., Hickson, D.J. and Wilson, D.C. (1996) 'Decision-making in organizations', in S.R. Clegg, C. Hardy and W. Nord (eds), *Handbook of Organization Studies*, London: Sage.

Mills, C. (2014) 'The Great British Class Fiasco: a comment on Savage et al', *Sociology*, 48(3): 437– 444.

Mills, C.W. (1970) *The Sociological Imagination*, Harmondsworth: Penguin.

Millward, N., Bryson, A. and Forth, J. (2000) *All Change at Work? British Employment Relations 1980–1998, as Portrayed by the Workplace Industrial Relations Survey Series*, London: Routledge.

Minssen, H. (2006) 'Challenges of teamwork in production: demands of communication', *Organization Studies*, 27(1):103–124.

Mintzberg, H. (1973) *The Nature of Managerial Work*, New York: Harper and Row.

Mirowski (2013) *Never Let a Serious Crisis Go to Waste: How Neoliberalism Survived the Financial Meltdown*, London: Verso.

Mische, A. (2011) 'Relational sociology, culture, and agency', in J. Scott and P.J. Carrington (eds), *The Sage Handbook of Social Network Analysis*, New York: Sage, 80–97.

Moody, K. (1997) *Workers in a Lean World: Unions in the International Economy*, London: Verso.

Mooney, J.D. and Riley, A.C. (1931) *Onward Industry*, New York: Harper.

Morgan, G. (1990) *Organisations in Society*, London: Macmillan.

Morgan, G. and Whitely, R. (2012) *Capitalisms and Capitalism in the Twenty-First Century*, Oxford: Oxford University Press.

Morris, J., Hassard, J. and McCann, L. (2008) 'The resilience of "institutionalised capitalism": managing managers under "shareholder capitalism" and "managerial capitalism"', *Human Relations,* 61(5): 687–710.

Morris, L. (1988) 'Employment, the household and social networks', in D. Gallie (ed), *Employment in Britain*, Oxford: Blackwell: 376–405.

Morris, T. and Morris, P. (1973) 'The prison officer', in D. Weir (ed), *Men and Work in Modern Britain*, Glasgow: Fontana.

Moses, J.A. (1990) *Trade Union Theory from Marx to Walesa*, New York: Berg.

Moule, C. (1998) 'The regulation of work in small firms', *Work, Employment and Society*, 12: 635–654.

MOW International Research Team (1987) *The Meaning of Work*, London: Academic Press.

Muehlberger, U. (2007) *Dependent Self-Employment: Workers on the Border between Employment and Self-Employment*, Basingstoke: Palgrave Macmillan.

Mulholland, K. (2003) *Class, Gender and the Family Business*, Basingstoke: Palgrave Macmillan.

Mulkay, M. (1988) *On Humour: Style and Technique in Comic Discourse*, Cambridge: Polity.

Muzio, D., Ackroyd, S. and Chanlat, J-F. (eds) (2007) *Redirection in the Study of Expert Labour: Established Professions and New Expert Occupations*, Basingstoke: Palgrave Macmillan.

Neal, M. and Morgan, J. (2000) 'The professionalization of everyone? A comparative study of the development of the professions in the UK and Germany', *European Sociological Review*, 16: 9–26.

Newby, H. (1977) *The Deferential Worker*, Harmondsworth: Penguin.

Newsome, K., Taylor, P., Bair, J. and Rainnie, A. (2013) *Putting Labour in Its Place: Labour Process Analysis and Global Value Chains*, Basingstoke: Palgrave Macmillan.

Newton, T. with Handy, J. and Fineman, S. (1995) *'Managing' Stress: Emotion and Power at Work*, London: Sage.

Ngai, P. (2005) *Made in China: Women Factory Workers in a Global Workplace*, Durham, NC: Duke University Press.

Nichols, T. (1997) *The Sociology of Industrial Injury*, London: Mansell.

Nichols, T. and Beynon, H. (1977) *Living with Capitalism*, London: Routledge and Kegan Paul.

Nickson, D., Warhurst, C., Witz, A. and Cullen, A.M. (2001) 'The importance of being aesthetic: work, employment and service organization', in A. Sturdy, I. Grugulis and H. Willmott (eds), *Customer Service*, Basingstoke: Palgrave: 170–190.

Nicolini, D. (2013) 'Practice theory, work, and organization: an introduction, occupational community', *Information, Communication & Society*, 18(10): 1238–1252.

Nippert-Eng, C.E. (1996) *Home and Work: Negotiating Boundaries through Everyday Life*, Chicago: University of Chicago Press.

Nisbet, R. (1970) *The Sociological Tradition*, London: Heinemann.

Nolan, P. and Wood, S. (2003) 'Mapping the future of work', *British Journal of Industrial Relations*, 41(2): 165–174.

Noon, M. and Delbridge, R. (1993) 'News from behind my hand: gossip in organisations', *Organisation Studies*, 14: 23–36.

Nordenmark, M. and Nyman, C. (2003) 'Fair or unfair? Perceived fairness of household division of labour and gender equality among women and men', *European Journal of Women's Studies,* 10(2): 181–209.

Nordenmark, M. and Strandh, M. (1999) 'Towards a sociological understanding of mental well-being among the unemployed: the role of economic and psychosocial factors', *Sociology*, 33: 577–597.

O'Connell Davidson, J. (1994) 'Resistance in a privatised utility', in J. Jermier, D. Knights and W.R. Nord (eds), *Resistance and Power in Organisations*, London: Routledge: 69–101.

O'Connell Davidson, J. (1995) 'The anatomy of "free choice" prostitution', *Gender, Work and Organisation*, 2: 1–10.

O'Connell Davidson, J. (1998) *Prostitution, Power and Freedom*, Cambridge: Polity.

O'Connor, E. (1999) 'Minding the workers: the meaning of "human" and "human relations" in Elton Mayo', *Organization*, 6: 223–246.

O'Doherty, D. and Willmott, H. (2001) 'Debating labour process theory: the issue of subjectivity and the relevance of poststructuralism', *Sociology*, 35: 457–476.

Oakley, A. (1974) *Housewife*, London: Allen Lane.

Orzack, L. (1959) 'Work as a central life interest of professionals', *Social Problems*, 6: 125–132.

Pahl, R.E. (1984) *Divisions of Labour*, Oxford: Blackwell.

Parker, J. (2004) *Women's Groups and Equality in British Trade Unions,* Lampeter: The Edwin Mellen Press.

Parker, M. (1993) 'Life after Jean-François', in J. Hassard and M. Parker (eds), *Postmodernism and Organizations*, London: Sage: 204–212.

Parker, M. (1999) 'Capitalism, subjectivity, and ethics: debating labour process analysis', *Organization Studies*, 20: 25–45.

Parker, M. (2000) *Organizational Culture and Identity: Unity and Division at Work*, London: Sage.

Parker, M., Cheney, G., Fournier, V. and Land, C. (2014) *The Routledge Companion to Alternative Organization*, London: Routledge.

Parker, S. (1982) *Work and Retirement*, London: Allen and Unwin.

Parker, S. (1983) *Leisure and Work*, London: Allen and Unwin.

Parkin, F. (ed) (1974) *The Social Analysis of Class Structure*, London: Tavistock.

Parzefall, M-R. and Salin, D.M. (2010) 'Perceptions of and reactions to workplace bullying: a social exchange perspective' *Human Relations*, 63(6): 761–780.

Paulsen, R. (2013) *Empty Labor: Subjectivity and Idleness at Work*, Uppsala, Sweden: Uppsala Universitet.

Paulsen, R. (2015) 'Non-work at work: resistance or what?', *Organization*, 22(3): 351–367.

Pavot, W. and Diener, E. (2013) 'Happiness experienced: the science of subjective well-being', in S.A. David, I. Boniwell, and A.C. Ayers (eds), *The Oxford Handbook of Happiness*, Oxford: Oxford University Press: 134–151.

Peccei, R. and Rosenthal, P. (2000) 'Front-line responses to customer orientation programmes: a theoretical and empirical analysis', *International Journal of Human Resource Management*, 11(3): 562–590.

Perrow, C. (1970a) 'Departmental power', in M. Zald (ed), *Power in Organisations*, Nashville, TN: Vanderbilt University Press: 59–89.

Perrow, C. (1970b) *Organisational Analysis*, London: Tavistock.

Perrow, C. (1977) 'Three types of effectiveness studies', in P.S. Goodman and J.M. Pennings (eds), *New Perspectives on Organizational Effectiveness*, San Francisco: Jossey-Bass: 96–105.

Peters, T.J. and Waterman, R.H. Jr (1982) *In Search of Excellence*, New York: Harper and Row.

Pettigrew, A.M. (1973) *The Politics of Organisational Decision Making*, London: Tavistock.

Pettigrew, A.M. and McNulty, T. (1995) 'Power and influence in and around the boardroom', *Human Relations*, 48: 845–873.

Pettinger, L. (2006) 'On the materiality of service work', *The Sociological Review*, 54: 1– 48.

Pettinger, L., Parry, J., Taylor, R. and Glucksmann, M. (eds) (2006) *A New Sociology of Work?* Oxford: Blackwell/Sociological Review.

Pfeffer, J. and Salancik, G.R. (1978) *The External Control of Organisations: A Resource Dependence Approach*, New York: Harper and Row.

Phizacklea, A. and Wolkowitz, C. (1995) *Homeworking Women*, London: Sage.

Phoenix, H. (1999) *Making Sense of Prostitution*, Basingstoke: Macmillan.

Pickford, L.J. (1985) 'The superstructure of myths supporting the sub-ordination of women', in B.A. Stead (ed), *Women in Management* (2nd edn), Englewood Cliffs, NJ: Prentice-Hall: 165–174.

Piketty, T. (2014) *Capital in the Twenty-First Century*, Cambridge, MA: Harvard University Press.

Pilcher, J. (2000) 'Domestic divisions of labour in the twentieth century: "change slow a coming"', *Work, Employment and Society*, 14: 771–780.

Piore, M. and Sabel, C.F. (1984) *The Second Industrial Divide: Possibilities of Prosperity*, New York: Basic Books.

Piore, M.J. (1986) 'The decline of mass production and challenge to union survival', *Industrial Relations Journal*, 17: 207–213.

Poggi, G. (1983) *Calvinism and the Capitalist Spirit*, London: Macmillan.

Pollert, A. (1981) *Girls, Wives, Factory Lives*, London: Macmillan.

Poole, M., Mansfield, R., Gould-Williams, J. and Mendes, P. (2005) 'British managers' attitudes and behaviour in industrial relations: a twenty year study', *British Journal of Industrial Relations*, 43(1): 117–134.

Powell, G.N. and Greenhaus, J.H. (2010) 'Sex, gender, and decisions at the family → work interface', *Journal of Management,* 36 (4): 1011–1039.

Poynter, G. (2000) *Restructuring in the Service Industries: Management Reform and Workplace Reform and Workplace Relations in the UK Service Sector*, London: Mansell.

Prandini, R. (2015) 'Relational Sociology: a well-defined sociological paradigms or a challenging relational turn are you in sociology', *International Review of Sociology,* 25(1): 1–14.

Pratt, M.G., Schulz, M., Ashforth, B.E. and Ravasi, D. (2016) *The Oxford Handbook of Organizational Identity*, Oxford: OUP.

Pringle, R. (1989) *Secretaries Talk: Sexuality, Power and Work*, London: Verso. *Process* (2nd edn), London: Macmillan.

Procter, S.J. and Mueller, F. (2000) *Teamworking*, Basingstoke, Macmillan.

Pugh, D.S. and Hickson, D.J. (1976) *Organisational Structure in Its Context: The Aston Programme I*, Farnborough: Saxon House.

Pugh, D.S. and Hinings, C.R. (eds) (1976) *Organisation Structure: Extensions and Replications, the Aston Programme II*, Farnborough: Gower.

Pugh, D.S. and Payne, R.L. (1977) *Organisational Behaviour in Its Context: The Aston Programme III*, Farnborough: Saxon House.

Purcell, K. (1982) 'Female manual workers: fatalism and the reinforcement of inequality', in D. Robbins (ed), *Rethinking Inequality*, Aldershot: Gower: 43–64.

Putnam, L.L., Myers, K.K. and Gailliard, B.M. (2014) 'Examining the tensions in workplace flexibility and exploring options for new directions', *Human Relations*, 67(4): 413–440.

Quinney, E.R. (1963) 'Occupational structure and criminal behaviour', *Social Problems*, 11: 179–185.

Radcliffe-Brown, A.R. (1965) *Structure and Function in Primitive Society*, New York: Free Press.

Radkau, J. (2009) *Max Weber*, Cambridge: Polity Press.

Radnor, Z., Holweg, M. and Waring, J. (2012) 'Lean in healthcare: the unfulfilled promise?', *Social Science and Medicine*, 74(3): 364–371.

Rainnie, A. (1989) *Industrial Relations in Small Firms*, London: Routledge.

Ram, M. (1994) *Managing to Survive: Working Lives in Small Firms*, Oxford: Blackwell.

Ram, M., Edwards, P., Gilman M. and Arrowsmith, J. (2001) 'The dynamics of informality: employment relations in small firms and the effects of regulatory change', *Work, Employment and Society*, 15: 845–861.

Ray, C.A. (1986) 'Corporate culture: the last frontier of control?', *Journal of Management Studies*, 23: 287–297.

Ray, L.J. and Reed, M. (eds) (1994) *Organizing Modernity: New Weberian Perspectives on Work*, London: Routledge.

Reay, D. (2005a) 'Doing the dirty work of social class? Mothers' work in support of their children's schooling', in L. Pettinger, J. Parry, R. Taylor, and M. Glucksmann (eds), *A New Sociology of Work?* Oxford: Blackwell/Sociological Review: 104–116.

Reay, D. (2005b) 'Beyond consciousness: the psychic landscape of social class', *Sociology*, 39(5): 911–928.

Reed, M. (2005) 'Beyond the iron cage? Bureaucracy and democracy in the knowledge economy and society', in P. du Gay, (ed), *The Values of Bureaucracy*, Oxford: Oxford University Press: 115–140.

Riach, K. and Wilson, F. (2014) 'Bodyspace at the pub: sexual orientations and organizational space', *Organization*, 21(3): 329–345.

Ribeiro, V.E. and Blakely, J.A. (1995) 'The proactive management of rumor and gossip', *Journal of Nursing Administration*, 25: 43–50.

Rice, A.K. (1958) *Productivity and Social Organisation*, London: Tavistock.

Richman, J. (1969) 'Busmen v. the public', *New Society*, 14 August: 243–245.

Richman, J. (1983) *Traffic Wardens: An Ethnography of Street Administration*, Manchester: Manchester University Press.

Rifkin, J. (1995) *The End of Work: The Decline of the Global Labour Force and the Dawn of the Post-Market Era*, New York: Putnam.

Rifkin, J. (1996) *The End of Work*, New York: Tarcher/Putnam Press.

Rinehart, J., Huxley, J. and Robertson, D. (1997) *Just Another Car Factory? Lean Production and its Discontents*, Ithaca, NY: Cornell University Press.

Ritzer, G. (1993) *The McDonaldization of Society*, Thousand Oaks, CA: Pine Forge.

Ritzer, G. (1998) *The McDonaldization Thesis*, London: Sage.

Ritzer, G. (1999) 'Assessing the resistance', in B. Smart (ed), *Resisting McDonaldization*, London: Sage: 234–255.

Roberts, K. (1975) 'The developmental theory of occupational choice', in G. Esland, G. Salaman and M. Speakman (eds), *People and Work*, Edinburgh: Holmes McDougall: 134–146.

Roberts, K. (1977) *The Fragmentary Class Structure*, London: Heinemann.

Robertson, R. (1992) *Globalisation: Social Theory and Global Culture*, London: Sage.

Rodrigues, S.B. and Child, J. (2010) 'The development of corporate identity: a political perspective', *Journal of Management Studies*, 45(5): 885–911.

Rodrigues, R.A. and Guest, D. (2010) 'Have careers become boundary-less?' *Human Relations*, 63(8): 1157–1175.

Rodriguez, J.K., Holvino, E., Fletcher, J.K. and Nkomo, S.M. (2016) 'The theory and practice of intersectionality in work and organisations', *Gender, Work and Organization*, 23(3): 201–222.

Roe, R.A., Solinger, O. and Van Olffen, W. (2009) 'Shaping organizational commitment', in S.R. Clegg and C.L. Cooper (eds), *The Sage Handbook of Organizational Behaviour, Vol 2 Macro Approaches*, London: Sage.

Roethlisberger, F.J. (1945) 'The foreman: master and victim of double talk', *Harvard Business Review*, 23: 283–298.

Roethlisberger, F.J. and Dickson, W.J. (1939) *Management and the Worker*, Cambridge, MA: Harvard University Press.

Roper, M. (1994) *Masculinity and the British Organisation Man since 1945*, Oxford: Oxford University Press.

Rose, D. and O'Reilly, K. (eds) (1997) *Constructing Classes: Towards a New Social Classification for the UK*, Swindon: Economic and Social Research Council/Office for National Statistics.

Rose, M. (1985) *Re-Working the Work Ethic*, London: Batsford.

Rose, M. (1988) *Industrial Behaviour*, London: Allen Lane.

Rosenfeld, J. (2014) *What Unions No Longer Do*, Cambridge, MA: Harvard University Press.

Rouncefield, M. and Tolmie, P. (eds) (2011) *Ethnomethodology at Work*, Farnham: Ashgate.

Roy, D. (1952) 'Quota restriction and goldbricking in a machine shop', *American Journal of Sociology*, 57: 427–442.

Roy, D. (1953) 'Work satisfaction and social reward in quota achievement: an analysis of piecework incentives', *American Sociological Review*, 18: 507–514.

Roy, D. (1954) 'Efficiency and "the fix": informal inter-group relations in piecework machine shops', *American Journal of Sociology*, 60: 255–266.

Roy, D. (1958) 'Banana time: job satisfaction and informal interaction', *Human Organization,* 18: 158–168.

Russell, B. (2008) 'Call centres: a decade of research', *International Journal of Management Reviews,* 10(3): 195–219.

Sabel, C. and Zeitlin, J. (1997) *World of Possibilities: Flexibility and Mass Production in Western Industrialisation,* Cambridge: Cambridge University Press.

Saks, A.M. (2011) 'Workplace Spirituality and employee engagement', *Journal of Management, Spirituality and Religion,* (4): 317–340.

Saks, M. (2015) 'Inequalities, marginality and the professions', *Current Sociology Review,* 63(6): 850–868.

Salaman, G. (1974) *Community and Occupation,* Cambridge: Cambridge University Press.

Salaman, G. and M. Speakman (eds) (1973) *People and Work,* Edinburgh: Holmes McDougall.

Sallaz, J.J. (2010) 'Service labour and symbolic power: on putting Bourdieu to work', *Work and Occupations,* 37(3): 295–319.

Samuel, P. (2007) 'Partnership consultation and employer domination in two British life and pensions firms', *Work, Employment and Society,* 21(3): 459–477.

Sanders, C.R. (2010) 'Working out back: the veterinary technician and "dirty work"', *Journal of Contemporary Ethnography,* 39(3): 243–272.

Sanders, T. (2004) 'Controllable laughter: managing sex work through humour', *Sociology,* 38(2): 273–291.

Sanders, T. (2005) *Sex Work: A Risky Business,* Cullompton: Willan Publishing.

Sandiford, P. and Seymour, D. (2007) 'The concept of occupational community revisited: analytical and managerial implications in face-to-face service occupations', *Work, Employment and Society,* 21(2): 209–226.

Savage, M. (2000) *Class Analysis and Social Transformation,* Buckingham: Open University Press.

Savage M., Devine F. and Cunningham, N. (2013) 'A new model of social class? Findings from the BBC's Great British Class Survey Experiment', *Sociology,* 47(2): 219–250.

Sayer, A. (2000) *Realism and Social Science,* London: Sage.

Sayles, L.R. (1958) *The Behavior of Industrial Work Groups,* New York: Wiley.

Scase, R. (2003) 'Employment relations in small firms', in P. Edwards (ed), *Industrial Relations: Theory and Practice* (2nd edn), Oxford: Blackwell: 471–488.

Scase, R. and Goffee, R. (1982) *The Entrepreneurial Middle-Class,* London: Croom Helm.

Scase, R. and Goffee, R. (1989) *Reluctant Managers: Their Work and Lifestyles*, London: Unwin Hyman.

Schacht, R. (1970) *Alienation*, London: Allen and Unwin.

Schein, E. (1965) *Organizational Psychology*, Englewood Cliffs, NJ: Prentice-Hall.

Schein, E. (1978) *Career Dynamics: Matching Individual and Organizational Needs*, Reading, MA: Addison Wesley.

Schienstock, G. (1981) 'Towards a theory of industrial relations', *British Journal of Industrial Relations*, 19(2): 170–189.

Schor, J. (1991) *The Overworked American: The Unexpected Decline of Leisure*, New York: Basic Books.

Schwab, K. (2017) *The Fourth Industrial Revolution*, London: Penguin Portfolio.

Schwartzman, H.B. (1993) *Ethnography in Organisations*, Newbury Park, CA: Sage.

Scott, J. (1997) *Corporate Business and Capitalist Classes*, Oxford: Oxford University Press.

Scott, W.R. (2008) *Institutions and Organizations* (2nd edn), London: Sage.

Selznick, P. (1949, 1966) *TVA and the Grassroots*, Berkeley: University of California Press.

Selznick, P. (1957) *Leadership in Administration: A Sociological Interpretation*, New York: Harper and Row.

Sennett, R. (1998) *The Corrosion of Character: The Personal Consequences of Work in the New Capitalism*, New York: Norton.

Sennett, R. (2003) *Respect*, Harmondsworth: Penguin.

Sennett, R. and Cobb, J. (1977) *The Hidden Injuries of Class*, Cambridge: Cambridge University Press.

Seymour, D. and Sandiford, P. (2005) 'Learning emotion rules in service organizations: socialization and training in the UK public house sector', *Work, Employment and Society,* 19(3): 547–564.

Shantz, A., Alfes, K. and Truss, C. (2012) 'Alienation from work: Marxist ideologies and twenty-first-century practice', *The International Journal of Human Resource Management,* 25(18): 2529–2550.

Sharpe, S. (1984) *Double Identity: The Lives of Working Mothers*, Harmondsworth: Penguin.

Shenav, Y. (1999) *Manufacturing Rationality: The Engineering Foundations of Managerial Rationality*, Oxford: Oxford University Press.

Siciliano, M. (2016) 'Disappearing into the object: aesthetic subjectivities and organizational control in routine cultural work', *Organization Studies*, 37(5): 687–708.

Sillince, J.A.A. and Brown, A.D. (2009) 'Multiple organizational identities and legitimacy: the rhetoric of police websites', *Human Relations*, 62(12):1829–1856.

Silverman, D. (1970) *The Theory of Organisations*, London: Heinemann.

Silverman, D. (1994) 'On throwing away ladders: rewriting the theory of organisations', in J. Hassard and M. Parker (eds), *Towards a New Theory of Organisations*, London: Routledge: 1–23.

Silverman, D. and Jones, J. (1976) *Organisational Work*, London: Collier Macmillan.

Simms, M. and Holgate, J. (2010) 'Organising for what? Where is the debate on the politics of organising?' *Work, Employment and Society*, 24(1): 157–168.

Simon, H.A. (1957) *Models of Man*, New York: Wiley.

Simpson, R. (2004) 'Masculinity at work: the experiences of men in female dominated occupations', *Work, Employment and Society*, 18(2): 349–368.

Simpson, R., Hughes, J., Slutskaya, N. and Balta, M. (2014) 'Sacrifice and distinction in dirty work: men's construction of meaning in the butcher trade', *Work, Employment and Society*, 28(5): 754–770.

Simpson, R., Slutskaya, N., Lewis, P. and Höpfl, H. (eds) (2012) *Dirty Work: Concepts and Identities*, Basingstoke: Palgrave Macmillan.

Skipper, J. and McCaghy, C. (1970) 'Stripteasers', *Social Problems*, 17: 391–405.

Smart, B. (ed) (1999) *Resisting McDonaldization*, London: Sage.

Smith, A. (1974, orig. 1776) *The Wealth of Nations*, Harmondsworth: Penguin.

Smith, C. (2005) 'Beyond convergence and divergence: explaining variations in organizational practices and forms', in S. Ackroyd, R. Batt,, P. Thompson and P. Tolbert, (eds), *The Oxford Handbook of Work and Organization*, Oxford: Oxford University Press: 602–625.

Smith, J.H. (1987) 'Elton Mayo and the hidden Hawthorne', *Work, Employment and Society*, 1: 107–120.

Smith, V. (1990) *Managing in the Corporate Interest: Control and Resistance in an American Bank*, Berkeley, CA: University of California Press.

Sørensen, B.M. and Spoelstra, S. (2011) 'Play at work: continuation, intervention and usurpation', *Organization*, 19(1): 81–97.

Soylu, S. and Sheehy-Skeffington, J. (2015) 'Asymmetric intergroup bullying: the enactment and maintenance of societal inequality at work', *Human Relations*, 68(7): 1099–1129.

Spradley, J.P. and Mann, B.J. (1975) *The Cocktail Waitress*, New York: Wiley.

Standing, G. (2014) *The Precariat: The New Dangerous Class*, London: Bloomsbury Academic.

Starkey, K. (1998) 'Durkheim and the limits of corporate culture: whose culture? Which Durkheim?', *Journal of Management Studies*, 35: 125–137.

Stedman Jones, S. (2001) *Durkheim Reconsidered*, Cambridge: Polity Press.

Steel, T. (2016) 'Encounters on the waterfront: identities in the context of Sailortown culture', in B. Beaven, K. Bell, and R. James (eds), *Port Towns and Urban Cultures*, Basingstoke: Palgrave Macmillan: 111–132.

Stiglitz, J. (2010) *Freefall: Free Markets and the Sinking of the Global Economy*, London: Allen Lane.

Storey, J. (1992) *Developments in the Management of Human Resources*, Oxford: Blackwell.

Storey, J. (ed) (2001) *Human Resource Management: A Critical Text* (2nd edn), London: Thomson Learning.

Storey, J. and Harrison, A. (1999) 'Coping with world class manufacturing', *Work, Employment and Society*, 13: 643–664.

Storey, J. Salaman, G. and Platman, K. (2005) 'Living with enterprise in an enterprise economy: freelance and contract workers in the media', *Human Relations*, 58(8): 1033–1054.

Strangleman, T. (2004) *Work Identity at the End of the Line? Privatisation and Culture Change in the UK Rail Industry*, Basingstoke: Palgrave.

Strangleman, T. (2006) 'Dignity, respect and the cultures of work', *Work, Employment and Society*, 20(1): 181–188.

Strauss, A. (1978) *Negotiations*, New York: Wiley.

Strauss, A., Schatzman, L., Erlich, D., Bucher, R. and Sabsin, M. (1963) 'The hospital and its negotiated order', in E. Friedson (ed), *The Hospital in Modern Society*, New York: Macmillan: 147–169.

Streek, W, (2015) *Buying Time: The Delayed Crisis of Democratic Capitalism*, London: Verso.

Stuart, M. and Lucio, M.M. (eds) (2005) *Partnership and Modernisation in Employment Relations*, London: Routledge.

Sturdy, A. (1992) 'Clerical consent: "shifting" work in the insurance office', in A. Sturdy, D. Knights, and H. Willmott (eds), *Skill and Consent: Contemporary Studies in the Labour Process*, London: Routledge: 115–149.

Sturdy, A., Wright, C. and Wylie, N. (2015) *Management as Consultancy: Neo-Bureaucracy and the Consultant Manager*, Cambridge: Cambridge University Press.

Super, D.E. (1957) *The Psychology of Careers*, New York: Harper and Row.

Susskind, R. and Susskind, D. (2015) *The Future of the Professions*, Oxford: Oxford University Press.

Svarc, J. (2016) 'The knowledge worker is dead: what about professions?', *Current Sociology*, 64(3): 392–410.

Sveningsson, S. and Alvesson, M. (2003) 'Managing managerial identities:

organizational fragmentation, discourse and identity struggle', *Human Relations,* 56: 1163–1193.

Swingewood, A. (2000) *A Short History of Sociological Thought*, Basingstoke: Macmillan.

Sykes, A.J.M. (1969) 'Navvies: their work attitudes', *Sociology*, 3: 21–35.

Symonds, M. and Pudsey, J. (2008) 'The concept of "paradox" in the work of Max Weber', *Sociology,* 42(4): 223–241.

Taksa, L. (1992) 'Scientific Management: technique or cultural ideology?', *Journal of Industrial Relations*, 34: 365–397.

Taleb, N.N. (2007) *The Black Swan: The Impact of the Highly Improbable*, New York: Random House.

Taylor, F.W. (1911a) *The Principles of Scientific Management*, New York: Harper.

Taylor, F.W. (1911b) *Shop Management*, New York: Harper.

Taylor, I. and Walton, P. (1971) 'Industrial sabotage: motives and meanings', in S. Cohen (ed), *Images of Deviance*, Harmondsworth: Penguin.

Taylor, P. and Bain, P. (2003) '"Subterranean Worksick Blues": humour as subversion in two call centres', *Organization,* 24(9): 1487–1509.

Taylor, R. (1982) *Workers and the New Depression*, London: Macmillan.

Taylor, R.F. (2005) 'Rethinking voluntary work', in L. Pettinger, J. Parry, R. Taylor, and M. Glucksmann (eds), *A New Sociology of Work?*, Oxford: Blackwell/Sociological Review: 117–135.

Taylor, S. (1998) 'Emotional labour and the new workplace', in P. Thompson and C. Warhurst (eds), *Workplaces of the Future*, Basingstoke: Macmillan: 84–103.

Tebbut, M. and Marchington, M. (1997) '"Look before you speak": gossip and the insecure workplace', *Work, Employment and Society*, 11: 713–735.

Tengblad, S. (2012) *The Work of Managers*, Oxford: Oxford University Press.

Terkel, S. (1977) *Working*, Harmondsworth: Penguin.

Terry, M. (2003) 'Employee representation: shop stewards and the new legal framework', in P. Edwards (ed), *Industrial Relations: Theory and Practice* (2nd edn), Oxford: Blackwell: 183–203.

Theodosius, C. (2008) *The Unmanaged Heart of Nursing*, London: Routledge.

Thomas, R. and Linstead, A. (2002) 'Losing the plot? Middle managers and identity', *Organization*, 9: 71–93.

Thompson, E.P. (1967) 'Time, work discipline and industrial capitalism', *Past and Present*, 38.

Thompson, P. (1989) *The Nature of Work: An Introduction to Debates on the Labour Debate*, London: Macmillan.

Thompson, P. (1993) 'Fatal distraction: postmodernism and organisational analysis', in J. Hassard and M. Parker (eds), *Postmodernism and Organizations*, London: Sage: 169–184.

Thompson, P. (2003) 'Disconnected capitalism: or why employers can't keep their side of the bargain', *Work, Employment and Society*, 17(2): 359–378.

Thompson, P. (2013) 'Financialisation and the workplace: extending and applying the disconnected capitalism thesis', *Work, Employment and Society*, 27(3): 472–488.

Thompson, P. and Ackroyd, S. (1995) 'All quiet on the workplace front: a critique of recent trends in British industrial sociology', *Sociology*, 29: 615–633.

Thompson, P. and Alvesson, M. (2005) 'Bureaucracy at work: misunderstandings and mixed blessings', in P. du Gay (ed), (2005) *The Values of Bureaucracy*, Oxford: Oxford University Press, 89–114.

Thompson, P. and Newsome, K. (2016) 'The dynamics of dignity at work', in L.A. Keister ,Vi.J. Roscigno (eds), *A Gedenkschrift to Randy Hodson: Working with Dignity* (Research in the Sociology of Work, Volume 28), London: Emerald: 79–100.

Thompson, P. and Smith, C. (2009) 'Labour power and labour process: contesting the marginality of the sociology of work', *Sociology*, 43(5): 913–930.

Thompson, P. and Smith, C. (2010) *Working Life: Renewing Labour Process Analysis*, Basingstoke: Palgrave Macmillan.

Thornton, P. and Ocasio, W. (2008) 'Institutional logics', in R. Greenwood, C. Oliver, C. K. Sahlin, and R. Suddaby (eds), *The Sage Handbook of Organizational Institutionalism*, London: Sage: 99–129.

Thornton, P.H., Ocasio, W. and Lounsbury, M. (2012) *The Institutional Logics Perspective: A New Approach to Culture, Structure and Process*, Oxford: Oxford University Press.

Thursfield, D. (2012) 'The social construction of professionalism among organizers and senior organizers in a UK trade union', *Work, Employment and Society*, 26(1):128–144.

Thursfield, D. (2015) 'Resistance to teamworking in a UK research and development laboratory', *Work, Employment and Society*, 29(6): 989–1006.

Tichy, N.M., Fombrun, C.J. and Devanna, M.A. (1982) 'Strategic human resource management', *Sloan Management Review*, 23(2): 47–61.

Tietze, S. and Musson, G. (2005) 'Recasting the home-work relationship: a case of mutual adjustment?', *Organization Studies*, 26 (9): 1331–1352.

Tilgher, A. (1930) *Work: What It Has Meant to Men through the Ages*, New York: Harcourt Brace.

Tilly, C. and Tilly, C. (1998) *Work under Capitalism*, Oxford: Westview Press.

Timming, A.R. (2016) 'The effect of foreign accent on employability: a study of the aural dimensions of aesthetic labour in customer-facing and non-customer-facing jobs', *Work, Employment and Society. DOI 10.1177/0950017016630260.*

Tinker, T. (2002) 'Spectres of Marx and Braverman in the twilight of postmodernist labour process research', *Work, Employment and Society*, 16(2): 251–281.

Tolbert, P.S. and Zucker, L.G. (1996) 'The institutionalization of institutional theory', in S. Clegg, C. Hardy and W. Nord (eds), *Handbook of Organizational Studies*, London: Sage: 169–184.

Tomlinson, J. (1999) *Globalization and culture,* Cambridge: Polity Press.

Toynbee, P. (2002) *Hard Work*, London: Bloomsbury.

Trist, E.L., Higgin, G.W., Murray, H. and Pollock, A.B. (1963) *Organisational Choice*, London: Tavistock.

Tsai, C., Sengupta, S. and Edwards, P. (2007) 'When and why is small beautiful? The experience of work in the small firm', *Work, Employment and Society*, 60(12): 1779–1807.

Turnbull, P. and Sapsford, D. (1992) 'A sea of discontent: the tides of organised and "unorganised" conflict on the docks', *Sociology*, 26: 291–309.

Turner, B.S. (1996) *For Max Weber: Essays in the Sociology of Fate*, London: Sage.

Turner, J.H. (2001) 'The origins of positivism: the contributions of Auguste Comte and Herbert Spencer', in G. Ritzer and B. Smart (eds), *Handbook of Social Theory*, London: Sage: 30–42.

Turner, S.P. (2000) 'Introduction', in S.P. Turner (ed), *The Cambridge Companion to Weber*, Cambridge: Cambridge University Press.

UBS (2015) *The New Global Context: Could economic transformations threaten stability?* White Paper from the World Economic Forum Annual Meeting, Zurich: UBS.

Umney, C. and Kretsos, L. (2015) '"That's the experience": passion, work precarity, and life transitions among London jazz musicians', *Work and Occupations*, 42(3): 313–334.

Undy, R., Fosh, P., Morris, H., Smith, P. and Martin, R. (1996) *Managing the Unions: The Impact of Legislation on Trade Unions' Behaviour*, Oxford: Clarendon Press.

Vallas, S.P. (2012) *Work*, Cambridge: Polity.

Van de Ven, A. (2007) *Engaged Scholarship*, Oxford: Oxford University Press.

Van der Bly, M. (2005) 'Globalization: a triumph of ambiguity', *Current Sociology*, 53(6): 875–893.

Van Maanen, J. (1991) 'The smile factory: work at Disneyland', in E.J. Frost, L.F. Moore, M.R. Louis, C.C. Lundberg and J. Martin (eds), *Reframing Organizational Culture*, Newbury Park, CA: Sage: 58–76.

Vardi, Y. and Wiener, Y. (1996) 'Misbehavior in organizations: a motivational framework' *Organization Science*, 7: 151–165.

Vega, G. and Comer, D.R. (2005) 'Bullying and harassment in the workplace', in R.E. Kidwell and C.L. Martin (eds), *Managing Organizational Deviance*, Thousand Oaks, CA: Sage: 183–203.

Vie, O.E. (2010) 'Have post-bureaucratic changes occurred in managerial work?', *European Management Journal*, 28:182–194.

von Zugbach, R. (1995) *The Winning Manager: Coming out on Top in the Organization Game*, London: Souvenir Press.

Wacjman, J. and Martin, B. (2001) 'My company or my career: managerial achievement and loyalty', *British Journal of Sociology*, 52: 559–578.

Waddington, J. (2003) 'Trade union organization', in P. Edwards (ed), *Industrial Relations: Theory and Practice* (2nd edn), Oxford: Blackwell: 214–256.

Wainwright, D. and Calnan, M. (2002) *Work Stress: The Making of a Modern Epidemic*, Buckingham: Open University Press.

Wajcman, J. (1998) *Managing Like a Man: Women and Men in Corporate Management*, Cambridge: Polity Press.

Wajcman, J. and Martin, B. (2002) 'Narratives of identity in modern management: the corrosion of gender difference', *Work, Employment and Society,* 36(4): 985–1002.

Walby, S. (1986) *Patriarchy at Work: Patriarchal and Capitalist Relations in Employment*, Oxford: Polity.

Walby, S. (1997) *Gender Transformations*, London: Routledge.

Walby, S. (2006) *Globalization and Difference*, London: Sage.

Walker, C.R. and Guest, R.H. (1952) *The Man on the Assembly Line*, Cambridge, MA: Harvard University Press.

Walsh, J. (1999) 'Myths and counter-myths: an analysis of part-time female employees and their orientations to work and working hours', *Work, Employment and Society*, 13: 179–203.

Walton, R.E. (1985) 'From control to commitment in the workplace', *Harvard Business Review*, March–April: 76–84.

Warde, A. and Hetherington, K. (1993) 'A changing domestic division of labour? Issues of measurement and interpretation', *Work, Employment and Society*, 7: 23–45.

Warhurst, C. and Nickson, D. (2001), *Looking Good, Sounding Right: Style Counselling in the New Economy*, London: The Industrial Society.

Warhurst, C. and Nickson, D. (2007) 'Employee experience of aesthetic labour in retail and hospitality', *Work, Employment and Society*, 21(1): 103–120.

Warhurst, C., Eikhof, D.R. and Haunschild, A. (2008) *Work Less, Live More: Critical Analysis of the Work-Life Boundary*, Basingstoke: Palgrave Macmillan.

Waring, J. (2014) 'Restratification, hybridity and professional elites: questions of power, identity and relational contingency at the points of 'professional–organisational intersection', *Sociology Compass*, 8(5): 688–704.

Warr, P. (1987) *Work, Unemployment and Mental Health*, Oxford: Oxford University Press.

Warren, D.E. (2003) 'Constructive and destructive deviance in organizations', *Academy of Management Review,* 28(4): 622–632.

Warren, T. (2003) 'Class- and gender-based working time: time poverty and the division of domestic labour', *Sociology,* 37(4): 733–752.

Warren, T. (2016) 'Work and social theory', in S. Edgell, H. Gottfried, and W. Granter (eds), *The Sage Handbook of the Sociology of Work and Employment*, London: Sage: 34–51.

Waters, M. (1995) *Globalization*, London: Routledge.

Watson, C. (2014) 'A sociologist walks into a bar (and other academic challenges): towards a methodology of humour', *Sociology*, 49(3): 407–421.

Watson, D.H. (1988) *Managers of Discontent: Trade Union Officers and Industrial Relations Managers*, London: Routledge.

Watson, T.J. (2015) 'Work and Industry, Sociology of', in James D. Wright (editor-in-chief), *International Encyclopedia of the Social and Behavioral Sciences* (2nd edn), Vol 25. Oxford: Elsevier: 657–661.

Watson, T.J. (1977) *The Personnel Managers: A Study in the Sociology of Work and Employment*, London: Routledge.

Watson, T.J. (1982) 'Group ideologies and organisational change', *Journal of Management Studies*, 19: 259–275.

Watson, T.J. (1986) *Management, Organisation and Employment Strategy*, London: Routledge and Kegan Paul.

Watson, T.J. (1994) 'Management "flavours of the month": their role in managers' lives', *The International Journal of Human Resource Management*, 5: 889–905.

Watson, T.J. (1995) 'Rhetoric, discourse and argument in organisational sense-making: a reflexive tale', *Organisation Studies*, 16: 805–821.

Watson, T.J. (1996a) 'Motivation: that's Maslow, isn't it?', *Management Learning*, 27: 447–464.

Watson, T.J. (1996b) 'How do managers think? - morality and pragmatism in theory and practice', *Management Learning*, 27(3): 323–341.

Watson, T.J. (1997) 'Theorising managerial work: a pragmatic pluralist approach to interdisciplinary research', *British Journal of Management*, 8(special issue): 3–8.

Watson, T.J. (2001, originally 1994) *In Search of Management: Culture, Chaos and Control in Managerial Work* (2nd edn), Harlow: Prentice-Hall.

Watson, T.J. (2002a) 'Professions and professionalism: should we jump off the bandwagon better to study where it is going?', *International Studies of Management and Organization*, 32: 94–106.

Watson, T.J. (2002b) 'Speaking professionally – occupational anxiety and discursive ingenuity among human resourcing specialists', in S. Whitehead and M. Dent (eds), *Managing Professional Identities*, London: Routledge: 99–115.

Watson, T.J. (2003a) 'Strategists and strategy-making: strategic exchange and the shaping of individual lives and organisational futures', *Journal of Management Studies,* 40(5): 1305–1323.

Watson, T.J. (2003b) 'Ethical choice in managerial work: the scope for managerial choices in an ethically irrational world', *Human Relations*, 56: 167–185.

Watson, T.J. (2004) 'Human resource management and critical social science analysis', *Journal of Management Studies*, 41(3): 447–467.

Watson, T.J. (2006) *Organising and Managing Work: Organisational, Managerial and Strategic Behaviour in Theory and Practice* (2nd edn), Harlow: FT Prentice-Hall.

Watson, T.J. (2007a) 'Organization theory and HRM', in P. Boxall, J. Purcell, and P. Wright (eds), *The Oxford Handbook of Human Resource Management*, Oxford: Oxford University Press.

Watson, T.J. (2007b) 'HRM, ethical irrationality, and the limits of ethical action', in A. Pinnington, R. Macklin and T. Campbell (eds), *Human Resource Management: Ethics and Employment*, Oxford: Oxford University Press: 223–236.

Watson, T.J. (2008a) 'Managing identity: identity work, personal predicaments and structural circumstances', *Organization*, 15(1): 121–143.

Watson, T.J. (2008b) 'Identity Work, Managing and Researching', in A. Pullen, N. Beech and D. Sims (eds), *Exploring Identity Concepts and Methods*, Basingstoke: Palgrave Macmillan: 135–150.

Watson, T.J. (2008c) 'Social construction of reality', in Y. Gabriel (ed), *Organizing Words*, Oxford: Oxford University Press: 270–271.

Watson, T.J. (2009a) 'Narrative, life story and the management of identity: a case study in autobiographical identity work', *Human Relations,* 62(3): 425–452.

Watson, T.J. (2009b) 'Work and the sociological imagination: the need for continuity and change in the study of continuity and change', *Sociology,* 43(5): 861–877.

Watson, T.J. (2010) 'Critical social science, pragmatism and the realities of HRM' *International Journal of Human Resource Management*, 21(6): 915–931.

Watson, T.J. (2011) 'Ethnography, reality and truth: the vital need for studies of 'how things work' in organisations and management', *Journal of Management Studies*, 48(1): 202–217.

Watson, T.J. (2012) 'Making organizational ethnography', *Journal of Organizational Ethnography*, 1(1): 15–22.

Watson, T.J. (2013a) 'Entrepreneurial action and the Euro-American social science tradition: pragmatism, realism and looking beyond 'the entrepreneur', *Entrepreneurship and Regional Development*, 25(1–2): 16–33.

Watson, T.J. (2013b) 'Entrepreneurship in action: bringing together the individual, organizational and institutional dimensions of entrepreneurial action', *Entrepreneurship and Regional Development*, 25(5–6): 404–422.

Watson, T.J. (2015) 'Organizations: Negotiated Orders', in James D. Wright (editor-in-chief), *International Encyclopedia of Social and Behavioural Sciences, Second Edition*, Amsterdam: Elsevier: 411–414.

Watson, T.J. (2016) 'Organizational identity and organizational identity work as valuable analytical resources', in B.E. Ashforth, M.G. Pratt, D. Ravasi and M. Schultz, (eds), *The Oxford Handbook of Organizational Identity*, Oxford: Oxford University Press: 123–139.

Watson, T.J. and Harris, P. (1999) *The Emergent Manager*, London: Sage.

Watson, T.J. and Watson, D.H. (1999) 'Human resourcing in practice: managing employment issues in the university', *Journal of Management Studies*, 36: 483–504.

Watson, T.J. and Watson, D.H. (2012) 'Narratives in society, organizations and individual identities: an ethnographic study of pubs, identity work and the pursuit of 'the real', *Human Relations*, 65(6): 683–704.

Watson, T.J. (2013) 'Pragmatism, organisations and getting to grips with reality', in M. Keleman and N. Rumens, (eds), *American Pragmatism and Organisations: New Directions in Theory and Practice*, London: Gower: 59–72.

Watson, W. (1964) 'Social mobility and social class in industrial communities', in M. Gluckman and E. Devon (eds), *Closed Systems and Open Minds*, Edinburgh: Oliver and Boyd: 129–157.

Watts, J.H. (2009) 'Leaders of men: women "managing" in construction', *Work, Employment and Society*, 23(3): 512–530.

Webb, J. (2004) 'Organizations, self-identities and the new economy', *Work, Employment and Society*, 38(4): 719–738.

Weber, M. (1927) *General Economic History*, New York: Free Press.

Weber, M. (1965) *The Protestant Ethic and the Spirit of Capitalism*, London: Allen and Unwin.

Weber, M. (1978) *Economy and Society*, Berkeley: University of California Press.

Webster, F. and Robbins, K. (1993) '"I'll be watching you": comment on Sewell and Wilkinson', *Sociology*, 27: 243–252.

Weick, K.E. (1979) *The Social Psychology of Organizing*, Reading, MA: Addison-Wesley.

Weick, K.E. (1995) *Sensemaking in Organisations*, Thousand Oaks, CA: Sage.

Welch, D. and Welch, C. (2015) 'How global careers unfold in practice: evidence from international project work' *International Business Review*, 24(6): 1072–1081.

West, J. and Austrin, T. (2005) 'Markets and politics: public and private relations in the case of prostitution', *The Sociological Review*, 53(s2): 136–148.

Weststar, J. (2015) 'Understanding video game developers as an occupational community', *Information, Communication and Society*, 18(10): 1238–1252.

Westwood, R. and Rhodes, C. (2007) 'Humour and the study of organisations', in R. Westwood and C. Rhodes, (eds), *Humour, Work and Organization*, London: Routledge: 1–13.

Wheelock, J. (1990) *Husbands at Home: The Domestic Economy in a Post Industrial Society*, London: Routledge.

Whipp, R. (1990) *Patterns of Labour: Work and Social Change in the Pottery Industry*, London: Routledge.

White, M., and Smeaton, D. (2016) 'Older British employee's declining attitudes over 20 years and across classes', *Human Relations*, 69(8): 1619–1641.

White, M. Hill, S., Mills, C. and Smeaton, D. (2004) *Managing To Change? British Workplaces and the Future of Work*, Basingstoke: Palgrave Macmillan.

Whitehead, T.N. (1938) *The Industrial Worker*, New York: Oxford University Press.

Whitley, R. (1994) 'The internationalisation of firms and markets: its significance and institutional structuring', *Organisation*, 1: 101–134.

Whitley, R. (2000) *Divergent Capitalisms: The Social Structuring and Change of Business Systems*, Oxford: Oxford University Press.

Whitley, R. and Morgan, G. (2012) 'Capitalisms and capitalism in the twenty-first century: introduction', in G. Morgan and R. Whitley (eds), *Capitalisms and Capitalism in the Twenty-First Century*, Oxford: Oxford University Press.

Wilkinson, A., Dundon, T., Donaghey, J. and Townsend, K. (2014) 'Partnership, collaboration and mutual gains: evaluating context, interests and legitimacy', *International Journal of Human Resource Management*, 25(6): 737–747.

Wilkinson, R. and Pickett, K. (2009) *The Spirit Level: Why Equality Is Better for Everyone*, Harmondsworth: Penguin.

Williams, C.C. (1988) *Examining the Nature of Domestic Labour*, Aldershot: Avebury.

Williams, C.C. (2004) *Cash-in-Hand Work: The Underground Sector and Hidden Economy of Favours*, Basingstoke: Palgrave Macmillan.

Williams, C.C. (2007) *Re-Thinking the Future of Work: Directions and Visions*, Basingstoke: Palgrave Macmillan.

Williams, C.C. and Nadin, S. (2012) 'Work beyond employment: representations of informal economic activities', *Work, Employment and Society*, 26(1): 1–10.

Williams, C.L. and Connell, C. (2010) '"Looking good and sounding right": aesthetic labor and social inequality in the retail industry', *Work and Occupations,* 37(3): 349–377.

Williams, C.L., Giuffre, P.A. and Dellinger, K. (1999) 'Sexuality in the workplace: organizational control, sexual harassment and the pursuit of pleasure', *Annual Review of Sociology*, 25: 73–93.

Willis, P.E. (1977) *Learning to Labour*, London: Saxon House.

Willman, P. (1980) 'Leadership and trade union principles: some problems of management sponsorship and independence', *Industrial Relations Journal*, 11(4): 39–49.

Willmott, H. (1995) 'Strength is ignorance; slavery is freedom: managing culture in modern organisations', *Journal of Management Studies*, 30: 511–512.

Willmott, H. (2011) 'Making sense of the financial meltdown' *Organization*, 18(2): 239–260.

Wilson, F. (1999) 'Genderquake? Did you feel the earth move?', *Organization*, 6: 529–541.

Wilson, S. (2004) *The Struggle over Work: The End of Work and Employment Options for Post-Industrial Societies*, London: Routledge.

Wilson, W.J. (1987) *The Truly Disadvantaged*, Chicago: University of Chicago Press.

Wilson, W.J. (1996) *When Work Disappears,* New York: Alfred Knopf.

Wise, S. and Stanley, L. (1987) *Gorgie Porgie: Sexual Harassment in Everyday Life*, London: Pandora.

Witz, A., Warhurst, C. and Nickson, D., (2003), 'The labour of aesthetics and the aesthetics of organisation', *Organisation*, 10(1): 33–54.

Wolkowitz, C. (2006) *Bodies at Work*, London: Sage.

Wolkowitz, C. (2009) 'Challenging boundaries: an autobiographical perspective on the sociology of work', *Sociology,* 43(5): 846–860.

Womack, J.P., Jones, D.J. and Roos, D. (1990) *The Machine That Changed the World*, New York: Rawson.

Woodfield, R. (2000) *Women, Work and Computing*, Cambridge: Cambridge University Press.

Woodward, J. (1994) *Industrial Organisation*, Oxford: Oxford University Press (originally 1965).

Woolgar, S. (1988) *Science: The Very Idea*, London: Ellis Horwood.

Wray, D. (1949) 'Marginal men of industry: the foremen', *American Journal of Sociology*, 54: 298–301.

Wright, C. (2008) 'Reinventing human resource management: business partners, internal consultants and the limits to professionalisation' *Human Relations*, 61(8): 1064–1086.

Zaidman, N., Goldstein-Gidoni, O. and Nehemya, I. (2009) 'From temples to organizations: the introduction and packaging of spirituality', *Organization,* 16(4): 597–621.

Zeitlin, M. (1989) *The Large Corporation and Contemporary Classes*, Oxford: Polity Press.

Zilber, T.B. (2013) 'Institutional logics and institutional work: should they be agreed?', in M. Lounsbury and E. Boxenbaum (eds), *Institutional Logics in Action, Research in the Sociology of Organizations*, Volume 39, Part A, Bingley, UK: Emerald Group Publishing Limited, pp. 77–96.

Zimmerman, D.H. (1973) 'The practicalities of rule use', in J.D. Douglas (ed), *Understanding Everyday Life: Toward the Reconstruction of Sociological Knowledge*, London: Routledge: 221–238.

Zucker, L.G. (ed) (1988) *Institutional Patterns and Organisations*, Cambridge, MA: Ballinger.

Author index

Subject index

Taylor & Francis eBooks

Helping you to choose the right eBooks for your Library

Add Routledge titles to your library's digital collection today. Taylor and Francis ebooks contains over 50,000 titles in the Humanities, Social Sciences, Behavioural Sciences, Built Environment and Law.

Choose from a range of subject packages or create your own!

Benefits for you

» Free MARC records
» COUNTER-compliant usage statistics
» Flexible purchase and pricing options
» All titles DRM-free.

Benefits for your user

» Off-site, anytime access via Athens or referring URL
» Print or copy pages or chapters
» Full content search
» Bookmark, highlight and annotate text
» Access to thousands of pages of quality research at the click of a button.

REQUEST YOUR FREE INSTITUTIONAL TRIAL TODAY | **Free Trials Available** We offer free trials to qualifying academic, corporate and government customers.

eCollections – Choose from over 30 subject eCollections, including:

Archaeology	Language Learning
Architecture	Law
Asian Studies	Literature
Business & Management	Media & Communication
Classical Studies	Middle East Studies
Construction	Music
Creative & Media Arts	Philosophy
Criminology & Criminal Justice	Planning
Economics	Politics
Education	Psychology & Mental Health
Energy	Religion
Engineering	Security
English Language & Linguistics	Social Work
Environment & Sustainability	Sociology
Geography	Sport
Health Studies	Theatre & Performance
History	Tourism, Hospitality & Events

For more information, pricing enquiries or to order a free trial, please contact your local sales team: **www.tandfebooks.com/page/sales**

 Routledge
Taylor & Francis Group

The home of
Routledge books

www.tandfebooks.com